# KILLER HIGH

# KILLER HIGH

## A HISTORY OF WAR IN SIX DRUGS

PETER ANDREAS

OXFORD
UNIVERSITY PRESS

# OXFORD
UNIVERSITY PRESS

Oxford University Press is a department of the University of Oxford. It furthers the University's objective of excellence in research, scholarship, and education by publishing worldwide. Oxford is a registered trade mark of Oxford University Press in the UK and certain other countries.

Published in the United States of America by Oxford University Press
198 Madison Avenue, New York, NY 10016, United States of America.

Library of Congress Cataloging-in-Publication Data
Names: Andreas, Peter, 1965– author.
Title: Killer high : a history of war in six drugs / Peter Andreas.
Other titles: History of war in six drugs
Description: New York, NY : Oxford University Press, [2020] |
Includes bibliographical references and index.
Identifiers: LCCN 2019005585 | ISBN 9780190463014 (hardback)
Subjects: LCSH: Medicine, Military—History—Miscellanea. |
Soldiers—Drug use—History. | Soldiers—Substance use—History. |
Drug utilization—History. | Drug abuse—History. | Military art and science—
Miscellanea. | Military history—Miscellanea. |
BISAC: HISTORY / Military / General.
Classification: LCC RC971 .A53 2020 | DDC 616.9/8023—dc23
LC record available at https://lccn.loc.gov/2019005585

9 8 7 6 5 4 3 2 1

Printed by Sheridan Books, Inc., United States of America

# CONTENTS

# PREFACE

THE DEPLOYMENT OF SOLDIERS to battle drugs is what first got my attention. It was the evening of September 5, 1989. The Cold War was ending, but a new war was ramping up, not against a foreign military threat but a psychoactive substance. In his first prime-time address to the nation, President George H. W. Bush held up a clear plastic bag of a chalky substance in front of the camera at his desk in the Oval Office. "This is crack cocaine," Bush said in a somber voice. The president declared war, calling for "an assault on every front." Urging Americans to "face this evil as a nation united," Bush proclaimed that "victory over drugs is our cause, a just cause." He announced that "when requested, we will for the first time make available the appropriate resources of America's armed forces." Late that December, the United States launched Operation Just Cause, invading Panama and arresting its leader, General Manuel Noriega, on cocaine-trafficking charges—surely the most expensive drug bust in history. In the years that followed, fighting cocaine replaced fighting communism as the driver of Washington's military relations with its southern neighbors.

But it wasn't until years later that I began to fully grasp the deeper and more expansive links between drugs and war. Part of this discovery was by accident: while writing a book about the 1992–1995 siege of Sarajevo, I could not help but notice the pervasive role of cigarettes as a substitute currency in keeping the city alive, including their use as payment to soldiers for defending the siege lines. Black-market booze was also in high demand, so much so that United Nations aid workers would bribe Serb checkpoint guards with bottles of whiskey to lubricate the passage of food convoys into the besieged city. Later, in the midst of researching a book on the history of smuggling in America, I was struck by the importance of rum and tea in provoking the War of Independence, the use of "ardent spirits" as an ethnic cleanser during westward expansion, and the crucial role of World War I in enabling the prohibition of alcohol. And this made me want to dig more, much more, to untangle the historical roots of the drugs–war relationship.

Tracing this relationship across centuries, continents, and psychoactive substances has been a long journey, one that I could not have embarked on by myself—and, I must confess, one that I could not have completed without heavy daily doses of my own drug of choice, caffeine. I owe much to a talented team of research assistants over the years: Dakota Fenn, Kyra Foose, Richard Gagliardi, Benjamin Giampetroni, Miriam Hinthorn, and especially Jerome Marston and Rebecca Martin (who were involved at various stages from beginning to end). The book would not have been possible without the generosity of Brown University, particularly the Watson Institute for International and Public Affairs, the Department of Political Science, and the Office of the Dean of Faculty. Some of the final revisions were completed during a summer visiting appointment at the Free University of Berlin's John F. Kennedy Institute, and I thank David Besold and Christian Lammert for making my stay there possible. I gave presentations based on the book at Brown University, Georgetown University, the Free University of Berlin, the German Institute for International and Security Affairs, Swarthmore College, McGill University, Providence College, the University of New Mexico, Tufts University, and the University of California at Berkeley, as well as at the annual conferences of the American Political Science Association and the International Studies Association. Part of chapter 6 draws from Peter Andreas, *Smuggler Nation: How Illicit Trade Made America* (Oxford University Press, 2013), and the introduction and conclusion draw from my essay, "Drugs and War: What Is the Relationship?" in the *Annual Review of Political Science* (2019).

Many friends and colleagues gave much-appreciated feedback and advice at various stages of the project, including Nick Barnes, David Courtwright, Cornelius Friesendorf, Rich Friman, Paul Gootenberg, Pat Herlihy, Jim Kurth, Rose McDermott, Rahul Mediratta, Tom Naylor, and Mark Schrad. My editor, Dave McBride, took this project on when it was merely a rough draft of a proposal, generated detailed external reader reports that greatly improved the book, and gently prodded me at just the right moments. Emily Mackenzie at Oxford University Press helped me check off all the boxes before final submission and shepherded the manuscript into production. My agent, Rafe Sagalyn, was wonderful and wise, as always.

The writing was slowed down, and indeed momentarily derailed, by the arrival of Stella and Annika into this world. I dedicate this book to Kristen, who somehow managed to handle me and our two rambunctious girls without resorting to either drugs or war.

# KILLER HIGH

# Introduction: How Drugs Made War and War Made Drugs

AFTER YEARS OF UNCHECKED drug trafficking and the bribing of local officials to look the other way, the frustrated government authorities finally cracked down, seizing and destroying tons of illicit shipments. Undeterred, the furious traffickers retaliated with military force, provoking an all-out drug war. It was both a war against drugs and a war for drugs. Drugs won.

This may sound like a Mexican border town in recent years. But the year was 1839, and the place was the Chinese port city of Guangzhou, also known as Canton. For decades, the British East India Company, by far the largest drug-trafficking organization in the history of the world, had orchestrated the shipping of ever-increasing amounts of Indian opium into China in flagrant violation of official bans. And when the Chinese authorities finally got serious about enforcement, Britain responded by sending troops and gunships to keep the opium floodgates open. The Opium War profoundly shaped the fate of China and the imperial reach of Britain for the next century. Britain, it turns out, was not only the world's first true "narco-state" but also a "narco-empire."

This episode is only one particularly prominent example of the age-old relationship between warfare and psychoactive substances. This relationship has ranged from using drugs to motivate soldiers to using drug profits to pay them, from going to war to secure drug markets to

*Killer High*, Peter Andreas. Oxford University Press (2020). © Peter Andreas.
DOI: 10.1093/actrade/9780190463014.001.0001

using the instruments of war to suppress them. In various ways and in various forms, the drugs–war relationship has fueled imperial expansion, provoked rebellion and revolution, built up states, and helped to create not only addicted armies but also nations of addicts.

In this book, I tell the story of this long, symbiotic relationship between drugs and war and the politics that surrounds it. I show how drugs made war and war made drugs.[1] I do so by tracing the history of war through the lens of drugs and the history of drugs through the lens of war. In other words, drug history is retold as military history, and military history is retold as drug history. I do not simply reduce war to drugs or drugs to war, of course, but I do stress that there are key questions about both war and drugs that we cannot adequately answer without understanding their relationship.

Take the most devastating war of the twentieth century. What explains the astonishing speed of the Blitzkrieg? What sustained the morale of Londoners during the darkest days of the Battle of Britain? How did the Japanese finance their occupation of China, and how did Japanese military industry workers stay so productive during wartime? Drugs are only part of the answer to these questions, but a crucial and too-often-overlooked part.

Similarly, war helps us answer all sorts of questions about the history of drugs. For instance, how did cigarette smoking become the favored vehicle for tobacco consumption, and how did it become globalized? How was the legal cocaine industry dismantled, and why is the drug now prohibited across the globe? How did Coca-Cola become the world's leading caffeinated soft drink? Why is Afghanistan the world's largest opium producer? As *Killer High* shows, these questions simply cannot be answered without taking into account the essential role of war.

An underlying theme throughout this book is that the drugs–war relationship has been a major enabler of states and their military ambitions. To be sure, states have found the drugs–war relationship to be a double-edged sword: drugs have enhanced troop morale and battlefield performance yet also created drugged-out foot soldiers; funded imperial conquest but also insurrection; propped up governments while at times subverting them. Nevertheless, as we will see again and again in the pages that follow, more often than not the drugs–war relationship has been about statecraft—serving state interests and contributing to state-building projects. This has often been true even when states have appeared most threatened. For instance, drug traffickers with their own private armies have at times violently defied and even confronted the state, yet going to war against traffickers has also provided a mechanism to expand the power and reach of the state and its security apparatus. At the same time, states have made alliances of convenience with traffickers when strategically useful.

The big-picture story of the relationship between drugs and war is largely missing—up to now we mostly have pieces and fragments. Many accounts treat the relationship as a contemporary stateless phenomenon involving illegal drugs, drawing our attention to so-called narco-terrorists in Afghanistan and doped-up child soldiers wielding AK-47s in Sierra Leone. History beyond the last few decades tends to be glossed over. Drug-fueled conflicts are therefore too often characterized as a distinctly post–Cold War phenomenon, inflating their contemporary novelty at the expense of downplaying their historical significance.[2]

This book is therefore a corrective of sorts, placing both history and a wider range of drugs front and center in our story. The standard narrow focus on the present obscures a much longer and bloodier history, one in which perfectly legal drugs have in many ways played an even more lethal role than their illegal counterparts in wars of all types, from traditional interstate wars to less conventional intrastate conflicts. After all, the selective and uneven criminalization of drugs such as heroin and cocaine occurred rather late in the history of war. And this, in turn, introduced a far greater criminal element to war itself, with warlords, clandestine intelligence operatives, insurgents, and traffickers all rubbing shoulders in a shadowy underworld.

Countless volumes have been written about the history of war, and, to a much lesser extent, the history of drugs, but it is striking how little the recountings of these two histories overlap.[3] War histories occasionally mention drugs but rarely focus on them. Drug histories typically examine a particular drug, place, and time period. Those few that put war at the center of analysis tend to focus on a specific war or type of war, such as the Opium Wars of the mid-nineteenth century or insurgency and counterinsurgency in more recent decades.[4] This book connects the historical dots, piecing together and building on these vital accounts to more widely trace the drugs–war relationship across time, place, and psychoactive substance.

## The Drugs of War

*Killer High* covers a lot of historical ground, from wine and war in ancient times to cocaine and counterinsurgency in more recent years. But the coverage is also necessarily selective. I paint in broad strokes, identifying and making sense of the defining moments, underlying dynamics, and core dimensions of the drugs–war relationship. The book does not try to cover all wars and all drugs throughout history. Indeed, although the drugs–war relationship dates back to antiquity, most of the world's leading drugs only became globalized commodities during and after the sixteenth century—what historian David Courtwright calls the "psychoactive revolution."[5] In this regard, one could argue that during the past 500 years or so, war has become progressively more drugged with the introduction, mass production, and global proliferation of more (and more potent) mind-altering substances. And their wartime impact has often been as profoundly felt on the home front as on the war front.

Defined simply as chemicals that alter the mind of the user, psychoactive drugs are certainly not an inherent part of war. Rather, certain drugs have particular attributes that make them especially exploitable for war-making—whether preparing for, carrying out, or recovering from battle. The most war-facilitating attributes of drugs are their psychoactive effects, habit-forming potential, ease of production and transport, and high value and profitability relative to weight and bulk.

But in their relation to war, not all drugs are created equal: some drugs are more potent than others as war ingredients, and there is considerable variation in their significance across time and place. I focus on six drugs in particular: alcohol, tobacco, caffeine, opium, amphetamines, and cocaine. Why these six? At various times and in varying ways these are the ones that have most defined the drugs–war relationship. They range from old to relatively new, mild to potent, licit to illicit, natural to synthetic. And although all have had medical applications, all have become extraordinarily popular and profitable global commodities through their nonmedical use.

When I first started to work on this book I was agnostic about which drugs to focus on. For example, I took a close look at the history of cannabis, assuming that the world's most widely consumed illicit drug must surely be an important piece of the story. But while weed and war have crossed paths here and there—Napoleon's soldiers introduced hashish to France on their return from Egypt, and American GIs smoked plenty of pot in Vietnam—this has not been as significant as the other drugs in this book. And indeed, in the late 1960s cannabis even came to be viewed as an *antiwar* drug. It is also interesting to note that its most important war role has been not as a drug but rather as a strategically valued fiber for naval warfare in the form of hemp for rope. Hallucinogens are also missing in our story. Psychedelic mushrooms were apparently popular among Siberian warriors on the eve of battle centuries ago, and the Central Intelligence Agency (CIA) used LSD for brainwashing experiments during the Cold War, but these are nevertheless niche rather than mass-produced drugs with global reach and appeal. Similarly, chewing qat (or khat), the stimulant of choice for Somali combatants and pirates and a wildly popular drug crop in war-ravaged Yemen, is not covered because, unlike the truly globalized drugs highlighted in the pages ahead, its use has been almost entirely confined to the Horn of Africa and southwestern Arabia. At the same time, I was initially not expecting to include caffeinated beverages such as tea, coffee, and Coca-Cola. Caffeine is certainly not the first drug that comes to mind when thinking about drugs and war—sometimes we forget that it is even a drug—but the research led me to conclude that I had to make it part of the story.

The chapters that follow are organized around these six leading war drugs, with each introduced into the story based on when it became a major war ingredient. Our story therefore begins with alcohol, the oldest mass-consumption drug, dating back to the establishment of sedentary agricultural societies. Alcohol has been a powerful war lubricant for thousands of years, from wine in the Greek and Roman empires, to rum in late colonial America, to vodka in the lead-up to the Russian Revolution. As we will see, alcohol in its many concoctions has long been used both for liquid courage and to raise war revenue through taxation. As such, its sheer longevity and popularity have made alcohol unrivaled in its importance as a war drug. But it has also clearly been a mixed blessing, desensitizing soldiers but also debilitating them; filling war chests but also enraging taxpayers.

We next turn to nicotine, ingested in the form of tobacco, which became globalized in the aftermath of the conquest of the Americas. Nicotine is one of the world's most addictive substances and has also had a particularly addictive relationship to war. Starting in the seventeenth century, soldiers were the perfect vehicle for the spread of tobacco smoking throughout Europe and eventually across the world. Tobacco turned out to be especially useful for both calming nerves and coping with boredom. And later, particularly with the invention of the cigarette as a highly effective and portable delivery mechanism, tobacco was added to standard soldier rations. When soldiers returned home after war, they brought with them their new smoking habit. At the same time, major powers turned to tobacco taxes to pay for their ever-more expansive and expensive war machines.

We then examine a much milder drug, caffeine, mostly consumed via coffee and tea. The globalization of coffee and tea sipping came to rival the globalization of tobacco smoking. The British Empire was an empire of tea, and the most successful armed rebellion against the empire started with the Boston Tea Party. Later, soldiers became heavily caffeinated, nowhere more evident than during the American Civil War, when coffee was the most valued item in troop rations, and during the First and Second World Wars, when coffee reached new heights as a mild stimulant and instant coffee was popularized.

Opium is an ancient drug but is introduced at the middle point of our story because its role in major warfare didn't fully take off until the nineteenth-century Opium Wars, when Britain forced China to keep its doors open to opium imports. Indeed, it is precisely due to these imperial battles that opium is the drug most famously associated with war. After China's defeat, opium and its derivatives continued to be a key war ingredient in subsequent decades and centuries, from the chaotic warlord era of early twentieth-century China, to the Vietnam War at the height of the Cold War, to the Afghan wars in more recent decades.

Amphetamines enter relatively late in our story because they did not fully arrive on the battlefield until World War II. With the development and commercialization of amphetamines, World War II became the first major war involving widespread use of synthetic drugs. The high point of the industrialization of war was the ingesting of industrial-strength pills to produce more efficient, fast, and effective soldiers. Amphetamines reduced fatigue and appetite and increased wakefulness. World War II was a war on speed, from Germany's Blitzkrieg to Japan's kamikazes. Allied troops also turned to amphetamines to stay awake and alert, with little awareness or concern about the health hazards. And in the aftermath of the most destructive war in human history, massive stockpiles of amphetamines were dumped on civilian populations in Japan, with long-lasting consequences.

Finally, more than any other drug, cocaine became the target of an increasingly militarized drug war from the last decades of the twentieth century to the present. To a large extent, the US-led drug war turned into a cocaine war, in which the main battlefields were the source and transit countries of the Americas. In the escalating effort to combat the northward flow of cocaine, soldiers became cops, old Cold War equipment and technologies were recycled for new drug war tasks, and a massive injection of US military training and assistance to Colombia blurred the distinction between antidrug and anti-insurgency missions. At the same time, traffickers beefed up their own fighting capacities, ranging from cocaine-financed Colombian paramilitaries to Mexican smuggling organizations composed of ex-military personnel using military-grade arms. From Rio de Janeiro to the Rio Grande, the cocaine war took on some of the characteristics of an actual war, with mounting casualties and no end in sight.

In tracing the histories of these six particularly prominent war drugs, I weave together what I consider to be the core dimensions of the drugs–war relationship: war *while on* drugs (drug consumption by combatants and civilians during wartime), war *through* drugs (the use of drugs to finance war or to weaken the enemy), war *for* drugs (the use of war to secure drug markets), war *against* drugs (the use of military means to suppress drugs or to attack or discredit military rivals in the name of drug suppression), and drugs *after* war (different drugs as winners or losers in the aftermath of war). The six drugs examined in this book vary widely across these dimensions. As previewed below, these dimensions are distinct but can interact and shape each other, and often do.

## War *While on* Drugs

Mind-altering substances have long been essential for both relaxing and stimulating combatants on the war front and workers on the home front. War is exceptionally demanding and traumatic work, and those tasked with war-related jobs often turn to chemical assistance. Drugs provide chemical assistance in all sorts of ways, whether to boost courage, morale, and group bonding or to cope with boredom, stress, and exhaustion. No wonder then that, as one historian points out, "of all of civilization's occupational categories, that of soldier may be the most conducive to regular drug use."[6] By manipulating the central nervous system, psychoactive drugs have long helped to inhibit or to heal war-shattered nerves.

Soldier drug use has often been tolerated, facilitated, and even encouraged by states, though not without considerable risks. Take alcohol, for example. Drink has helped soldiers brace for battle, toast victories, and numb defeats, but in excess has made them unreliable and inept. This was embarrassingly evident in imperial Russia's defeat in the Russo-Japanese war, in which Russian commanders, soldiers, and sailors were more often drunk than sober. Despite the downside of combatant alcohol use, governments have often been enablers, as evidenced by a long history of including alcohol in soldier rations, a practice that persisted well into the twentieth century.

Other psychoactive substances, such as tobacco, have for centuries been used to manage the trauma of war before, during, and after battle. "Fear creates a desire for tobacco," noted Benjamin Rush. "Hence it is used in greater quantities by soldiers and sailors than by other classes of people."[7] No wonder, then, that tobacco has often been treated as essential to troop morale. As US Army General John Pershing explained during World War I, "You ask me what we need to win this war. I answer tobacco as much as bullets. Tobacco is as indispensable as the daily ration; we must have thousands of tons without delay."[8] Other drugs, most notably the stimulants caffeine and amphetamines, have been embraced not only as morale boosters but as performance enhancers, helping soldiers fight off sleep and fatigue and build up energy and stamina.

## War *Through* Drugs

There has been a great deal of hand-wringing in policy circles in recent years about drug-financed insurgents and terrorists, as well as traffickers who use drug profits to fund their own private armies. These anxieties are certainly understandable, yet they are also too easily simplified and politicized. This is reflected in the popularization of the terms "narco-guerrillas" and "narco-terrorists" to bolster support for counterinsurgency and counterterrorism campaigns while simultaneously glossing over the drug ties of unsavory but politically useful allies, such as those the United States has at different times propped up in Southeast Asia, Central America, and Afghanistan.

In fact, drugs as a funder of war is an old story, one in which legal drugs have played an especially prominent role. One rebel group that was particularly hooked on drug revenue in the late eighteenth century was George Washington's Continental Army. Tobacco money was used to pay soldiers, purchase war supplies, and cover war debts.

However, the historical record reveals that states, not rebels, have more often been dependent on drug revenue to finance war. For centuries, taxing drugs such as tobacco and alcohol was a cornerstone of major power war financing. In the eighteenth and nineteenth centuries, rival European imperial powers, including France and England, were able to build up their massive war machines and keep them running thanks to heavy taxes on high-demand commodities such as tea, alcohol, and tobacco. As Napoleon III is said to have quipped, "This vice [tobacco smoking] brings in one hundred million francs in taxes each year. I will certainly forbid it at once—as soon as you can name a virtue that brings in as much revenue."[9] In Britain, war provided a convenient rationale to impose new taxes on alcohol, and collecting such taxes in turn created an ever-more capable taxation bureaucracy—making it possible for the state to collect even more revenue to pay for its increasingly costly military campaigns. "War and national defense were the public goods that rulers used to justify taxation," explains Margaret Levi in her classic *Of Rule and Revenue*.[10] And in the case of Britain in the eighteenth and nineteenth centuries, no tax was more important than the excise on alcohol, helping to transform it into the world's leading military power.

## War *for* Drugs

From Burma to Mexico to Colombia, drug traffickers have built up their military capacities to violently defend and compete for drug markets. Turf wars between rival traffickers have taken an especially heavy toll in Mexico in recent years, where the death count has exceeded that of most civil wars. However, the use of military force to secure drug markets goes back at least to the nineteenth-century Opium Wars. The main change that has occurred is that violent competition for drug markets has gone from being state-sponsored—epitomized by the British opening the Chinese opium market via the barrel of a gun—to being largely the domain of heavily armed stateless actors.

Perhaps today's battles between rival drug gangs should be viewed as a form of criminal commercial warfare, made possible by both the criminalization of drugs and the easy availability of military hardware and military-trained foot soldiers. Traditional security scholars, as well as many legal scholars, may scoff at categorizing this type of organized violence as "war." Yet the sheer number of deaths involved in some of these conflicts and the heavily armed nature of their most powerful players suggest that we may need to rethink our conventional definitions of war.[11]

It should be emphasized that "war for drugs" can closely interact with and be fueled by "war against drugs." For example, looking at the Mexico case again, it is clear that the government's strategy of decapitating major drug-trafficking organizations has unintentionally helped to fuel brutal battles between rival traffickers. When one trafficking organization has been taken down or weakened by the "war against drugs," other trafficking organizations have aggressively engaged in "war for drugs," violently competing for the newly vacated turf—especially the major corridors and border entry points for US-bound drug shipments. These bloody clashes are also "wars through drugs" in that they are financed through drug revenue.

Another interactive effect is that drug traffickers can launch a "war for drugs" in defensive response to a "war against drugs," including assassinating judges, police, and politicians. The standard practice for most drug traffickers is to evade rather than violently confront the state—after all, too much violence can be bad for business by attracting unwanted attention—but the exceptions have included going so far as to declare an all-out war on the state. The most famous case was that of Pablo Escobar and his Medellin cocaine-trafficking organization in the 1980s and early 1990s. However, as the Opium Wars demonstrate, responding to a "war against drugs" with a "war for drugs" is far from new.

## War *Against* Drugs

Declaring war against drugs moved from metaphor and political slogan in the early 1970s to reality in the 1980s. This was dramatically evident in the increased use of military tools, strategies, and personnel for antidrug missions, especially in the United States and Latin America. The militarization of drug control ranged from a loosening of the US Posse Comitatus Act, which prohibited the use of the military for domestic law enforcement, to support for the use of local militaries on the frontlines of antidrug campaigns across the Americas. The "war against drugs" even provided the pretext for the US military invasion of Panama. More generally, the drug war helped to prompt and perpetuate a post–Cold War shift of the national security state's focus away from traditional military threats and toward "new transnational threats." Conventional distinctions between crime fighting and war fighting became increasingly blurred, changing the very nature of warfare itself.

But while going to war against drugs is for the most part a recent development, it has some striking historical precedents. Often forgotten, these include the militarized British crackdown on the smuggling of molasses for rum production in the New England colonies, which provoked such an intense backlash that it helped spark the American War of Independence. The British Royal Navy's crusade against the smugglers was not called a "war against drugs," but it was certainly militarized. The Royal Navy was unleashed against colonial smugglers because civilian customs agents had proven too corrupt and unreliable. Smuggler resistance not only defied the imperial authorities but led to armed revolution, making it a far greater threat to the state than any modern-day drug-trafficking organization.

Finally, it should be recognized that a war against drugs, even while not particularly effective in suppressing drugs, can serve as an effective tool to further other strategic objectives, including those of attacking and delegitimizing adversaries. This was evident during the Cold War, when the United States accused Red China and Castro's Cuba of flooding the United States with drugs, when in fact China had largely removed itself from the international drug trade and the main Cubans involved in the illicit business were anticommunist exiles in Miami and elsewhere. And after the Cold War came to an end, when the US Congress and the American public were no longer so willing to fund anticommunist counterinsurgency campaigns, counternarcotics provided a convenient alternative funding channel for Washington strategists to militarily support the Colombian government's war against leftist guerrillas.

## Drugs *After* War

Too often overlooked is that not only have drugs shaped war, but war has shaped drugs well beyond wartime. Specifically, war has profoundly influenced postwar drug production, regulation, and consumption patterns. The use of a particular drug can increase sharply in the aftermath of war. This was strikingly evident, for instance, after the Opium Wars, in which the British victory made possible the export of even more Indian opium to China, and China itself eventually became a major opium producer. Fast forward to the Chinese Revolution, however, when the Communist victory dealt a fatal blow to the China opium market. Opium production and trafficking were then pushed south across the border to Laos, Burma, and Thailand, which became known as the "Golden Triangle."

Wars can also lead to a surge in drug use by returning soldiers. For example, combatants on all sides of World War II developed an amphetamine habit, and the wartime availability of the drug extended into peacetime. Japan in particular experienced a postwar amphetamine epidemic, the first drug epidemic in the history of the country. Many soldiers and factory workers who had become hooked on the drug during the war continued to consume it into the postwar years.

The popularity of certain drugs can rise and fall as a result of war. For instance, the split from the British Empire brought a shift in the drinking habits of the new American nation. By the early eighteenth century, whiskey had replaced rum as the most popular spirit in

America. Drinking whiskey came to be seen as more patriotic, since it was associated with self-reliance and independence. Rum, in contrast, represented dependence on foreigners and was associated with the British. Tea was similarly a casualty of the American Revolution, eventually supplanted by coffee as the caffeinated drink of choice by a newly independent nation that negatively associated tea drinking with British rule. The popularity of coffee again surged in the aftermath of the Civil War and the two world wars. Thanks to World War II, the coffee break was even institutionalized in the American workplace, where it had become routine for defense industry workers. Instant coffee, first popularized on the battlefield, also became entrenched in postwar drinking habits.

A particularly dramatic example of a drug losing out from war is cocaine. World War II and its aftermath killed off legal cocaine. The US military occupation wiped out the Japanese cocaine industry that had grown up in the 1920s and 1930s, and the United States also uprooted the last remnants of coca production in Java, which Japan had invaded during the war. More generally, postwar US hegemony also meant the hegemony of the US antidrug agenda, which included the global criminalization of cocaine. But legal cocaine's loss was illegal cocaine's gain: cocaine would reemerge in later years as an enormously profitable illicit drug pushed by criminal organizations rather than pharmaceutical companies.

There is also an age-old pattern in which wars can introduce entirely new drugs to conquered lands. Invaders have long brought their drug tastes with them. The military expansion of the Roman Empire included the expansion of wine drinking, while beer came to be identified with the still-unpacified Germanic tribes. The fall of the Roman Empire in turn led to a diversification of alcohol preferences, with beer making a comeback, wine retreating even while remaining entrenched in some locales, and mead and ale becoming increasingly common. Similarly, the conquest of the Americas brought distilled spirits to new regions, sometimes with devastating effects on native communities. However, the adoption of drug habits is not always a one-way street: the conquerors can sometimes make a local drug their own—as was the case with the European (and subsequently global) adoption of Native American tobacco smoking. Alternatively, conquerors may shun a local drug themselves but still exploit it to help pacify the population, as was the case with coca in postconquest Peru, where the Spanish rulers turned it into a mass-consumption crop once they realized they could use it to push native laborers in the fields and mines to work longer and harder.

LET ME MAKE ONE final note before turning to a more detailed telling of the history of war in six drugs. A heavy dose of caution is called for when it comes to the subject matter of this book. "Bringing drugs in" to better understand the history of war inevitably runs the risk of "drugging" the narrative. In its crudest form, this can sloppily reduce all wars to being about drugs, drugs, and more drugs. It is much too easy and tempting to simply blame drugs for violent conflict—as reflected in the popularization of terms such as "narco-terrorists" and "narco-guerrillas"—drawing attention away from other causes and contextual factors. Oliver North, the incoming head of the National Rifle Association, even went so far as to conveniently blame drugs for school shootings: Shooters have "been drugged in many cases," he said in the immediate aftermath of yet another shooting spree, noting that young boys have often "been on Ritalin" most of their lives.[12] This sort of extreme distortion, exaggeration, and simplification is not what I have in mind when I underscore the role of drugs in fueling wars. Rather than invalidating or supplanting other accounts, my more modest aim is to instead incorporate and illuminate the often-overlooked or misunderstood psychoactive side of the history of war.

# I

# Drunk on the Front

THE BOOK COVER OF John Mueller's *The Remnants of War* shows a soldier chugging down a bottle of booze during the bloody disintegration of the former Yugoslavia in the early 1990s. The striking image conveys the main message of the book: war is in such decline across the globe that it is increasingly fought by undisciplined, thuggish, and inebriated irregular combatants rather than the traditional, disciplined, and presumably dry armies of the past.[1] As Mueller and others point out, there were certainly plenty of drunk thugs carrying out the genocidal killing sprees in Bosnia and Rwanda.[2]

But were wars in earlier eras actually more sober? Far from it. In fact, alcohol—the world's oldest mass-consumption drug—has long been a powerful war lubricant for soldiers and leaders alike. Indeed, outside of predominantly Muslim societies, no mind-altering substance has been more synonymous with warfare. While drinking habits and attitudes toward drinking have changed over time, drinking and war-making have gone hand in hand since antiquity. And this relationship holds all the way to the top ranks, from Alexander the Great to Churchill and Stalin.

It is not difficult to understand why combatants may find comfort in the bottle. Alcohol releases endorphins in the brain, reducing stress and increasing a person's sense of well-being. Depending on the dose, it can have both stimulant and sedation effects. What is most notable

*Killer High*, Peter Andreas. Oxford University Press (2020). © Peter Andreas.
DOI: 10.1093/actrade/9780190463014.001.0001

about the long, intimate relationship between alcohol and war is its double-edged character. Drink has helped soldiers prepare for combat, boost their confidence and willingness to take risks, anesthetize the injured, celebrate wins, and cope with losses, but excessive drinking has also made them unreliable and even self-destructive. Back on the home front, alcohol has helped civilian populations endure wartime hardships but has also provoked charges that it undermines worker productivity and the mobilization for war. Temperance advocates and government leaders alike have campaigned to restrict and even prohibit the consumption of alcohol in the name of war, sometimes with consequences that have lasted well beyond wartime. Last but not least, alcohol taxes have been major funders of wars, even as such tax burdens have fueled popular discontent and even helped to provoke rebellion.

### Ancient Brews, Wines, and Wars

For much of human history, alcohol mostly meant beer and wine, which by all accounts spread from the Near East to Europe. Some archeological evidence suggests that these alcoholic beverages were included in the military rations of the Mesopotamian army some 5,500 years ago.[3] Beer-making may extend as far back as 10,000 BC, when cereal grains—notably wheat and barley—were first domesticated. Indeed, archaeologists have debated whether beer was actually more important than bread in stimulating the early proliferation of grain agriculture.[4] The status of beer as a staple beverage can be explained by its relative affordability and ease of production, not to mention its nutritional and health benefits—beer has been referred to as "liquid bread" and has often been considered safer than water.

The Sumerians, who inhabited the lands between the Tigris and Euphrates rivers in what is today Iran and Iraq, left records of many beer types and recipes in the text "A Hymn to Ninkasi." Ninkasi was not only the Sumerian goddess of brewing, but also the goddess of harvesting, lovemaking, and war-making. After the Babylonians conquered the Sumerians around 2,000 BC, brewing was turned into a mass production business to supply both civilians and soldiers. King Hammurabi recorded twenty different styles of beer in what came to be known as the Code of Hammurabi.[5] In ancient Egypt and Mesopotamia, beer was widely used as a currency, serving as payment for soldiers, policemen, and the workers who built the pyramids.[6]

The importance of wine for war for the ancient Greeks is hinted at in the *Iliad* and *Odyssey*, written in the eighth century BC: Homer makes reference to wine in recounting the sacking of Troy and the return home of one of its leaders. The Greeks, who enjoyed an ideal climate and terrain for wine-making, were the first to mass produce and make the drink available beyond elite circles. In classical Greece, "wine was the drink of fighting men, the indispensable lubricant of their culture of death and honor, of sacking cities, of carrying off armor, cattle, and women. All their rituals were punctuated with libations of wine—the gods did not pay attention otherwise."[7] One of the many siege strategies employed by the Greeks was to attack at a time, such as during a festival, when the defenders would be least prepared or drunk.[8]

Alexander the Great was as fond of wine as he was of conquest, which often went together. During his time in India, Alexander apparently introduced his habit of binge drinking to the locals, which included participating in one of the first recorded drinking games. But drinking was not all about fun and games. Following his conquest of Persepolis in 330 BC, Alexander razed the city to the ground to avenge the burning of the Acropolis by the Persian ruler Xerxes. The destruction of Persepolis supposedly came after a procession of his intoxicated men, who sang:

> *The jolly god in triumph comes*
> *Sound the trumpets, beat the drums . . .*
> *Bacchus' blessings are a treasure*
> *Drinking is the soldier's pleasure.* [9]

The Romans not only came to embrace the wine-drinking culture of Greece but perfected the art of wine-making and became major exporters of the product to their expanding territories. The flamboyant politician and general Mark Antony even went into his last battle dressed up in fawn skins to impersonate the wine god Bacchus. Wine was treated as a strategic resource: a secure supply was crucial to ensure the daily wine rations of Roman legions spread out across the far-flung empire. Often diluted, the wine was of poor quality, but its absence would have been unacceptable. Leaders could also use wine to pacify disgruntled troops: in 38 BC, Herod the Great, a Roman client king of Judea, quashed a threatened mutiny by distributing extra wine and other foodstuffs.[10] The daily wine ration was not only good for troops' morale but also good for their health: adding wine with its antibacterial properties to water shielded many from the waterborne illnesses that plagued armies.[11] Moreover, a Roman soldier's success on the battlefield was often rewarded with a tract of farmland, and the most coveted crop was the vine.[12]

As the reach of Rome spread, so too did the vine. Vineyards followed supply routes for legions and garrisons.[13] Consequently, the edge of wine-drinking territory tended to be the edge of the Roman Empire. Most of today's leading wine-producing regions in Europe had their start under Roman rule.[14] In the middle of the first century AD, a Roman legion established a port city that would later come to be known as Bordeaux. Gaul, which included the present-day French wine-making areas of Bordeaux, the Rhone Valley, Burgundy, and Champagne, was firmly beer-drinking territory until the Roman invasion. The Gauls used wooden barrels to transport beer, which the Romans adopted to more easily ship their wine, ending the age-old use of amphorae (tall clay vessels for storing wine).[15]

The Germanic tribes in the heavily forested areas east of the Rhine continued to prefer beer. The historian Tacitus considered their beer-guzzling a weakness: "If you will but humor their excess in drinking, and supply them with as much as they covet, it will be no less easy to vanquish them by vices than by arms." Their favored drink, Tacitus observed, was "a liquor prepared from barley or wheat," and their thirst seemed unquenchable: "It is no disgrace to pass days and nights, without intermission, in drinking." Furthermore, "the frequent quarrels that arise amongst them, when inebriated, seldom terminate in abusive language, but more frequently in blood."[16]

These tribes' lack of familiarity with wine meant that it could be exploited by the Romans as a weapon of war. In 105 BC, the beer-drinking Gauls, unaccustomed to the higher alcohol content of wine, turned themselves into an easy, slow-moving target upon ingesting large quantities of Roman wine they found in the Alban district.[17] According to one account, "the tactic of inebriating opponents before slaughtering them seems to have been a standard Roman military stratagem and was employed with great success over the centuries against various barbarian hordes."[18]

Not all Romanized lands were fully overtaken by the vine, especially as one went farther north, where the climate for viniculture was less hospitable. The Romanization of Britain, which began in AD 43, gave rise to an increasing taste for wine, but local ale-drinking persisted, especially outside of the Roman towns and camps, and ultimately outlasted the Roman Empire.

While the Romans spread wine through war, wine was also a casualty of the wars that ultimately brought an end to their rule. In AD 406, the Vandals, a Germanic tribe, swarmed across the Rhine to Roman Gaul, burning not only towns and villages but also vineyards. The nomadic Huns brought even more devastation, uprooting vineyards, slaughtering their workers, and drinking the spoils.[19] By midcentury, wave after wave of invasions—by Goths, Visigoths, Ostrogoths, and Huns—had left the Roman Empire and its empire of wine in shambles.

Viniculture survived Rome's decline, especially in the Mediterranean, but as power in Europe fragmented, so too did drinking habits. The hard-drinking Germanic tribes moving west mostly imbibed ale, a preference nowhere more evident than in Britain, which the Romans had abandoned in AD 406. Romanized Britain's wine-drinking culture was soon drowned out by Anglo-Saxon ale.[20]

The next round of barbarians to invade Britain, this time bands of Viking warriors attacking by sea from the north, also preferred ale as well as mead (a fermented honey beverage). Drinking and fighting were inseparable for the Norsemen. Indeed, they believed that the afterlife for those who died in battle was a battlefield where they could continue fighting during the day and spend their nights being served mead in the great hall of Valhalla (the hall of the slain) by blond Valkyries. At their height, between the middle of the ninth century and the twelfth century, the Vikings sacked English towns and monasteries near the coast, extended their raids as far south as Spain, and were the first to reach the coast of North America via their outposts in Iceland and Greenland.[21] The thirsty Vikings even managed to brew beer on board their longships during raiding campaigns. The skulls of their dead victims were turned into drinking containers—the Nordic toast "Skål!"

comes from the word *scole*, which means skull.[22] Alcohol also played a role in Viking power struggles: brother kings Alf and Yngve attacked and killed each other in a mead hall, and King Ingjald burned his hall down after getting his royal guests drunk on mead, killing them to usurp their lands.[23]

Wine and ale drenched the battlefields of medieval Europe. The enormous Bayeux Tapestry, illustrating the Norman conquest of England in 1066, depicts a cask of wine carried by wagon. French and other soldiers received wine and ale rations during this era. According to historian Rod Phillips, alcohol was of great use in war, particularly during marches and wherever water supplies were contaminated with bacteria that gave rise to illness. The siege of Dover Castle in 1216 was one such instance: the soldiers, numbering around 1,000, drank 600 gallons of wine and over 20,000 gallons of ale while they encircled the castle over 40 days.[24] In 1316, King Edward II of England made sure that his army deployed to Scotland received 4,000 barrels of wine. In 1406, the half-dozen soldiers tasked with guarding the Château de Custines were given a daily ration of two liters of wine.[25]

Figure 1.1 Norman soldiers pull a cart bearing a large cask of wine, spears, and helmets to be loaded onto ships for the invasion of England. Detail from the Bayeux Tapestry (Granger Collection).

Meanwhile, beer increasingly supplanted ale on the battlefield thanks to its greater longevity. Ale, which was made without hops, lasted no more than a few weeks. But beer, which contained hops, lasted for months. One historian points out that in the early-fifteenth-century siege of Rouen, Londoners were still sending their army both ale and beer. But by the turn of the next century, the English military drank only beer, so much so that in 1515 a brewery was built in Portsmouth to supply Henry VIII's maritime fleet with the beverage.[26] Subsequently, beer, which had not been a common civilian drink, became as popular as ale in London pubs.

Through the Middle Ages, alcoholic drinks in Europe—largely wine, ale, and beer, but also mead and cider—were produced through fermentation. The Islamic science of distillation had appeared in Europe by the twelfth century, producing limited quantities of alcohol mostly for medicinal uses, but did not become entrenched in drinking cultures until the late sixteenth century.[27] Brandy (distilled from wine) came first, followed by whiskey and gin (distilled from cereals) and vodka (distilled from potatoes). Rum (distilled from molasses) was introduced in the seventeenth century. Historian Rudi Matthee notes that brandy grew in popularity after it became routine for European soldiers to drink it on the eve of battle, and Louis XIV's campaign against Holland in 1672, and other land wars of the age, may have played an especially important role in spreading the consumption of spirits.[28]

As a much more compact, concentrated, and durable form of alcohol, distilled spirits had a clear advantage over ale, beer, and wine. The fact that spirits did not spoil—regardless of exposure to air, heat, or cold—made them ideal for long-distance transport. They could also be diluted with water, which in turn made the water safer to drink. The introduction of distilled spirits, perfectly timed to coincide with the Age of Exploration, revolutionized drinking and in the process fueled imperial power and shaped the fate of the New World.

## The Spirits of the Americas

Although Ferdinand Magellan spent almost twice as much on wine rations than on the cost of his flagship, the *San Antonio*, wine was not well suited for crossing vast oceans.[29] Much of Hernan Cortes's supply had spoiled by the time he arrived in the New World. It is little surprise, then, that the Spanish conquistadores dreamed of producing wine in the new colonies. Cortes required new settlers in what is now Mexico City to plant grape vines. But the results were disappointing, with pests and disease conspiring to frustrate Cortes's wine-making ambitions.[30] Distilled spirits fared much better. The arrival of distillation in Mexico led to the creation of mezcal—a distilled form of pulque, the mild indigenous alcoholic beverage made from the agave plant. The Spanish authorities encouraged the local Indians to drink the much stronger mezcal instead of pulque, adding to their subjugation and dependence on the colonial power.[31]

But the transformative impact of distilled spirits on the New World was not fully evident until the introduction of rum. First documented in Barbados, rum was much cheaper than the brandy imported from Europe. The potent drink could be locally produced using the raw molasses left over from sugar production, of which there was more and more as sugarcane plantations spread throughout the Caribbean. A traveler visiting Barbados in 1651 commented that the inhabitants' favorite drink was "Rumbullion, alias Kill-Devill, and this is made of sugar-canes distilled, a hot, hellish and terrible liquor." Rumbullion was a slang word for "a brawl or violent commotion."[32]

Rum's early claim to fame was its close association with pirate identity. The pirates who roamed the Caribbean in the early eighteenth century, attacking settlements and commercial ships, were organized into loose associations that were remarkably democratic. The right to rum was affirmed in these groups' governance documents. One such document stipulated that "Every Man has a Vote to Affairs of Moment; has equal Title to the fresh Provisions, or strong Liquors, at any Time seiz'd, and may use them at Pleasure."[33] Pirates' fondness for rum could also be their undoing. In 1720, after pirate John Rackman and his men became drunk on a captured shipload of rum, they were easy targets for the Royal Navy and were promptly hanged.[34]

Some captured pirates tried to blame their crimes on drinking. As he was about to be executed in 1724, John Archer exclaimed that the "one wickedness that has led me as much as any, to all the rest, has been my brutish drunkenness. By strong drink I have been heated and hardened into the crimes that are now more bitter than death unto me." Before his hanging in 1723, John Browne warned youth "to not let yourselves be overcome with strong drink."[35] At the same time, other pirates pleaded for a last drink of rum before being put to death, and some, such as Captain William Kidd, were visibly intoxicated at the moment of their execution.[36]

The era's most notorious pirate, Edward Teach—known as "Blackbeard"—was also a notorious drunkard. He wrote in his ship's journal: "Such a Day, Rum all out—Our Company somewhat sober:— A Damn'd confusion amongst us!—Rogues a plotting:—great Talk of Separation. So I look'd sharp for a Prize:—such a day took one, with a great deal of Liquor on board, so kept the Company hot, damn'd hot, then all Things went well again."[37] Appropriately, Blackbeard died in his last battle with the authorities after downing a glass of liquor. His skull was then turned into a receptacle for rum punch at the Raleigh Tavern in Williamsburg.[38]

Beyond its connection with pirates, rum came to be known as the sailor's drink, with the British Royal Navy its biggest consumer.[39] A pint of rum replaced a gallon of beer as the alcohol ration on Royal Navy ships as early as 1655, following the British conquest of Jamaica.[40] In 1740 Admiral Edward Vernon came up with the idea of adding water to the rum and then mixing in sugar and lime juice. This not only stretched rum supplies and left the men less tipsy but also made the water on board ships both safer (by killing bacteria) and more palatable. Vernon's concoction—a forerunner of the cocktail—came to be known as grog, after his nickname, "Old Grogram," which he got from wearing a waterproof grogram cloak.[41] By the time of the Seven Years' War, "grog" had been formally incorporated into the Admiralty's naval regulations, and while the ration was reduced over the years, it remained an integral part of the Royal Navy's identity until 1970.

An unexpected side effect of the introduction of the grog ration was to drastically reduce in the British Royal Navy the incidence of scurvy, which in the eighteenth century was a leading health hazard on ships. Although it was unknown at the time, scurvy was caused by a vitamin C deficiency, which the lime juice in grog greatly helped to ameliorate. The growing health of British crews gave them a notable advantage over their French counterparts, who instead received three-quarters of a liter of wine (containing very little vitamin C) as their daily drink

Figure 1.2  Sailors serve up "grog" as part of daily life on a British troop ship. From *The Illustrated London News*, vol. 63, December 20, 1873 (De Agostini/Biblioteca Ambrosiana/Getty Images).

ration. On longer voyages, their drink ration was three-sixteenths of a liter of eau-de-vie (containing no vitamin C at all). One naval physician claimed that the unique British capacity to guard against scurvy had the effect of doubling crew performance and was instrumental in the British victories against the French and Spanish fleets at Trafalgar in 1805.[42]

### Rum and Revolution

But while rum helped Britain maintain mastery over the seas, it also helped fuel rebellion in its American colonies. Rum production was the lifeblood of the New England economy in the eighteenth century, and keeping the region's 159 rum distilleries running depended on the colonists' ability to smuggle molasses from the French West Indies. This worked fine as long as British customs agents were willing to ignore their own trade laws and take bribes in exchange for turning a blind eye. For decades, British authorities tolerated smuggling through a combination of neglect, incompetence, and corruption. But after the costly Seven Years' War with France, the Crown was eager to refill its coffers and decided to finally get serious about collecting taxes on trade. The Royal Navy was unleashed against colonial smugglers because civilian customs agents had proven so corrupt and unreliable.

Benjamin Franklin was among the many who denounced this punitive move. As he sarcastically wrote:

Convert the brave, honest officers of your *navy* into pimping tide-waiters and colony officers of the *customs*. Let those who in the time of war fought gallantly in defense of their countrymen, in peace be taught to prey upon it. Let them learn to be corrupted by great and real smugglers; but (to show their diligence) scour with armed boats every bay, harbor, river, creek, cove, or nook throughout your colonies; stop and detain every coaster, every wood-boat, every fisherman. . . . O, *this will work admirably!*[43]

The militarized crackdown provoked a violent backlash. Starting in the 1760s, bullying—in the form of mob riots, the burning of customs vessels, and the tarring and feathering of informants—became increasingly common as bribery became a less dependable way of doing business. The authorities proved overconfident: instead of imposing order, they created more disorder. In trying to tighten its grip, Britain lost its grip entirely. John Adams would later write, "I know not why we should blush to confess that molasses was an essential ingredient in American independence."[44] Molasses meant rum, since most of the imported supply went to the rum distilleries. Rum, in short, was the spirit of '76.

Nowhere did rum fuel more revolutionary sentiment than in Rhode Island, where the economy was dependent on keeping the distilleries running. One of the most brazen attacks against the Crown occurred on June 9, 1772, when the royal cutter *Gaspee* was stormed and burned late at night in Narragansett Bay. Earlier that day, the *Gaspee* had run aground while chasing a suspected smuggling vessel. Realizing it was stranded and vulnerable, local merchants quickly formed a raiding party that snuck up on the ship under cover of darkness and overwhelmed the crew. Today Rhode Islanders annually celebrate the burning of the *Gaspee* as a heroic episode in the push for independence.[45]

Alcohol lubricated the road to revolution in other ways. It was not only the sheer amount of alcohol consumed that mattered—by the 1770s per capita drinking in the American colonies was nearly twice what it is today—but *where* the drinking took place and *who* was meeting there. Taverns, not churches or schoolhouses or town halls, were the favored meeting spots to plot against the Crown. One writer has described the local taverns as "the cradle of the American Revolution, the place where people allowed their anger at the king and his loyalists to surface and be supported by other drinkers."[46] Virginia's Committee of Correspondence met at Williamsburg's Raleigh Tavern. Ethan Allen and his Green Mountain Boys set up their headquarters at the Catamount Tavern in Bennington, Vermont. The first meeting between John Adams and George Washington was at Philadelphia's City Tavern. Captain John Parker turned Buckman's Tavern on Lexington Green into the headquarters for the Minutemen. Thomas Jefferson later wrote the Declaration of Independence at the Indian Queen Tavern in Philadelphia. John Hancock—whose ship *Liberty* had been impounded for smuggling Madeira wine—was the first to sign that document, but many other signatories also had ties to the alcohol business, including a maltster, a cooper, a distiller, a handful of smugglers, and quite a few hard cider–makers.[47]

Boston had some ninety licensed taverns by 1769; twenty of these establishments' license holders were members of the Sons of Liberty.[48] Samuel Adams, who ran a malting business and was the founder of the Boston chapter of the Sons of Liberty, met with his conspirators at the Green Dragon Tavern in Boston's North End. Some of the Sons of Liberty drank from a special punch bowl known as the Liberty Bowl, made by the silversmith and engraver Paul Revere, and engraved along the rim with the names of prominent Sons, including John Hancock.[49] During Paul Revere's famous ride on April 19, 1775, to warn the colonists of the arrival of British soldiers, he stopped at the home of Isaac Hall, a rum distiller and captain of the Medford Minutemen, who reportedly gave Revere enough rum to make "a rabbit bite a bulldog."[50] The militiamen who first confronted the Redcoats on Lexington's green and fired the shot heard around the world had assembled at Buckman's Tavern.[51]

Rum proved essential during the war as well. Rum was such a valued commodity that it served as a form of currency. For instance, New Hampshire politician John Langdon donated about 150 hogsheads of rum to raise a militia, and this militia in turn repelled the British troops entering the colony from Canada under the command of General John Burgoyne.[52] Most critically, the daily four-ounce rum ration helped keep both the Redcoats and the Continental Army marching on. General Henry Cox informed George Washington in 1780 about his supply needs: "Besides beef and pork, bread & flour, Rum is too material an article, to be omitted," he wrote. "No exertions ought to be spar'd to provide ample quantities of it."[53] According to one observer, "Without New England rum, a New England army could not be kept together."[54] Rum could also be used as a reward: one band of rebel soldiers was given a rum bonus for retrieving incoming cannon balls, which were then reloaded and returned to the original sender.[55]

General Washington, who owned four stills on his Virginia estate, considered rum a priority provision and forcefully argued to keep the rum rations going: the "benefits arising from the moderate use of strong liquor have been experienced in all Armies and are not to be disputed," he advised Congress in 1777.[56] He had doubled the rum rations for his troops at Valley Forge during the harsh winter that same year.[57] Washington even advocated setting up public distilleries to avoid rum shortages. The general strongly favored rum over wine: he told John Hancock in 1781 that "Wine cannot be distributed [to] the soldiers instead of Rum, except the quantity is much increased."[58] Hancock subsequently wrote to Major General Benjamin Lincoln in Boston that rum "is of such importance that the army should be fill'd up & regularly supplied."[59]

But soldiers' thirst for rum was also a handicap. Washington's victory over the Hessian mercenaries at Trenton was aided by the fact that the enemy was intoxicated. Washington's troops in turn defied his orders to destroy the Hessians' rum and instead got so drunk that they slowed down their return trip across the Delaware, with many of them falling out of their boats.[60] After the Americans pushed the British out of their camp at Eutaw Springs and drank the captured rum rations in celebration, the British successfully launched a surprise counterattack.[61]

As the six-year war dragged on, rum supplies for the Continental Army became increasingly scarce, threatening to undermine troop morale. The British were well aware of the morale-boosting importance of rum and targeted the enemy's shrinking supplies. For instance, the British 64th Regiment of Foot attacked Washington's stores along the Hudson River, destroying at least 400 hogsheads of the beverage.[62] In August 1780, just as Brigadier General Horatio Gates was preparing to engage British troops under the command of General Charles Cornwallis in South Carolina, his rum supplies ran out. His mess officers panicked and decided to distribute molasses instead, apparently not realizing that this would function as a laxative. The next day, as the soldiers ran back and forth to the bushes, preoccupied with their stomach attacks, the British attacked and routed them.[63]

After the war, rum remained the British military's drink of choice. Indeed, it was deemed vital to keeping the troops in line. In 1791, an army surgeon in Jamaica warned that when deprived of their rum ration for even a single day, "discontent immediately begins to shew itself among the men. If with-held for any length of time, complaints sometimes rise to a state of mutiny, and desertions become notorious."[64] At the same time, officers could push their men to work harder and longer with the promise of extra rations of "fatigue rum."[65] Rum drinking was such an integral part of British military culture that one observer at the time went so far as to suggest it had magical powers: "I am sure there is some elixir of life in rum ration; I have seen wounded men, all but dead, come to life after having some rum given to them. Be this as it may, I am convinced there is something very extraordinary about it."[66]

It is therefore perhaps not surprising that at the Battle of Waterloo in 1815, the victorious soldiers were given rum to help prepare them for battle.[67] An estimated 550,000 gallons of rum were dispensed to the British Army every year during the second half of the nineteenth century. In 1875 alone, the British armed forces drank 5,386 million gallons of rum.[68] And as the global reach of the British military grew, so too did the disruptive reach of rum production and consumption, stretching from Australia to India.[69]

## Whiskey, Rebellion, and Westward Expansion

But while the British continued to favor rum, the new American nation's break from the empire brought a break in its people's drinking habits. By the early eighteenth century, whiskey had supplanted rum as America's favorite spirit. Whiskey was easier and cheaper to produce. It could be made from surplus domestic grain and corn instead of imported molasses, the supply of which had been disrupted during the war and never fully recovered. Most New England rum distilleries eventually shut down. Whiskey, which was associated with self-reliance and independence, came to be viewed as the more patriotic drink. Rum, on the other hand, was thought of as a British drink and symbolized dependence on foreigners.

Whiskey also replaced rum as the preferred drink in both the US Navy and the US Army. In 1830, according to the War Department's annual report, the army issued an estimated 72,537 gallons of whiskey— equivalent to 13.6 gallons per man in the military.[70] In his 1834–1836 travel journal, English journalist Charles A. Murray wrote that in observing the US military, he witnessed "more cases of drunkenness than I ever saw among any troops in the world."[71] In the first decades of the nineteenth century, alcohol helped with recruitment by "enticing" drunk civilians to enlist and then kept them motivated in the face of harsh conditions.[72] According to one estimate, some "12 to 20 percent of general courts-martial and about 60 percent of regimental courts-martial were alcohol-related."[73] Drunkenness in the military became an easy target for temperance activists. But even after President Andrew Jackson eliminated alcohol rations in 1832, whiskey was still included in army supplies.[74]

Whiskey's earliest claim to fame in America was its leading role in the country's most well-known tax protest since independence—the "Whiskey Rebellion." Burdened by war debts, the adolescent nation faced the same revenue collection problem that the British had, and taxing spirits was one of the most tempting solutions. In 1791, Alexander Hamilton came up with the idea of imposing an excise tax on domestic spirits, and Congress agreed, giving rise to the nation's first tax bureaucracy. In addition to needing to pay off burdensome war debts and place the country on a sound financial footing, the official rationale for the excise tax was that it was needed to fund a naval force to battle the Barbary pirates in the Mediterranean. Senator William Maclay of Pennsylvania was not convinced there was a real threat: "The trifling affair of our having eleven captives at Algiers . . . is made the pretext for going to war . . . and fitting out a fleet." He saw the government's desire for excise dollars as just the beginning. "Farewell freedom in America," he warned.[75]

Nowhere was whiskey more entrenched than in western Pennsylvania, where there were more than 5,000 pot stills—one for every six inhabitants.[76] Many outraged distillers not only refused to pay the new tax but intimidated and attacked the tax collectors, even going so far as to tar and feather them. The American collectors were as hated as their British predecessors had been. In 1794, a band of disgruntled western Pennsylvania settlers, calling themselves the "Whiskey Boys," denounced the excise tax as a threat to their liberty and called for secession. Apparently, they believed in no taxation even with representation. The revolt began when the band burned down the home of General Neville, the tax inspector for the region—but not until they had finished drinking the contents of his cellar. The Whiskey Boys, who soon grew to a force of over 5,000, proceeded to assemble in Braddock's Field, near Pittsburgh, to contemplate their next move. Local residents greeted them with free whiskey. Hugh Brackenridge, editor of the *Pittsburgh Gazette*, explained why: "I thought it better to be employed in extinguishing the fire of their thirst, than of my house."[77]

When news of the revolt reached President Washington, he denounced the Whiskey Boys as traitors and, at Hamilton's urging, mobilized a militia army of 13,000. Hamilton considered the refusal to pay the tax to be particularly offensive, since the federal government, through its purchases for the military, had been the most important customer of the Pennsylvania distillers.[78] Dispatched to the Pennsylvania backcountry, the troops apparently spent much of their time enjoying the local product. The account of one of the militiamen, published in the *American Daily Advertiser*, summarized the daily routine:

> No sooner does the drum beat in the morning, than up I start, and away to my canteen, where a precious draft of new distilled whiskey animates and revives me. This being done, away to fire, where in

CAPTURE OF THE WHISKEY-TAX COLLECTORS.

Figure 1.3 This wood engraving depicts the capture of a tax collector at Pigeon Creek, Pennsylvania, during the Whiskey Rebellion in 1794 (Granger Collection).

ten minutes you will hear more genuine wit than Philadelphia will afford in a month. When we halt at night, our tents being pitched, we sit down on the straw, cover ourselves with blankets, and push about the [whiskey] canteen so briskly that at length we are obliged to lie down: A sound sleep then enables us to endure a repetition of fatigue—and so on.[79]

The army met no local resistance, and the short-lived rebellion was put down without bloodshed. It helped matters that the federal soldiers paid cash for all the whiskey they consumed—giving the distillers the funds they needed to pay the excise.[80]

Spirits also proved to be a key ingredient in how the West was won. As part of the process of being displaced or wiped out, Indian populations became dependent on "White Man's Wicked Water."

Their consumption of alcohol started with rum during the colonial period and then switched mostly to whiskey during the nineteenth century. Introducing heavy drinking to Native American communities with no previous exposure to alcohol had devastating consequences. White colonists were alarmed by the Native Americans' resolve to drink until drunk and the behavior this incited.[81] Alcohol researchers have pointed to the widespread Native American drinking pattern of "maximal dosing," which exhausts available alcohol supplies in the absence of social controls.[82] Such bouts of binge drinking reinforced white stereotypes of Native Americans as out-of-control "savages" who were morally deficient and racially inferior.

In 1763, near the end of the Seven Years' War, the commissary of the Detroit post, James Sterling, identified the thirst for rum as the motive for an expected attack by Pontiac: "I believe the main Attack is design'd against the Rum Cags [kegs]." But he also anticipated that rum would motivate the defenders: "I'll be hang'd if ever one of them offers to come past them 'till the last Drop is expended," promised the custodian of the fort's rum supplies.[83] After Pontiac's unsuccessful attack, the commander of the British troops, Major Henry Gladwin, advised General Jeffrey Amherst that the most effective reprisal would be to supply the Indians with alcohol: "If yr. Excellency still intends to punish them further for their barbarities, it might easily be done without any expense to the Crown, by permitting a free sale of rum, which will destroy them more effectually than fire and sword."[84] Later, an English trader paid an Indian from the Peoria tribe a barrel of rum to kill Pontiac.[85]

"Rum was a potent ethnic cleanser," Ian Williams notes in tracing the history of the beverage in America.[86] In the early 1770s, a British official visited the Choctaws and reported that he "saw nothing but Rum Drinking and Women Crying over the Dead bodies of their relations who have died by Rum."[87] Colonial leaders were well aware of the lethal effects that alcohol was having on Indian communities, as is evident in this startling passage from Benjamin Franklin's *Autobiography*: "If it be the Design of Providence to extirpate these Savages in order to make room for Cultivators of the Earth, it seems not improbable that Rum may be the appointed means. It has already annihilated all the Tribes who formally inhabited the Sea-Coast."[88]

In 1837, an anonymous Boston poet came to a similar conclusion:

> *When our bold fathers cross'd the Atlantic wave,*
> *And here arrived—a weak, defenseless band,*
> *Pray what became of all the tribes so brave—*
> *The rightful owners of this happy land?*
> *Were they headlong to the realms below.*
> *"By doom of battle?" friend, I answer no.*
> *Our Fathers were too wise to think of war:*
> *They knew the woodlands were not so quickly past:*
> *They might have met with many an ugly scar—*
> *Lost many a foretop—and been beat at last;*
> *But Rum, assisted by his son Disease,*
> *Perform'd the business with surprising ease.*[89]

As white settlers and soldiers moved west, so too did alcohol. Federal Indian agents routinely reported that "alcohol was destroying the tribes more rapidly than gunpowder or the advance of white yeomen with the plow."[90] Indian leaders occasionally made impassioned pleas to the federal government to stem the tide of alcohol. A leader of the Miamis, Little Turtle, said to President Jefferson in 1802: "When our white brothers came to this land, our forefathers were numerous and happy; but since their intercourse with the white people, and owing to the introduction of this fatal poison [alcohol], we have become less numerous and happy."[91] Several decades later, in 1831, a Kickapoo tribal spokesman told U.S. Commissioner E. A. Ellsworth: "We are afraid of the wicked water brought to us by our white friends. We wish to get out of its reach by land or water."[92]

Government authorities used such concerns about alcohol as a convenient rationale to push for Indian removal to more distant lands. In its efforts to negotiate a removal treaty, an executive commission warned the Miamis: "If you continue here where you now are . . . and let the white people feed you whiskey and bring among you bad habits, in a little while where will be the Miami nation? They will all be swept off." But the commission also suggested an alternative: "Situated as you are, your Great Father cannot prevent his white people from coming among you. He wants to place you in a land where he can take care of you [and] protect you against all your enemies, whether red men or white."[93] From 1825 to 1847, the federal government relocated some 70,000 Indians to Indian Country, west of Missouri and Arkansas. And as Indian tribes moved west, so too did alcohol peddlers. So while alcohol can be viewed as a weapon of war, in many ways it was such a lethal facilitator of westward expansion that it can also be thought of as a substitute for war.

Whiskey's more conventional war functions were to fortify soldiers and fill government coffers, roles that were especially evident during the American Civil War. Whiskey helped keep both North and South soldiering on. Equally important, the Union's military supplies were partly paid for by the imposition of a new excise tax on spirits. General Ulysses Grant was perhaps the war's most notorious drunk, but President Abraham Lincoln was apparently unconcerned by his general's habit. He replied to a complaint about Grant's heavy drinking by announcing that he would request "the quartermaster of the army to lay in a large stock of the same kind of liquor, and would direct him to furnish a supply to some of my other generals who have never yet won a victory."[94] While there is little evidence that drinking impaired Grant's military abilities (which perhaps explains why Lincoln was so tolerant of it), the same cannot be said of General Thomas Meagher, who was apparently so drunk while leading his men into battle at Antietam that he fell off of his horse.[95] Meanwhile, the Union kept its soldiers well supplied with whiskey to help them endure the hardships of the battlefield, despite the drink's considerable downsides. General George McClellan complained in February 1862 that "no one evil agent so much obstructs this army . . . as the degrading vice of drunkenness. It is the cause of by far the greater part of the disorders which are examined by courts-martial."[96]

Whiskey was equally popular on the Confederate side. Tennessee general Benjamin Franklin Cheatham, whose picture appeared on an early Jack Daniel's label, reportedly rode drunk into the Battle of Stones River.[97] Some rebel leaders blamed alcohol for subverting the war effort. Drunkenness, argued General Braxton Bragg, was causing "demoralization, disease, and death" among the troops: "We have lost more valuable lives at the hands of the whiskey sellers than by the balls of our enemies."[98] In 1862, at Middletown, Virginia, Confederate soldiers seemed more interested in drinking captured booze than in fighting: when they intercepted Union supply trains that included whiskey and other liquors, they became so drunk that the trapped Union forces were able to sneak away.[99] Alcohol was banned in some Confederate camps, but smugglers easily subverted the restrictions.

At the same time, alcohol was used as the main anesthetic on both sides. "Our most valued medicament was the alcoholic liquors," wrote Confederate doctor William Henry Taylor. "As alcoholic liquors were indispensable on a battlefield, it is conceivable that the sudden and complete vanishing to which they were liable might at some time prove to be a serious matter. And so it would have been but that one of our staff, being in tolerably constant communication with his own home, where there was a distillery, was able to keep on hand a full keg of his own."[100]

Following the war, alcohol also took its toll on US soldiers stationed at remote western outposts. Ryan Kennedy notes that at Fort Hays in Kansas, many enlisted men coped with low morale and the banality of daily life by turning to the bottle, which proved to be a bigger threat to their health than clashes with Native Americans: between 1867 and 1884, there was only one soldier wounded by arrow at the outpost, but in just the first six years of that same time period, the post's surgeon saw twenty-two cases of soldiers afflicted with delirium tremens (alcohol withdrawal). In 1873 alone, one in twenty soldiers stationed at the post suffered the shaking, confusion, and hallucinations associated with intensive withdrawal.[101] Dismayed, Army Lieutenant Duane Merritt Greene observed that soldiers "tremble on the brink of a drunkard's grave—men who might have made themselves famous as warriors, but preferred to expend their genius in dissipation and revelry."[102]

On February 22, 1880, General William T. Sherman ordered, with the approval of President Rutherford B. Hayes, a ban on the sale of alcohol to soldiers, which, due to the immediate backlash, was amended to permit "light" beverages (wine, beer, cider) to be sold at posts. Enforcement of the ban, however, was uneven and varied from fort to fort.[103]

But even as the government tried to wean its soldiers off the bottle, its coffers relied on taxing it. After the Civil War, alcohol taxes and customs duties were the twin pillars of federal finances, with the former providing up to 40 percent of government funds in the 1880s.[104] Postbellum military campaigns depended on alcohol revenue. As historian E. Elliot Brownlee notes, alcohol taxes financed Southern Reconstruction, military incursions against the Native Americans, and the buildup of the US Navy. In fact, twofold increases in alcohol and tobacco taxes were responsible for most of the tax revenues necessary to fund the Spanish-American War.[105]

## Taxing Booze, Building Empire

The British proved much better at collecting taxes closer to home than in their rebellious colonies. Indeed, taxing alcohol funded Britain's emergence as the world's leading military power. War costs provided the impetus for new alcohol taxes, and the alcohol revenue in turn helped to build up the state's taxation apparatus—enabling extraction of even more revenue to pay for ever-more-costly military ventures.[106] Even with the repeal of the Corn Laws in the 1840s and Britain's embrace of free trade, tariffs on alcohol (as well as on coffee and tea) remained in place because of their importance to state revenue.[107]

This dynamic dated back to the English Civil War, when England imposed the first excise tax on alcohol.[108] Whiskey from Scotland was a lucrative target for the tax authorities as early as 1643, when Parliament first imposed taxes on distilled spirits. As Kevin Kosar puts it, "Whenever England found itself at war, it looked for money in whisky." The government first taxed the malt and stills used to make Scotch and then levied another tax on the alcohol once it was distilled. In 1781 Parliament outlawed private distillation and endorsed the seizure of any apparatus used in whiskey production and transportation, including stills, horses, and wagons.[109] The alcohol tax also created friction with Ireland: "Perhaps especially galling to the Irish was that their drinks were being taxed to finance England's army."[110]

The pressure to raise tax revenue grew as the business of war became more financially burdensome. Britain's average annual expenditures went from nearly £5.5 million in the Nine Years' War to more than £20 million in the American War of Independence.[111] Britain's tax bureaucracy mushroomed in size during this period, with the Excise Office eventually dwarfing all other fiscal offices. Between 1793 and 1815, malt yielded £41.7 million in taxes to finance wars, spirits £28.7 million, wine £20.8 million, beer £11.8 million, and imported spirits £30.6 million. According to historian Patrick Karl O'Brien, alcohol (and tobacco) accounted for 27 percent of British taxes used in war-making. He argues that without Britons' widespread smoking and drinking habits, the government would have had far more trouble financing the defeat of Napoleon.[112]

The reason Britain was able to so significantly boost its tax revenue and fund its rise to become such a dominant global military power, historian John Nye documents, was that the domestic alcohol industry was increasingly oligopolistic, making the collection of taxes easier and more efficient. Moreover, local producers greatly benefited from trade restrictions (especially against French wine and brandy) imposed during wartime and were therefore more willing and able to pay the excise taxes. From 1788 to 1792, alcohol (and tobacco) taxes accounted for over 43 percent of British government tax revenue.[113] As was true in the US case, collecting excise taxes was easier and met less domestic resistance than direct taxation on income and wealth. For instance, "the gradual acceptance of the beer excises," Nye notes, "would lead to its use to finance a variety of government ventures, notably the wars with France."[114]

The long period of war with France from 1689 to 1713 provided the opportunity for Britain to virtually cut off trade relations with France and eliminate the trade deficit, the greatest portion of which was due to wine imports. The political repercussions of this move would be long-lasting, with brewers and distillers, as well as British traders and investors in Portuguese wine, pushing for high tariffs on French wine and spirits once trade with France was reinitiated in 1714.[115]

One of the many consequences of the Anglo-French conflict was the reshaping of drinking habits. When Britain's growing fondness for French brandy came to an abrupt end with the outbreak of hostilities between the two countries, Dutch gin took its place, sparking a long-lasting gin craze in England and the proliferation of domestic gin distillers to meet the surging demand.[116] The British love of gin would later lead to the invention of the "gin and tonic," which started out as a military drink in India, where soldiers were receiving gin rations. The public drunkenness that came to be associated with what has been dubbed the

"Gin Age" fueled the temperance movement and prompted more government restrictions on where gin could be produced and sold.[117] Wine remained popular, but the supply now flowed from Portugal and Spain rather than from France, and it was overshadowed by the growth of domestic beer production in the early to mid-eighteenth century, which was concentrated in a dozen or so big porter brewers in London.[118]

Alcohol continued to be the leading target of British excise taxes in the nineteenth century. Between 1819 and 1900, Britain raised at least 30 percent of its tax revenue from alcohol.[119] As Britain had done in prior wars, it passed higher taxes on malt and spirits to finance the Crimean War, fought between 1853 and 1856.[120] And by 1880, the tax on alcohol was responsible for more than 43 percent of total tax revenue.[121]

### Alcoholic Empire

Russia has been called the "alcoholic empire," not only because of societal addiction to alcohol, but because of the state's addiction to alcohol revenue.[122] This began as early as 1474, when Ivan III established a state monopoly on the vodka industry to help fund his wars of conquest.[123] At the height of the tsarist empire in the eighteenth and nineteenth centuries, alcohol taxes funded one-third of the Russian state's budget, covering the cost of not only building the royal family's Winter Palace in St. Petersburg but also maintaining Europe's largest army.[124] Indeed, from 1839 until the Russian Revolution, vodka stood out as the single most important source of revenue for the government.[125]

The more Russians drank, the more money poured into state coffers. But a drunk nation also meant a drunk army. Heavy drinking became embedded in Russian military culture.[126] Drinking while soldiering was encouraged from the very top. In the early eighteenth century, Peter the Great—a heavy drinker himself (reportedly drinking between thirty and forty glasses of wine per day)—authorized thrice-weekly vodka rations. Daily rations (*charkas*) of the beverage became standard by 1761, and by the end of the century Emperor Paul had formalized the right to daily alcohol rations by incorporating it into naval regulations.[127] Vodka rations also became widespread in the infantry, especially in combat situations.

But while alcohol boosted Russian troops' morale, it also undermined their effectiveness on the battlefield, as Napoleon discovered in the 1805 Battle of Austerlitz. Napoleon's spies informed him that the Russian army was "marked by riot and intemperance; and that they spent the night preceding the day on which the battle of Austerlitz was fought, in drunkenness, noise and revelry. . . .This circumstance may have assisted to produce, or at least to heighten the disasters of that fatal day."[128] After this decisive defeat, Russian troops withdrew to their own territory.

In 1812, an overconfident Napoleon invaded Russia, determined to capture Moscow and force Tsar Alexander I to surrender. But this time, vodka worked against Napoleon's war aims. Rather than hand the city over to Napoleon and his exhausted soldiers, Moscow governor Fyodor Rostopchin "ordered the withdrawal of all of Moscow's fire pumps and the emptying of the prisons before turning the highly flammable taverns and vodka storehouses into firebombs and igniting boats loaded with alcohol that burned three-quarters of the city to the ground."[129] As the French failed to put out the flames, chaos spread. "The army had dissolved completely," recalled French major Pion des Loches. "Everywhere one could see drunken soldiers and officers loaded with booty and provisions seized from houses which had fallen prey to the flames."[130] Deprived of food and shelter for his dwindling army, a frustrated Napoleon retreated, losing thousands more men to disease, fatigue, cold, and hunger on the long march home.

Less than two years after Napoleon's Russia disaster, Tsar Alexander I's troops invaded France and took Paris, forcing Napoleon to abdicate and go into exile. Prussian and Austrian armies joined the invasion of eastern France. The Prussian soldiers, aware of their commander's particular fondness for champagne, wrote a verse in anticipation of their victory:

> *Throw bridges over the Rhine.*
> *I must drink Champagne wine,*
> *It is at its best, straight from the nest,*
> *Soon it will all be mine.*[131]

"The Prussians are insatiable," complained one of Napoleon's generals. "You cannot believe the amount of champagne they drink."[132] The

Russians were equally thirsty: "Cellars throughout Champagne were plundered, the worst being those of [Jean-Remy] Moet, which saw six hundred thousand bottles emptied by Russian soldiers camped on the premises."[133] Moet, an old friend of Napoleon,[134] viewed this event as a longer-term business opportunity: "All of those soldiers who are ruining me today will make my fortune tomorrow. I'm letting them drink all they want. They will be hooked for life and become my best salesmen when they go back to their own country." Indeed, another champagne maker observed that before they returned home, the victorious rulers "came back to Champagne because they said they did not have time to taste champagne while they were busy fighting. They were curious about this new kind of wine that sparkled, so they returned."[135] Champagne soon became the most famous wine in the world.

While the French champagne industry rebounded after the Napoleonic Wars, the Russian army continued to drown itself in vodka. "By the mid-nineteenth century," Mark Lawrence Schrad writes in *Vodka Politics*, "the autocratic vodka politics that had long enriched the state while wedding the people to the bottle started backfiring on the Russian state by corroding its military might."[136] Russians were fond of vodka, and none more so than the Russian soldier. Drinking's centrality to Russian military culture led to peer pressure and the conversion of former teetotalers. In the mid-nineteenth century, company commander Nikolai Butovskii wrote in the official military journal *Voennyi sbornik* that the state vodka ration encouraged new recruits to turn to drink. Of the "non-drinkers," most of whom were new recruits, he wrote: "By their faces you notice that they are depressed, or more accurately embarrassed by something—and it is all too simple to see why: they not only cannot join in the general merriment but on the contrary, have become targets for their inebriated comrades who, for lack of any other kind of entertainment, begin to mock them, giving them various annoying nicknames which excite a general scorn and contemptuous laughter."[137]

In the Crimean War (1853–1856), drunkenness reached all the way up to the army high command. On one occasion Russian lieutenant general Vasily Kiryakov hosted a champagne party instead of leading the left flank of the army's defenses. Often described as intoxicated, Kiryakov ordered his soldiers to open fire on his own Kiev Hussars, mistaking them for the French enemy. This led much of his Minsk regiment to retreat, having lost faith in their commander.[138]

Alcohol sales later underwrote Russia's war with Japan (1904–1905). As former finance minister Sergei Witte wrote in his memoirs about his successor: "When the war with Japan began, the then finance minister Vladimir Nikolaevich Kokovtsov began to use the liquor monopoly primarily as a means of increasing revenue, by raising liquor prices and increasing the number of liquor stores. And the work of excise officials was judged by increase in revenue rather than by decrease in alcoholism."[139]

But while the booze paid for arms, those carrying the arms were too boozed up to fight. After the first torpedo attack on the Russian fleet at Port Arthur in February 1904, the drunken chaos that surrounded mobilization slowed reinforcements, placing Russia at a disadvantage from the start. An American journalist observed that "in the mobilization for the Japanese war the soldiers were carried, dead with intoxication, to the train."[140] Schrad notes that "the tearful send-offs at assembly points often turned into orgies of mayhem, as recruitment officers corralled drunken conscripts with bayonets. With surprising frequency commanders were overwhelmed by the drunken masses, as vodka-fueled mobs ransacked local taverns and businesses and murdered recruitment officers."[141] Such behavior gave birth to the expression "drunk as a recruit."[142]

And the drinking continued as Russian soldiers were sent into battle. Reporting from Port Arthur, Associated Press journalist Frederick McCormick observed a "pile of perhaps ten thousand cases of vodka" near the train station.[143] Schrad provides numerous examples of the strategic implications of alcohol abuse during the war, from tales of commanders of military supply ships shooting at fishing ships after confusing them with enemies to cases of Russian naval men undercutting military efficiency with drunken fights, insubordination, and even several drunk officers falling overboard.[144] One war correspondent described the entire campaign in Manchuria as "a scuffle between a drunken guardsman and a sober policeman."[145]

McCormick reported that the Russian commanders appeared to drink as much as the soldiers, and indeed seemed more interested in the bottle than the battle:

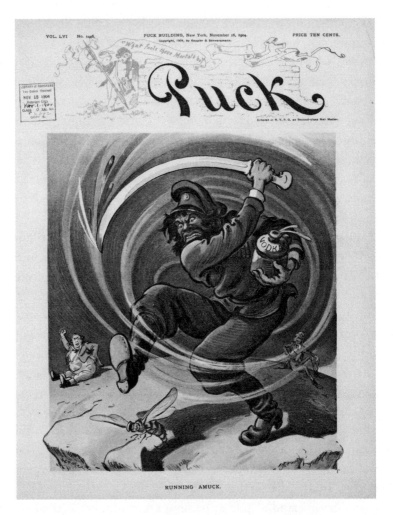

Figure 1.4  A drunken Russian man holds a jug of vodka and wildly swings a bloody sword at a wasp representing Japan in this illustration of the Russo-Japanese War from 1904. John Bull and Uncle Sam sit in the background (Library of Congress).

Up to this time, although the troops had been continually beaten, the army seemed outwardly, at least to the casual observer, as care-free as possible. In the back court in the International Hotel, captains, colonels and generals could be found any day, and occasionally from late morning breakfast to late at night, repeatedly greeting each other with kisses through their heavy beards and making merry over liquor, champagne and beer. It reminded one of Port Arthur just before the opening of the war. Every night had its orgy, and out of these grew many troubles for the commander-in-chief. It seemed to be a natural characteristic to begin breakfast with champagne. A young officer . . . would begin in the morning on a bottle of liquor, and at night was always certain of being carried out to his room by the Chinese waiters. It took a fortnight by military process to transfer him from the army base to the rear. A staff officer and three companions, who mixed their champagne with beer and vodka, and among them could not raise fifty rubles with which to pay their bill, would monopolize the hotel.[146]

By the middle of 1904 the Japanese had blockaded the Russians at Port Arthur and had won repeated land battles at the Yalu River. On January 2, 1905, the Russians surrendered Port Arthur to the Japanese. Inland, meanwhile, many of the retreating Russians were in a drunken stupor. According to a Russian journalist of the *Vilna Military Leaflet*, "The Japanese at Mukden found several thousand dead-drunk soldiers, whom they bayoneted like pigs."[147] Meanwhile, the retreating military high command drank champagne aboard their luxurious train. "Through the windows could be watched the scene of headlong flight of the soldiers up the railway," McCormick wrote. "The foreigners were plunged into a state of confused and sympathetic embarrassment, for in no country which any one of them represented was it possible to drink to such a state of affairs. But all thoughts of chagrin and mortification as far as the Russian officers were concerned seemed to vanish under the spell of the opportunity to drink."[148]

A Russian officer summarized the extent of the problem: "Drinking and more drinking—what victories could there be? All, or almost all of our forces suffered from alcoholism. That is why we lost battles. And can it be that this poison has become less pervasive after the war? The Treasury can go on enriching itself on revenues from the monopoly, but what's the sense of that if the military will not be able to prevent the Treasury from being seized by foreign forces?"[149] A German war correspondent noted, " 'Who defeated the Russians?' ask foreigners, and they answer, 'The Japanese did not conquer, but alcohol triumphed, alcohol, alcohol.' "[150] A British war correspondent similarly wrote of the Russian loss: "A great people with a great army, who could not defeat the Japanese in a single battle, must first have been victims not of their enemy, but of themselves."[151]

It took a hugely embarrassing defeat for Tsar Nicholas II to turn against vodka. Rightly or wrongly, the Russian loss in the Russo-Japanese War of 1904–1905 was widely blamed on booze. It is impossible to say what the outcome of the war would have been in the absence of such rampant drinking within the ranks, but it is clear that the tsar's eventual embrace of prohibition as a solution to the alcohol problem was a disastrous overreaction, so much so that it ended up contributing to the downfall of the government and outbreak of revolution.

In the years after the Russo-Japanese War, vodka became politicized like never before, giving rise to growing public criticism of the tsar's "drunken budget."[152] In January 1914, Nicholas II fired Finance Minister Vladimir Kokovtsov, who had been blamed for the state's excessive reliance on the vodka monopoly. He was replaced by Pyotr Lyovich Bark, whom Nicholas charged with making sure that the Treasury was no longer "dependent on the ruination of the spiritual and economic forces of the majority of My faithful subjects."[153]

The tsar's decision to then ban alcohol both alienated the public and took away the single most important source of state revenue. According to Tsar Nicholas's biographer Sergei Oldenburg, World War I provided the crucial opening to impose prohibition: "Only wartime conditions, which upset all normal budgetary considerations, made it possible to adopt a measure that amounted to a renunciation of the state's largest source of income. Before 1914 no other nation had adopted such a radical measure in the struggle against alcoholism."[154] This bold move would backfire. Not only was prohibition financially self-destructive, but politically it further weakened the tsar's already fragile public support. And this in turn set the stage for political radicalization and revolution.[155]

The first steps toward prohibition were taken when the government ordered a ban on selling alcohol during mobilization in August 1914, a measure that was declared permanent by Nicholas II in October of the same year.[156] This unprecedented move impressed outside observers. Stanley Washburn, a war correspondent with the Russian army, wrote in the *London Times* in early 1915:

One cannot write of the Russian mobilization or of the rejuvenation of the Russian Empire without touching on the prohibition of vodka; the first manifest evidence of the increased efficiency was, of course, in the manner and promptness with which the army assembled; but, from that day, the benefits have been increasingly visible, not only in the army, but in every phase of Russian life. . . . At one stroke she freed herself of the curse that has paralyzed her peasant life for generations. This in itself is nothing short of a revolution.[157]

But the reality on the ground was considerably messier. According to a British military attaché in Russia in 1914, one group of soldiers ordered to destroy a supply of vodka on an estate could not resist getting drunk off it first. Dmitry Shlapentokh wrote that many mobilized troops resented the alcohol ban and turned to looting liquor supplies before reporting for duty. Boris Segal blamed desertions after February 1917 on the scarcity of vodka. According to Shlapentokh, "by the first days of the February Revolution bands of excited 'drunk soldiers and hooligans' roamed the streets shooting in doors and windows," and "by March–April of 1917, Petrograd was in a condition of unrestricted drunken frenzy, with contemporary cartoons depicting the Russian mob as drunken whores."[158]

On the front, meanwhile, during holidays and other breaks from battle, Russian soldiers traded food for vodka and other alcoholic drinks.[159] The Austrians and Germans were well aware of the Russian fondness for the bottle. Indeed, they would intentionally leave vodka bottles in the trenches and in houses at the battlefronts, hoping the enemy would not advance owing to drunken stupors and internecine quarrels.[160]

As morale declined with mounting battlefield losses, Russian troops deserted en masse, often looting liquor stores and wine cellars in the process. For instance, some 20,000 soldiers from the Russian Fifth Platoon based near Oryol looted a private wine cellar and emptied a local distillery. A detachment sent to restore order ended up joining the drunken festivities.[161]

Meanwhile, the state was starving for vodka revenue. "From time immemorial countries waging war have been in want of funds," wrote Andrei Shingarev, the official rapporteur of the imperial

Figure 1.5 A German political cartoon from World War I depicts unhappy Russian soldiers after Russia prohibits alcohol. From *Simplicissimus*, August 12, 1914, Carl Olof Petersen (Alamy).

Duma's budget and finance committees, in a report assessing the monetary impact of the alcohol ban, "but never since the dawn of human history has a single country, in a time of war, renounced the principal source of its revenue."[162] It was financial suicide. Russia's alcohol-free budget projections were based on wildly unrealistic expectations of increased worker productivity and economic growth, ignoring the simultaneous need to pay for the world's largest army. With the start of World War I, the timing of prohibition could not have been worse.[163] A desperate imperial government resorted to printing more and more money, with predictable hyperinflationary results. Adding to the financial strain, the costs of enforcing prohibition continued to mount. Thus, not only had the government deprived itself of desperately needed alcohol revenue, but it was further impoverished by trying to police the spread of illegal distillers and alcohol traders.[164]

The overthrow of the royal family in February 1917 and of the short-lived Provisional Government the following October were often defined by drunken chaos and disorder that the new Communist leadership struggled to control. Many of the soldiers and sailors who sacked the Winter Palace in late October first went after the wine cellars. "In the wine cellars of the Winter Palace, which were the first to be smashed, many unfortunate souls have already died from over-drinking," reported Lenin's advisor Vladimir Bonch-Bruevich. "Crates of wine were thrown into holes in the river ice, but crazed people dove in after it, and drowned in the Neva trying to catch that cursed potion. From there a drunken pogrom erupted, as with furious and rabid joy the crazed and drunken crowd stormed private apartments throughout the city."[165] Bessie Beatty, the war correspondent for the *San Francisco Bulletin*, described the scene at the Winter Palace that night as follows: "We thought the whole populace was going to be killed; but it later developed that the sounds we had taken for shots were nothing more fatal than popping corks, and the soldiers who lay on the white snow were not dead, but merely drunk."[166]

Over the next two months, Petrograd routinely experienced soldier-led alcohol riots, which targeted the more than 800 wine cellars scattered throughout the city. Lenin blamed counterrevolutionaries: "The bourgeoisie perpetuates the most evil crimes," he wrote in December 1917, "bribing the cast-offs and dregs of society, getting them drunk for the pogroms."[167] A Bolshevik order distributed in the Petrograd neighborhoods of Vasily Island called for the immediate confiscation and destruction of all alcohol. The order began: "The bourgeoisie has chosen a very sinister method of fighting against the proletariat; it has established in various parts of the city huge wine depots, and distributes liquor among the soldiers, in this manner attempting to sow dissatisfaction in the ranks of the Revolutionary Army."[168]

The Bolsheviks considered drunkenness counterrevolutionary, and in the Red Army, alcoholism was an offense listed as punishable by death. "If we don't stamp out alcoholism, then we will drink up socialism and drink up the October Revolution," declared Leon Trotsky, the leader and founder of the Red Army.[169] Lenin similarly warned that

Figure 1.6  Revolutionary workmen and soldiers rob a wine shop in Petrograd during the Russian Revolution (State Museum of Revolution/Alamy).

"vodka and other narcotics will draw us back to capitalism, rather than forward to Communism."[170] Lenin set up an antiriot committee and appointed a commissar to fight drunkenness and pogroms. In cities across the country, Red Guard forces sworn to be "sober and loyal to the revolution" were dispatched to confront drunken soldiers, leading to violent clashes. "The duty of the Red Guard," stated its own pledge, "includes the struggle with drunkenness so as not to allow liberty and revolution to drown in wine."[171]

Lenin remained staunchly prohibitionist, but his death in 1924 conveniently helped his successors change course. Alcohol simply proved too irresistible for a cash-strapped Bolshevik state desperately trying to recover from the twin devastations of a world war and a civil war.[172] The vodka ban was gradually loosened in order for the state to once again access alcohol revenue. A state monopoly was set up to control alcohol production. "Which is better: enslavement to foreign capital or the introduction of vodka?" Joseph Stalin remarked. "Naturally, we decided on vodka, because we figured that if we have to dirty our hands a little for the cause of the victory of the proletariat and the peasantry, we would resort even to this extreme in the interest of our cause."[173] Stalin not only came to depend on vodka revenue, but also used vodka as a political weapon to manipulate and control those closest to him in government and to inebriate visiting foreign dignitaries—Franklin Roosevelt claimed that between thirty and thirty-six rounds of drinks would be consumed at drunken dinners for British, French, and American delegates.[174]

### Drinking on the Western Front and on the Home Front

The mobilization of entire societies for full-scale mechanized warfare during World War I fundamentally shifted attitudes toward alcohol and provided an opening for temperance advocates to push for new government restrictions on recreational drinking. In England, Munitions Minister David Lloyd George even went so far as to declare that "we are fighting Germany, Austria, and Drink, and as far as I can see, the greatest of these deadly foes is Drink."[175] To set a good example, King George V vowed to eliminate alcohol from royal households until the war was over. Taxes on alcohol were increased, and new limits on beer production and drinking hours were imposed; the "temporary restrictions" on pub hours would last the rest of the century.[176] Beer was watered down, and production declined by a third. To a lesser extent, new laws were also introduced in France, including a ban on absinthe in 1915, restrictions on the opening hours of bars and cafes, and classification of public intoxication as a criminal offense for the first time.[177]

Yet even as Britain and France introduced measures to reduce drinking on the home front, they made sure to provide alcohol to their soldiers on the frontlines. Indeed, part of the rationale for limiting civilian drinking was to assure adequate supplies for the troops in the trenches. In the first sixteen months of the war, Britain shipped a quarter of a million gallons of rum to its troops in France.[178] The official army rationale for the rum rations was that the beverage was a medical remedy for fatigue, stress, and hardship[179]—consequently, additional shots were doled out before battle. One British soldier explained that "the second ration [administered before battle] is supposed to give us Dutch courage. It might fulfill its purpose if it were handed out in more liberal doses. . . . It does not even make us merry. But every one of us welcomes it."[180] Rum rations were distributed in jars marked "S.R.D.," which meant Special Rations Department, though soldiers joked that it stood for Soon Runs Dry and Services Rum Diluted.[181] In his book *The Great War and the Modern Memory*, Paul Fussell recalls daily life in the trenches, including starting out each early morning with the rum ration: "Some put it into their tea, but most swallowed it straight. It was a precious thing, and serving it out was almost like a religious ceremonial."[182] Another soldier wrote that during combat, "pervading the air was the smell of rum and blood."[183] A few years after the war, a medical officer went so far as to testify: "Had it not been for the rum ration I do not think we should have won the war."[184]

For their part, the French considered the wine ration essential not only to the war effort but to their national identity. When the war began, the wine ration was a quarter of a liter per day, but it was increased to three-quarters per day in 1918. In 1917, the French army consumed 1,200 million liters of wine.[185] Wine (referred to as *pinard*) was touted as a sophisticated drink, reflecting France's superiority over crude beer-drinking Germans. This image of wine was enthusiastically promoted by grapevine growers and wine producers, who relied on government contracts to stay in business.

On the other hand, the Americans, who were late arrivals to the Western Front, were caught up in prohibitionist fervor. A prohibition on alcohol in the military was a precursor to nationwide prohibition. The Canteen Act of 1901 banned "the sale of, or dealing in, beer, wine, or any intoxicating liquors by any person in any post exchange or canteen or army transport or upon any premises used for military purposes by the United States." In 1917, Section 12 of the Selective Service Act aimed to create the soberest fighting force in the world. It called for a five-mile radius of all US camps to be an alcohol-free zone and outlawed the sale of alcohol to uniformed military personnel.[186] The reality on the ground for the doughboys in France, however, was rather different, and General John Pershing even went so far as to make it possible for soldiers to have access to light wines and beers.[187]

Dry advocates back home masterfully exploited the war to push their own agenda, and indeed their eventual success in imposing prohibition is difficult to imagine in the absence of the war. They made frightening

Figure 1.7  Barrels of wine stored at the French Lemnos Island military base during the Dardanelles Campaign of World War I, 1915 (Everett Collection Historical/ Alamy).

claims about how alcohol was putting the country at risk: "Brewery products fill refrigerator cars, while potatoes rot for lack of transportation, bankrupting farmers and starving cities. The coal that they consume would keep the railroads open and the factories running."[188] The Anti-Saloon League declared that "Kaiser kultur was raised on beer." Going dry was the best way to beat the wet Germans: "Prohibition is the infallible submarine chaser we must launch by thousands. The water-wagon is the tank that can level every Prussian trench. Total abstinence is the impassable curtain barrage which we must lay before every trench. Sobriety is the bomb that will blow kaiserism to kingdom come."[189]

The 1917 U.S. Food Control Act, meant to secure the nation's scarce resources in wartime, became a prohibitionist tool: even though there was no serious food shortage, the law was used to curtail the use of food for the production of distilled spirits. The law also stipulated that the president could "limit or prohibit the manufacture of beer or wine as

Figure 1.8 French soldiers warm wine in a trench during World War I, 1917 (SOTK2011/Alamy).

he saw fit." President Woodrow Wilson opted to cut the supply of grain to brewers by 30 percent and limited the alcohol content of beer to 2.75 alcohol by volume (ABV).[190] Not only was beer drinking portrayed as Germanic and therefore unpatriotic, but the German roots of American brewers were used to paint them as traitors. The leader of the Anti-Saloon League wrote to the federal custodian of alien property: "I am informed that there are a number of breweries in this country which are owned in part by alien enemies. It is reported to me that the

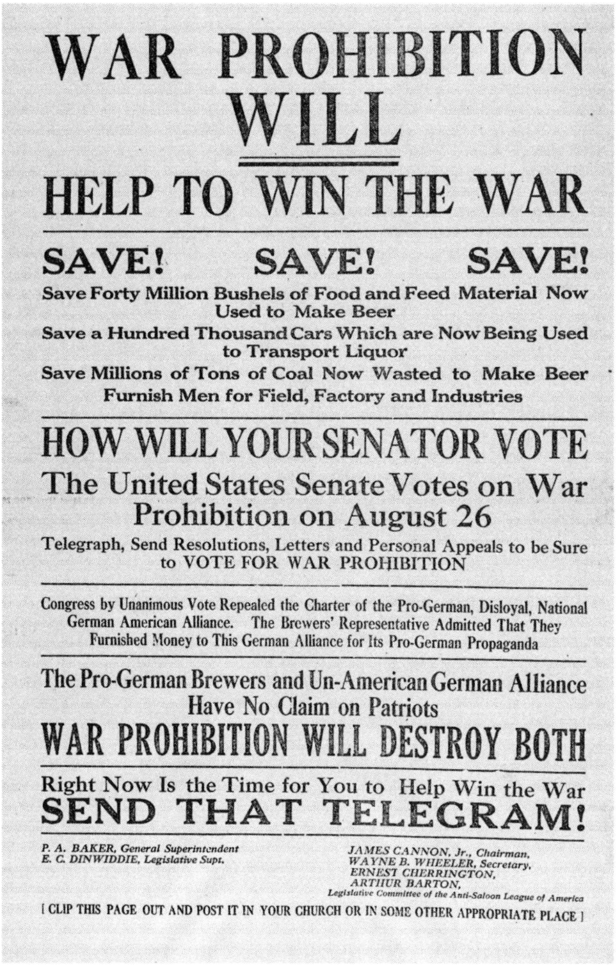

WAR PROHIBITION
WILL
HELP TO WIN THE WAR

SAVE! SAVE! SAVE!

Save Forty Million Bushels of Food and Feed Material Now Used to Make Beer
Save a Hundred Thousand Cars Which are Now Being Used to Transport Liquor
Save Millions of Tons of Coal Now Wasted to Make Beer
Furnish Men for Field, Factory and Industries

HOW WILL YOUR SENATOR VOTE

The United States Senate Votes on War Prohibition on August 26

Telegraph, Send Resolutions, Letters and Personal Appeals to be Sure to VOTE FOR WAR PROHIBITION

Congress by Unanimous Vote Repealed the Charter of the Pro-German, Disloyal, National German American Alliance. The Brewers' Representative Admitted That They Furnished Money to This German Alliance for Its Pro-German Propaganda

The Pro-German Brewers and Un-American German Alliance Have No Claim on Patriots

WAR PROHIBITION WILL DESTROY BOTH

Right Now Is the Time for You to Help Win the War
SEND THAT TELEGRAM!

P. A. BAKER, General Superintendent
E. C. DINWIDDIE, Legislative Supt.

JAMES CANNON, Jr., Chairman,
WAYNE B. WHEELER, Secretary,
ERNEST CHERRINGTON,
ARTHUR BARTON,
Legislative Committee of the Anti-Saloon League of America

[ CLIP THIS PAGE OUT AND POST IT IN YOUR CHURCH OR IN SOME OTHER APPROPRIATE PLACE ]

Figure 1.9 A poster pullout from a 1918 American newspaper calls on citizens to support the war effort by encouraging their legislative representatives to vote for alcohol prohibition (Indiana Historical Society).

Anheuser-Busch Company and some of the Milwaukee Companies are largely controlled by alien Germans. . . . Have you made any investigation?"[191] It was this heated wartime context that helped fuel calls for a nationwide prohibition on alcohol.

By the time World War I began, the Treasury was generating as much as one-fifth of its total annual revenues from the taxation of alcohol. And, as was true elsewhere, the war prompted even higher taxes on alcohol through the War Revenue Act of 1917. This measure continued an old pattern: starting with Hamilton's establishment of an alcohol tax to help pay off war debts, every major US military engagement had brought with it a spike in the alcohol tax.[192]

But this time there was a crucial difference: the first peacetime income tax in American history had also been introduced in 1913 and was generating more revenue every year.[193] This gave the Anti-Saloon League another opening: in lobbying the government, it argued that not only was prohibition the righteous thing to do, but it was also becoming more fiscally viable as reliance on alcohol taxes declined.

Prohibition advocates were far less successful in persuading European allies to follow their lead. The US government suggested that the Allies should cease brewing beer in the interest of rationing. The British declined, pointing to "the difficulties and dangers of imposing upon the working classes any sweeping measures of prohibition especially at a moment when drastic compulsory rations are coming into force."[194]

Back on the Western Front, the trenches were drenched in alcohol—nowhere more so than in the French region of Champagne, which was not only the source of the country's most celebrated wine but historically the location of some of its bloodiest battles. And none were bloodier than those fought during World War I, when the region lost half of its population. Early in the war, the Germans occupied Reims, the main city in the region, and ransacked its champagne cellars. When the Germans were forced out, they left thousands of empty bottles on the road. Fortunately for the residents of Reims, the city's vast network of limestone caves used to store champagne reserves could also be used as refuge from continuous German bombardment. Some 20,000 people moved underground, essentially creating a city under the city that withstood more than 1,000 consecutive days of shelling.[195]

The web of caves, tunnels, and corridors under Reims also provided cover for French troops to safely move around for miles. Many of the 50,000 French soldiers stationed there could not resist helping themselves to the bubbly local beverage. "We took the opportunity to liberate quite a few bottles," one soldier admitted.[196] At the same time, champagne became a rallying cry for the troops to defend the city. When the commander of the French soldiers based in Reims was instructed to retreat and abandon the city in anticipation of a German offensive, he ignored the order. "As long as there is champagne here," he declared, "we will defend it."[197] Champagne even became an international rallying cry. Winston Churchill told his colleagues during World War I that "it's not just France we are fighting for, it's Champagne!"[198]

As the war dragged on, the French made it a policy to distribute champagne to boost troop morale, with those in the trenches closest to Reims receiving two bottles per day.[199] Even French prime minister Aristide Briand drank champagne at lunch every day to improve his mood, claiming that it helped him stay upbeat "in these sad times."[200]

In July of 1918, the advancing Germans were so sure that Reims and the rest of the region would fall that they had empty trains waiting in eastern France, ready to haul hundreds of thousands of bottles of champagne back to Germany to be sold to help pay for the war effort.[201] The city's defenders managed to hold the line largely thanks to the arrival of several divisions of African colonial soldiers—each of whom had been promised two bottles of champagne per day in exchange for keeping the enemy at bay. Deterred, the kaiser's troops opted to go around the city but again met fierce resistance, and it soon became clear that their plan to take Paris would fail. The war would continue to grind on for four more months, but the French realized the end was near. Their festive mood was captured by a cartoon in a Paris newspaper depicting the kaiser's son unable to open a champagne bottle and complaining, "I'm thirsty, thirsty for glory, and I can't uncork it." Another cartoon depicted a German soldier running back to Germany holding bottles of champagne while a French soldier pursued him yelling, "You call that harvesting?"[202]

When the war came to an end, the French troops stationed at Reims were forgiven for their overindulgence. "What would have become of Reims and all its 'buried treasures,'" one champagne producer explained, "if our brave defenders hadn't taken advantage of the situation to comfort themselves physically and morally with our incomparable champagnes? The enemy was defeated and our stocks were saved, so it's better to pull a veil over these sad events and accept that what we have lost sustained the courage of the defenders of champagne."[203]

Indeed, wine was hailed as a savior of France. A doctor who had served on a recruiting board during the war asserted that "we were able to note that among the young men called for army duty, those from wine growing regions were the most muscular, alert, and lithe, as well as the strongest, biggest, and leanest."[204] French politician Edouard Barthe declared, "Wine, the pride of France, is a symbol of strength; it is associated with warlike virtue."[205] Joining the loud chorus celebrating the war-enhancing virtues of wine, Marshal Philippe Petain claimed that "of all the shipments to the armies, wine was assuredly the most awaited and most appreciated. To procure his ration of wine, the French soldier braved perils, challenged artillery shells and defied the military police. In his eyes, the wine ration had a place almost equal to that of ammunition supplies. Wine was a stimulant that improved his morale and physical well-being. Wine, therefore, was a major partner in the victory."[206]

While the French celebrated the wartime role of wine, the British celebrated rum, which in turn provided ammunition to fight off prohibition. In November 1919, American prohibitionist William "Pussyfoot" Johnson gave an invited speech at Essex Hall in London about the benefits of prohibition and was quickly shouted down by the students in attendance. "We say that if Britain wants to be wet or dry," one of them came up to the front to proclaim, "that is a thing for Britishers alone to decide. We don't want Americans coming over here with elaborate and ornate speeches, telling us what we ought to do. We won the battle of the Somme on rum, and rum only, and the sooner Mr. Johnson realises that the better." The raucous crowd cheered him on, and the event soon devolved into a riot through the streets of London in which Johnson lost his right eye.[207]

## Goodbye Prohibition, Hello War

America's battle against alcohol failed to attract many foreign allies and ended in defeat. By the time World War II broke out, the nation's short-lived prohibition experiment had long ended. In some countries, such as France, drinking had been celebrated and encouraged during the interwar years, and consumption surged. Indeed, the French remained so devoted to their wine that securing enough wine for the troops was deemed essential in mobilizing for the next war. A third of the country's railroad cars designed to carry liquid in bulk were reserved for transporting wine to the frontlines. When Germany attacked France in

May 1940, 3,500 trucks were tasked with delivering 2 million liters of the beverage per day to the troops.[208]

But when France fell to the Germans within two months, praise turned to condemnation. Wine was blamed for making the country soft. Petain, the World War I hero who had credited wine with saving France, now pointed a finger at drunkenness for "undermining the will of the army."[209] He became the leader of the collaborative Vichy government, under which new restrictions on the sale of alcohol were quickly imposed, including the setting of a minimum drinking age for the first time (no one under the age of fourteen could purchase alcohol).

The British fought on with their daily rum rations. "We simply kept going on rum," recalled one soldier. "Eventually it became unthinkable to go into action without it."[210] But German U-boats targeting shipping lanes made it much harder for the British to secure rum supplies from the West Indies. "Things became so critical in 1943," writes James Pack, "that the Admiralty was forced to seriously consider discontinuing rum which, for reasons of morale, the board was loathe to do."[211] Instead, the Treasury opted to purchase expensive and immature rum from Cuba and Martinique in order to continue the rum ration.[212]

With alcohol prohibition long since abandoned, American soldiers sent off to fight were no longer expected to stay dry. Beer in particular was considered so important to troop morale that the government instructed the brewing industry to allocate 15 percent of its production for the military effort. Brewers were more than happy to oblige, launching an aggressive public relations campaign touting their many contributions to the war, including their payment of taxes that went toward supporting war production. Having made a full recovery from their abject vilification in World War I, American brewers were now considered promoters of patriotism. Beer was portrayed as a patriotic drink and a morale booster. It was even touted for its nutritional value because of the vitamin B in brewers' yeast. The industry viewed GIs as a target consumer group with long-term potential: a 1941 issue of *Brewers Digest* described army camps as "a chance . . . to cultivate a taste for beer in millions of young men who will eventually constitute the largest beer-consuming section of our population." The government also supplied defense workers with beer in the belief that it would help their productivity. To keep the beer flowing, the government gave brewers

Figure 1.10  British purse calendar advertising rum (Amoret Tanner/Alamy).

privileged access to rationed goods (such as rubber, gasoline, and tin cans) and granted them status as an essential wartime industry.[213]

The British government also had a noticeably more relaxed attitude toward alcohol than it had during World War I. This was symbolized by Winston Churchill's candid views on the matter: "My rule of life prescribe[s] as an absolutely sacred rite smoking cigars and also the drinking of alcohol before, after, and if need be during all meals and in the intervals between them."[214] Churchill typically started his day with a glass of champagne or a weak whiskey and water, drank more whiskey and water between meals, and enjoyed wine with lunch and dinner.[215]

In 1940, Lord Woolton, the British minister for food, declared beer drinking to be essential for public morale: "If we are to keep up anything like approaching the normal life of the country, beer should continue to be in supply, even though it may be beer of a rather weaker variety than the connoisseurs would like. It is the business of the Government not only to maintain the life but the morale of the country."[216] Unstated was that beer was also helping to pay for the war: the beer tax was increased three times between September 1939 and July 1940.[217] The tax on increasingly scarce whiskey supplies was also nearly doubled.[218]

Whereas pubs and alcohol were treated as threats during World War I, now they were promoted as essential to the war effort. As one beer advertiser observed, "At no other time in British history had an intoxicating drug enjoyed so much symbolic importance."[219] Keeping the beer flowing, however, became increasingly challenging as the war dragged on. Many London breweries suffered direct hits from German bombers. Finding a place to drink also became harder: by 1943, 1,300 pubs had been destroyed by German attacks.[220]

Meanwhile, the Nazis denounced drunkards but did plenty of drinking. Hitler himself rarely drank, and soldiers who committed crimes under the influence faced the death penalty. The victims of a sterilization program included several thousand alcoholics, and thousands more were shipped off to concentration camps as "undesirables" and "deviants."[221] The government announced that "no dangerous alcoholic, no person who has fallen under the influence of alcohol may . . . remain unknown to the state and party."[222] In 1939, the Bureau Against the Dangers of Alcohol and Tobacco was created, initiating a wave of restrictions on alcohol. Alcohol taxes were increased, and new limits on its production and sale were introduced.

The new rules also included restrictions on alcohol use in the military, but Hitler's commanders on the ground often had a more tolerant attitude. One German soldier on the Eastern Front wrote, "Those who were neither asleep, on guard, playing cards, nor writing letters were absorbing the alcohol which was freely distributed along with our ammunition."[223] A wounded German soldier observed: "There's as much vodka, schnapps and Terek liquor on the front as there are Paks [antitank guns]. It's the easiest way to make heroes. Vodka purges the brain and expands the strength. I've been doing nothing but drinking for two days now. It's the best way to forget that I've got seven pieces of metal in my gut, if you can believe the doctor."[224]

Alcohol, which facilitated desensitization, was also supplied to German soldiers and police tasked with carrying out some of the most horrendous atrocities of the war.[225] Extra alcohol rations were given to the men in the Reserve Police Battalions in Poland who shot tens of thousands of Jewish men, women, and children at close range.[226]

Historian Edward Westermann documents how alcohol not only lowered inhibitions but also fostered social bonding and helped to incentivize and reward genocidal killing.[227] In the occupied eastern territories, members of the ruthless *Schutzstaffel* (SS) regularly participated in celebratory postexecution drinking rituals. One teenage Polish girl working at a restaurant in Zakrzewo testified that SS members often came in to drink beer and schnapps in late 1939: "They were half-drunk, and the mood was very merry, as if they were intoxicated. They sang and danced. . . . Such drinking bouts were repeated after every mass shooting . . . sometimes several times a week."[228]

Alcohol also flowed freely among SS personnel at both the Auschwitz and Treblinka concentration camps during mass killings. One Treblinka survivor recalled observing "SS-men who held a pistol or truncheon in one hand, [and a] whiskey bottle in the other."[229] The doctors charged with running the gas chambers were also well lubricated with alcohol. By their own admission, drinking was part of the job: "The selections [of people to be gassed] were mostly an ordeal. Namely to stand all night. And it wasn't just standing all night— but the next day was completely ruined because one got drunk every time. . . . A certain number of bottles were provided for each section and everybody drank and toasted the others. . . . One could not stay out of it."[230]

To the west, meanwhile, the German-occupied territories of France included the country's most prized wine-producing areas—Burgundy, Bordeaux, and Champagne. The Nazis extracted an average of almost 900,000 bottles a day during the occupation period. The extraction of French wine was overseen by Hermann Goering, who expressed no remorse: "In the old days, the rule was plunder. Now, outward forms have become more humane. Nevertheless, I intend to plunder, and plunder copiously."[231] In addition to securing wine shipments for his fellow military officers, he stocked his private cellar with more than 10,000 bottles of the country's best wines.[232]

In Champagne, producers frantically hid their prized supplies. But their efforts failed to keep the Germans from quenching their thirst for France's most famous drink. An estimated 2 million bottles of champagne were stolen in the first chaotic months of occupation.[233] Some producers resisted by relabeling bad wine as good, watering down the good wine, using bad corks, and even substituting water for wine in barrels being shipped to Germany.[234] German orders for French wine provided an opportunity to unload unwanted wine: "They were incredibly sloppy when they placed orders for wine," recalled Alsace's Johnny Hugel. "We'd get a piece of paper saying send ten thousand bottles to such and such a place, but they never designated precisely which wine they wanted, so we would always send our worst, like the 1939, which was absolute rubbish. If the Germans hadn't arrived, we would still have that vintage unsold in our cellars."[235] Technically, the occupiers paid for what they consumed, but since they set the value of the mark at five times its prewar value, their payment essentially amounted to what one producer bitterly described as "legalized plunder."[236]

German champagne orders sometimes provided military intelligence, which the French Resistance happily passed on to the British: the Germans celebrated victories with champagne, and therefore the destination specified on orders provided an advance warning of their attacks. So when the Germans put in an order in late 1941 for the shipment of thousands of cases of champagne to "a very hot country," the British were tipped off to Field Marshal Erwin Rommel's North Africa campaign before it began.[237]

The tunnels and caverns beneath the champagne houses that had provided refuge from German bombardment during World War I now facilitated French Resistance efforts to hide weapons, ammunition, and persons from the Nazis.[238] For several years, one French producer even managed to use his wine barrels to smuggle Resistance leaders in and out of the occupied zone.[239]

Meanwhile, in the wake of the failed Bolshevik temperance campaign, alcohol returned in full force to the Red Army, with the vodka ration in 1942 set at 100 grams per man per day.[240] And toward the end of the war, as Soviet forces advanced into Germany they supplemented their ration with looted alcohol. One Soviet colonel complained that "when our soldiers find alcohol, they take leave of their senses. You can't expect anything from them until they have finished the last drop." He even blamed booze for extending the war: "If we hadn't had drunkenness like this we would have beaten the Germans two years ago."[241] An Allied observer accompanying the Soviet forces reported: "Russians are absolutely crazy about vodka and all alcoholic drinks. They rape women, drink themselves into unconsciousness, and set houses on fire."[242]

As they retreated, the Germans purposefully left their alcohol stocks behind, calculating that a drunk Soviet soldier would be less effective. But the reality was that the Soviets had such an abundance of manpower that no amount of alcohol was going to stop them, and in the end it was the German civilian population, especially its women, who suffered the most at the hands of intoxicated Soviet soldiers.[243] Heavy drinking within the Soviet military went all the way to the top of the ranks: Stalin told British foreign minister Anthony Eden that his generals "fought better when they were drunk."[244]

In the Pacific, where the war raged on even after the German surrender, the Japanese also turned to alcohol, but more in preparation

Figure 1.11 A Russian soldier drinks hard liquor before going to fight, Leningrad, 1941 (Chandogin, Nikolaj. I. [1909–1989] ©bpk Bildagentur/German-Russian Museum Berlin-Karlshorst, Berlin, Germany/Art Resource, NY).

for battle than during battle itself. Part of the goodbye ceremony for kamikaze pilots was to toast the emperor with shots of sake. Many also turned to alcohol during the stressful days leading up to their suicide missions. One pilot wrote to a friend: "The farewell party was fun. I, the brave warrior, will definitely destroy our enemy, even if it takes seven lives. Hopefully, you won't forget about me after I go. Since I am intoxicated, I don't know what I write. I am sure you understand. Forgive me if I said anything nasty to you. As long as you are alive, it is OK. I am lonely."[245]

### Drunk Superpowers

Even as the standard provision of alcohol in soldier rations generally declined after World War II, the two Cold War superpowers remained strikingly tolerant of drinking while soldiering. In September 1950, despite pressure from temperance advocates back home to ban alcohol rations, General Douglas MacArthur reportedly ordered that US soldiers deployed to fight in Korea receive one free can of beer per day. The Milwaukee brewing companies, Blatz and Schlitz, together donated more than a million cans or bottles of beer to American GIs on the frontlines, with the shipments reaching military units at chow lines on Christmas Day 1950. And when the war came to an end in 1953, soldiers used empty beer cans as a creative way to safely store 25,000 unused hand grenades, saving the army $20,000 in packaging costs.[246]

During the Vietnam War (1964–1973), American soldiers received a beer ration of two cans per person per day, and they could also purchase up to three cases of beer per month per person at the PXs (post exchanges). In addition, soldiers had access to beer at the enlisted man clubs, known as malt shops. Since the average age of conscripts serving in Vietnam was nineteen, the US minimum drinking age of twenty-one was ignored.[247] A Pentagon-sponsored study reported that nearly 90 percent of servicemen acknowledged drinking during their tour of duty, frequently in "prodigious amounts."[248] Heavy drinking within the military was not only tolerated but in some ways encouraged. Many officers rewarded kills with free alcohol, which promoted the practice of cutting off ears and penises as evidence of kills. One soldier testified that "the person who had the most ears was considered the number one

Figure 1.12 A US Marine guards the Corps' beer rations during the Korean War (Science History Images/Alamy).

'Vietcong' killer. When we'd get back to base camp, they would get all the free beer and whiskey they could drink."[249]

While the war came to be associated with illicit drug use, alcohol was the most abused drug. As one observer described it: "While there were rumors about soldiers fucking up because of drugs, the only cases I knew of were with alcohol; guys drunk or hung-over who couldn't do their jobs or [who] made mistakes like stepping on a land mine, which cost lives. Drinking was simply part of the culture in Vietnam and it was everywhere. A beer was cheaper to get than a soda."[250] One private bluntly acknowledged that "everybody in Vietnam drank like fish, and every chance you got you drank yourself silly. Us infantry guys, we were a bunch of alcoholics."[251] Many brought their drinking problem back home with them.

The American military dried out to some extent after Vietnam, which included eliminating the beer ration. But the alcohol-soaked military culture persisted: a 1991 study reported that heavy alcohol use was twice as prevalent within the military as in a matched civilian sample.[252] The wars in Iraq and Afghanistan in the early twenty-first century brought a spike in alcohol-related problems. The possession or consumption of alcohol in five countries—including Afghanistan and Iraq—was prohibited by the military's General Order No. 1, of which every soldier received a laminated copy. Nevertheless, alcohol filtered into bases, camps, and outposts via smuggling, care packages, or soldiers from other countries, or disguised as mouthwash (typically by adding blue-green food coloring to gin or vodka).[253] Binge drinking in the army reportedly increased by nearly a third from 2002 to 2005. While alcohol use declined in the navy and air force, it went up in the army and marines—the services doing the bulk of the fighting in Iraq.[254] More than 9,000 soldiers sought help for alcohol abuse in 2009, representing a more than 50 percent increase since the start of the Iraq War.[255] According to a 2009 study, alcohol abuse cost the US military over $1 billion per year, with more than 34,000 drinking-related arrests and crimes.[256] A 2012 Pentagon-commissioned Institute of Medicine report described drinking in the military as a "public health crisis"—some 20 percent of soldiers were reported to be heavy drinkers, and binge drinking had increased substantially between 1998 and 2008.[257]

But while the wars in Iraq and Afghanistan appeared to continue the long tradition of drinking while soldiering, in the early twenty-first century there was much greater awareness of it as a problem—after all, by this time it was hard to imagine the US military giving out a daily alcohol ration. One army veteran described the difference: "Back when I was in the Army, back in the 1970s and 1980s, we assumed drinking was mandatory." He added, "Drinking was as big a problem then as it is now. It just wasn't as highlighted."[258]

The place where there appeared to be the greatest historical continuity was in Russian military drinking habits. "Even if you are not an alcoholic when you go into the Army," a Soviet soldier commented in the 1970s, "you are when you come out."[259] Soldiers' ability to drink during the war in Afghanistan (1979–1989) was inhibited by limited supplies, which inflated alcohol prices to the point at which only officers could typically afford it. Soldiers tried to compensate by using clever smuggling schemes: "Customs regulations permitted two bottles of vodka, four of wine, but unlimited beer, so we'd pour out the beer and fill the bottles with vodka," one recalled. "Or else you might open a bottle of mineral water and find it was 40 proof!"[260]

Alcohol was more readily available during the Chechen Wars (1994–1996, 1999–2006), so much so that it aided the enemy. Russian soldiers routinely traded with the Chechens they were fighting, providing them weapons, ammunition, and other war supplies in exchange for booze—some of which was allegedly mixed with bleach to blind Russian soldiers.[261] One Chechen leader claimed the Russians traded an armored vehicle for two chests of vodka, with the understanding that the Chechens not attack their site for a week while they got drunk. According to one Chechen rebel, "We never drank vodka in action, but Russians were always drunk to ward off fear."[262] Russian commanders often required a bottle of vodka before handing over dead Chechen fighters to their families.[263]

The heavy drinkers included former defense minister and leader of the Russian forces in Chechnya Pavel Grachev, who often arrived at press conferences drunk.[264] One journalist covering the war described the state of the Russian military: "They are nearly all drunk out there, 'no limits' appears to be the order of the day."[265] One unit commander who boasted of bombing civilian homes commented that "street fighting is hell. We were all drunk and high. Otherwise we couldn't have stood it. There was no other way."[266] Another commander claimed that soldiers "get drunk as pigs, lob out a few shells, claim combat pay and get drunk again."[267]

It should therefore be no surprise that alcohol contributed to the terrorization of the local population. One village leader claimed that "as a rule, [the soldiers] fire every time they get drunk."[268] At the Russian base in Khankala, an estimated 29 percent of shelling was primarily due to accidents, drunkenness, or some combination of the two.[269] Some accidents involved soldiers shelling their own side. And alcohol may have even played a role in Boris Yeltsin's decision to go to war in the first place. Shrad points out that Yelstin gave the order for Russia to retake Chechnya under the heavy influence of alcohol, during a meeting at his dacha in which drinking friends outnumbered government ministers. The bold order was given despite the absence of military planning and there being too few troops at the ready.[270]

RUSSIA WAS ADMITTEDLY AN extreme case.[271] At least by historical standards, most modern militaries had sobered up considerably by the turn of the century, even if they were far from dry. The same could not be said of the less disciplined irregular forces mentioned in the opening of this chapter—certain types of organized killing by certain types of killers in places such as Bosnia and Rwanda continued to go hand in hand with heavy drinking in the post–Cold War era. But for the professional militaries of major powers, drinking on the job (as opposed to during downtime) became less and less tolerable with the development of ever-more mechanized and sophisticated warfare utilizing complex and costly equipment requiring high levels of coordination and precision. So, while alcohol had been the drug of choice on the battlefield for centuries, not to mention a leading source of revenue to fill war chests, its importance as a fuel for advanced modern military forces waned. Yet, as we'll see in the next chapter, smoking on the job was an entirely different matter. Tobacco arrived on the battlefield much later than alcohol, yet once it took hold, it remained entrenched despite growing health concerns. More and more, where there was smoke, there was war.

# 2

## Where There's Smoke There's War

IN WILLIAM COSGROVE'S 1693 British comedy *The Old Bachelor* one character tells another, "You stink of brandy and tobacco, most soldier-like."[1] By the end of the seventeenth century, tobacco had come the closest to rivaling alcohol as the wartime drug of choice. It was an ideal war drug, with distinct advantages over alcohol. It could calm nerves, inhibit hunger, relieve boredom, comfort the wounded, facilitate camaraderie, and boost morale—all without impairing fighting capacity, even if it would eventually kill the user. Inhaling tobacco smoke could deliver nicotine to the brain particularly fast, providing an almost instant "kick" caused by a temporary release of adrenaline and endorphins. These momentary pleasurable effects could only be maintained through repeated dosing, making nicotine highly addictive.

As they had with alcohol, governments became addicted to the tax revenue tobacco could generate to fund their war machines. And similar to alcohol, tobacco consumption spread through military campaigns. But in the case of tobacco, the leaf was first introduced by the conquered rather than the conquerors, moving from the New World to the Old. From the Thirty Years' War in the early seventeenth century to the world wars of the first half of the twentieth century, every major military encounter brought with it a surge in tobacco use, with soldiers leading the way.[2] Importantly, war not only spread tobacco *use*

*Killer High*, Peter Andreas. Oxford University Press (2020). © Peter Andreas.
DOI: 10.1093/actrade/9780190463014.001.0001

but also profoundly shaped the *way* it was consumed: the industrialization of tobacco in the form of mechanized, mass-produced cigarettes was perfectly timed to coincide with the industrialization of warfare. And indeed, total mobilization for industrial-scale war in the first half of the twentieth century enabled the cigarette to overcome deep societal resistance and triumph as the premier form of tobacco consumption across the globe.

## From the New World to the Old

Originating in the Americas, tobacco was first grown by humans between 5000 and 3000 BC, first in the Andean region and then spreading across the Western Hemisphere, where it was firmly rooted by the time Europeans arrived.[3] The tobacco leaf served many ritual functions, including some related to battle: to bless or reward warriors, to honor the war gods, and to declare war.[4] Its methods of consumption varied as much as its purposes: "Tobacco was sniffed, chewed, eaten, drunk, smeared over bodies, used in eye drops and enemas, and smoked. It was blown into warriors' faces before battle, over fields before planting and over women prior to sex, it was offered to the gods, and accepted as their gift, and not least it served as a simple narcotic for daily use by men and women."[5]

In pre-Columbian North America, the preferred method of tobacco use was smoking via the pipe.[6] Indeed, the pipe itself may have been more socially significant than what was in the pipe: tribal leaders used such instruments to both make sworn pledges and to announce war. The Omaha Indians, for instance, had both war pipes and peace pipes with distinct markings, and "the peace pipe of any particular tribe was as easily recognizable to other tribes as was the banner or the coat of arms of a feudal lord."[7]

Beginning with members of Columbus's crew, some of the newly arrived Europeans soon became habitual tobacco users.[8] Although it is not entirely clear who first brought tobacco back from the New World to the Old, or who was the first to use tobacco outside of the Americas, all agree that the starting point was conquest.[9] As one writer puts it, "The Aztecs and the Incas may have been destroyed by the Spaniards but their tobacco habits have been adopted since by the entire world.

If an Aztec and a Roman were transported to the twenty-first century the Aztec might be the less mystified. He would know why people were smoking."[10]

Tobacco was slow to take hold in continental Europe. But once it did in the seventeenth century, Spain, France, and other countries were quick to exploit its revenue-generating potential through monopolization and taxation. The financial strains of war and empire were key drivers. With his kingdom spread thin, Spain's Philip IV was constantly in search of new means to fill his coffers, especially after war broke out again with the Low Countries in 1621.[11] France followed Spain's lead, making tobacco production and sale a state monopoly. Soon after, the rest of Europe followed suit. Few governments could resist taxing tobacco, the revenues from which were primarily used to finance war-making.[12]

*Spaniards discovering tobacco.*

Figure 2.1 This wood engraving depicts Spanish explorers in the New World discovering tobacco upon observing native Indians smoking leaves in their pipes (Granger Collection).

Although there is disagreement about who first introduced tobacco to Britain, Sir Walter Raleigh is typically credited with popularizing its use, especially smoking via pipes, which became a national habit.[13] Queen Elizabeth I, who was captivated by Raleigh's worldly adventures and love of tobacco, made him captain of her guards and vice admiral of the West. Approved by the queen and embraced by her inner circles, tobacco smoking soon gained wider popularity within British society— so much so that it turned into the country's favorite leisure activity.[14] Later sentenced to death for treason, Raleigh took one last puff of the pipe before being beheaded.[15]

The British helped to disseminate tobacco smoking across continental Europe, partly through military campaigns: English soldiers, who smoked on and off the battlefield during the Thirty Years' War (1618–1648), are credited with spreading tobacco as far east as Bohemia, and from there into Austria and Hungary.[16] To the north, tobacco was also introduced for the first time to countries such as Sweden. Dutch armies proved to be the most energetic disseminators of the smoking habit, having originally acquired the leaf from the English.[17]

Tobacco also proliferated well beyond Europe, though not without considerable initial resistance. Suspicious of outside influences, Japanese rulers repeatedly tried to ban tobacco, but each ban failed despite stiffer penalties, and the leaf was legalized in 1625. Even the shogun's own bodyguards had openly defied the ban.[18] Samurai became particularly avid smokers: they formed smoking associations, and members possessed ornate silver pipes that they carried next to their swords or tied to their backs.[19] The Japanese in turn likely introduced tobacco to Korea and Manchuria through their occupation of the Korean peninsula.[20]

In China's northern borderlands, soldiers, privateers, and freebooters were among the first to take up smoking in the early seventeenth century.[21] The Manchus amassing on China's northeast border spread tobacco to Chinese military men posted there.[22] Meanwhile, far from the northeast border, the Shanghainese resisted tobacco smoking for some time, reinforced by a ban from the regional military commander, until soldiers from the new dynasty arrived in 1645 and brought their smoking habit with them.[23] Having conquered China, the Manchus legalized tobacco use and cultivation, which spread rapidly.[24] Tobacco was even believed to be a cure for malaria: "When our forces entered this malaria infested region," wrote a physician in the service of the emperor in Yunan Province, "almost everyone was infected by this disease with the exception of a single battalion. To the question why they had kept well, these men replied that they all indulged in tobacco. For this reason it was diffused to all parts of the country."[25]

In some cases, tobacco was violently resisted, at least initially. When Shah Abbas I of Persia was informed during the Safavid-Ottoman War of 1609 that his soldiers had developed a fondness for tobacco, he immediately banned it. Violators had their noses and lips cropped. But despite such draconian measures, the ban failed, and the leaf became so popular that Persian soldiers were soon carrying the water pipes they used to smoke it with them.[26] Ottoman rulers proved equally incapable of stopping tobacco's spread. During a military campaign in 1625–1626, Sultan Murad IV punished some of his officers for violating his smoking prohibition. When the offenders "were put to death with the severest torture in the imperial presence," noted the Ottoman scholar Kātib Chelebi, "some of the soldiers carried short pipes in their sleeves, some in their pockets, and they found the opportunity to smoke even during the executions." Despite the ban and such extreme punishments, smokers in the military continued to sneak away to the barracks latrines in Istanbul for a quick puff.[27]

### Lighting Up, Sparking Rebellion

Back in the New World where tobacco had originated, meanwhile, the leaf became a cornerstone of some colonial economies. Indeed, in the decades leading up to the American War of Independence, tobacco was a leading export crop—especially in the largest and wealthiest colony, Virginia—while providing a lucrative source of tax revenue for the Crown.[28] By the time of the rebellion, tobacco was providing the exchequer with £300,000 sterling in export duties.[29] Tobacco exports made up about three-quarters of the value of all Virginia and Maryland exports. Tobacco was so valuable that it served as a form of currency in Virginia and the Carolinas. And indeed, the Virginia militia was paid in tobacco in the years before the Revolutionary War.[30]

Prior to the war, the colonists enjoyed special access to the British market, but this had considerable downsides: the Crown determined the prices, all tobacco shipments had to use vessels flying the British flag, and non-British markets were closed to the leaf. There were other restrictions on planters, too, including the requirement that they pay freight and duty charges set in London.[31] Tobacco debts and dependence on Britain fueled colonial resentment, helping to foment rebellion. As historian Allan Brandt puts it, "For those who grew tobacco during the eighteenth century, debt was strongly tied to their emergent political ideology and commitment to independence." The peculiar characteristics of the tobacco economy "helped to create a relatively rare historical conjunction: elites with a powerful bent toward rebellion and revolution."[32]

For tobacco farmers, revolution brought with it the prospect of breaking free from their heavy debts to British creditors.[33] The Virginia tobacco farmer debtors included Thomas Jefferson, who complained that "these debts had become hereditary, from father to son, for many generations, so that the planters were a species of property annexed to certain Mercantile houses."[34] Other tobacco farmers, including Patrick Henry and George Washington, were equally bitter.[35] It is perhaps no coincidence that a majority of the signatories of the Declaration of Independence had direct ties to the tobacco trade. As Iaian Gately observes, "If one were to search for similarities among the fifty-six men who drew up the birth certificate of the most powerful nation in history, one would discover a belief in God, and tobacco interests. The Declaration began with a preamble enumerating the colonists' grievances against Britain, many of which were inspired by tobacco, the foundation stone of their overseas trade and hence national identity."[36]

Tobacco also helped finance the Revolutionary War itself. Soldiers were sometimes paid in tobacco, and essential supplies from Europe, including weapons and food, were purchased with the leaf. Perhaps the most critical role that tobacco played was to provide the collateral for the key wartime loan that Benjamin Franklin secured from France.[37] After the fighting was over, tobacco exports helped pay off war debts.[38]

And, of course, tobacco was used by revolutionary soldiers to relax and distract themselves from the strains and stresses of battle. Indeed, George Washington considered tobacco so important to soldier morale and daily life that he told civilians who wanted to support the war effort, "If you can't send money, send tobacco."[39] Tobacco similarly maintained civilian morale, and as a result, tobacco consumption also increased off the battlefield.[40] The British were well aware of the importance of tobacco to the rebellion and were particularly outraged that tobacco was used as collateral for a wartime loan from France.[41] In retaliation, General Charles Cornwallis launched what came to be dubbed the "Tobacco War," resulting in the burning of some 10,000 hogsheads of cured Virginia leaf in 1780–1781, some of which belonged to Thomas Jefferson.[42]

Beyond promoting a surge in tobacco's use, the push for independence also shifted *how* tobacco was consumed. While pipes were the most common way to smoke tobacco, cigars were introduced to and popularized in the colonies through war. Cigars were first brought to the colonies by the military officer Israel Putnam, who picked up the habit while fighting in Cuba during the Seven Years' War (1756–1763). In the midst of the American Revolution, many Americans replaced their pipes with cigars as a patriotic statement and symbolic gesture to distinguish themselves from the British.[43] Although American tobacco exports never recovered to their prewar levels, this decrease was partially offset by increased domestic consumption.

### Tobacco Taxes, Revolution, and the Napoleonic Wars

The French Revolution was spurred in part by grievances similar to those of the American Revolution—taxes in general, but in this case tobacco taxes in particular. France's involvement in conflicts such as the Seven Years' War and the American Revolution contributed to a fiscal crisis in 1788.[44] The state increasingly turned to taxes to solve its financial woes, and one of the most resented of these solutions was the tobacco tax. Taxing tobacco was "all the more reasonable," explained the Sun King, Louis XIV, given the "extraordinary expenses of the current war [against Holland]" and the fact that tobacco was not "necessary for . . . the maintenance of life."[45] Many Frenchmen, however, certainly considered tobacco to be an absolute necessity, and French peasants in particular were regular smokers who relied on tobacco to suppress hunger.[46] To boost revenue, the state had aggressively encouraged their addiction to tobacco, setting up state retailers across the country. By the mid-eighteenth century, more than 20 percent of the proceeds from all

French indirect taxation came from tobacco, representing more than 7 percent of all government revenue.[47]

The state tobacco monopoly increasingly antagonized French citizens through a combination of high tobacco prices and highly invasive enforcement measures against smuggling and domestic cultivation. The heavy-handed enforcement apparatus included an army of over 20,000 guards patrolling both the capital and the hinterlands. The law even called for the death penalty for smugglers who could not pay the steep fines imposed on them for their crimes, prompting further public outrage.[48]

The French Revolution began in July 1789. On July 12, three days before the storming of the Bastille, the first target of the angry crowds was the customs gate of the ten-foot-high, fourteen-mile-long new wall that had been built around Paris to deter smugglers, especially of tobacco and wine. Among those arrested that day were many smugglers, who also played a major role in mobilizing the crowds.[49] The attack on the customs gate had ripple effects across the provinces, which experienced a "rash of fiscal rebellions." The province of Picardy had its checkpoints burned down, jails forced open to free smugglers, and tax agents chased off. In Roye and San Quentin, rebels expressed their defiance by allowing smugglers to conduct business unimpeded.[50]

On May 1, 1791, indirect taxation was ended on tobacco and many other consumer goods.[51] With the end of the state tobacco monopoly, the production and sale of the leaf was liberalized throughout the country.[52] At the time, the French were the only Europeans who could enjoy tobacco tax-free.[53] This did not last long, although even when a tax was reintroduced, it was far less burdensome than before and lightly enforced. A higher tobacco tax would have been considered an affront to the revolution.[54] The sharp fall in income from indirect taxation on tobacco and other consumption goods, however, added to the fiscal woes of the new revolutionary regime, which found itself financially strained from war with Austria and Prussia in 1792 and with Britain in 1793.

At the same time, antiroyalists were as fond of tobacco as ever, but they turned their noses up at snuff (dry pulverized tobacco for inhaling), the favored tobacco of the monarch.[55] In fact, snuffing virtually disappeared, as Gately recounts: "The habit was indelibly tainted by its association with courtiers and kings, and in the early, guillotine happy years of the French Revolution, even committed snuffers were forced to switch to smoking lest a dust-covered lip or a bad sneezing habit might cause them to lose their heads."[56]

The minimal and loosely enforced tobacco taxes of postrevolutionary France did not survive Napoleon's rise to power. The tobacco monopoly was brought back in 1810. Indeed, Napoleon's tobacco taxes were soon raising more revenue than taxation of the leaf ever had before the French Revolution. Napoleon himself was an avid user of snuff—consuming a kilo per week, equivalent to 100 cigarettes per day—and collected snuffboxes with pictures of his favorite tyrants, such as Alexander the Great and Julius Caesar.[57] Such taxation patterns would continue beyond Napoleon and well into the nineteenth century in France as tobacco use grew and the state tobacco monopoly stood ready to benefit.

Napoleon's military campaigns fundamentally altered the way Europeans engaged with tobacco. The hardships of war, both at home and on the battlefield, led to a spike in demand among warring nations and combatants. In addition, war changed the modes of consumption. The popularity of cigars in particular was facilitated by both the practical wartime convenience of the cigar and interaction between combatants from different countries. Napoleon's men first took up cigar smoking as a result of exposure to Spanish cigars during the French occupation of that country, which began in 1808.[58] Troops based in Andalusia, the site of the Spanish state-run Fabrica del Tobacos, were early adopters of the cigar. French troops then introduced cigars to their Russian counterparts. Until then, smoking in Russia had largely been a leisure activity of the wealthy, who consumed tobacco via hookahs. Hookahs were cumbersome and not well suited for everyday soldiering, but in their long campaigns across Russia, the cigar-puffing French demonstrated that there was a viable alternative.[59]

During the Napoleonic Wars, the British troops—whose home society favored snuff over smoking—faced harsh conditions and frequent hunger and, like so many soldiers before and after them, relied on tobacco to suppress appetites and ease the strains of war. They soon abandoned the then-dominant snuff habit in favor of the readily available Spanish habit of smoking cigars. The British also found cigars to be more practical than their clay pipes. In time, British officers and soldiers alike became as avid cigar smokers as the French.[60]

British officers returning from the battlefield brought their new preference for cigars back with them, and they were embraced as role models at home. The cavalry played an outsized role in spreading the habit of cigar smoking to Britons of all social classes. Cavalry officers had smoked cigars out of practicality: snuffboxes were difficult to open while riding a horse, but a cigar freed up the hands.[61] Between 1800 and 1830, British cigar imports skyrocketed, increasing from 26 pounds of cigars to 250,000 pounds.[62]

The cigar spread elsewhere in Europe. After participating in the Battle of Waterloo, Prussian troops brought cigars back with them, helping to popularize a form of tobacco use that previously had had little appeal at home. Until 1848, however, smoking in Prussia remained tightly restricted. The freedom to smoke in public was a key demand in the Revolution of 1848.[63]

In Italy, meanwhile, protestors clamored for the freedom *not* to smoke. Smoking tobacco was associated with Austrian oppression and occupation. Nonsmokers turned violent in Milan in 1848 when they forced cigars from the mouths of smokers in the streets. Austrian troops responded by entering restaurants smoking cigars, and some officers ordered their soldiers to light up while on patrol.[64] The antismoking protests spread to Padua and Venice before turning into an uprising in Lombardy, and as fighting spread beyond Piedmont, the Austrians retreated from Milan. The rebellion was stamped out within months, but "it was the first blow struck for a free and united Italy."[65]

Smoking in Europe was further popularized through the Crimean War (1854–1856), but in this case via the dissemination of cigarettes— short, miniature twists of tobacco wrapped in crude paper that provided a faster and cheaper nicotine hit than pipes or cigars. The rise of the cigarette began with exchanges between English, French, Russian, and Turkish forces.[66] With cigars in short supply, the British turned to the more readily available cigarette favored by their Turkish allies and Russian enemies. They then carried their new habit home, where cigarettes had previously been considered only diluted cigars, smoked by those either too weak or too poor to enjoy the real thing.[67] The new popularity of cigarette smoking among military men countered this negative portrayal, and civilian imitation soon followed.[68] Robert Gloag, who had fought in the Crimean War, opened the first British cigarette factory in 1856.[69] Philip Morris, a tobacco shop owner on London's Bond Street who had previously specialized in selling Havana cigars and Virginia pipe tobacco, catered to the new demand for cigarettes among returning Crimean soldiers by introducing the brands Oxford and Cambridge Blues.[70]

## Southern Tobacco Fields and Civil War Battlefields

Around the same time, American visitors to England were introduced to cigarettes and brought them home. As an unfamiliar way to smoke tobacco, the cigarette did not receive a warm welcome in America, however, and indeed experienced many ups and downs. It did not become the premier form of tobacco consumption until the early twentieth century—with war as the great enabler of its adoption. Although as a leading tobacco producer the United States consumed more of the leaf per capita than any other country in the world by the mid-nineteenth century, cigarettes were considered little more than a novelty compared to pipes, cigars, chew, and snuff.[71] Chewing tobacco was especially popular, though the cigar became increasingly common in the wake of the Mexican-American War (1846–1848), during which American soldiers had been exposed to Latin cigar-smoking habits.

As had been the case in the War of Independence, tobacco was a strategic resource in the Civil War. This was especially evident when retreating Confederate soldiers resorted to burning Richmond, their capital and the center of southern tobacco production, rather than letting their tobacco stockpiles fall into Union hands. Taxes on tobacco made the crop a key source of wartime revenue.[72] The Revenue Act of 1862, a direct response to the Civil War, assessed taxes on cigars, chewing tobacco, smoking tobacco, and snuff.[73] Revenue from the tobacco tax was approximately $3 million in 1863 and $8 million in 1864. In an effort to raise even more funds for the Union war effort, the Revenue Act of 1864 doubled or tripled taxes on the various tobacco products.[74] This would leave a lasting legacy: the wartime federal excise tax on cigarettes was reintroduced after the war, and the excises on alcohol and tobacco, in addition to import duties, became the primary sources of revenue for the federal government from 1868 to 1920.[75]

Tobacco was equally sought after on the battlefield. Troops on both sides received a tobacco ration. As Eric Burns notes, "Commanding officers wanted their men to smoke, knowing that they needed distraction from the ennui and horrors around them and much preferring tobacco to booze. A man who smoked too much could still aim his gun and hit the enemy; one who drank to excess might pull the trigger and amputate his toe."[76] Some military leaders were themselves equally fond of the leaf. Most famously, General Ulysses S. Grant enjoyed his cigars as much as his whiskey and would later die of throat cancer.[77]

The geography of the conflict—which often unfolded in the heart of southern tobacco country—was certainly convenient for smokers. Indeed, some battles took place in tobacco fields, and soldiers were at times housed on tobacco farms.[78] This may have influenced postwar tobacco preferences. Union soldiers posted around Durham, North Carolina, for example, continued to order "bright leaf" tobacco, which had a distinct flavor, from the area's producers after returning home. Washington Duke, whose family would found Duke University, was among the local producers who profited from this growing national demand.[79]

The Civil War also influenced Americans' *mode* of tobacco consumption. Like the Crimean War before it, the American Civil War boosted the popularity of cigarettes, at least for a time. The conveniences of cigarettes made tobacco an especially war-ready drug. Compared to a cigar or to a pipe and pouch, cigarettes were lighter, more compact, and more portable—all desirable wartime attributes. On top of that, they were more potent: Cuban cigars had a nicotine content of only about 2 percent, whereas the Virginia tobacco used to make cigarettes had a content as high as 10 percent.[80]

Yet the gains in popularity the cigarette enjoyed during the Civil War were short-lived, as soldiers returned to their more familiar cigars and pipes once the war ended, and few women had taken up cigarette smoking during the war. A number of factors conspired to hold the cigarette back in the United States: cigars and pipes were associated with masculinity and postwar patriotism, and the cigarette market was further limited by the low-efficiency hand-rolling required for production prior to the advent of the Bonsack cigarette-rolling machine in 1880, which could roll more than 200 cigarettes a minute.[81]

Cigarettes had such a poor public image in the last decades of the century that they even came to be negatively depicted in national security terms as the anticigarette Americans geared up to fight the cigarette-loving Spanish. A *New York Times* editorial went so far as to declare, "The decadence of Spain began when the Spaniards adopted cigarettes, and if this pernicious practice obtains among adult Americans the ruin of the Republic is close at hand."[82] Observers portrayed Spain as a nation that was weak and backward due to its love of the cigarette, while the United States was seen as a stronger, more advanced nation that would lose its vitality if cigarette smoking were to spread.[83] Spain's defeat in the Spanish-American War only reinforced this view. US news outlets quoted a British parliamentarian as claiming that Spain had lost the war because of cigarettes. But this criticism only targeted a particular mode of smoking, not smoking in general.[84] The US government, meanwhile, imposed an extra tax on tobacco to pay for its war with Spain—the War Revenue Act of 1898 increased the tobacco duty by 200 percent, continuing a well-established pattern of using the leaf to pay for military conflicts.[85]

## World War and the Triumph of the Cigarette

World War I was the best thing that ever happened to the cigarette, and nowhere was this more evident than in the United States. In 1914, cigarettes accounted for less than 7 percent of US tobacco consumption. By 1920 their share of the market had grown to 20 percent. Not only had the cigarette market tripled in size, but the anti-tobacco and anticigarette campaigns that had been gaining ground earlier in the century—bolstered by new knowledge about possible health hazards of tobacco use—had been rolled back. On the eve of World War I, eight states had banned the sale of cigarettes, and at least twenty other states were considering passing new anticigarette laws. By the conclusion of the war, the measures passed in this flurry of legislative activity had mostly been repealed or abandoned.[86]

The war not only saved the cigarette but gave it new life: after all, at the end of the war, almost all of the returning American soldiers brought their cigarette habit back with them. Unlike the years after the Civil War, this time the habit stuck. Cigarette use by soldiers and civilians alike surged. Assistant Secretary of War Benedict Crowell estimated that virtually all of the American Expeditionary Forces used tobacco, with cigarettes the overwhelmingly favorite mode of ingestion.[87]

Military leaders encouraged cigarette smoking to maintain morale and discipline, relax nerves, maintain alertness, foster camaraderie, and suppress hunger.[88] Cigarettes became so important to soldier maintenance that General George W. Goethals reasoned that tobacco was as vital to troops as food.[89] Major Grayson M. P. Murphy claimed that "a cigarette may make the difference between a hero and a shirker," and that "in an hour of stress a smoke will uplift a man to prodigies of valor; the lack of it will sap his spirit."[90] Despite growing anticigarette sentiment leading up to the war, some military doctors even endorsed soldiers' smoking habit.[91] A navy physician concluded that cigarettes were "a means of diversion which, far from interfering with a man's performance of duty, attaches him to it and renders it less burdensome."[92] The army's chief medical officer, William Gorgas, argued that the utility of tobacco in promoting "contentment and morale" trumped any health concerns and urged an antismoking group to not oppose tobacco use by the troops.[93]

The support of military officials is especially remarkable since military leaders initially disapproved of the habit after many soldiers began smoking during the Spanish-American War. The army and the navy had campaigned against cigarettes at the start of the century. The US Military Academy at West Point even prohibited cigarettes in 1903.[94] Rear Admiral Seaton Schroeder, commander-in-chief of the Atlantic battleship fleet, went so far as to advocate a ban on cigarette smoking by enlisted men. The *New York Times* supported this recommendation, arguing that "the excessive use of cigarettes is not conducive to good shooting or clear thinking."[95]

Cigarette use nevertheless continued to spread among the troops, and by the time the country entered World War I, the military had reversed course and even supported the habit. One might argue that the proliferation of cigarettes during the war was merely due to the addictive properties of nicotine. But cigarettes were much more than simply a drug-delivery mechanism. Beyond their physiological effects, cigarettes came to possess enormous cultural value. Soldiers especially valued smoking as a show of camaraderie.[96] And, not to be overlooked, smoking was a potent antidote to boredom. "Contrary to popular opinion, war is not a state of perpetual activity, not even for soldiers at the front," one volunteer for the Ambulance Corps wrote to his mother back home. "For every hour of activity there are many more when there is nothing to do but wait at one's post—and these hours of waiting are unspeakably gummy. Here is the chief explanation of why soldiers smoke so much."[97]

Smoking while soldiering was pushed by the US government, so much so that it quickly became the world's biggest purchaser of cigarettes.[98] Tobacco was designated an essential industry, cigarettes were added to the rations for deployed soldiers, and cigarette sales to soldiers were subsidized at PXs and canteens. While the daily ration also included chewing tobacco, and military post exchanges offered tobacco of all sorts—often below wholesale prices—cigarettes were the overwhelming preference of soldiers. Tobacco rations mostly meant cigarettes. Until World War I, wartime tobacco rations had been limited to pipe or chewing tobacco.[99] The government sent an average of 425 million cigarettes per month to its soldiers on the frontlines in France. All in all, it ended up sending approximately 5.5 billion cigarettes abroad, while providing troops with merely 200 million cigars.[100]

The government's promotion of cigarettes during the war is particularly notable since cigarettes had so recently been socially scorned by anticigarette activists and the country was experiencing a wave of moral temperance at the time. Congress in fact briefly considered a proposal to ban cigarette sales for the well-being of soldiers, but it was quickly shut down. Smoking cigarettes was promoted as a lesser evil compared to other soldierly vices like drinking and prostitution. As a retired medical officer put it at the time, soldiers "have got to do something, and smoking, in my opinion, injures them less than any other 'vice' they could acquire."[101]

Cigarettes came to be viewed as a necessary vice for soldiers.[102] But the intent of declaring cigarette manufacturing an essential wartime industry in the United States was not only to avoid shortages among troops abroad, but also to prevent domestic shortages. Civilian cigarette consumption shot up during the war. Though the government considered rationing tobacco at home to ensure supplies for the troops, the head of the War Industries Board maintained that tobacco was critical to civilian morale in the same way it was critical to soldier morale.[103] The government asked the tobacco industry to increase production, and producers were more than happy to comply. Cigarette production tripled during the war years.[104]

Cigarettes were considered so vital to the war effort that citizens, charities, and nongovernmental organizations like the Young Men's Christian Association (YMCA), the Salvation Army, and the Red Cross collected both cigarettes and monetary donations to provide the soldiers with cigarettes. These drives were conducted through programs such as the "Smokes for Soldiers Fund," which were enthusiastically supported by President Woodrow Wilson and enjoyed exemptions from tobacco taxes and export restrictions.[105] Supplying the troops with smokes became a way to publicly demonstrate one's patriotism. The *New York Sun* urged its readers to collect donations as a method of "proving your patriotism and testing that of your friends."[106] Red, white, and blue collection boxes were set up in department stores, theaters, and restaurants across the country, and walls were plastered with posters asking for donations. These charities and their shared purpose provided a much-needed unifying bond between the home front and the war front.[107]

Celebrities helped raise funds for the tobacco programs, and even organizations that had maintained anticigarette positions in the years prior to the war jumped on the smokes-for-soldiers bandwagon. One such organization was the YMCA, which alone shipped more than $12 million worth of tobacco to the frontlines and set up hundreds of YMCA-run cigarette canteens in war zones. It ended up providing over 2 billion cigarettes to soldiers in France, in addition to 50 million cigars, turning the YMCA into one of the world's leading tobacco distributors.[108]

In only a few years, YMCA magazines had gone from publishing antismoking articles to touting how many cigarettes the organization was delivering to the frontlines. The magazine featured photographs of YMCA volunteers passing out cigarettes to wounded soldiers, with one such photograph captioned: "Just What the Doctor Ordered."

**"SEND SMOKES TO SAMMY!"**

"FIFTY-FIFTY ON MY LAST SMOKE, BILL!"

Mail Your Contributions to

**"OUR BOYS IN FRANCE TOBACCO FUND"**

West 44th Street    Endorsed by War Department    New York City

Figure 2.2  A World War I poster from the United States calls on citizens to donate to the "Our Boys in France Tobacco Fund" (Corbis Historical/Getty Images).

"Stop this talk against tobacco," Reverend Perry Atkins, president of the YMCA's War Work Council, scolded an audience in Ann Arbor, Michigan. "God knows what a comfort it is to men in the trenches. Let them have it."[109]

The about-faces of organizations such as the YMCA, Salvation Army, and Red Cross may be understood as both a recalibration of risk under wartime conditions and a "lesser of evils" mentality. One previously anticigarette activist who later affiliated with the YMCA explained:

There are hundreds of thousands of men in the trenches who would go mad, or at least become so nervously inefficient as to be useless, if tobacco were denied them. Without it they would surely turn to worse things. Many a sorely wounded lad has died with a cigarette in his mouth, whose dying was less bitter because of the "poison pill." The argument that tobacco may shorten the life five or ten years, and that it dulls the brain in the meantime, seems a little out of place in the trench where men stand in frozen blood and water to wait for death.[110]

Meanwhile, the American public shifted its views on the risks associated with cigarettes. All arguments against cigarettes were set aside in light of wartime exigencies, as the horrors of war paled in comparison to any potential health consequences of smoking cited by the anticigarette movement. As one critic put it, "We might as well discuss the perils of gluttony in a famine as those of nicotine on the battlefield."[111] Commentary in a 1914 edition of the *Lancet* reflected the changed attitude: "We may surely brush aside much prejudice against the use of tobacco when we consider what a source of comfort it is to the sailor and soldier engaged in a nerve-racking campaign . . . tobacco must be a real solace and joy when he can find time for this well-earned indulgence."[112]

As the war brought more women into the American workplace and opened up better-paying jobs to them—which in turn made them more independent and gave them more disposable income—they also became an increasingly important segment of the cigarette market. And this trend continued into the postwar period: cigarette smoking by women doubled between 1920 and 1930. It certainly helped that the war had curtailed imports of the stronger Turkish tobacco, prompting US companies to produce a milder cigarette that was more appealing to women.[113]

The wartime disruption of Turkish tobacco supplies had other repercussions. Cigarette manufacturers such as Lorillard that had depended on Turkish imports suffered, while domestic manufacturers such as Reynolds (the maker of Camels) thrived. Since government contracts were based on domestic market share, brands such as Camel (which represented more than a third of domestic cigarette sales) enjoyed a huge advantage. Not only did Camel become a favorite brand of US soldiers on the front, but its market dominance continued into the postwar period.[114]

American cigarette producers were also advantaged during the war because they were not hurt by the same supply disruptions faced by their European competitors.[115] US tobacco companies not only enjoyed a privileged market position but took full advantage of the patriotic fervor surrounding the war. Being associated with the war effort was not only good for business but good for a company's public image.[116] It is therefore not surprising that many cigarette advertisements featured military-related or patriotic messages and images. Bull Durham, for example, advertised that "when our boys light up, the Huns will light out."[117]

By capitalizing on patriotic support for American soldiers, the cigarette companies were able to overcome the earlier wave of anticigarette sentiment in the country. Wartime exports skyrocketed, quadrupling from approximately 2.5 billion cigarettes in fiscal year 1914 to over 9 billion in 1918.[118] Military service meant that men who otherwise might have refrained from the habit picked it up—and soldiers smoked 60 to 70 percent more cigarettes every day, on average, than civilians. Most factories were forced to run overtime to keep up.[119]

By the end of the war, the US consumer base had grown exponentially. Prewar per capita cigarette consumption was 134 per year; by the end of the war, that figure had jumped to 310 per year.[120] The cigarette's public image had also been transformed, from one of weakness and degeneracy, evident during the Spanish-American War, to one of strength and patriotism. Now, not only was smoking cigarettes acceptable, but being against them was downright unpatriotic. The Red Cross even greeted returning soldiers with gifts of cigarettes. The War Department announced that the daily ration for soldiers on active duty in future conflicts should be increased from four to sixteen cigarettes.[121]

The triumph of the cigarette extended far beyond the United States. Consumption increased worldwide during the war. Soldiers from nearly every country involved in the conflict received state-sanctioned tobacco rations in various forms that ranged from one to four ounces per week.[122] Some Belgians reportedly pleaded to their minister of war, "Give us worse food if you like, but let us have tobacco."[123] Britain experienced one of the biggest spikes in smoking.[124] In many ways, Britain's wartime experience mirrored that of the United States. Both soldier and civilian cigarette use accelerated during the war, and anti-tobacco sentiment was obliterated. Nearly all those who made it back from the front were smokers. By the time the war ended, cigarettes dominated British tobacco sales.[125]

And, as in the United States, the British state and its citizens rallied to support the smoking habits of the British soldier through state-provided rations and charitable donations. To complement the War Office's ration of two ounces of tobacco per week, newspapers ran drives urging readers to contribute to their Tobacco Funds.[126] Women also joined the ranks of cigarette smokers in post–World War I Britain, for all the same reasons that women in the United States had taken up cigarettes, including newfound financial freedom achieved by getting out of the house and working in jobs previously held by men on the front, with part of their new disposable income spent on smokes.[127]

## More War, More Smoke

If World War I made the triumph of the cigarette possible, World War II made sure it would remain triumphant for decades. Tobacco in general and cigarettes in particular were once again treated as a strategic wartime resource. All of the military forces of the warring countries received a tobacco ration, most commonly in the form of cigarettes. In Britain, tobacco was classified as an essential product and as such was exempt from civilian rationing. In the United States, the tobacco industry was protected by the government and was handsomely rewarded. President Roosevelt, who himself was famously photographed enjoying his smokes through a cigarette holder, declared tobacco an essential crop and even mandated that draft boards give deferrals to tobacco-growing draftees. US tobacco production increased by nearly a fifth between 1940 and the end of the war in 1945. Prices for tobacco soared, and although the tobacco companies did offer discounted product to the troops, demand was so high that they did not donate cigarettes as they had in the previous war. Any tobacco going to a military recipient was tax-free.[128]

Figure 2.3 A British World War I advertisement requests donations to the "Sailors' and Soldiers' Tobacco Fund." Designed by Frank Brangwyn, 1915 (Everett Historical/Shutterstock).

In Germany, meanwhile, Adolf Hitler staunchly opposed smoking, insisting that tobacco was the "wrath of the Red Man against the White Man for having been given hard liquor."[129] He often noted that he, Mussolini, and Franco were all nonsmokers, unlike Churchill, Stalin, and Roosevelt. Smoking was proclaimed a threat to "racial hygiene," and indeed Nazi government-sponsored medical research (which was largely ignored by postwar scientists) was the first to establish a link between lung cancer and tobacco use.[130] Hitler himself was frequently featured in official warnings about smoking, with declarations such as "Brother national socialist, do you know that your Fuhrer is against smoking and thinks that every German is responsible to the whole people for all his deeds and omissions, and does not have the right to damage his body with drugs?"[131]

But despite the Nazi government's formal antismoking stance and increasingly strict controls, tobacco was never banned in Germany. Indeed, the country was the world's top importer of tobacco in the years leading up to the war, taking in about 100,000 tons of the leaf per year, and tobacco taxes covered 12 percent of the Reich's annual budget. An estimated 80 percent of German men were smokers, smoking on average 12.5 cigarettes a day in 1937.[132]

To soften government opposition, German cigarette manufacturers made sizeable financial donations to the Nazi Party and even handed out coupons to civilians to receive a coffee-table book of photographs of Hitler. Even though the Nazi government was officially opposed to smoking, it still allocated six cigarettes per day to each soldier. A limited additional amount could also be purchased, subject to heavy taxation. The German SS, on the other hand, had more privileged access to tobacco, and indeed even had their own label brand of "Sturmzigaretten" ("Storm-Cigarettes"), manufactured by the Sturm-Abteilung.[133]

Wartime rationing prompted many Germans to grow tobacco plants at home, with each family limited to no more than 200 plants (and only 25 plants were exempt from taxes, with the remainder subject to a heavy tax).[134] Families grew more than they declared. As one grower recalled, "We too grew tobacco, although nobody in our family smoked. But money was worthless, and you could get everything for tobacco. We had some land and cultivated wheat which we had to cede to the state. Everything was strictly regulated at the time. But right in the middle of the wheat, where you could not see it, we planted tobacco."[135]

World War II tobacco use habits mimicked those of World War I, except that cigarette use was already widespread at the outbreak of hostilities in 1939. Cigarettes were used for the same reasons as they had been in the prior world war, including to soothe nerves, lift morale, and foster camaraderie.[136] And, as before, military leaders made sure that their soldiers had access to their smokes. American military

Figure 2.4 American troops take a cigarette break near Laneuveville, France, during World War II, October 1944 (Granger Collection).

personnel, whether in training or on the frontlines, smoked an average of thirty cigarettes per day. As this military force swelled to some 12 million strong, it came to consume almost a third of all US tobacco production. It is no surprise, then, that the popular image of the American soldier was of a cigarette smoker: "The classic renderings of weary, dirt-caked GIs by cartoonist Bill Mauldin invariably showed young soldiers with butts dangling from their grimly wisecracking lips," Richard Kluger observes.[137] In response to a charity group's inquiry about how it should spend the $10,000 it had raised for the troops, General Douglas MacArthur advised, "The entire amount should be used to purchase American cigarettes which, of all personal comforts, are the most difficult to obtain here."[138] MacArthur himself preferred to enjoy his tobacco through a pipe but apparently thought cigarettes were the best way to keep his soldiers happy.

The US government further supported its troops' smoking habit by incorporating smoking breaks into marches. The American soldiering

Figure 2.5 Red Cross workers pack boxes of cigarettes to be sent to American soldiers and prisoners of war, 1943 (Granger Collection).

experience was so tightly linked with cigarettes that even the camps where American soldiers waited to be shipped back home from France late in the war were named after cigarette brands, including Camp Chesterfield, Camp Lucky Strike, and Camp Philip Morris, among others.[139] It is little surprise that, as in World War I, US soldiers returned home from the war addicted to tobacco.[140]

Like their US counterparts, the other world powers also promoted cigarette use among their fighting forces. Red Army soldiers, for example, received daily rations of a handful of Makhorka tobacco (a coarse, low-grade variety), which they then rolled in newspaper. British combatants were allocated seven cigarettes per day, with more available for purchase at military canteens.[141] Cigarettes were an integral part of daily life among the top echelons of British war planners, evidenced by the elaborate cigarette accessories built into Winston Churchill's War Rooms.[142] Members of the Japanese military also received cigarettes from the government, and their favorite brand was a Chinese one named "Ko-ah" ("Golden Peace") that was readily available following the invasion of China.[143]

Smoking on the home front increased as well during the war years, among both men and women. Perhaps not surprisingly, a spike in British smoking was most evident in those areas targeted by German bombs.[144] As one British woman explained, "In London during the heavy raids I found smoking a great help. My consumption has gone up over 100 per cent. It started in September—during the Blitz. I found smoking kept me from getting jittery."[145]

In the United States, cigarette use had grown dramatically in the 1930s but increased even more during the war years. In 1945, some 267 billion cigarettes were sold at home—12 percent more than in 1944, 48 percent more than in 1940, and 124 percent more than in 1930.[146] Wartime supply limits were the main constraint on domestic consumption. With priority given to the military, the availability of cigarettes to civilians at home was often tight, producing hoarding, long lines, and a thriving black market.

As had been the case during World War I, US tobacco companies capitalized on wartime spikes in demand and patriotic sentiment. Cigarette manufacturers routinely ran advertising campaigns that linked the cigarette with the American soldier.[147] Cigarette advertising slogans included "Keep 'em Smoking, Our Fighting Men Rate the Best" (Chesterfield); "Camels are the favorite! In the Army . . . In the Navy! . . . In the Marine Corps! . . . In the Coast Guard!" (Camel); and "You Want Steady Nerves When You're Flying Uncle Sam's Bombers Across the Ocean." (Camel).[148] Another way tobacco companies in the United States capitalized on the wartime context was to claim that their cigarettes were made with "modern" technology like that used to produce the cutting-edge weaponry of the time.[149]

Meanwhile, cigarettes also came to serve as currency within prisoner-of-war (POW) camps. The experience of POW George Rosie of the US 106th Airborne and Ross Millhiser illustrates this:

Of the four camps George had been in, Stalag 4B was by far the best run camp. . . . The Red Cross parcels and the food could be bartered at their exchange store; the money was cigarettes, and every parcel had a cigarette price. . . . Canadian people would get names of POWs

Figure 2.6 This American magazine advertisement from 1943 features two US Marines smoking Chesterfield cigarettes (Rue des Archives/Granger Collection).

from their newspapers and send them cartons of cigarettes. Because these Canadians had been in Stalag 4B for so long, they were getting as many as twelve cartons of cigarettes a month, which made them rich men in POW camp economy.[150]

In his personal account of the economic organization of a POW camp, economist R. A. Bradford explains the utility of cigarettes: "Although cigarettes as currency exhibited certain peculiarities, they performed all the functions of a metallic currency as a unit of account, as a measure of value and as a store of value, and shared most of its characteristics. They were homogenous, reasonably durable, and of convenient size for the smallest or, in packets, for the largest transactions."[151]

## Cold War, Hot Smoke

The bloodiest war in history finally came to an end, perhaps appropriately, with the lighting of a cigarette. When the Japanese emperor delivered his country's official surrender, General MacArthur handed him a cigarette, recalling "how his hands shook as I lighted it for him."[152]

The smoky aftermath of the war included not only heavy smoking but heavy reliance on cigarettes as an alternate currency. The Marshall Plan delivered more than 200 million cigarettes to Germany, the equivalent of a massive injection of cash. Cigarettes were the most reliable medium of exchange in France, Italy, and especially Germany in the immediate postwar years.[153] With little confidence in the official currency and fearful memories of hyperinflation, many Europeans saw cigarettes as a more stable substitute. As German criminologist Henner Hess recalls:

> Cigarettes, in fact, were in many ways ideal as a commodity reserve currency. They were easy to transport, easy to store, relatively durable, they came in norm units, and larger units could easily be divided: cartons into packs, packs into pieces. . . . They were internationally recognized, by Moroccans in the French forces as well as by Uzbeks in the Red Army, on the fish market in Hamburg as well as on the black market next to Munich's railway station. And they kept their value, because they were rare and everybody could be sure of a continuous high demand for them. Even massive imports posed no menace of inflation, because cigarettes had—unlike money—a direct use-value and any surplus literally went up in smoke: no currency in the world can boast of such a wonderful mechanism of quantity regulation.[154]

Hess recounts his own family's reliance on cigarettes as currency when the war ended in Germany: "As a small child I got first-hand experience of their [cigarettes] miraculous properties. When, in the spring and summer of 1945, my mother was on the move with her children, as twelve million other people were, from the East into and within the Reich until we reached my grandparents' home, her most valuable luggage were a few cartons of cigarettes which fed her children and opened many doors." Unfortunately, as Hess adds, his mother began to smoke herself, reducing the amount they had for currency.[155]

American soldiers stationed in Germany profited from their privileged access to scarce cigarettes at the PX, using them to buy pretty much anything. A favorite activity of American diplomats in Berlin was to visit the Barter Market, where they provoked the ire of the locals by using cheap cigarettes to buy high-value goods ranging from art and antiquities to Leica cameras.[156]

The Cold War was a boom time for smoking in general and for cigarettes in particular. Scientific evidence of the health hazards of tobacco would not generate a backlash until later in the century. Smoking

Figure 2.7  Cigarettes are used to barter for food and clothing in Berlin, August 1946 (Imagno/Votava/Ullstein bild/Granger Collection).

in the United States, for example, reached record levels—by the late 1940s, Americans were smoking twice as many cigarettes as they had in the 1920s.[157] Just as World War I had done much to build up a future cigarette consumer base, World War II added greatly to that base by securing a fresh batch of young cigarette recruits, with millions of previously nonsmoking Americans now hooked on nicotine in the postwar era.[158]

And, just as foreign tobacco companies had been decimated in World War I while certain American companies thrived, World War II created in some cases and solidified in others the winners and losers of the tobacco industry both in the United States and abroad. In the United States, the war further strengthened the market position of the top cigarette manufacturers, with long-lasting consequences. The top three companies quickly came to dominate the market. And while tobacco companies abroad were stymied by the war, American tobacco companies gained overseas markets.[159] A decade after the end of the war, US cigarette makers "began actively to exploit the war-nurtured taste for the American blended product that would eventually become the world standard."[160]

After the patriotic cigarette fervor of World War II faded and concerns about the potential health consequences of smoking began to resurface, at least one cigarette company turned to the postwar defense industry for a technological solution. A chemist for Lorillard applied to cigarettes a recently declassified filter technology developed during wartime by the US military. This "Kent" cigarette came to fruition, though ironically, the filter material was a form of asbestos, the health consequences of which were not yet understood.[161]

Meanwhile, there was plenty of smoke in Cold War hot spots. Revolutionary Cuba, for instance, was a haven for smokers. Both Fidel Castro and Che Guevara were heavy smokers. In *Guerrilla Warfare*, Che writes, "A customary and extremely important comfort in the life of the guerrilla fighter is a smoke. . . . [A] smoke in moments of rest is a great friend to the solitary soldier."[162] Castro is quoted as saying: "There is nothing in the world more agreeable than having a place where one can throw on the floor as many cigar butts as one pleases without the subconscious fear of a maid who is waiting like a sentinel to place an ashtray where the ashes are going to fall."[163] Well aware of Castro's love of smoking, the CIA at one point even devised a plan to assassinate him by poisoning his cigars. While the cigars were indeed poisoned with botulinus toxin, they never reached the Cuban leader.[164]

The Vietnam War escalated alongside the growth of an anti-tobacco movement in the United States that was supported by mounting scientific evidence. This movement provoked new government regulations on the cigarette industry, including the mandatory inclusion of health warnings on cigarette packaging. Yet, as they had been in World War I and World War II, concerns about the consequences of smoking tobacco were sidelined by the immediacies of war. Soldiers fighting in Vietnam kept on smoking despite the health warnings on their cigarette rations. Lung cancer was not the most immediate threat to their lives.[165] The North Vietnamese Army, in contrast, had to scrape together smoking supplies, sometimes supplemented by captured Americans' stockpiles.[166]

Amid broader societal concerns about the health hazards of smoking, it became less politically acceptable for the US military to be directly doling out cigarettes to its troops. Vietnam was therefore the last major American military encounter in which cigarettes were included in

Figure 2.8 Fidel Castro (center), smoking a cigar, is surrounded by peasants of the Sierra Maestra before entering the hut that was his headquarters during the Cuban Revolution, May 1959 (Bettman/Getty Images).

soldier rations. In 1986, the Pentagon went further, implementing various measures to curb cigarette use within the military, including banning tobacco during army basic training. The years leading up to the Gulf War saw increasing awareness of the health hazards of tobacco use, especially links between cigarette smoking and cancer. As a result, the US government imposed new regulations that limited troops' exposure to tobacco advertising, including a prohibition on any kind of battlefield cigarette promotion. Still, the restrictions seemed half-hearted: when the troops were withdrawn from the Middle East in 1991, Marlboro was allowed to post "Welcome Home" signs in more than forty locations, and Philip Morris even hosted a welcome home event attended by 80,000 people at the Camp Lejeune marine base.[167]

Elsewhere, the enduring link between cigarette smoking and war-making was nowhere more dramatically evident than during the bloody breakup of Yugoslavia in the early 1990s. All of the historical war-related functions of tobacco were on full display during the long siege of Sarajevo from 1992 to 1995, including the payment of soldiers with tobacco and the use of cigarettes as an exchange currency. As one Sarajevo resident wrote in her diary, "Everything is traded for cigarettes and cigarettes are traded for everything." One liter of milk could be traded for a pack of cigarettes—described as "the best exchange between babies and smokers known in history." One foreign journalist in Sarajevo put such high value on cigarettes that he called them "the lucky charms of war, more useful than a flak jacket."[168]

Cigarettes were supplied to the city via smuggling, but also locally via the Sarajevo tobacco factory. With cigarettes acting as a substitute currency, the tobacco factory essentially functioned as a government mint. Well-stocked before the siege with tobacco meant to supply the entire region, the factory was officially designated a priority building during the conflict and managed to operate throughout the war, maintaining about 20 percent of its prewar production capacity. When the paper for rolling and packaging cigarettes was depleted, the factory resorted to using paper from 100 tons of books as a substitute.[169]

The Bosnian government distributed cigarette rations as a form of salary for individuals ranging from soldiers on the frontline all the way up to members of the presidency. These cigarette rations in turn could be either consumed to calm nerves and satisfy addictions or traded for food and other goods. Soldiers in the 1st Mountain Brigade were paid one pack of cigarettes per day (with cigarettes delivered every ten days), and ten packs could be sold for 100 to 150 German marks. Individual cigarettes also came in handy as a substitute for small bills, which were in short supply. When buses were running, drivers would give out cigarettes when they did not have small bills for change. Smokers were at a clear disadvantage in this exchange system (having to consume rather than exchange cigarettes for other items), but smoking also inhibited hunger and calmed nerves. The psychological importance of cigarettes is starkly illustrated in a passage from a local journalist's wartime diary: "My neighbor Zulfo is depressed because there are no cigarettes, and is contemplating suicide. I gave him a packet of cigarettes as a Bajram [Muslim holiday] gift and restored his self-confidence."[170]

Elsewhere, smoking while soldiering remained ubiquitous well into the post–Cold War era. In the United States, nearly one-third of military personnel smoked in 2005—a rate that was more than 10 percent higher than that found among the civilian population, and those deployed to Iraq and Afghanistan reportedly smoked at double the rate of American civilians. "Although we stopped distributing cigarettes to Service members as part of their rations, we continue to permit, if not encourage, tobacco use," two senior Pentagon officials observed in a March 2014 memo circulated to all four branches of the military. "The prominence of tobacco in [military] retail outlets and permission for smoking breaks while on duty sustain the perception that we are not serious about reducing the use of tobacco."[171] Smoking within the military was even more prevalent elsewhere—almost 40 percent of Israeli soldiers, for example, were smokers by the time they finished their military service, which was twice the national average.[172] Some militaries even continued the cigarette ration: in Russia, the military expressed concern that its nicotine-addicted troops might revolt if deprived of their ten free cigarettes a day.[173]

Even the Islamic State (IS), which imposed a strict smoking ban in territories under its control, had a difficult time kicking the habit. After all, about half of Syrian men were smokers. Those caught in the act of smoking faced a minimum of forty lashes, yet many continued to sneak a smoke in defiance of the ban, and some militants who were publicly opposed to tobacco were privately complicit in a thriving black market of contraband cigarettes. One busted smuggler bought his release from captivity by paying off the IS commander who was detaining him with two cartons of cigarettes. The tobacco ban also certainly did not help with recruitment. One French recruit deserted within a few weeks, complaining that giving up smoking had simply proved too difficult (he received a seven-year prison sentence upon his return to France). Not surprisingly, territory liberated from Islamic State rule immediately reverted to public smoking, with smokers flaunting their cigarettes as an expression of newfound freedom.[174]

WARTIME SMOKING BANS HAVE been strikingly rare and short-lived, with the Islamic State campaign the most recent failure. Instead, as we've seen, smoking and war-making have gone hand in hand for centuries, so much so that soldiers have proved the perfect instruments for the globalization of tobacco use. Even shifts in the favored methods of ingestion, from pipes to cigars to cigarettes, have been profoundly shaped by the ease and efficiency of battlefield application. And once the battles have ended, soldiers have brought their smoking habit home with them, much to the delight of tobacco producers and tobacco tax collectors. Despite growing public awareness of its serious health hazards, the leaf's popularity on and off the battlefield has stubbornly endured—no doubt partly because nicotine is one of the world's most addictive substances. But addictiveness alone does not explain a drug's popularity. After all, as we'll now see, an even more popular but far less addictive drug, caffeine, has had an equally intimate connection to war.

# 3

## Caffeinated Conflict

CAFFEINE—A MILD STIMULANT TYPICALLY ingested in the form of coffee or tea but also consumed via caffeinated energy drinks and soft drinks such as Coca-Cola—is the world's most popular mood-altering drug. Billions of people rely on it for a daily jolt to boost energy and mental alertness and fend off drowsiness. It is also considered one of the world's most benign drugs, though its relationship to war has certainly been far from harmless. Unlike alcohol and tobacco, caffeine does not kill—at least not short of extreme doses equivalent to sixty to ninety strong cups of coffee for a 200-pound adult.[1] Nevertheless, the drug has been complicit in plenty of killing. Caffeine has kept armies awake, energized empires and rebellions, and popularized wartime drinks that percolate long after the fighting has ended.

Caffeine was first isolated in 1819 by German chemist Friedlieb Ferdinand Runge.[2] Caffeine is certainly not restricted to coffee beans and tea leaves—more than 100 other plants contain the alkaloid, including the guarana climbing vine, the kola nut, the yerba mate tree, and the guayusa holly tree—but no other source of the drug compares to the twin dominance of tea and coffee, the most widely consumed beverages on the planet apart from water. Our story of caffeine and conflict therefore mostly revolves around the tales of these two extraordinarily popular plants.

*Killer High*, Peter Andreas. Oxford University Press (2020). © Peter Andreas.
DOI: 10.1093/actrade/9780190463014.001.0001

## Tea Drinking and Warhorse Trading

We know little about the exact origins of the tea plant, *Camellia sinensis*, other than that it first developed in the foothills of the eastern Himalayas, which stretch from southwest China and Indochina to the northern reaches of Burma and Thailand, and across to the northeast Indian province of Assam. We know even less about its initial discovery and use by humans, but it appears that tea first became a domestic drink in China during the Han dynasty (206 BC–220 AD) and grew steadily in popularity. By the Tang dynasty (609–907) it had established itself as China's favorite beverage, and it became fully entrenched in daily life during the subsequent Northern Song (960–1126) and Southern Song (1126–1279) dynasties. In addition to the energizing effects of its caffeine content, tea possessed bacteria-killing tannic acid that made water safer to drink.[3] And tea had other convenient attributes: it was easy to prepare and transport, and it did not spoil. In the form of highly portable, uniform, compact bricks, tea was often used as a currency. The tea habit eventually spread to China's immediate neighbors, including the Tibetans, Mongols, and Japanese, and ultimately expanded across the globe by land and sea, turning tea into one of the first global products.[4]

As the tea trade grew, so too did the temptation to tax it, especially to fund wars. And increased taxes in turn prompted evasion and protest. Tang rulers imposed the first tea tax in 782, set at 10 percent, and the tax rate increased substantially in subsequent decades. The prime minister under Emperor Wen Zong (r. 827–840) went even further, imposing a virtual state monopoly on tea. This move sparked a popular revolt that culminated in the prime minister's dismemberment and the lifting of the monopoly. The tax rate nevertheless continued to rise, leading to widespread smuggling that even the death penalty failed to deter. In the ninth century, revenue from tea smuggling enabled locals in remote mountainous tea-growing areas to buy contraband loot from gangs of river bandits plundering boats on the Yangtze.[5]

The biggest threat to Chinese rulers, however, came not from within, but from the nomadic horse-borne tribes in the frontier zones of the north and northwest, including the Khitans, Jurchens, Tanguts, and Mongols. The key advantage of these nomads—which led at one point to the Mongols overtaking the southern capital of the Chinese empire—was their warhorses. China had superior equipment and technology (including gunpowder), more fortified defenses (most famously, the Great Wall), and greater manpower (a sizeable standing army) but was woefully inferior when it came to the quality of horses.[6] "Horses are the foundation of military strength, the state's great resource," wrote Han dynasty general Ma Yuan.[7] Later, when the Song dynasty was chronically harassed by the Tangut Xixia nomads, government official Song Qi, the director of herds and pastures, identified the root of the problem as follows: "The northern Liao and western Xixia are able to oppose China only because they have numerous horses and practice riding. China has few horses, and its men do not practice riding. This is China's weakness."[8]

Song rulers turned to tea to try to solve the warhorse deficit. For centuries, the growing and selling of tea had been strategically organized to meet the needs of war-making through measures including the reestablishment of a virtual government monopoly. In 1074, the government created the Tea and Horse Agency in order to exchange Sichuan tea for Tibetan warhorses.[9] The need for Tibetan horses to fend off nomads from the north and west placed an enormous burden on Sichuan tea producers and traders, who were ordered to hand over their entire supply to the government at low prices.[10]

For a time, the tea-for-horses trade helped the Song fend off the nomadic invaders from the north. But a chronic horse shortage persisted, and the amount of tea necessary to purchase capable warhorses kept going up. Moreover, despite harsh penalties, part of the tea supply slipped out of government control via smuggling, further impeding the state's ability to acquire warhorses. After being on the defensive for years, the Southern Song finally surrendered to the Mongols in 1276.[11]

The Ming dynasty (1368–1644) unified China and brought back the Tea and Horse Agency as a cornerstone of Chinese defense. The government appropriated one million catties (more than 600 tons) of Sichuan tea annually, and soldiers were deployed to grow tea on unused lands.[12] With the northern nomadic tribes now avid tea drinkers, any sale of tea to them without authorization was strictly prohibited. Those caught smuggling the plant could be executed or drafted into the military. Yet as in the past, the state monopoly suffered from serious leakage, with two damaging consequences outlined in a 1505 government memorandum: not only were Ming rulers unable to raise the funds to purchase enough warhorses, but they were also unable to deprive attacking nomads of tea, making those tribes' frontier incursions bolder and more frequent.[13]

In neighboring Japan, meanwhile, the most important connection between tea and war was more cultural than strategic. After crossing the East China Sea, the tea leaf gradually became entrenched in Japanese military culture between the eleventh and sixteenth centuries. The popularity of tea received a critical boost in the early thirteenth century, when Japan's military leader, or shogun, Minamoto Sanetomo was brought back to health with tea, making him an enthusiastic promoter of the drink.[14] The extraordinarily intricate ceremony that developed around tea, and the ornate utensils used in it, became as cherished as the tea itself. At the time, warlords controlled Japan. In their fighting among one another and their efforts to unite their various fiefs, tea was ever-present. It was served in portable tea huts during battle and to celebrate victories, and an enemy's tea utensils were among the most sought-after spoils of war.[15]

For the rising samurai, who were often of humble origins, tea drinking—or, more accurately, the elaborate tea ceremony surrounding it—facilitated upward social mobility. They used tea and tea gatherings as an instrument to improve their social status.[16] The samurai class, who ruled during the Kamakura era (1192–1333), known as the "Age of Warriors," was instrumental in the proliferation of tea houses, the tea ceremony, and tea drinking more generally.[17] One description of the samurai code of honor known as *bushido*—the "way of the warrior"— noted that "a samurai whose only attribute is strength is not acceptable. He must use his leisure time to practice poetry and understand the tea ceremony."[18]

Toyotomi Hideyoshi (1536–1598), a peasant-turned-samurai warlord who rose to become Japan's second great unifier after more than 100 years of civil wars, was as committed to mastering the art of the tea ceremony as he was to the military unification of Japan. Indeed, fancying himself a great tea master, he went so far as to insist on bringing a portable teahouse onto the battlefield. According to one account, "Hideyoshi would then calmly practice the tea ceremony in view of both his own troops and his enemies, inspiring confidence in the first and fear in the second."[19] Hideyoshi also appointed Sen-no-Rikyu (1522–1591)—the tea master who more than any other shaped Japan's tea ceremony, tea garden, and teahouse—as curator of the palace tea ceremony, only to later order him to commit suicide out of envy and resentment.[20]

## From Coffee to Coffeehouses

Most accounts of the origins of coffee, the main caffeinated rival of tea, place it in the highlands of present-day Ethiopia at least as far back as the ninth century. Who first discovered coffee is unknown, though there are plenty of stories. According to one recent history of caffeine, it is likely that the nomadic Galla tribe was the first to take advantage of the caffeine boost provided by the coffee bean, which its members consumed for sustenance when participating in war parties.[21] When Scottish explorer James Bruce traveled to Ethiopia in 1768, he reported on what appeared to be a continuation of this ancient use of coffee:

> The Gallae is a wandering nation of Africa, who, in their incursions into Abyssinia, are obliged to traverse immense deserts, and being desirous of falling on the towns and villages of that country without warning, carry nothing to eat with them but the berries of the Coffee tree *roasted* and *pulverized*, which they mix with grease to a certain consistency that will permit of its being rolled into masses about the size of billiard balls and then put in leathern bags until required for use. One of these balls, they claim will support them for a whole day, when on a marauding incursion or in active war, better than a loaf of bread or a meal of meat, because it cheers their spirits as well as feeds them.[22]

Coffee was eventually brought to Yemen, where it was grown outside of the coastal town of Mocha and became popular as a drink ingredient in the mid-fifteenth century. After the Ottomans occupied Yemen in 1536, they exported coffee from the port of Mocha to the rest of their empire.[23] Their conquest of Mesopotamia greatly enabled the proliferation of coffee. Soon, coffeehouses sprang up across the Middle East, from Cairo to Constantinople. In his seven-volume history of the Ottomans, the French nineteenth-century historian Mouradgea

D'Ohsson writes that by 1570 there were more than 600 coffeehouses in Constantinople.[24] At various times, anxious Ottoman leaders banned coffeehouses as brewers of social instability, secular gathering places where locals could plot rebellion. Grand Vizier Kuprili shut down the Constantinople coffeehouses as a deterrent to sedition during his war with Candia.[25] Persian leaders took a subtler approach, deploying spies to coffeehouses to report back on any potential threats to their rule.[26]

It took another century for coffee to reach Europe, where it was embraced as an alternative to (and antidote for) alcoholic drinks, and where the coffeehouse came to be viewed as more respectable than the tavern. Coffee arrived in Europe at different times and through multiple routes in the seventeenth century. The most famous account of coffee's journey west involved the failed Ottoman siege of Vienna in 1683, remembered as both the end of Ottoman imperial ambitions in Europe and the beginning of Viennese coffee drinking. When the siege was repelled, the retreating Turks left behind dozens of sacks filled with mysterious green beans that the locals mistook for camel fodder. The messenger-spy Georg Franz Kolschitzky insisted he could put the beans to good use. He gladly accepted them as a reward for his service during the siege, in which he had disguised himself as a Turkish soldier to cross enemy lines and reach nearby Polish troops to request reinforcement. Having spent years among the Turks, Kolschitzky knew not only what the beans were but also the basics of coffee preparation and service, and he soon opened the Blue Bottle coffeehouse. His signature coffee was as sweet as the Turkish version, but he filtered out the muddy grounds and added a bit of milk. Soon, coffeehouses were popping up throughout the city, transforming Vienna's intellectual culture and the drinking habits of its residents.[27]

Or so the story goes.[28] Kolschitzky was undoubtedly not the only person in the city familiar with coffee, but his heroic story is the one the Viennese most like to tell, and they have even erected a statue of him outside the Café Zwirina. The Vienna café "has become a model for a large part of the world," writes William Ukers in his classic *All About Coffee*, and "Kolschitzky is honored in Vienna as the patron saint of coffeehouses."[29]

Mirroring the earlier experience in the Arab world, coffee and coffeehouses spread throughout Europe, though unevenly and not always without controversy and opposition. The Prussian ruler Frederick the Great issued a proclamation against coffee on September 13, 1777:

> It is disgusting to notice the increase in the quantity of coffee used by my subjects, and the amount of money that goes out of the country in consequence. Everybody is using coffee. If possible, this must be prevented. My people must drink beer. His Majesty was brought up on beer, and so were his ancestors, and his officers. Many battles have been fought and won by soldiers nourished on beer; and the King does not believe that coffee-drinking soldiers can be depended upon to endure hardship or to beat his enemies in case of the occurrence of another war.[30]

Failing to eradicate coffee drinking, Frederick instead created a royal monopoly on roasting that proved enormously profitable. As one might expect, this also generated a flourishing black market, which Frederick attempted to police with a team of spies—composed largely of wounded or retired soldiers—known as "coffee smellers" and "coffee sniffers." Their job was to wander the streets and alleys to sniff out and find unauthorized coffee roasters.[31]

In England, King Charles II thought the coffeehouse rather than coffee was the real menace. In 1675 he issued a "Proclamation for the Suppression of Coffee-houses," which accused them of having "very evil and dangerous effects . . . for that in such Houses . . . divers False, Malitious and Scandalous Reports are devised and spread abroad, to the Defamation of His Majestie's Government, and to the Disturbance of the Peace and Quiet of the Realm; His Majesty hath thought it fit and necessary, That the said Coffee-Houses be (for the future) Put down and Suppressed."[32] But the public backlash made it clear the ban would be unenforceable. The government backed down and instead insisted that coffeehouse owners swear an oath of allegiance and promise to keep out spies and troublemakers.[33]

European rulers had good reason to be wary of coffeehouses as incubators of rebellion. This was particularly true in France in the time before the French Revolution. In the words of one eyewitness in Paris in 1789, coffeehouses "are not only crowded within, but other expectant crowds are at the doors and windows, listening *à gorge déployée* [open-mouthed] to certain orators who from chairs or tables harangue each his little audience; the eagerness with which they are heard, and the thunder of applause they receive for every sentiment of more than common hardiness or violence against the government, cannot easily be imagined."[34] The French Revolution "literally began at a café," notes Tom Standage. "It was at the Café de Foy, on the afternoon of July 12, 1789, that a young lawyer named Camille Desmoulins set the French Revolution in motion. Crowds had gathered in the nearby gardens of the Palais Royal. . . . Desmoulins leaped onto a table outside the café, brandishing a pistol and shouting, 'To arms, citizens! To arms!' His cry was taken up, and Paris swiftly descended into chaos; the Bastille was stormed by an angry mob two days later."[35]

## From Rebellious Coffeehouses to Tea Party Rebellions

A taste for coffee, and the popularity of the coffeehouse as the place to sip it, soon spread not only across Europe but also across the Atlantic to the New World. In the British colonies, the first coffeehouse opened in Boston in 1689. But here, a tavern and a coffeehouse were the same thing, a place where one could order beer or ale as easily as coffee or tea. And as it had in Europe, such a setting offered a convenient spot for men to talk politics and plot rebellion. At Boston's Green Dragon, colonists such as John Adams, James Otis, and Paul Revere drank and strategized, leading Daniel Webster to dub it "the headquarters of the Revolution."[36] And it was at the Bunch of Grapes, another prominent Boston coffeehouse, that the Declaration of Independence was first read in public.[37]

By the 1770s, tea had become the favorite caffeinated beverage in the British colonies, mirroring the drinking preference of the mother country. But that taste abruptly shifted as the colonies rejected tea as a symbol of oppressive imperial rule. What became known as the "Boston Tea Party" served not only as a lightning rod for colonial opposition but also as a trigger for British overreaction. On the evening of December 16, 1773, a group of irate Boston colonists, some thinly disguised as Mohawk Indians, boarded three ships of the British East India Company and for the next three hours proceeded to dump 342 chests of tea into Boston Harbor—cheered on by the crowds watching

THE DESTRUCTION OF TEA AT BOSTON HARBOR.

Figure 3.1 An 1846 lithograph portrays the Boston Tea Party (GraphicaArtis/Getty Images).

from the dock. The whole thing had been planned out ahead of time at the Green Dragon by Paul Revere and his collaborators.

The episode had a polarizing effect. Colonial opposition leaders celebrated and defended the "party" as a principled protest. John Adams, the future second president of the United States, wrote, "This is the most magnificent Movement of all. . . . This Destruction of the Tea is so bold, so daring, so firm, intrepid, and inflexible, and it must have so important Consequences and so lasting, that I cannot but consider it as an Epocha in History."[38] Once word of Boston's defiance spread, other colonies followed suit, turning the destruction of tea into a collective and unifying act of defiance against British rule. London retaliated by closing the port of Boston and introducing a series of punitive measures known as the Coercive Acts. These events proved to be a tipping point: both the Boston Tea Party and the punishing British response served as catalysts for the mobilization of opposition throughout the colonies.

What provoked this incident that turned tea into fuel for the American Revolution? The Boston Tea Party is remembered in the popular imagination as a protest against taxes, but it actually had more to do with smuggling interests than tax burdens. Relatively low-priced tea supplied to the colonists by the British East India Company—which had been given a monopoly on tea imports to the colonies—undercut the sale of smuggled Dutch tea, which up until that point had dominated the local market in violation of the Townsend duty on tea. "The smugglers not only buy cheaper in Holland but save the 3d duty," complained Governor Thomas Hutchinson.[39] In the summer of 1771 Hutchinson guessed that more than 80 percent of the tea consumed in Boston had been smuggled in.[40] No doubt many colonists found the granting of monopoly trade rights to the British East India Company irksome. But most threatened were the economic interests of those co-lonial merchants who had invested heavily in the illicit Dutch tea trade and enjoyed wide profit margins.[41]

The colonists not only broke from British rule but also tried to break their British-inspired tea habit. An "anti-tea hysteria" spread through the colonies, with the Continental Congress ultimately passing a res-olution against the drink.[42] John Adams wrote his wife in 1774: "Tea must be universally renounced and I must be weaned, and the sooner the better."[43] Later, he wrote to his wife about an episode at an inn that had occurred on his way to sign the Declaration of Independence. He had asked the barmaid, "Is it lawful for a weary traveler to refresh himself with a dish of tea, provided it has been honestly smuggled and has paid no duty?" "No, sir!" she had replied. "We have renounced tea under this roof. But, if you desire it, I will make you some coffee."[44] Coffee was therefore one of the victors of the American Revolution, with average coffee consumption jumping sevenfold between 1772 and 1799, from 0.19 pounds to 1.41 pounds per person per year.[45]

Still, unpatriotic tea-drinking quietly returned after independence, with the leaves now supplied directly from the Far East via American ships. But even with America's taste for tea revived, coffee continued to make inroads in the new nation and by the mid-nineteenth century had eclipsed tea as the country's caffeinated drink of choice. By the end of the nineteenth century, the United States would be consuming al-most half of the world's coffee supply. This consumption was a matter not just of patriotic sentiment and shifting tastes, but of access and cost: with importers freed from restrictive British trade rules, coffee could now be secured directly from nearby producers in the Americas and thus became cheaper than tea.[46]

Coffee production did not fully take off in the Western Hemisphere until the wars of independence from Portugal and Spain in the early 1820s. Napoleon had inadvertently contributed to Brazil's future coffee boom, which would propel it to become the world's top coffee producer. After Napoleon's troops sacked Lisbon in November 1807 and the Portuguese royal family fled to Rio de Janeiro, Prince Regent (and later King) João VI from his new royal seat declared Brazil to be a kingdom and promoted agricultural development there—including the breeding of new strains of coffee plants obtained by planters as seedlings from the Royal Botanical Gardens in Rio.[47]

As coffee gained ground in the United States, so too did the temptation to tax it, especially during wartime. In the 1790s, the federal government imposed an import tax on the beans of a few cents a pound, but this increased to ten cents a pound during the War of 1812. The coffee tax was halved after the war and entirely lifted by 1832, greatly enabling the accessibility of the drink. The coffee tax was only brought back with the outbreak of the Civil War, rising to five cents per pound in 1862, and was again repealed in 1872.[48]

## Empire of Tea

Meanwhile, Britain's addiction to tea—especially black tea, which was more durable than green tea for long-distance transport—continued to grow, so much so that Britain became the largest consumer of tea in the world in the nineteenth century. And as the nation became addicted to tea, the Crown became addicted to tea revenue.[49]

Supplying Britain's enormous—and enormously profitable—caffeine habit became an imperial imperative, placed largely in the hands of the British East India Company and its monopoly on trade with the East Indies. Through the tea trade, the British East India Company morphed into the most powerful corporation in history, possessing state-like powers that included maintaining its own army and waging war.[50] Through its trading posts established in China in the early eighteenth century, the company secured enough tea to make the drink affordable and accessible to every British citizen, and indeed tea was cheaper at this time than any drink other than water.[51]

There was only one problem: How to pay China for all that tea? China had little interest in European goods and insisted on being paid in silver. Consequently, silver represented 87.5 percent of East India Company exports to China between 1708 and 1760.[52] And the price of silver kept rising. Even worse, the Seven Years' War (1756–1763) and the American War of Independence (1775–1783) severely strained British silver supplies, making it that much harder for the British to keep up with payments for Chinese tea. Britain tried to cover its mounting war costs by increasing the import duty on tea—from a tax of 64 percent in 1772 to 106 percent in 1777, and up to 119 percent in 1784—but this only prompted massive smuggling. Indeed, in the 1770s there was probably more bootlegged tea in Britain than legally imported tea, with some 250 European ships engaged in the illicit trade.[53] The Crown thus faced a double shortage of both silver and tax revenue.

Opium (the focus of the next chapter) provided the unofficial solution to Britain's fiscal woes. In the wake of the Battle of Plassey and the annexation of Bengal, Indian opium production, which had previously been in the hands of the nawab of Bengal, had by 1763 come under the control of the British East India Company. There was a ready market for the drug in China, despite an official ban on it since 1729. The politically delicate task of illicitly trading opium for tea was handled through an elaborate scheme mostly run through intermediaries— merchants subcontracted out to smuggle opium to the port of Canton, from which it was then transferred to Chinese trading vessels (with bribed local customs officials turning a blind eye) in exchange for silver. The silver, in turn, was used to pay for Britain's tea imports, with handsome profits for all involved. Opium imports to China quadrupled between 1770 and 1800, remained high through the first three decades of the nineteenth century, and then skyrocketed again in the first half of the 1830s.[54]

Meanwhile, most Britons paid little attention to the fact that their tea habit was made possible by illicitly feeding China's opium habit. It was not exactly a secret. In 1836, John Davis, having returned from a stint as joint superintendent of British trade in Canton, published *The Chinese: A General Description of the Empire of China and Its Inhabitants*, in which he acknowledged that "opium has of late formed about *one-half* of the total value of British imports . . . and that tea has constituted something less than the same proportion of our exports. . . . The pernicious drug, sold to the Chinese, has exceeded in market-value the wholesome leaf that has been purchased from them."[55] One reviewer of Davis's treatise commented that "it is a curious circumstance that we grow the poppy in our Indian territories to poison the people of China, in return for a wholesome beverage which they prepare, almost exclusively, for us."[56] Some expressed unease, including future prime minister William Gladstone, who wrote in his diary: "I am in dread of the judgment of God upon England for our national iniquity toward China."[57] But for the most part, the British attitude was defined more by denial and tolerance than by revulsion and protest. As William Jardine, one of the world's leading opium traffickers at the time, explained in a letter to a friend, "The good people in England think of nothing connected with China but tea and the revenue derived from it, and to obtain these quietly will submit to any degradation."[58]

Angry Chinese leaders kept denouncing the opium trade and passing more laws against it, but the British and their trading accomplices simply ignored them. The authorities finally resorted to confiscating and destroying opium stockpiles at Canton. The ensuing merchant outcry led to Britain's declaration of war, officially to protect free trade, but unofficially to protect the opium-for-tea trade.[59]

The Opium War of 1839–1842 was overwhelmingly one-sided from the start, with the Chinese hopelessly outgunned by Britain's superior weaponry on both land and water. The outcome was inevitable, with a humbled China forced to cede Hong Kong, open five ports for free trade, and pay reparations in the form of silver.[60] China would eventually be forced to legalize the opium trade after the Second Opium War (1856–1860).[61] The remaining decades of the century would be defined by China's rapid decline, including violent turmoil, economic hardship, and repeated foreign intervention.

Even China's massive tea export business came undone. At the same time that the British were militarily forcing China to open its ports to opium, they were busily trying to diversify their source of tea beyond one lone supplier.[62] When the British East India Company lost its trade monopoly with China in 1834, it became especially motivated to find land under its control in India that was suitable for tea growing. The company had previously used its troops to battle local tribes for control of Assam in the 1820s. In 1823, Robert Bruce, an ex-army businessman who doubled as a mercenary and illicit trader in Assam, discovered that tea was indigenous to the area. This was of particular interest to his brother, Charles Alexander Bruce, a commander of a division of gunboats placed in charge of the area, who would go on to become the most important early developer of the commercial tea industry in India. After helping to drive the Burmese out and imposing British rule in Assam, he managed to secure local tea samples and would eventually be appointed superintendent of tea forests, using both indigenous strains and strains brought in from China.[63]

War-making paved the way for tea planting.[64] British-run tea farms began to proliferate in Assam, prompting further military incursions for more land. While the conflict over these lands largely predated British tea ventures in the Indian heartland, imperial conquest, especially the Anglo-Burmese wars of the 1820s, was a prerequisite for the transformation of the area into a leading global tea exporter. And it was the profits from the Chinese tea trade, after all, that empowered the British East India Company to militarily conquer and administer India in the first place.[65]

With the Treaty of Yandabo in 1826, the Burmese ceded not only all of their possessions in India but also a third of Burma to Britain. British rule replaced Burmese rule, with the East India Company taking over direct administration of the territories in 1838. Its eye was clearly on expanding tea cultivation.[66] The British would later also pacify Darjeeling, laying the groundwork for production of some of the highest-quality tea in the world.[67]

## Caffeinated Soldiers

While conquering and tea growing went hand in hand for the British Empire, British soldiers came to enjoy sipping tea as part of their daily rations. It was not until the nineteenth century that it became common to add tea or coffee to military rations, with the emergence of the caffeinated soldier nowhere more pronounced than in Britain and the United States. Caffeine made tea a particularly uplifting wartime drink for the British. It energized soldiers and sailors, yet a warm cup of it could also fight off cold and soothe war-rattled nerves.[68] In addition to the warmth and caffeine rush tea provided, in many cases it was the only safe means of drinking water because of the boiling necessary for its preparation.

In the United States, soldiers became officially caffeinated when coffee was added to their rations in 1832.[69] But it was not until the Civil War (1861–1865) that the country experienced its first large-scale caffeinated conflict. With the South's secession, the Union imposed a hefty duty on coffee imports to help pay for the war while at the same time blockading southern ports. Far from depressing the coffee trade, the war made it more profitable. The price of Brazilian coffee increased to fourteen cents a pound in 1861, and it jumped all the way to forty-two cents a pound before the end of the war. The US Army's insatiable thirst for coffee drove demand, so much so that victories on the battlefield provoked more trading and price jumps. By 1864, the Union government was importing some 40 million pounds of coffee beans.[70]

A former Massachusetts artilleryman described the importance of the coffee ration for the average soldier:

> Little campfires, rapidly increasing to hundreds in number, would shoot up along the hills and plains and, as if by magic, acres of territory would be luminous with them. Soon they would be surrounded by the soldiers, who made it an almost invariable rule to cook their coffee first, after which a large number, tired out with the toils of the day, would make their supper of hardtack and coffee, and roll up in their blankets for the night. If a march was ordered at midnight, unless a surprise was intended it must be preceded by a pot of coffee. . . . It was coffee *at* meals and *between* meals; and men going on guard or coming off guard drank it at all hours of the night.[71]

In his account of his regiment in the Civil War, William F. Scott described the thirst for coffee at length: "For, next to fire, the one thing indispensable to the soldiers was coffee. There must have been very many who, when they enlisted, were not in the habit of drinking it, or drank it very little; but camp-life soon made it a necessity to all.

Figure 3.2 Army of the Potomac soldiers wait for coffee at a camp during the Civil War. Lithograph published by L. Prang after a sketch by Winslow Homer, 1863 (Granger Collection).

The active campaigner was sure to take it as often as he could get it. No other article of either food or drink could approach it in value in the estimation of a man who had to march or work by day or watch by night." He went on: "It was a luxury to the Southerners, who were deprived of their usual supply by the blockade and their poverty. To them it was something like the visit of an angel when a Union soldier appeared with a little coffee to trade. With that coin he could buy anything, everything, he might fancy." Scott also recounted how the drink was produced and consumed on a daily basis:

Of course boiling was the one method of producing the drink. In a regular camp this was done in camp-kettles, in quantity sufficient for a mess of six or eight men or more, but on a march and in bivouac each man was provided with a small tin pail (usually made by himself from an emptied fruit can), in which he could make a quart for one or two men. This rude little kettle was seen hanging to every saddle on a march, and three or four or half a dozen times a day, if halts were made long enough, or opportunity offered, small fires were started and water set on for making coffee. If the column should move before the boiling was done, why, a soldier's blessing upon the inconsiderate commander; if while the cooling was in progress, the steaming pails would be carried along in the hand until the liquor could be drunk in the saddle. Many a time the little pots were set a-boiling in the halt that preceded an engagement, to provide a brace against the coming contest.[72]

The most celebrated Civil War coffee story involved a nineteen-year-old commissary sergeant with Company E of the 23rd Ohio Infantry at the Battle of Antietam in September 1862. The young man, William McKinley, braved enemy fire to haul vats of hot coffee to exhausted soldiers who had been fighting since before dawn. Their officer described the magical effect of the hot brew as the equivalent of "putting a new regiment in the fight." Historian Jon Grinspan writes that "three decades later, McKinley ran for president in part on this singular act of caffeinated heroism."[73] A monument at Antietam—which includes a panel depicting McKinley offering a cup of coffee to a soldier—memorializes the event.

In Union soldier diaries, the word "coffee" appears more often than "rifle," "cannon," or "bullet." As one diarist put it, "Nobody can 'soldier' without coffee."[74] Another soldier wrote home that "what keeps me alive must be the coffee."[75] General Benjamin Butler was well aware of the effect of coffee on his soldiers, insisting they carry coffee in their canteens and timing attacks to coincide with when his men would have the most caffeine in their system. He promised another general before a battle in October 1864 that "if your men get their coffee early in the morning you can hold."[76] The great irony and contradiction, of course, is that while fighting to end slavery, these soldiers were drinking coffee imported from Brazilian slave plantations.[77]

The Union Army allocated each soldier approximately thirty-six pounds of coffee per year. Men ground their own beans—some carbines had built-in hand-cranked grinders in the buttstock. As one historian describes it: "The massive Union Army of the Potomac made up the second-largest population center in the Confederacy, and each morning this sprawling city became a coffee factory. . . . [T]he encampment buzzed with the sound of thousands of grinders simultaneously crushing beans."[78] In his 1952 classic *The Life of Billy Yank*, Bell Irvin Wiley noted, "Coffee was one of the most cherished items in the ration. . . . The effect on morale must have been considerable. And if it cannot be said that coffee helped Billy Yank win the war, it at least made his participation in the conflict more tolerable."[79]

Confederate soldiers, meanwhile, were forced to fight decaffeinated, thanks to the Union's blockade of southern ports. One Alabama nurse joked that the desperate need for a caffeine fix would be the Union's "means of subjugating us."[80] What little coffee was available had to be smuggled in through the blockade or clandestinely traded across enemy lines.[81] Those who suffered through the war without coffee on the Confederate side included captured Union soldiers. After being released from a Confederate prison camp where he had gone without coffee for more than a year, one Union soldier described how much he had missed the beverage: "Just think of it, in three hundred days there was lost to me, forever, so many hundred pots of good old Government Java." He blasted "those Confederate thieves for robbing me of so many precious doses."[82]

In documenting the history of the US military's procurement of coffee, Franz Koehler points to the long-lasting repercussions of the Union Army's coffee habit: "It is not so generally known that the part played by the military forces in promoting the popularity of coffee has not only been a large one but has been a pioneering one. After the Civil War, soldiers brought the flavor of coffee from mess hall and campfire to civilian pursuits and post war contemporaries. And it was only thereafter that the growth in national popularity for coffee was assured."[83]

World War I had an even more transformative impact on coffee, both on and off the battlefield. The United States quickly supplanted Europe as Latin America's most important importer.[84] In 1914, American importers were suddenly in a position to take advantage of wartime disruptions to carve out a much greater share of the trade while also enjoying lower prices. In fact, the United States wooed Brazil into the war with the promise of buying a million pounds of Brazilian coffee for American soldiers.[85]

Meanwhile, the war years were hard times for many Germans in Latin America, including those in the coffee business. In Guatemala, Germans owned 10 percent of the country's coffee plantations, which produced about 40 percent of the harvest before the war. The United States claimed that almost two-thirds of German-owned coffee-producing land was "enemy property" and applied intense pressure on the Guatemalan government to confiscate it. Guatemalan dictator Estrada Cabrera was more than happy to comply with US wishes as a way to add to his own property.[86]

The US Army was a leading coffee consumer during this period, with more than 29 million pounds of the beans requisitioned by the Quartermaster-General's Department in 1917.[87] As one journalist reported, coffee was available at every meal, making it "THE most popular drink of the camp."[88] The quality of the beverage, however, did not match the quantity. Roasted and ground in the United States, the coffee was predictably stale by the time it reached the frontlines, and army regulations made matters worse by watering it down and reusing the grounds. E. F. Holbrook, the purchaser of coffee for the Quartermaster's Department, was eventually able to convince the military to ship green beans closer to the front for roasting there. By the end of the war, the US Army was roasting 750,000 pounds of coffee beans per day.[89]

Instant coffee was an instant hit on the battlefield. As Ukers puts it, "It was the World War that brought soluble coffee to the front."[90] Packed in envelopes, soluble coffee became part of the reserve ration, and meeting the surging demand for soluble coffee in the trenches became one of the biggest challenges of the Subsistence Division in Washington.[91] By the end of the war, production had increased by more than 3,000 percent, reaching 42,500 pounds daily.[92]

One of the most popular brands of instant coffee was "G. Washington's Refined Coffee." In 1906, a Belgian residing in Guatemala named George Washington experimented with further refining the crystals from brewed coffee. A few years later, after moving to New York and becoming a US citizen, he started selling his product under the "G. Washington" name. It was quick, convenient, and came close enough to resembling conventionally brewed coffee—including in caffeine content—that it was a success. But it was the war that gave it the biggest boost. The US Army bought up the entire supply in the summer of 1918, leading the company to proudly boast in its advertisements, "G. Washington's Refined Coffee has gone to WAR." One soldier wrote, "There is one gentleman I am going to look up first after I get through helping whip the Kaiser, and that is George Washington, of Brooklyn, the soldiers' friend."[93] Soldiers would sometimes even ask for a cup of "George" rather than coffee.[94] Demand soared, prompting other producers to rush to market with their own instant coffee concoctions.[95]

Although the popularity of instant coffee ended with the war, the conflict had made the coffee-drinking nation even more hooked. During the war, US troops consumed some 75 million pounds of coffee, and the American Army of Occupation in Germany consumed an additional 2,500 pounds per day. "The war had addicted veterans to coffee," notes Pendergrast.[96] "It shall not be forgotten," one coffee roaster proclaimed, "that a good cup of coffee is one of the vital blessings of their every-day life which should not and must not be denied to them, our boys, the unbeatable, happy warriors of a coffee-loving nation!"[97]

In 1919, *Simmons Spice Mill*, a business publication promoting the coffee, tea, and spice trades, asked E. F. Holbrook, who had been in charge of coffee supplies for the US War Department during World War I, to write an article about soldier coffee drinking. He wrote the following:

> I have been asked often how much coffee was required by the army. The quantity was huge and, taken as a whole, formed a basis for the biggest coffee business the world has ever seen. In round figures, the amount of green coffee required daily for both "issue" coffee and soluble coffee, based on the size of the army at the time of the signing of the armistice, was 750,000 lbs.—a terrifying figure to contemplate

when the rapidly vanishing visible supply of green coffee in this country was considered. The country would surely have been put on limited rations of coffee had the war continued.[98]

In the wake of armistice, promoters of the coffee business took out advertisements in leading newspapers and popular magazines, boasting of their patriotic role during the war, one of which read:

Your Uncle Sam provided his boys with COFFEE.

Our government sent 3,000,000 fighting men abroad. And, to keep them physically fit, it sent millions of pounds of coffee.

A most careful diet was planned in order to maintain health and strength. While bread and beans and beef were needful, there was one item recognized as absolutely indispensable—*coffee.*

So—whatever else they had, our boys had their coffee,—plenty of it, *four times a day!* It cheered and comforted and encouraged them. It helped them do their job,—and do it well. Who shall say how *grand* a part coffee played in this great war?[99]

Coffee consumption increased steadily in the interwar years. William Ukers, founder of the *Tea & Coffee Trade Journal,* wrote that "the 2,000,000 American soldiers who went overseas, and there had their coffee three times a day, learned to have a keener appreciation of coffee's benefits, and since returning to civilian life are using it more than ever before."[100]

World War II would prove to be an even more caffeinated conflict. During that conflict the US Army developed a 32.5-pound annual per-capita habit. Sustaining this habit required the army to purchase 140,000 bags of coffee a month.[101] Pendergrast points out that coffee and soldiers became so closely identified that the former took on the name of the latter: a "cuppa Joe."[102] Between 1941 and 1942, the US military's coffee-roasting, -grinding, and -packaging capacity massively expanded, increasing from 50,000 to 250,000 pounds per day.[103]

At first the coffee was roasted, ground, and vacuum-packed domestically, but after D-Day the military shipped green beans abroad for roasting closer to the front.[104] Some 300 Red Cross "clubmobiles" in

Figure 3.3  US Marines take comfort in a hot cup of coffee after two days and two nights of fighting in the Enewetak Atoll in the Marshall Islands, 1944 (George Eastman House/Getty Images).

Europe served coffee and doughnuts to the troops.[105] Coffee's particular appeal to the soldier was readily evident by the fact that the average annual consumption of a soldier was almost twice the average domestic consumption during the war.[106]

As they had done during the previous war, US coffee sellers promoted their product as patriotic. Maxwell House boasted: "Coffee's in the fight too! With the paratroopers . . . in the bombers . . . on board our Navy ships . . . the crews turn to a steaming cup of hot coffee for a welcome lift."[107]

American defense workers at home were also kept caffeinated with the introduction of the "coffee break," a short rest and caffeine boost to stimulate productivity. More than $4 billion in coffee was imported into the country during the war—amounting to 10 percent of *all* US imports.[108] The year after the war ended, annual per capita consumption of the beverage rose to nearly twenty pounds—double the amount in 1900.[109]

Instant coffee, which had been given a huge stimulus during World War I, saw demand spike again during the World War II. It was globally distributed to the frontlines: as Koehler described it, "In small envelopes for individual servings and in olive-drab cans for group use, it appeared almost overnight at the 'four corners of the earth' in the many special operational rations, food packets, and ration supplements in which soluble coffee became an essential component."[110] By 1944, a dozen companies were all producing soluble coffee, including Maxwell House and Nescafé—all of which was requisitioned for the war effort.[111]

For the Germans, in contrast, the war was defined by an acute coffee shortage. All coffee advertising in Germany was banned in 1938 to help wean the country off of foreign imports. In early 1939 coffee imports were cut by 40 percent, and what remained of the country's coffee supply was confiscated and diverted to the military right before the war began.[112] In the Nazi-occupied Netherlands, coffee cost $31 a pound, making it out of reach for the average consumer. And even when beans were available, roasting was a chronic challenge given that Allied bombings had destroyed roasting plants.[113]

Meanwhile, the British kept their soldiers caffeinated through tea, so much so that in 1942 Winston Churchill declared that tea was more important than ammunition.[114] The restorative and uplifting powers of tea became part of the mythology of the war. Tea, long entrenched in British culture, was now also an essential ingredient of the war effort, equally important on the war front and the home front.[115] The popular image of the British soldier included a cup of tea in his hand, printed again and again in tea industry ads. In one such ad, a soldier exclaims that a cup of tea "snaps" him back to normal after "handling those hefty tanks."[116]

The British tea industry had anticipated the war early on. As early as 1937, it had planned out supply routes and storage locations that it could use in the event of war that were more comprehensive than those plans eventually enacted by the government during the conflict.[117] Tea was of such importance that, rather than leaving it in London's thirty storehouses, where bombings were more likely, most of the supply was dispersed throughout storehouses in hundreds of locations across the country.[118] The British were so hooked on tea that they came up with contingency plans to ensure they would still have the brew even in the event of German occupation.[119]

As had been the case during World War I, tea was rationed, starting with a "temporary" measure in July 1940 that was not fully lifted until 1952.[120] However, the tea ration never applied to the military, the home defense services, or workers in war-related industries such as munitions.[121] John Griffiths points out that the average adult in Britain measured the progress of the war and its immediate aftermath by the availability of tea, with the ration based on the level of the tea reserve. The two-ounce weekly ration established in July 1940 increased to four ounces in July 1945.[122]

To assure delivery of the cherished energizing drink, the Empire Tea Bureau set up a "Tea Car" service in the form of a mobile canteen mounted on a van or truck. The BBC journalist Richard Dimbleby reported that the "tea van" was "one of the most popular vehicles" wherever it went, "swaying on its way to a camp, hospital, or aerodrome, delivering hundreds of cups of tea to troops who had not expected it." These "mobile tea kitchens" brought "food and hot tea to civilians bombed from their homes, to air raid wardens standing watch, to firefighters battling against incendiaries, and to men in the three armed services."[123] Defense industry workers were also provided tea by the Tea Bureau's trolley service.[124]

One journalist writes that "the Tea Cars' finest hours on the home front were during the blitz. Often in conditions of great danger, those who operated them calmly and cheerfully doled out tea to rescued and rescuers alike."[125] So too were the Tea Cars a sight for sore eyes on the frontlines. After serving tea to the troops on the beaches of Dunkirk awaiting rescue, the undersecretary of war declared that the Tea Cars "had done more than any single factor to maintain the morale of the forces and to keep the troops happy."[126] Between the home front and the war front, by war's end nearly 100,000 people were rationing out tea from over 500 Tea Cars.[127]

By 1942, tea supplies from the Far East had been cut off by Japan, but Britain and its allies could still secure the leaf from India, Ceylon, and East Africa. Production around the world dwindled to about 730 million pounds in 1943 (below 1905 levels), but the upside for Britain was

Figure 3.4 A member of the Women's Voluntary Service serves tea from the back of her WVS tea car in the wake of an air raid, 1941 (Imperial War Museums/Getty Images).

that by the end of the war, the global tea trade was monopolized by British firms.[128] The tea supply from India was secured by keeping the Japanese out of Assam. British and Commonwealth troops, especially Indians and Gurkhas, stopped the Japanese advance into the heartland of Indian tea production in Assam.[129]

With the tea supply secured, the tea break came to be seen as an essential aid to workers' focus, alertness, and productivity. And once

Figure 3.5 The British Army's mobile tea canteen serves soldiers in the forward operating area of North Africa, July 1942 (Imperial War Museums).

embedded in the workplace, it outlasted the war itself. Griffiths notes that "the majority of industrial enterprises had no experience of simultaneous catering on such a scale, so many factories were largely supplied by the National Canteen Service. This was set up by the tea industry at the beginning of the war from a genuine sense of patriotism, but also with an understandable glance toward the future benefits of inculcating the tea habit."[130] British workers came to view the tea break as a right, so much so that they even went on strike to defend it.[131]

Similarly, the wartime coffee break in the American workplace, which became common for defense workers during the conflict, outlasted the war. The phrase "coffee break" was a 1952 invention of the Pan American Coffee Bureau, which adopted the campaign slogan "Give Yourself a Coffee-Break—And Get What Coffee Gives to You."[132]

Almost unheard of before the war, the coffee break had been instituted by a vast majority of firms polled in 1952.[133]

Instant coffee also became entrenched in postwar American drinking habits. As Stewart Lee Allen describes it, "Millions of soldiers and nurses returned with Proustian associations linking the taste of instant with some of their most vivid life experiences. Domestic consumption skyrocketed, and by 1958 one third of America's coffee was instant."[134] And the product's appeal extended well beyond the United States. "It was as if World War and the concomitant World Peace had opened the door to instant coffee in countries that previously had little acquaintance with it," writes Antony Wild. "Even the European heartland of traditional coffee drinking found itself assailed by the new beverage."[135] He points to "the ubiquitous presence of U.S. troops" as a key factor driving this global explosion.[136]

## How Coca-Cola Conquered the World Through War

Coffee and tea were not the only caffeinated drinks that got a massive stimulus from World War II. At the start of the war, Coca-Cola was mostly a domestic beverage. Beyond Cuba, Canada, and Germany, Coca-Cola had little reach outside the United States. But a global war transformed it into a global drink. As Pendergrast puts it in *For God, Country, and Coca-Cola*, "The Japanese didn't realize that by bombing Pearl Harbor they were indirectly giving The Coca-Cola Company a worldwide boost that would ensure the soft drink company's unquestioned global dominance of the industry."[137]

Coca-Cola, the pioneer of caffeinated soft drinks, was named after the coca leaf and the kola nut.[138] As the first advertisement for the drink in the *Atlanta Journal* on May 29, 1886, put it, "Coca-Cola. Delicious! Refreshing! Exhilarating! Invigorating! The new and popular soda fountain drink containing the properties of the wonderful Coca plant and the famous Cola nut."[139] Andean coca leaves contain small quantities of an alkaloid drug, cocaine, while the nuts of the West African kola plant contain about 2 percent caffeine. The cocaine content of Coca-Cola was removed early in the twentieth century, but the caffeine remained (albeit at a lower level than the original formula).[140]

As America entered World War II, Robert Woodruff, head of the Coca-Cola Company, boldly ordered that "every man in uniform gets a bottle of Coca-Cola for five cents, wherever he is, and whatever it costs the company."[141] This patriotic gesture was also a savvy business move. And the demand was certainly there: "We sincerely hope that your Company will be able to continue supplying us during this emergency," one officer wrote in a letter. "In our opinion, Coca-Cola could be classified as one of the essential morale-building products for the boys in the Service."[142] Coca-Cola, with the army's blessing, used 100 such letters to successfully lobby Washington to be exempted from the sugar ration in 1942. Coca-Cola's Washington lobbyist even managed to get a company executive appointed to the sugar-rationing board.[143] Rival soft-drink makers did not receive similar preferential treatment and were forced to make sharp cuts in production. Complaints by Pepsi that Coca-Cola had unfair access to military bases fell on deaf ears in Washington.[144] The war was therefore a double win for Coca-Cola, which was able to use the conflict to simultaneously beat domestic rivals and boost foreign sales.

Still, there was the logistical challenge of actually getting Coke into the eager hands of the more than 16 million thirsty American soldiers fighting overseas. Shipping the bottles was inefficient and cumbersome, especially in wartime. The solution was to set up bottling plants within military bases wherever possible so that only the syrup had to be brought in. The company deployed 248 employees to build and maintain sixty-four bottling facilities across the world—mostly paid for by the military—which would serve 10 billion Cokes during the course of the war.[145] Coca-Cola representatives were even deemed "technical observers"—the official status granted to civilians necessary to the war effort—wearing "T.O." as a shoulder patch on their army uniforms and nicknamed "Coca-Cola Colonels."[146]

Far from being resented for having avoided the draft and staying safe behind the frontlines, the technical observers from Coca-Cola "were deemed as vital as those [T.O.s] who fixed tanks or airplanes."[147] They even developed a portable soda dispenser for use in the jungle and a slimmed-down version that could squeeze through a submarine hatch door. And the company made sure its product was accessible to those living near US military bases abroad: "People around the world, from Polynesians to Zulus, tasted Coca-Cola for the first time."[148]

The Coca-Cola archives are filled with letters from appreciative servicemen who equated America with Coca-Cola. "To my mind, I am in this damn mess as much to help keep the custom of drinking Cokes as I am to help preserve the million other benefits our country blesses its citizens with. . . . May we all toast victory soon with a Coke," wrote one. "If anyone were to ask us what we were fighting for," another soldier wrote, "we think half of us would answer, the right to buy Coca-Cola again."[149]

And it wasn't only the foot-soldiers who felt this way. Generals such as Douglas MacArthur, Dwight D. Eisenhower, and George Patton were also famously fond of Coke. In June 1943, Eisenhower made sure the Allied campaign in North Africa did not go without its Coca-Cola supply, sending a telegram order for "three million bottled Coca-Cola (filled) and complete equipment for bottling, washing, capping same quantity twice monthly. Preference as to equipment is 10 separate machines for installation in different localities, each complete for bottling twenty thousand bottles per day. Also sufficient syrup and caps for 6 million refills."[150] Quartermasters at US bases lobbied equally hard for their Coke supplies: Colonel John P. Nau, the quartermaster at an American base in Dutch Guiana, pleaded for bottling equipment in early 1942, which he argued was "vital to the maintenance of contentment and well-being of the military personnel stationed at this far away post."[151]

Coca-Cola also entered Western Europe immediately after D-Day, and indeed its name was even adopted as a password by US soldiers as they battled across the Rhine.[152] After the invasion of Normandy, one US soldier joked in a letter to his sister:

> The most important question in amphibious landings: Does the Coke machine go ashore in the first or second wave? I've told you before what a problem this is. If you send the Coke machine in with the first wave, future waves come pouring in without enough nickels. Obviously, getting change for a dime or a quarter on an enemy beach is quite difficult. On the other hand, if you hold the Coke machine

up until the second wave, the men of the first wave wait on the beach for it to come in, instead of driving forward to attack the enemy.[153]

Back in the States, the company's advertisements promoted a patriotic image, highlighting its contribution to the war effort. One advertisement depicted American sailors enjoying a Coke on board a ship, with the caption underneath "Wherever a U.S. battleship may be, the American way of life goes along. . . . So, naturally, Coca-Cola is there, too."[154] At the same time, Germany and Japan, who before the war had imported Coca-Cola, now denounced the drink. Japanese propagandists proclaimed, "With Coca-Cola we imported the germs of the disease of American society," and their counterparts in Germany derided America for having "never contributed anything to world civilization except chewing gum and Coca-Cola."[155]

Behind the scenes, company executives scrambled to secure the key ingredients to keep the Coke flowing. This included encouraging Monsanto Chemical Company to build special caffeine manufacturing plants in Brazil and Mexico and turning to recycled bottle caps to cope with metal shortages. The company faced a chronic potential shortage of both vanilla extract (25,000 gallons needed per month) and the coca leaf and kola nut extract referred to as Merchandise No. 5 (a million pounds needed per year).[156]

When the fighting finally came to an end, few companies were as well positioned as Coca-Cola to take advantage of the postwar business opportunities. After all, the startup costs of its extraordinary global reach had been almost entirely paid for by the US military.[157] And indeed, the military-sponsored bottling facilities kept running for another three years before shifting to civilian operation. By that time, Standage observes, "with the exception of Antarctica, Coca-Cola had established itself on every continent on Earth, carried on the coattails of the American military."[158] In the words of one company official, the war had guaranteed "the almost universal acceptance of the goodness of Coca-Cola."[159]

Even some Soviet leaders became secret Coke drinkers, including Georgy Konstantinovich Zhukov, the celebrated general who led the Red Army into Berlin at the end of the war. Eisenhower introduced Zhukov to Coca-Cola during their negotiations over the postwar carving

Figure 3.6 A 1940s advertisement portrays US soldiers enjoying Coca-Cola (Advertising Archives/Alamy).

up of Germany, and the Soviet general liked it so much that he asked if a special color-free version—to disguise its American origins and make it look like vodka—could be made just for him. With President Harry Truman's blessing, Coca-Cola was happy to comply with the request, and sent Zhukov shipments of bottles with no labels other than a white cap with a red Soviet star.[160]

During the Cold War, Coca-Cola came to be either denounced or embraced as a symbol of American consumer capitalism. Coca-Cola's

Figure 3.7  Coca-Cola reaches American forces on the frontlines in Italy for the first time, 1944 (Bettman/Getty Images).

aggressive postwar expansion into foreign markets was interpreted in many places as a form of US imperialism. The term *Coca-colonization* was coined by French communist sympathizers who hoped to block new bottling plants from being built in the country and even argued that the drink was poisonous and should be banned. French mobs overturned Coca-Cola trucks and broke bottles in protest. Austrian communists warned that the local Coca-Cola plant could double as an atom bomb factory. And Italian communists went so far as to charge that the drink turned children's hair white.[161] Yet nothing could deter Coca-Cola, which, despite political opposition in some quarters, became ever-more popular throughout Western Europe and across the globe. And when the Berlin Wall came down in 1989, East Berliners were soon seen standing in line to buy Coca-Cola by the crate from the Coca-Cola bottling plant in West Berlin.[162]

## Blood Coffee

Elsewhere, meanwhile, the world's most popular caffeinated beverage—coffee—was closely linked to both military repression and popular rebellion. Nicaragua, El Salvador, and Guatemala were torn apart by brutal civil wars in the late 1970s and 1980s. It is no coincidence that they were also heavily dependent on coffee exports. It was not so much coffee itself that was to blame for these rebellions, but rather the organization of coffee production, particularly the extraordinarily unequal distribution of coffee-producing lands. Jeffrey Paige explains in *Coffee and Power* that such stark inequality in access to the fruits of coffee helped fuel such conflicts:

> Although North American policy makers saw the Central American conflicts as episodes in the Cold War, they were in fact deeply rooted in the social and economic structures of the region. These structures in turn were shaped by a single commodity that has dominated these small export economies from the nineteenth century to the present—coffee. . . . Coffee and power have been closely linked in Central America since the nineteenth century. Coffee created the dynastic elites and shaped the political institutions that faced revolutionary crisis in the 1980s.[163]

It is striking that there were no rebellions in Costa Rica and Honduras, where the coffee sector was defined by small and medium-sized farms. Costa Rica in particular had long avoided the vicious dynamic of concentrated coffee holdings and bloody repression of popular revolts by coffee-financed regimes. Unlike Guatemala and El Salvador, large coffee *fincas* relying on coerced labor were not the norm in Costa Rica. In the absence of an easily available and exploitable labor force, Costa Rica's coffee growers instead developed smaller family-run farms.[164] In contrast, Guatemala's coffee sector was defined by enormous coffee *fincas*, with Nicaragua and El Salvador following Guatemala in terms of level of concentrated ownership.[165] And it was precisely these three regimes that faced rebellions.

Guatemala's coffee export sector, which took off in the last decades of the nineteenth century, was not only concentrated in the hands of relatively few but relied on the native Indian population to work the fields as virtual slave labor. As Paige describes it, "Guatemala had so many soldiers that it resembled a penal colony because it *was* a penal colony based on forced labor."[166] The profits from coffee financed the government's brutal repression of the native Indian population whenever it rebelled.[167] The military regime of Jorge Ubico Castañeda took over in 1931 and in the midst of the Depression moved to crush resistance by any means necessary. Debt bondage was abolished, but a new vagrancy law limited freedom of movement. Two years after taking office, Ubico ordered the killing of 100 labor organizers, political leaders, and student activists, and allowed plantation owners to execute their workers without consequence.[168]

After Ubico was overthrown in 1944, Guatemala's new president, Juan José Arévalo, moved to end all forms of forced labor but failed to initiate any agrarian reforms, even though a mere 0.3 percent of the country's farms accounted for more than half of its farmland.[169] Any redistribution of land would have to wait until General Jacobo Arbenz Guzmán became president in 1951 after promising to transform Guatemala "from a dependent nation with a semi-colonial economy into an economically independent country."[170] In 1952, Guatemala's Law of Agrarian Reform ordered the redistribution of all public lands, idle lands, and land holdings over 222 acres. Sellers would receive compensation based on tax assessments. The United Fruit Company, which primarily focused on the banana business but was also involved in coffee exports, owned vast tracts of unused land and therefore led the list of foreign companies most affected by the reforms. The first lands distributed to peasant cooperatives were former German coffee plantations that had been expropriated during wartime. Peasants also started to take over coffee plantations illegally with the encouragement of communist activists. "The land reform program has practically been taken over by communist agitators who exhort peasants to 'invade' private property," complained the *Tea & Coffee Trade Journal* in one report. "Owners have no recourse and objections only bring threats of fines and imprisonment." The report concluded that "if the present trend continues, the days of large privately owned and operated coffee Fincas are numbered."[171]

Washington viewed Arbenz and his reforms as a communist-inspired threat to US interests in the region, and in 1953 President Eisenhower gave the green light for a covert CIA operation to overthrow Guatemala's government. Following a US-backed military coup in 1954, Arbenz's replacement, General Carlos Castillo Armas, immediately rolled back the agrarian reform program—which had redistributed some 1.4 million acres of land to one-sixth of the country's population—and banned political parties and labor and peasant organizations.[172] During the three decades following the assassination of Armas in 1957, Guatemala's military rulers violently put down all opposition and sanctioned militias to maintain order in the countryside. The country's plantation owners, meanwhile, continued to depend on cheap labor to pick their coffee beans.[173] The subsequent leftist rebellion and government massacres that occurred between 1960 and 1996—with more than 200,000 people killed, mostly at the hands of state military forces—were therefore a continuation of this long and bloody history.

Neighboring El Salvador followed a similar pattern. New laws in the early 1880s expropriated Indian communal lands, which happened to be the lands most suitable for coffee cultivation. The resulting Indian revolts, which included burning down coffee fields, prompted the government to send in a mounted patrol force to extinguish uprisings. Thus began the country's decades-long dominance by fourteen coffee plantation–owning families, backed by export profits, a rural militia, and revolving military governments.[174] By the 1930s, coffee represented more than 90 percent of Salvadoran exports.

The Great Depression hit the coffee export sector particularly hard, and no one suffered more than the plantation workers, who saw their low wages and abysmal working conditions deteriorate even further. An Indian revolt on January 22, 1932, in the coffee-growing western highlands killed almost 100 people, the majority of whom were plantation overseers and army soldiers. The rebellion was easily and quickly squashed by the military, which went on to retaliate by killing some 30,000 people in just a few weeks. The brutal massacre, encouraged by the country's coffee elite, would be remembered as *La Matanza*.[175] The reaction of the Coffee Association of El Salvador was summarized in its journal: "There have always been two essential classes in every society: the dominators and the dominated. . . . Today they are called the rich and the poor." Any effort to change this, the association claimed, would "break the equilibrium and cause the disintegration of human society."[176]

A half-century later, El Salvador had descended into a full-blown civil war that claimed some 50,000 lives, with leftist guerrillas on one side battling against the US-supported military government, right-wing death squads, and the entrenched old coffee oligarchy on the other. In the 1980s, El Salvador's coffee elite worked as one against all opponents, especially the Farabundo Martí National Liberation Front (FMLN) guerrillas, and backed an extreme right-wing party founded by death-squad leader Roberto D'Aubuisson.[177]

A half-hearted land reform program initiated in 1980 left the coffee plantations largely intact. Still, this didn't protect coffee growers from the insurgents, who controlled about one-fourth of the country's coffee-growing areas by the mid-1980s. Coffee growers in guerrilla-controlled territory made accommodations, paying their workers higher wages and paying the insurgents a "war tax" to stay in business.[178] In the Usulutan highlands, guerrillas often targeted coffee mills, especially those owned by the Llach family (the family of the wife of President Alfredo Cristiani).[179]

By the end of the 1980s, the connection between coffee and violence in El Salvador had generated growing international calls for a boycott, led by the small grassroots organization Neighbor to Neighbor. Folgers was especially targeted. Robbie Gamble—a descendant of the founder of Procter & Gamble—gave away his inheritance as a protest against Folgers' (owned by Procter & Gamble) use of Salvadoran coffee beans.[180] The owner of several important coffee farms, President Cristiani dismissed Neighbor to Neighbor as a communist organization.[181] Anxious about its own public image, Nestlé temporarily suspended buying coffee from El Salvador.[182] Wishing to avoid further losses and public embarrassment, US coffee companies became active supporters of a negotiated settlement to El Salvador's civil war and even bought advertising space in Salvadoran papers to promote a peace agreement. As part of the 1992 settlement that finally brought the war to an end, about one-fifth of the country's coffee-growing land was distributed to peasants—all of which happened to be in the areas already under guerrilla control.[183] In 1990, coffee accounted for about half of the country's export earnings.[184]

In Nicaragua, coffee had never been as economically dominant as it was in Guatemala and El Salvador. But the best lands for coffee growing—in the north-central highlands—were initially in the hands of the indigenous population, which led the state to engage in coercive displacement that in turn sparked rebellion. In Matagalpa, the heart of coffee country, the army killed over 1,000 Indian peasants in response to an 1881 uprising against forced labor. Still, *campesino* organizing and opposition continued during the 1893–1909 rule of General José Santos Zelaya, who, from a coffee family himself, built up both the military and the coffee export sector.[185] After orchestrating the assassination of guerrilla leader Augusto César Sandino in 1934, General Anastasio Somoza García came to power, and then built up a coffee-based family dynasty that ruled the country with an iron fist for decades to come.[186]

The Nicaraguan revolution of 1979, led by the Marxist-inspired Sandinista insurgency, overthrew the country's longtime dictator, Anastasio Somoza Debayle. After their victory, the Sandinistas inherited a bankrupt country devastated by war, with some 40,000 dead, 1 million homeless, and $1.6 billion in foreign debt (the largest debt burden in the region). All Somoza family properties, including some 15 percent of the country's coffee *fincas*, were quickly expropriated, and an ambitious agrarian reform program was initiated to redistribute land.[187]

But reviving and transforming the coffee export sector, the country's most important source of foreign exchange, would not be so easy. Not only were the Sandinistas not particularly adept at managing coffee production, but the coffee harvest was a favorite target of the counterrevolution led by the US-backed Contras against the Sandinista government between 1979 and 1990. As a strategy of war, the Contras engaged in economic sabotage by attacking coffee farms and farmers, and the government responded with military force. The attacks were primarily carried out in the provinces of Matagalpa and Jinotega, where three-fourths of the crop was grown. In 1984 alone, the Contras destroyed eight state-owned and twelve private coffee farms in these provinces, and also killed or kidnapped hundreds of peasant leaders to keep workers away from the fields.[188]

This was a continuation of an old pattern. As Stephen Kinzer reported for the *New York Times* in 1983, "The highlands of northern Nicaragua are rich in revolutionary history. It was here that guerrillas led by Augusto Cesar Sandino fought United States marines in the 1930's. When the modern Sandinista Front was formed in 1961 by Carlos Fonseca Amador, a Matagalpa native, its first military operations were ambushes along the tortuous paths that wind among the coffee fields here." Kinzer further reported: "Government officials said this week that an estimated 2,000 anti-Government rebels had infiltrated the area where young volunteers are working. Armed patrols guard plantations, and officials fear that fire fights could shatter the routine on some plantations as insurgents try to disrupt the harvest. Economic sabotage has been as important a part of rebel strategy here as it is for leftist rebels in El Salvador."[189]

Desperate for the export revenue from coffee, the cash-strapped Sandinista government attempted to defend the coffee farms through military force. This in turn gave the Contras an added excuse to treat the farms as a legitimate military target. "There is no line at all, not even a fine line, between a civilian farm owned by the Government and a Sandinista military outpost," claimed Contra leader Adolfo Calero Portocarrero. "What they call a cooperative is also a troop concentration full of armed people. We are not killing civilians. We are fighting armed people and returning fire when fire is directed against us."[190]

As the war with the Contras escalated, the Sandinistas used the distribution of coffee lands to peasants as an instrument to keep them on the government's side. "We gave them land and a gun and said, 'This is yours. Now defend it,'" explained General Joaquin Cuadra Lacayo, the army chief of staff. "We called it 'agrarian reform,' but the logic was strictly military. We wanted to stop them from joining the *contras*."[191] In other words, coffee in Nicaragua became a weapon of war for all sides—for the Contras, targeting coffee was economic sabotage, whereas for the Sandinistas coffee was used as a reward for peasant loyalty in fighting the Contras.

BY THE END OF the century, with the Central American wars long over, caffeine's most enduring connection to war remained its stimulating effect on combatants. Indeed, even with the introduction of new drugs,

Figure 3.8 A soldier of the Sandinista Popular Army (Ejercito Popular Sandinista) addresses workers on a state coffee plantation in Nicaragua, 1986 (Scott Wallace/ Getty Images).

caffeine continued to be the military stimulant of choice across the world. The US military in particular was as high on caffeine as ever, with military researchers busily developing ever-more varied ways of delivering caffeine hits, including caffeinated chewing gum ("Stay Alert" gum), caffeinated beef jerky, mocha-flavored caffeinated energy bars ("First Strike Nutritious Energy Bar"), caffeinated applesauce ("Zapplesauce"), caffeinated apple pie, and caffeinated chocolate pudding. Any item labeled "First Strike" in an MRE (Meal Ready to Eat) was likely to be heavily spiked with caffeine.[192] But what proved most popular among US soldiers in Afghanistan and Iraq was the jolt provided by caffeinated energy drinks such as Red Bull and Rip It, which contained amounts of caffeine that were equivalent to as much as four cups of coffee. Guzzling down energy drinks was especially common among younger soldiers directly involved in combat, with a majority of caffeine-using troops in Afghanistan preferring these beverages over coffee.[193] One favorite energy drink brand, Rip It, aggressively cultivated its military connection in its advertising, boasting that the beverage had been "tested on the battlefield." Soldier testimonials suggested that Rip

It had indeed become the drink of choice in many deployments. As one Iraq War veteran recalled, "When platoons had to go on extended patrols their supply sergeants often did not ask for more M.R.E.'s but instead asked for more Rip It." Similarly, a noncommissioned officer in Iraq in charge of a chow hall commented that although "the quality of chow was a major concern, an overriding concern was the quantity of Rip Its in storage."[194]

Thus, even though caffeine no longer fueled imperial expansion in the same way that the tea trade had underwritten the growth of the British Empire, armed conflict remained as caffeinated as ever through soldier use, with an ever-growing menu of ingestion options. The story of caffeinated conflict suggests that a drug can have a highly addictive relationship to war even if the drug itself is not highly addictive or a major health hazard. However, the same cannot be said of the history of the next drug in our story, opium, particularly when it comes in the form of its semisynthetic derivatives morphine and heroin.

# 4

## Opium, Empire, and Geopolitics

MENTION OPIUM AND WAR and the first thing that comes to mind are the nineteenth-century "Opium Wars," when the British militarily forced opium imports on China. And indeed, this is the main starting point of our story. But it is far from the end point. From opiate-using soldiers to the use of opiates as a weapon and funder of war, opium and warfare have long been locked in a deadly embrace.

The nature of that embrace, however, fundamentally changed as the legal status of opium shifted in the early twentieth century. What had largely been a legally traded global commodity—comparable in importance to coffee, tea, and tobacco—at the turn of the century became the target of increasingly restrictive controls culminating in a global prohibition regime. The criminalization of opium brought with it a more prominent role for the criminal underworld in war, as can be seen in conflicts stretching from China's chaotic civil wars through the hot wars of the Cold War in Southeast and South Asia. In these opium-saturated conflict zones, military success on the battlefield came to be tied to business success in a murky underworld where warlords, traffickers, and intelligence agencies crossed paths and rubbed shoulders. At the same time, campaigns to suppress opium and its derivatives became a convenient political weapon to attack and discredit one's enemies.

*Killer High*, Peter Andreas. Oxford University Press (2020). © Peter Andreas.
DOI: 10.1093/actrade/9780190463014.001.0001

The use of opium—the thick, sticky sap extracted from the opium poppy plant when it blooms—extends back to Neolithic Europe, though the exact date and place of its origins remain a mystery. The Sumerians in Lower Mesopotamia cultivated the opium poppy some five thousand years ago—referring to it as *Hul Gil*, the "joy plant." Its narcotic effect, both blocking the perception of pain and causing feelings of euphoria, comes from the alkaloid morphine, which was first identified in 1806, and the potency of which vastly increased with the introduction of heroin in 1898.[1]

Early use of opium is hinted at in the *Odyssey*: Homer writes about "nepenthe," brought from Egypt, that is poured into the drinks of saddened soldiers returning from Troy to help them forget the horrors of war. The Greek physician Hippocrates (460–357 BC) was the first to write about the healing powers of opium. The Greek taste for opium—the word itself is derived from the Greek *opion*, or "poppy juice"—was passed on to the conquering Romans, who came to value it as both a painkilling medicine and a poison for assassins.[2]

As opium use spread across Europe and beyond, the drug was mostly valued for its medicinal uses, even as doctors became increasingly aware of its habit-forming potential.[3] Opium's blissful buzz made it the most potent anesthetic in the world. The poppy moved east via Arab merchants in the seventh and eighth centuries. It was not until the fifteenth century that opium's potential as a recreational substance was more fully realized, as evidenced by records of opium use in Persia and India during this period.[4] In 1546, the French naturalist Pierre Belon traveled to Asia Minor and Egypt and commented, with more than a bit of exaggeration, on the prevalence of opium use there: "There is not a Turk who would not purchase opium with his last coin; he carries the drug on him in war and in peace. They eat opium because they think they will thus become more courageous and have less fear of the dangers of war. At the time of war, such large quantities are purchased it is difficult to find any left."[5] Similarly, Francois Bernier, a French traveler who visited northern India in 1656, wrote that the Rajput warriors were regular opium users: "From an early age they are accustomed to the use of opium, and I have sometimes been astonished to see the large quantity they swallow. On the day of battle they never fail to double the dose, and this drug so animates, or rather inebriates them, that they rush into the thickest of the combat insensitive of danger."[6] The Rajputs shared their opium not only with each other but also with their horses and camels before setting out on desert patrols.[7]

## Opium and Empire

Nowhere did opium become more entrenched than in China, where it would become the focus of the world's first true "drug war." While Arab traders were the first to bring opium in substantial quantities to China, it was not until the arrival in the eighteenth and nineteenth centuries of Western imperial powers—the Portuguese, then the Dutch, and finally the British—that the opium business became fully commercialized. This was greatly facilitated by the introduction of the pipe by Western sailors in the seventeenth century, which made the smoking of opium—initially mixed with tobacco—the most popular form of ingestion. Compared to eating opium, smoking provided a more efficient delivery mechanism.

Opium trading and empire building went hand in hand for Western powers, especially Britain. London placed the opium trade in the hands of its East India Company, which initially also had a monopoly on imports of Chinese tea. As noted in the previous chapter, tea and opium transformed the British East India Company into the most powerful corporation the world has ever seen. These two drugs were the twin pillars of Britain's trading empire, and they became inescapably linked: supplying Chinese smokers with high-quality Indian-grown opium made it possible for Britain to supply its tea drinkers with tea grown in China, which at that point was the world's only source of the plant. The Chinese insisted on being paid for their tea in silver, and opium was the only commodity that could generate enough silver to fund Britain's rapidly growing taste for tea. With the exception of opium, the self-sufficient Chinese had little interest in foreign commerce, rejecting European pleas to open the country up to trade with the outside world. Most Britons either remained blissfully ignorant or conveniently overlooked the fact that their relatively mild and benign tea habit fueled a far more serious habit on the other side of the globe.

Chinese prohibitions on the drug repeatedly failed. Opium smoking was first banned by imperial edict in 1729, yet that same year an

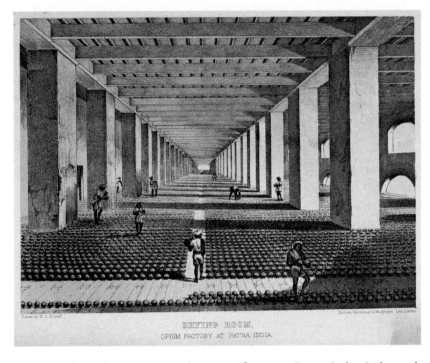

Figure 4.1 A busy drying room in the opium factory at Patna, India. Lithograph after W. S. Sherwill, c. 1850 (Wellcome Collection).

estimated 200 chests of opium were imported, and by 1790 the trade had jumped to 4,000 chests per year.[8] Alarmed by the ever-increasing inflow of opium—and even more alarmed by the ever-increasing outflow of silver—the Qing dynasty further criminalized opium in 1796 and 1799. But the British East India Company and its middlemen, with the connivance of local smugglers and corrupt officials, continued to defy government controls. The number of chests of Indian opium imported into China reportedly grew from 4,494 annually in the period between 1811 and 1821 to 9,708 chests annually between 1821 and 1828, to 18,835 chests annually between 1828 and 1835, and finally to more than 30,000 chests annually between 1835 and 1839.[9] At the same time the number of opium users soared—according to one estimate, increasing sixfold between 1820 and 1835.[10] What had started out as an upper-class niche drug with limited distribution and access had become cheap and plentiful enough to reach the masses. By the mid-1830s, China had perhaps

10 million opium users, with the country spending almost half of its revenue on maintaining the habit.[11]

Lin Zexu, the commissioner appointed by the emperor to stem the flood of opium into China, warned: "If we still hesitate to take any determined action to ban it, within ten years there would be no soldiers that can be deployed to defend the country from foreign invasion; nor would there be any money left to maintain our army."[12] There was already serious concern in the imperial court about the fighting capacity of opium-smoking soldiers: in 1832, opium use among troops deployed to put down the Yao rebellion in Northeast Guangdong Province was blamed for their poor battlefield performance and widespread desertion.[13] An estimated 7,000 of the 10,000 soldiers deployed were opium users.[14]

In a move that would remake China and its external relations for the next century, the emperor dispatched Lin Zexu to the port of Canton—where the import business was concentrated—with orders to put an end to the opium trade. In early June 1839, Lin Zexu ordered hundreds of his men to destroy all confiscated British opium stockpiles, which numbered more than 21,300 chests. This lengthy public spectacle outraged the foreign traders, who fled to Macao and appealed to London to retaliate with military force to recover their losses and keep the opium trade going. In other words, China went to war against opium and Britain responded by going to war for opium.

Britain deployed six warships and 7,000 troops, occupying Canton and then moving north to besiege the coastal cities. Shanghai was sacked in the early summer of 1842. The heavily lopsided British victory in what came to be dubbed the First Opium War (1839–1842), the outcome of which was assured from the start, given Britain's overwhelming technological advantage on land and sea, paved the way for skyrocketing opium imports. The British insisted they were merely promoting free trade, but what this actually meant was forced trade.

The Treaty of Nanking opened up five ports for foreign trade, provided compensation for prior losses, and handed Hong Kong to the British in 1842. The port, which would later emerge as a global commercial hub, owed its start to opium: it first came under British rule as a result of a war for opium and, within a year, had become the principal opium trading port in China.[15] By 1849, the vast majority of India's

Figure 4.2  British forces attack Chinese forts on Chuenpee Island during the First
Opium War, 1839–1843 (Everett Historical/Shutterstock).

opium was being traded through Hong Kong, with some 40,000 chests
on average stored in its warehouses.[16] More than a century later, Hong
Kong would also serve as the world's most important heroin distribution center.

But it took the Second Opium War (1856–1860)—bloodier than the
first, yet equally as lopsided—to actually legalize opium imports. As a
result of this conflict, more Chinese ports were opened to foreign trade,
and foreigners were given full access to the Chinese interior for the first
time. Sir Rutherford Alcock, a British ambassador to Peking, bluntly
described the situation to the British Parliament in 1871: "We forced
the Chinese Government to enter into a Treaty to allow their subjects
to take opium."[17]

Around the same time, a different type of war pressure also induced
China to legalize domestic opium production. The financial burden of
putting down the Taiping Rebellion (1850–1864) convinced the Chinese
court to impose a tax on opium crops for the first time—starting in
Shanghai in 1856 and then expanded to Fujian in 1857 and Yunnan in
1859—and this de facto legalization of opium planting eventually led
to full legalization. By the 1870s, domestic supplies surpassed imports.

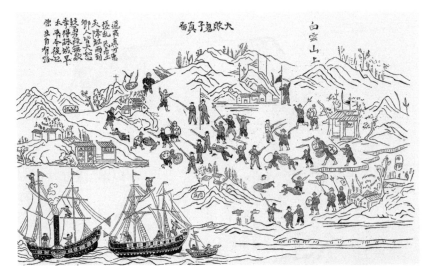

Figure 4.3 Depiction of the engagement between the British and Chinese at Fatsham Creek on Canton River during the Second Opium War. British wood engraving (HIP/Art Resource).

Chinese authorities saw domestic cultivation as an effective way to both put a brake on Indian imports and fund the military through opium taxes.[18] But the considerable downside was that both the economy and the population became increasingly hooked on opium. By the turn of the century, China had the distinction of being both the world's largest producer and its largest consumer of opium. An estimated 13.5 million (out of a population of 400 million) Chinese consumed a total of 39,000 tons of opium per year.[19] In 1906, the government estimated that more than a quarter of all adult males in the country smoked opium.[20] The opium poppy was so conspicuous that it was jokingly called the national flower.[21]

## Birth of the American Empire and the Global Anti-Opium Crusade

While the Americans sat on the sidelines during the First Opium War, they were more than happy to profit from the British victory. Largely overshadowed by their British counterparts, most of the US firms that began conducting trade in China had trafficked in opium in the years

Figure 4.4  A French cartoon satirizing the Second Opium War depicts opium being forced down the throats of the Chinese. Daumier, 1858 (Granger Collection).

leading up to the outbreak of war. Warren Delano II, the grandfather of Franklin Delano Roosevelt and the creator of the family fortune, profited from shipping opium to China, calling it a "fair, honorable and legitimate trade" that was no worse than trading in alcohol.[22]

Not all US merchants shared this view. The most prominent critic was Charles William King, a longtime anti-opium advocate from the trading firm Olyphant & Company, who wrote to British superintendent of trade Charles Elliot on the eve of the Second Opium War: "For nearly forty years, the British merchants, led on by the British East India Company, have been driving a trade, in violation of the highest laws, and the best interests of the Chinese empire. This course has been pushed so far, as to derange its currency, to corrupt its officers, and ruin multitudes of its people." King pleaded to no avail for Britain to "make this crisis an opportunity" to finally create an opium-free relationship with China.[23] Instead, the Second Opium War opened the floodgates. And while the United States was formally neutral during this conflict—despite shelling and seizing Chinese fortifications at the mouth of the Pearl River and assisting British and French forces during one skirmish—American merchants were once again beneficiaries of the treaty that ended the war.[24]

The treaty terms not only opened China to more opium but also opened the interior to foreign travelers—including American missionaries, who frowned on opium use. They were appalled by what they saw as the moral and social degeneration resulting from the opium trade, and they urged Washington to take a leadership role in an international effort to combat it. They circulated horror stories of opium's impact back home, where opiate consumption had also increased sharply in the decades following the American Civil War. The war had contributed to this problem through the widespread use of opium on both sides—as a painkiller and as a remedy for ailments ranging from diarrhea to dysentery—with the resulting drug habit common enough to be labeled the "army disease" or "soldier's disease."[25] The anti-opium stance of foreign missionaries converged with that of increasingly vocal Chinese nationalists: both blamed the drug and outside opium pushers for the country's moral decay and promoted prohibition as a defense against cultural imperialism.[26]

The full impact of missionary diplomacy became apparent after 1898, when the United States gained control of the Philippines after the Spanish-American War and emerged as a true imperial power. The nation was suddenly faced with the question of what to do about drug use in the annexed territory: under Spanish rule, users had been licensed and opium had been legal. After the turn of the century, there were nearly 200 opium dens in the Philippines catering to a community of 700,000 Chinese.[27] By 1903, opium smoking had also become popular among the American troops stationed there. The US War Department turned to the Right Reverend Charles H. Brent, the Episcopal bishop in the Philippines. Brent had been appointed in 1903 to the Philippine Opium Commission, which produced a report that led to a ban on nonmedical opium imports.

However, as smuggled opium from China undermined the import ban, a frustrated Bishop Brent extended his prohibitionist ambitions beyond the Philippines. He convinced President Theodore Roosevelt to call an international conference on controlling the opium trade in 1906. The State Department supported the request, realizing that it also served other strategic interests. In particular, it would facilitate increased US influence in the Pacific, notably at the expense of the country's major competitor, Britain, and would help to strengthen relations with the Chinese government, which was strongly opposed to the British-dominated trade. In early 1909, what became known as the International Opium Commission met in Shanghai and called for "drastic measures" to be taken by governments to "control the manufacture, sale and distribution of this drug."[28] Although powerless to force countries to actually carry out this sweeping recommendation, the International Opium Commission marked a turning point in the history of drugs and the first key step in constructing a US-led global drug prohibition regime.[29] And this move toward prohibition in turn would fundamentally reshape not only the opium trade but also the drug's relationship to war.

### Warlords, Invaders, and Revolutionaries

As world opinion turned against opium, so too did China, with anti-opium rhetoric closely linked to rising Chinese nationalism. In 1906, China's imperial government launched an ambitious campaign to suppress previously legal opium cultivation and use, closing down opium dens and eradicating poppy fields. Britain also finally agreed to curb Indian opium imports, bringing to an end what had once been a cornerstone of imperial finance. Suppression efforts, however, pushed opium underground rather than out of business. They also created black market incentives to deal in the drug's more compact, portable, concealable, and potent derivatives—first morphine and then increasingly heroin—instead of the much milder and less addictive traditional opium.

Although the initial results of the Chinese suppression campaign were encouraging, it took place in the midst of an economic upheaval and deepening political crisis that culminated in the overthrow of the government in 1911, ending the Qing dynasty's 270-year reign (and with it, the government's newfound commitment to drug prohibition). Not only had the failure of opium control helped to further delegitimize the empire, but opium had also helped to fund the revolution. As Martin Booth notes, "Sun Yat-Sen, the mastermind behind the revolution and the acknowledged father of modern, post-imperial China, raised money for his cause by taxing all the opium dens in Canton."[30]

A new republic was declared in 1912, led by theNationalist Party, also called Kuomintang, and the military strongman Yuan Shikai. As Yuan became more dictatorial, going so far as to declare himself emperor, he increasingly alienated many of his followers, including those within the military. Once-loyal officers in Yunnan Province staged a rebellion in 1916, forming the Protect the Nation Army. The rebellion succeeded in ousting Yuan, but this victory came at a high price: dependence on funding from the Shanghai underworld and the opium economy. The overthrow of Yuan paved the way for a decades-long struggle among opium-funded warlords vying for territorial control.[31]

By the 1920s, opium production had made a full comeback, with expansive cultivation in fourteen of eighteen Chinese provinces making the drug once again the country's most important cash crop.[32] Opium was at the heart of the highly decentralized warlord system that emerged in China in the early twentieth century. By one count, between 1912 and 1928, more than 1,300 men in China could be described as warlords, with their own subnational territories and private armies.[33] Since opium was commonly used to pay and supply these forces, it is little surprise that, as historian Alan Baumler describes it, "many of the military struggles between warlords were struggles over the opium trade."[34]

Having fought two external opium wars with Britain, China was now consumed by decades of internal opium wars between competing warlords. These took place both in opium-producing regions (such as the 1920 war among Sichuan, Yunnan, and Guizhou provinces) and in key transit zones.[35] Warlords battled each other over control of the opium trade but also cooperated to keep the trade going when it was mutually convenient.[36]

Even as they officially projected an anti-opium posture, provincial warlords earned revenue from the opium economy by imposing "fines" on the production, sale, and smoking of opium. In this manner, the anti-opium rhetoric that became standard after 1906 was maintained by warlords even while they still profited from the trade. "So-called economic opium suppression fines were the economic foundation of warlordism," acknowledged Huang Shaoxiong, a member of the clique that ran Guangxi Province from 1921 on, during which time it served as a key opium transit route.[37] Other warlords simply imposed taxes on opium. Indeed, there were over thirty different names for opium taxes.[38] In practice, there was little difference between a fine and a tax other than that the official rationale for the former was opium suppression. Warlords even imposed a "laziness tax" on peasants who refused to cultivate opium.[39]

Ambitious warlords saw opium as a key ingredient for success. As Guangxi warlord Li Zongren described it in an exchange with one of his opium tax officials, "If we want to achieve great things, building up Guangxi and restoring China, we first need money. . . . To get money we must rectify our finances. . . . To rectify our finances we must first get hold of opium suppression (*jinyan*). As opium suppression makes up almost half of our revenue, once it is controlled the rest will follow."[40]

Facing either heavy fines or taxes, peasant opium growers devised various strategies of resistance, ranging from bribery to trickery (hiding their opium crops) and sometimes even armed confrontation.[41] In the Huaibei region, Zheng Yangwen reports, "the greatest single cause of rural unrest . . . at this time [was] the opium tax."[42] Thousands of peasants in the area, organized by local Communists, staged a two-month revolt against the unpopular tax.[43]

As China descended into full-scale civil war in the 1920s and 1930s, the opium economy and the war economy became even more intertwined, so much so that in some places opium crops pushed out food crops. Anything opium-related was taxed, ranging from the harvest itself to its transport to the dens where it was smoked and the pipes used for smoking.[44]

Some combatants also turned to opium use as an everyday coping mechanism. In *Ten Weeks with Chinese Bandits*, published in 1926, Harvey J. Howard, an American ophthalmologist at Peking's Union Medical College, recalled his capture by opium-dependent rebels in Manchuria: "Opium smoking seemed to fill their every need. It often took the place of food, sleep and recreation with them. In fact every necessity and all other luxuries were as nothing compared to the indulgence in this one vice. When they had plenty of crude opium, their happiness appeared to be complete. When they were without it, they were demons to live with. Undoubtedly the craving for this drug had driven many of them into the bandit business."[45]

After 1927, Nationalists and Communists emerged as the strongest contending forces, battling each other while also facing a mounting Japanese military threat. Nationalist leader Chiang Kai-Shek turned to Du Yuesheng and his Green Gang, which controlled much of the smuggling of drugs in and out of Shanghai, to kill off thousands of Communist sympathizers within the Nationalists in 1927.[46] Green Gang execution squads systematically wiped out the Communist labor movement in the city. Chiang rewarded Du and several other Green Gang leaders with the title of "Honorary Advisors," a role equal in rank to major general. And in 1931, Chiang appointed Du to the post of Chief Communist Suppression Agent for Shanghai.[47] Chiang also relied on Du financially, and indeed, Du and his gang had funded Chiang's start in politics. Du profited from opium growing in Chekiang and Kiangsu provinces and dominated the Yangtze River and Shanghai opium trades.[48] In addition to supplying Shanghai's 100,000 opium users, Du ran ten morphine factories in the Shanghai area.[49]

Chiang made a strategic alliance with Du and the criminal underworld not so much for personal profit but for political and military advantage. The opium monopoly schemes that the Nationalist government set up in the 1930s helped meet revenue needs, including the funding of intelligence operations.[50] Chiang's government publicly promoted the suppression of opium consumption through measures including harsh new antidrug laws but in practice used opium to further its military goals. It even went so far as to appoint Du to the Shanghai Municipal Opium Suppression Committee while he was the city's biggest drug trafficker and was venturing into morphine and heroin production.[51] In a moment of extraordinary public hypocrisy, Du gave Chiang an American fighter aircraft for his fiftieth birthday that bore the name *Opium Suppression of Shanghai* on its nose.[52]

By the early 1930s, China was estimated to be the source of seven-eighths of the world's narcotics supply, which reached international markets via Hong Kong, Macao, and Shanghai.[53] British journalist H.G.W. Woodhead described the situation in a detailed investigation: "In general it may be stated that throughout China today with the exception of isolated instances, no effort is or can be made by the National Government to control the sale or smoking of opium. It can be purchased without difficulty, in practically every town and village of any size throughout the country. And the traffic is controlled by the military and big opium rings."[54] The Nationalists also illicitly exported narcotics to the United States and elsewhere to generate foreign exchange to pay for military supplies, including major aircraft purchases in the 1930s.[55]

While profiting from the opium trade, Chiang and the Nationalists used opium suppression as a tool to attack rivals, especially targeting areas of Communist activity. In June 1934, Chiang announced the Six-Year Opium Suppression Plan, with the stated aim of total eradication of the drug within six years. The new military-enforced prohibition policy included the execution of thousands of drug offenders.[56] The Six-Year Plan was a means to ensure that the government would exercise complete control over the opium economy while simultaneously depriving regional political rivals in the southwest of opium funds.[57]

The Japanese occupation of Shanghai in August 1937 diminished but did not end Nationalist influence over the opium trade, and its alliance with the criminal underworld remained as strong as ever. Pushed out of Shanghai by the Japanese occupiers, Du Yuesheng and his Green Gang retreated to Hong Kong and then moved on to Chongqing, joining Chiang and the Nationalists. There, elements of the Green Gang collaborated with Chiang's chief of espionage to work against the Japanese. Their efforts allegedly included setting up a company to distribute opium in Japanese-held areas as a way to fund their efforts.[58] Even though the Japanese had seized control over Chiang's most profitable opium markets, Chinese government finances remained dependent on the drug, which Chiang trafficked into occupied China and supplied to the local population.[59] Du Yuesheng's smuggling networks proved especially valuable in moving drugs between occupied and nonoccupied China.[60]

Well before Japan invaded China with soldiers, it had been invading the country with narcotics. While imposing strict controls at home— banning nonmedical opium use and carefully avoiding China's fate of having free trade in opium imposed from outside—Japan encouraged and facilitated the distribution and sale of opium and its derivatives to its neighbors, especially China.[61] Drug use by foreigners, which the Japanese were more than willing to exploit, was seen as an indicator of their inferiority: according to the manual of the Kwantung Army, a group within the Japanese Imperial Army, "The use of narcotics is unworthy of a superior race like the Japanese. Only inferior races, races that are decadent like the Chinese, Europeans, and East Indians, are addicted to the use of narcotics. This is why they are destined to become our servants and eventually disappear."[62]

Taiwan, a Japanese colony since 1895, and Korea, annexed by Japan in 1909, had long served as southern and northern hubs for the trafficking of drugs into China. In the 1930s the Japanese puppet-state of Manchukuo promoted both opium poppy cultivation and heroin production, turning northern China into a major supplier.[63] During the same decade, Japan reportedly earned more than $300 million annually from the Manchurian opium and heroin business.[64] The Nationalists publicly condemned the influx of Japanese-controlled narcotics from northern China yet at the same time profited from the trade by taxing their transport and sale.[65]

As the Japanese armies moved south into China following the outbreak of war in 1937, they gained control of drug crops and manufacturing facilities previously run by the Nationalist opium monopoly and Du Yuesheng's criminal enterprise.[66] This simultaneously provided funds for ongoing military operations and a way to continue to feed the habits of the sizeable local addict population.[67] Although the Nationalists were formally at war with the Japanese military occupiers, they also informally sold them large amounts of raw opium from the opium-producing regions of southern China.[68]

Many Chinese considered Japanese involvement in the narcotics trade a deliberate use of drugs as a weapon of war, meant to undermine their will to resist occupation.[69] In September 1938, Song Meiling, the wife of Chiang Kai-Shek, denounced the Japanese trade as a piece of "diabolical cunning" intended "to drench a land with opium and narcotics with the primary object of so demoralizing the people that they would be physically unfit to defend their country, and mentally and morally so depraved that they could easily be bought and bribed with drugs to act as spies when the time came in order that their craving might be satisfied."[70]

From the Japanese perspective, however, Japan was not engaged in a sinister plot to poison China but rather was simply being militarily pragmatic, using opium as a strategic resource. In other words, it was ultimately more about military finances than about drugging the local population.[71] This approach was not unlike that of the Chinese warlords who had preceded them, with a key difference being that the Japanese were pushing the production and trafficking of morphine and heroin and not just the less potent traditional opium that Chinese users had long been accustomed to smoking.

When Satomi Hajime, imprisoned after World War II as a Japanese war criminal for running Shanghai's opium monopoly at the start of the Japanese occupation, was questioned by American prosecutors who told him he had violated international law, he matter-of-factly replied, "Warfare itself is a violation of international law, and the violation of what I call the Opium Treaty was a necessary part of our warfare."[72] Prosecutors charged that the "march of Japan through China brought with it, as it had earlier in Manchuria, the enforcement of the Japanese policy of narcotization in the occupied areas for the purpose of raising revenue for Japan's plans of aggression and of debauching the people to keep them subservient to the will and desire of Japan."[73] Those accused of having directed Japan's opium policy in wartime occupied territories were sentenced as Class A war criminals. China's Kuomintang regime also put to death 149 imperial Japanese subjects on drug charges.[74]

Kumagai Hisao, acting head of Showa Trading, a firm created by the Japanese army in 1939, explained that "the army used opium as a 'treasured pharmaceutical' to pacify conquered areas and acquire food and other goods from the populace."[75] He claimed that by the middle of 1942, "gold and opium were the only things left with which to conduct operations," and so "the army made liberal use of opium, forcing coolies to lug sixty-kilogram crates, because we couldn't buy provisions with imperial scrip or the Wang regime's savings notes."[76]

Meanwhile, Mao Zedong and the Red Army, which was officially staunchly opposed to opium—and gained much propaganda value from the drug ties of the Nationalists and the Japanese occupiers—could not resist turning to opium in some areas, such as Shandong, to help underwrite their revolutionary campaign.[77] The Communists were far less complicit in the opium trade than the Nationalists, but the practical necessities of immediate wartime conditions could still trump ideological opposition. While the Communists banned opium smoking and closed opium dens in areas under their control, raising funds through confiscated opium was another matter. As Baumler notes, the Communists funded the Long March in part by seizing property. And some of the most valuable property was opium—a compact form of currency that actually increased in value when it reached urban centers.[78]

The Communists were also not averse to selling opium, but sales were largely restricted to areas under enemy control.[79] Peter Vladmirov, a Russian who worked with Chinese Communist comrades, kept a diary in which he recounted an exchange with a senior official who justified involvement in the opium business on the grounds that the drug was being sold in enemy zones and traded for much-needed arms.[80] In addition to opium's monetary value, some Red Army soldiers used the drug recreationally. As General Xiao Ke recalled, "It was not possible to recruit unless the Army accepted opium addicts."[81]

### The "Underworld Project"

Across the Pacific, meanwhile, World War II could not have come at a more opportune time for Charles "Lucky" Luciano, who had made a name for himself as a bootlegger but also engaged in heroin trafficking and organized prostitution. After his death, Arnold Rothstein's illicit drug import business was passed on to Luciano and others in the New York underworld, most notably Meyer Lansky, Louis Buchalter, and Frank Costello. In 1936, Luciano began a long prison sentence for running a New York prostitution ring. World War II proved to be the break that gave him his get-out-of-jail-free card. In 1946 he was pardoned and deported to freedom in Italy as a reward for his wartime collaboration with the US Office of Naval Intelligence (ONI)—and would go on to help revive the postwar international heroin trade.[82]

Luciano made a deal with the navy: using his business partner Lansky as a go-between, he agreed to gather intelligence from his contacts in New York's waterfront underworld to help protect the city's harbor against a mounting threat of German espionage and sabotage, including U-boat attacks.[83] The head of the New York staff of the

ONI, Lieutenant Commander Charles Radcliffe Haffenden, had no qualms about enlisting criminals for counterintelligence work given the gravity of the situation: "I'll talk to anybody, a priest, a bank manager, a gangster, the devil himself." As he saw it, "This is a war. American lives are at stake. It's not a college game where we have to look up the rule book every minute, and we're not running a headquarters office where regulations must be followed to the letter. I have a job to do."[84] As one of his subordinates later explained it, Haffenden "did not care from what source we got information as long as it was for the war effort."[85] Haffenden's "Underworld Project," as it came to be called by the navy, was apparently known to the higher-ups at headquarters in Washington.[86]

Getting Luciano on board was the key to the project's success. Lieutenant Commander Maurice Kelly, who was on the ONI team that ran the operation, explained the shift that occurred: Before Luciano got involved, naval intelligence "ran into great difficulty in obtaining reliable informants along the waterfront. . . . They just refused to talk to anybody, war effort or no war effort." Once Luciano's support was secured, however, there was "full and whole-hearted cooperation."[87] As a result, the US Navy detected and apprehended four German saboteurs.[88] "There'll be no German submarines in the Port of New York," Luciano proclaimed. "Every man down there who works in the harbor—all the sailors, all the fishermen, every longshoreman, every individual who has something to do with the coming and going of ships to the United States—is now helping the fight against the Nazis."[89]

When Federal Bureau of Investigation (FBI) director J. Edgar Hoover heard about the collaboration between the navy and Luciano, he declared in a memo: "This is an amazing and fantastic case. We should get all the facts, for it looks rotten to me from several angles." When informed that the Office of the Chief of Naval Operations "acknowledges that Luciano was employed as an informant," Hoover called the operation "a shocking example of misuse of Navy authority in interest of a hoodlum. It surprises me they didn't give Luciano the Navy Cross."[90]

The US Army drew a more positive lesson from the Luciano collaboration. As a US Army field manual on urban operations observes:

Criminal elements or organizations may not always work against Army commanders. They can be co-opted or influenced to serve friendly objectives. For example, during World War II the US Navy worked covertly with the Mafia in New York City to secure the New York harbor from German U-boats believed to be torpedoing ships there. The Mafia controlled most dock activities [in] New York harbor and was perfectly positioned to monitor other subversive waterfront activity. This capability provided needed information to the Navy for its counterintelligence and security tasks. New York civil authorities therefore agreed to permit a Navy-Mafia alliance to operate at the port for the greater good of the country.[91]

Luciano's criminal connections also proved handy in keeping potentially disruptive unionized port workers in line, which naval intelligence deemed crucial to ensuring the smooth outflow of supplies to the war effort in Europe. The navy's covert enlistment of the underworld for surveillance work included operations in factories, hotels, bars, nightclubs, and foreign embassies.[92]

Luciano's value as a wartime intelligence asset also extended to Italy, where he used his criminal contacts to help prepare the way for the 1943 American invasion of Sicily, Luciano's homeland and the birthplace of the Mafia. As the American forces mobilized to create a second front in Europe, they quickly realized that the necessary advance intelligence for an amphibious landing was woefully lacking. Haffenden's Underworld Project was tasked with helping solve the problem. Haffenden later acknowledged that "the greater part of the intelligence developed in the Sicilian campaign was directly responsible to the number of Sicilians that emanated from the Charles 'Lucky' Contact."[93] Luciano and his associates also provided names of "trustworthy" contacts in Sicily, and, according to an official inquiry, through these contacts "much valuable information was obtained relative to the position of mine fields, enemy forces and strong points."[94] Luciano was so enthused about the operation that he even offered to be parachuted in to use his personal clout to win over the locals to the American cause.[95] He suggested the Golfo di Castellammare near Palermo—long used by the Mafia for drug smuggling—as a landing point for the invading US forces. Haffenden was supportive of Luciano's proposal to accompany the invasion, but

Captain Wallace S. Wharton, head of the Counterintelligence Section of the ONI in Washington, rejected the idea out of fear that it could later become a scandal.[96]

After the war, Luciano was released from prison and, along with many other American crime figures of Italian descent, shipped off to Italy. New York governor Thomas Dewey issued a public statement explaining the pardon: "Upon the entry of the United States into the war, Luciano's aid was sought by the armed services in inducing others to provide information concerning possible enemy attack. It appears that he cooperated in such an effort though the actual value of the information procured is not clear."[97]

Bringing with them to Sicily their illicit business knowledge and connections, Luciano and his fellow mobsters proceeded to play a leadership role in resuscitating an international heroin-trafficking business that had been cut off with the disruption of global transportation during the war. As a *Rome Daily American* article reported in 1951, "An estimated fifty men deported from the U.S. to Italy on narcotics charges since the war are believed to have formed the nucleus of a far-flung dope smuggling network."[98] Luciano was singled out by the Federal Bureau of Narcotics as the heroin-smuggling ringleader, providing a face to blame for America's drug problem. But Luciano was just one of many traffickers feeding the nation's heroin habit. And some of these illicit suppliers were officially overlooked because it would have simply been too geopolitically inconvenient to do otherwise. Although always difficult to get a clear picture of the shadowy underworld where covert operations and heroin trafficking intersected, a pattern was emerging: fighting drugs was secondary to fighting communists, especially when those who were doing the fighting were also dealing drugs.

## Heroin and the Hot Wars of the Cold War

As the Cold War got going, heroin and national security increasingly bumped into each other, at times awkwardly, but also in politically useful ways. Geopolitics trumped drug enforcement, often to the advantage of politically protected traffickers who served larger strategic objectives. At the same time, anticommunist anxieties provided added ideological ammunition for America's antidrug campaign. In other words, the United States and some of its allies overlooked the heroin trade when strategically convenient while also disparaging geopolitical rivals as complicit in the trade.

Nowhere did geopolitics influence drug trafficking more forcefully than in Marseille, France, which became the main source of US-bound heroin in the 1950s and 1960s. France's second-largest city and biggest port was a key entry point for Marshall Plan aid shipments to Europe. It was also a French Communist Party stronghold and the epicenter of the country's labor movement, which during these decades launched strikes that threatened to disrupt shipping and the postwar economic recovery. Viewing French labor struggles through the prism of the East–West conflict, the CIA secretly recruited and funded Corsican gangs to harass local Communist leaders, intimidate trade unionists, and break the picket lines. The CIA's covert operation worked as planned—Communist influence and labor activism in Marseille were greatly reduced—but left a lasting, unintended legacy: newly empowered and politically protected, these very same gangs and their leaders came to dominate the Corsican underworld and control the Marseille waterfront.

Corsican-run heroin laboratories soon sprang up around Marseille, turning morphine base shipped in from Turkey and elsewhere into high-grade US-bound heroin. The product was of such high quality and purity, and the business was run so efficiently, that Luciano and his Sicilian partners also turned to the Marseille labs to process their heroin. From there, Luciano's old business partner Lansky and Mafiosi such as Santo Trafficante helped move the product into the US market. This infamous "French Connection"—the inspiration for the 1971 film by the same name—was America's main heroin supplier until the early 1970s. The French government overlooked the heroin laboratories as long as the product was for the export market.[99]

Meanwhile, Harry Anslinger, America's first "drug tsar" and director of the Federal Bureau of Narcotics, shrewdly tied the drug threat to the foreign threat of communism. "Red China" was publicly accused of trying to destroy Western society and of generating hard cash through heroin sales to US drug pushers. Anslinger declared that Mao's China was the "greatest purveyor in history of habit-forming drugs" and was "reaping tremendous amounts from its network of narcotics smugglers operating on a world-wide basis."[100] In 1953, Anslinger told the United Nations Commission on Narcotic Drugs that "there can be little doubt of the true purposes of Communist China in the organized sale of narcotics. Their purposes include monetary gain, financing political activities in various countries, and sabotage. The Communists have planned well and know a well-trained soldier becomes a liability and a security risk from the moment he first takes a shot of heroin."[101] While denouncing China, Anslinger was silent in public about the influx of heroin from allied France even as his own field agents were increasingly preoccupied by it.

The political atmosphere of the 1950s created a Congress receptive to Anslinger's designs. In the Senate, a subcommittee chaired by Texas Democrat Price Daniel embraced Anslinger's assertions about the Chinese communist threat, concluding that "subversion through drug addiction is an established aim of Communist China." Daniel's subcommittee recommended tougher penalties for heroin dealing. The resulting Narcotic Control Act of 1956 raised mandatory minimum penalties for the crime (five to twenty years for the second offense; ten to forty years for the third offense) and permitted juries to impose the death penalty on any adult who sold heroin to a minor.[102]

Conveniently overlooked by Washington was the fact that China had actually launched a sweeping crackdown on drugs, jailing or executing thousands of drug traffickers and dealers and largely removing the country from the heroin trade. Having used opium to help finance their revolution, the triumphant Communists quickly moved to eradicate it. After Mao and the Communists took power on October 1, 1949, the Chinese Revolution morphed into an anti-opium revolution. On February 24, 1950, the new government issued its General Order for Opium Suppression, marking the start of a nationwide anti-drug crusade. The General Order begins:

> It has been more than a century since opium was forcibly imported into China by the imperialists. Due to the reactionary rule and the decadent lifestyle of the feudal bureaucrats, compradors, and warlords, not only was opium not suppressed, but we were forced to cultivate it; especially due to the Japanese systematically carrying out a plot to poison China during their aggression, countless people's

lives and property have been lost. Now that the people have been liberated, the following methods of opium and other narcotic suppression are specifically stipulated to protect people's health, to cure addiction, and to accelerate production.[103]

Chinese antidrug rhetoric was wrapped up in the larger revolutionary cause—to be against opium was to be against foreign imperialism and capitalist decadence. The postrevolution antidrug movement, which took place alongside antiprostitution and antigambling movements— all targeting what were labeled "capitalist vices"—included rounding up and executing thousands of drug dealers and forcing addicts to choose between treatment or imprisonment. In 1952 alone, the antidrug crackdown generated 82,000 arrests, 35,000 prison sentences, and 880 public executions.[104] The Central Committee told local authorities that "it is easier to get people's sympathy by killing drug offenders than killing counter-revolutionaries. So at least 2 percent of those arrested should be killed."[105]

By 1953, domestic opium production and consumption had been virtually eradicated, making China's campaign the most successful "war against drugs" the world has ever seen. This reversed the legacy of a century in which opium had been popularly viewed as a bitter symbol of Chinese decline and humiliation and a tool for foreign exploitation and encroachment. The mass antidrug mobilization, largely unseen and unacknowledged by the outside world, was very much a state-building initiative, a rejection of the old as part of the creation of a "new China."[106] At the same time, tobacco—a state monopoly and major revenue generator—was promoted as opium's replacement, turning China into the world's largest consumer of cigarettes in the coming decades.

China's postrevolution exit from the opium trade prompted a fundamental reconfiguration of the political economy of narcotics in the region. Major traffickers, including the Shanghai underworld leadership, fled the country, with many of them relocating to Hong Kong.[107] New arrivals in Hong Kong included Green Gang master chemists who would turn the colony into the world's leading high-grade heroin laboratory.[108]

Opium production also shifted. Along with Nationalist forces, opium cultivation was pushed south—out of China and into remote borderland areas of Burma, Laos, and Thailand, which would later be called the "Golden Triangle." An area that until the 1950s produced only modest amounts of opium would in the next decade become the world's single largest supplier of the drug. By the end of the 1950s, it would produce about 700 tons of raw opium annually—about half of the world's supply.[109] The rugged, isolated hills and mountains of northern mainland Southeast Asia were already populated by tribes with knowledge of opium production, including the Hmong, who had fled southern China a century earlier after rebelling against Chinese rule. The terrain, located far from the reach of central government authorities, was ideal for an expansion of opium poppy cultivation.[110]

Secretly backed by the CIA starting in the early 1950s, the retreating Chinese Nationalists, already adept at using dope money to fund their military cause, now turned again to opium to carry out their anticommunist military operations along the southwestern Chinese border. These rebel remnants of the Kuomintang, operating in exile in Burma's Shan State, not only received clandestine military supplies from the CIA-owned Civil Air Transport (later renamed Air America) but also used this politically protected fleet of small aircraft as a cover for drug shipments.[111] The force soon swelled to a 12,000-strong guerrilla army, the leaders of which served as de facto rulers over the area—an area that also happened to be Burma's main source of opium. The strategic importance of opium was not difficult to understand. "To fight you must have an army," explained General Tuan Shi-wen, a veteran Nationalist commander in Burma, "and an army must have guns, and to buy guns you must have money. In these mountains the only money is opium."[112]

While the Chinese Nationalists failed to realize their dream of retaking China—their multiple invasions of Yunnan were easily driven back by the Red Army—they succeeded in turning the Golden Triangle into the world's largest opium poppy–growing area by the early 1960s.[113] In 1960–1961, Chinese and Burmese military campaigns drove many of the exiles to neighboring Laos and Thailand.[114] From there, they continued to move opium out of the Shan State via mule caravans, controlling nearly one-third of world opium supplies by the early 1970s.[115] They also enabled the emergence of local opium warlords, most notably

Khun Sa, who would use his own private army to dominate much of the trade in later years.[116]

Military rulers in neighboring Thailand also facilitated and profited from the opium boom, with Bangkok not only providing a consumer base but also serving as a regional distribution center and outlet to the rest of the world. Having occupied the Shan State during World War II, Thai leaders had already built close ties to local warlords and the Kuomintang across the border.[117] So when the war came to an end, the Thai government already had the requisite relations to engage in the opium business, which it would use to help bankroll its armed forces.[118] After taking power in an opium-financed coup in 1947, the country's military rulers and subsequent military regimes financed themselves through the opium trade. General Phao Sriyanond, the head of the CIA-trained and -supplied national police force, was also the de facto head of the opium trade. He helped to create and protect the Kuomintang's Burma-Bangkok opium-smuggling route.[119] According to historian Alfred McCoy, by the mid-1950s, Phao's police had become the biggest opium-trafficking organization in the country. The CIA provided Phao with the transport vehicles used to move his dope from field to port.[120]

The CIA became more deeply entangled in the region's drug trade after the French military defeat in Indochina in 1954. Colluding with Corsican traffickers who shipped opium from Indochina to Marseille, the French intelligence service had used opium funds to covertly pay local hill tribe leaders and warlords as part of its counterinsurgency campaign. Earlier, French colonial administrators had run an opium monopoly, with some 2,500 opium dens and retail shops serving more than 100,000 consumers in Indochina by the start of World War II. The French monopoly was closely associated with colonial rule, and it was therefore a favorite target of nationalist anticolonial voices.[121] Ho Chi Minh effectively exploited popular resentment against the French opium monopoly in his propaganda.[122]

To compensate for the cutting off of foreign opium supplies and opium revenue during World War II, the French encouraged the Hmong hill tribes of Laos and the Tonkin people of northwest Indochina to boost opium poppy cultivation, offering them political support in exchange for their cooperation.[123] Production shot up 800 percent, from less than 8 tons in 1940 to over 60 tons in 1944.[124] When French colonial administrators formally ended their opium monopoly after the war, French military intelligence informally took it over to finance their covert campaign in the first Indo-China War of 1946–1954. This secret revenue stream from what came to be known as "Operation X" was especially needed after the French Assembly cut back its funding in the midst of dwindling public support at home for an unpopular distant military campaign.[125] Opium funding helped the French slow down Viet Minh advances even if it ultimately failed to revive a dying empire and change the outcome of the war.

When the French withdrew after their defeat at the Battle of Dien Bien Phu, the CIA simply stepped in and took their place, building on the inherited opium trade relationships and infrastructure. This included supporting the same Hmong-based secret army in Laos headed by General Vang Pao. Pao and his soldiers provided intelligence and battled Laotian communists near the North Vietnamese border, and in exchange the CIA helped ship their opium out of the remote and difficult-to-access region.[126] The covert war in Laos required only a handful of CIA advisors, with the cost of supporting 30,000 Hmong troops (and a tribe of 250,000 to replenish battlefield losses with new recruits) cushioned by opium sales.[127] Senior US officials back at the CIA's Washington headquarters were not inclined to pay too much attention as long as Hmong loyalty was secured and the operation was producing results.[128]

As American intervention escalated and the war in Vietnam dragged on, CIA-backed anticommunist allies in the region increasingly profited from opium and its derivatives, with the Cold War context providing the necessary political cover. As McCoy documents in detail in his classic book *The Politics of Heroin*, the CIA was complicit not through corruption or direct involvement, but rather through what he describes as a radical pragmatism that tolerated and even facilitated drug trafficking by local allies when it served larger Cold War goals.[129] By 1970, more than two-thirds of the world's opium came from the Golden Triangle, and the region would retain this status of top producer until the end of the Cold War.[130]

The region's drug trade received an additional boost from the presence of American GIs, who in the early 1970s developed a serious heroin habit. With the help of master chemists brought in from Hong

Kong, by the late 1960s Golden Triangle laboratories were for the first time producing fine-grain No. 4 heroin (the classification for drugs of 80 to 99 percent purity). Previously, production had mostly been confined to refined opium or the lower-quality No. 3 heroin (only 20 to 40 percent purity).[131] Politically protected traffickers, including senior Laotian and Vietnamese military officials, supplied the American troops in Vietnam, who numbered half a million at the peak of the conflict. Some of these soldiers in turn helped to smuggle thousands of kilos into the United States through conveyances ranging from GI care packages to body bags.[132]

Most of the heroin was flown from the remote reaches of the Golden Triangle into Vietnam on Laotian and South Vietnamese military aircraft, overseen by corrupt senior officials. Later, the head of the Vietnamese navy, General Dang Van Quang, would use his fleet to ship heroin from Cambodia.[133] It was easy to reach consumers. As Booth notes, "Heroin was available at roadside stalls on every highway out of Saigon, and on the route to the main US military base at Long Binh, as well as from itinerant peddlers, newspaper and ice-cream vendors, restaurant owners, brothel keepers and their whores and domestic servants employed on US bases. No barracks was without a resident dealer."[134] Most soldiers preferred to smoke rather than inject the drug, a method of ingestion made possible by high purity levels. In mid-1971, US Army medical officers estimated that some 10 to 15 percent of the deployed rank-and-file troops were heroin addicts.[135] In 1973, the Pentagon estimated that one-third of American servicemen in Vietnam used heroin.[136]

Dramatic media reports of an epidemic of soldier drug use in Vietnam helped fuel public anxiety back home and provided a convenient new excuse for the war's failures. In November 1967 Walter Cronkite reported on the *CBS Evening News* that the "Communists are battling American troops not only with fire power, but with drugs."[137] And in May 1971 *Newsweek* printed a photograph of a syringe impaled in a soldier's helmet. A story in that same issue reported that "the drug epidemic" was so "horrifying" that it was "worse even than My Lai."[138]

Such shocking depictions gave added ammunition to President Nixon's declaration of a "war against drugs" in June 1971. Nixon noted that he was particularly "disheartened by the use of drugs among

American servicemen in Vietnam," who had brought shame on the country's proud citizen-soldier tradition.[139] He warned that "a habit which costs five dollars a day to maintain in Vietnam can cost one hundred dollars a day to maintain in the United States, and those who continue to use heroin slip into the twilight world of crime, bad drugs, and all too often a premature death."[140] Nixon therefore helped to construct an image of the addicted soldier as a threat not only to the country's fighting capacity in Vietnam but also to American society, by bringing a dangerous habit home with him. Heroin topped Nixon's list of drug threats: "It is no exaggeration to say that heroin addiction—if not checked by decisive action now—could cripple a whole generation or more of Americans in the critical years ahead. If we do not destroy the heroin menace, then it will surely and eventually destroy us and our great nation's future."[141]

The Pentagon responded to the growing alarm by subjecting returning soldiers to mandatory urine tests for the presence of heroin, dubbed "Operation Golden Flow." A positive test required the soldier to undergo a week-long methadone detoxification before flying home. Soldiers could trick the test by avoiding heroin five days before it was administered, a strategy that ensured the drug would not be detected. Getting drunk could also throw off the test, as could purchasing "clean" urine on the black market. Two positive tests in a row resulted in a dishonorable discharge, which certainly did not aid soldier recovery.[142]

One prominent psychiatrist, Thomas Szasz, argued that US soldiers were being turned into scapegoats in a losing foreign war that was being replaced by a war at home on drug users: "We claim that our troops are being stabbed in the back by heroin and the pushers responsible for supplying it to them. As we de-escalate against the 'Vietcong,' we will escalate against heroin. No doubt we shall find it easier to control Americans who shoot heroin than Vietnamese who shoot Americans."[143]

While Nixon's encouragement of public fears about drugs helped him distract attention from the disastrous consequences of his Vietnam strategy, some on the Left turned to the drug issue as a political weapon to criticize US intervention. The left-wing *Ramparts* magazine, for example, editorialized: "The U.S went on a holy war to stamp out Communism and to protect its Asian markets and its conscripted sons have come home with a blood-stained needle as their only lasting souvenir. It is a fitting trade-off—one that characterizes the moral quality of the U.S. involvement, which has radiated a nimbus of genocide and corruption. . . . This ugly war keeps coming back to haunt us, each manifestation more terrifying than the last."[144]

Drug use within the American military in Vietnam was real, but it had also been distorted through political handwringing and exaggerated media reporting. Far from presenting a grave societal threat, surveys of returned veterans suggested that the vast majority of them stopped taking drugs once they were back home.[145] The high remission rates suggested that wartime drug use was largely situational and contextual. Moreover, in the case of heroin, many veterans may have been deterred from continued use because the lower purity levels of the drug in the United States necessitated that it be injected intravenously instead of smoked.[146]

The US withdrawal from Vietnam and the fall of Saigon prompted major changes in the Southeast Asian drug trade. As GI demand dried up, traffickers sought new markets for the high-purity No. 4 heroin, with the United States a particularly promising outlet. The Golden Triangle, which was already producing the majority of the world's opium, would now also become a leading exporter of high-quality heroin, competing with Marseille and Hong Kong.[147] Trafficking routes also shifted: at the same time that the eastward flow of drugs across Southeast Asia was disrupted by the end of the war and the coming to power of communist regimes, the Bangkok route became increasingly important, with Thailand becoming the region's top opiate exporter.[148]

Meanwhile, in the opium-saturated Shan State of Burma, the warlord Khun Sa gained control of much of the drug business in the area. With a 3,500-strong personal army known as the Shan United Army, Khun Sa portrayed himself as the nationalist leader of the Shan State that was seeking independence from the Burmese government. Publicly acknowledging that opium was the basis of his power, in 1977 he boasted to the media that he was the "King of the Golden Triangle."[149] Repeated Thai and Burmese military attacks failed to dislodge him, as he easily moved back and forth across the borders of the two nations. He would remain the most influential opium warlord in the region for the next two decades, and at the peak of his power in the 1980s he

Figure 4.5 Burmese warlord Khun Sa, dubbed the "Opium King" as a result of his opium trading in the Golden Triangle region, 1974 (Granger Collection).

oversaw an army of tens of thousands of soldiers financed through the control of more than two-thirds of the Golden Triangle heroin trade.[150]

## Afghanistan from the Cold War to the War on Terror

Following earlier patterns in Southeast Asia, Washington looked the other way when CIA-backed Afghan insurgents battling the Soviets in the 1980s cultivated and smuggled opium to help fund their cause. In the CIA's biggest covert operation since Vietnam, the opium trade was once again one of the biggest winners. As McCoy summarizes, "To fight the Soviet occupation of Afghanistan, the CIA, working through Pakistan's Inter-Service Intelligence, backed Afghan warlords who used the agency's arms, logistics, and protection to become major drug lords."[151] US officials were apparently well aware of the situation but turned a blind eye in pursuit of larger geopolitical goals. "We're not going to let a little thing like drugs get in the way of the political situation," explained a Reagan administration official at the time. "And when the Soviets leave and there's no money in the country, it's not going to be a priority to disrupt the drug trade."[152]

When the Soviets invaded Afghanistan in late 1979, opium cultivation was a marginal activity compared to later years. Opium had long been present in what came to be known as the Golden Crescent—Afghanistan, Pakistan, and Iran. Zahiruddin Mohammad Babar, founder of the Mughal Empire, had written about using opium when he sacked Kabul in 1504, and the drug was being consumed socially across the region by the mid-sixteenth century.[153] But until the late 1970s the market was mostly self-contained, supplying local and regional customers and largely disconnected from the global heroin trade. All this changed thanks to the war-ravaged years of the 1980s and beyond, with Afghanistan eventually coming to dominate world opium production.

The Soviet Union's scorched earth strategy in the Afghan countryside, designed to starve the *mujahideen* resistance and force rural populations into more easily controllable urban centers, destroyed much of the infrastructure for food production. In addition to creating millions of refugees who fled to neighboring Pakistan and Iran, an unintended consequence of this strategy was to push the local population to grow opium to survive. Compared to many other crops, the hardy opium poppy could adapt to varied terrain and required little irrigation and fertilization. Opium production increased by more than twofold between 1984 and 1985—from an estimated 140 metric tons to 400—and then doubled again the next year.[154] By 1987, overall agricultural production was only one-third of 1978 levels, but opium cultivation had boomed.[155]

Mujahideen commanders became increasingly enmeshed in the opium trade. This involvement ranged from taxing and protecting crops to imposing road tolls on traders at checkpoints to smuggling opium out of the country through the same channels used to smuggle in arms supplied by the CIA and Pakistan's Directorate for Inter-Services Intelligence (ISI). Indeed, a fleet of trucks belonging to the Pakistani army's National Logistics Cell was allegedly used to move

CIA-provided arms into the country and then move opium and heroin out on the return trip. ISI documents assured those involved that the trucks would not be searched and seized by Pakistani police.[156] By 1988, there were as many as 200 heroin laboratories in Pakistan's North-West Frontier Province's Khyber district alone.[157] The heroin was not only exported to Europe and elsewhere but fed Pakistan's rapidly growing demand—a country that in the late 1970s did not have a serious heroin abuse problem soon had one of the largest addict populations in the world, skyrocketing from approximately 5,000 in 1980 to more than 1.3 million in the middle of the decade.[158]

Immediate military necessity overcame whatever religious qualms mujahideen leaders may have had about supporting the drug trade. "How else can we get money?" asked Mohammed Rasul, brother of the Helmand Province warlord Mullah Nasim Akhundzada. "We must grow and sell opium to fight our holy war against the Russian nonbelievers."[159] The Akhundzada family not only taxed opium crops but set up a system of production quotas and loans to farmers to induce them to grow opium poppy.[160]

Some mujahideen became directly involved in morphine and heroin manufacturing along the Pakistani border. They included Akhundzada's main rival, Gulbuddin Hekmatyar, an ISI protégé from the fundamentalist Hizb-i-Islami Party who received more than half of all CIA assistance to the anti-Soviet resistance.[161] "All the big traffickers in those days tended to be from Hizb-i-Islami and that was principally because Hekmatyar was a border person," recalled Edmund McWilliams, a special envoy to the resistance between 1988 and 1989. "He was very much operating along the border because he was so dependent on Pakistani support."[162] With CIA and Pakistani intelligence backing, Hekmatyar built up his small guerrilla force into the largest Afghan resistance army. He simultaneously became the country's most important drug trafficker, controlling half a dozen heroin laboratories in the Koh-i-Soltan district of Pakistan's Baluchistan Province, where opium brought in from Afghanistan's Helmand Valley was processed.[163]

American officials at the time preferred to look the other way because it was simply too politically inconvenient to do otherwise. "You have to put yourself in the mind-set of the period," McWilliams said. "Raising issues like Hekmatyar and the ISI's involvement in the drug trade was on no one's agenda."[164] In 1990, after the Soviets were gone and Afghanistan had lost its strategic importance, the *Washington Post* ran a front-page story detailing Hekmatyar's heroin operations and reported that US diplomats had "received but declined to investigate" on-the-ground accounts that Afghan fighters and Pakistani intelligence agents were "protect[ing] and participat[ing]" in the heroin trade.[165] The article indicated that the United States had turned a blind eye "because of its desire not to offend a strategic ally, Pakistan's military establishment."[166] "One of my great frustrations at the time was that the CIA would not give us information on narcotics," said former US ambassador to Pakistan Robert Oakley. "My belief was then and still is that they wanted to protect their contacts in Pakistani intelligence."[167]

Afghan dependence on the opium trade only deepened as the Soviet Union withdrew in early 1989. Agricultural recovery in the countryside was most evident in the drug trade: "Much of this renewed production took the form of opium growing, heroin refining, and smuggling; these enterprises were organized by combines of mujahideen parties, Pakistani military officers, and Pakistani drug syndicates," wrote prominent Afghan expert Barnett Rubin.[168] The labor-intensive opium business found easy recruits among the millions of desperate Afghan refugees repatriated from Pakistan.

With US assistance drying up, the countryside devastated by a brutal decade-long counterinsurgency campaign, and no effective government authority, Afghanistan descended into civil war in the early 1990s. The Soviet-supported government of Mohammad Najibullah, which was never able to exercise much control beyond Kabul or win support beyond its own ethnic base in the northeast, fell in April 1992.

Replaying some of the dynamics of China's early-twentieth-century warlord era of extreme political fragmentation, former mujahideen commanders brutally competed with each other over territory, especially the best opium land—except in this case, the market for the drug was external rather than internal, and there was no pretense of opium suppression. Mullah Nasim Akhundzada, for instance, oversaw most of the 250 tons of opium grown in the fertile Helmand Valley and was nicknamed the "King of Heroin." He imposed an opium quota and insisted that peasant growers devote half of their land holdings to the cultivation of opium poppy.[169] His competition with rival leader

Hekmatyar intensified, and in April 1990 Nasim was gunned down by Hekmatyar-allied troops. He was replaced by his brother, Mohammed Rasul, who maintained the family's grip on much of the Helmand Valley.

These former mujahideen factions, more preoccupied with fighting each other over control of the opium economy and building up their own personal fiefdoms than in uniting and governing the country, ultimately proved no match for the Taliban, a Pakistan-backed ultraconservative movement originating in the Islamic academies (*madrasas*) of the Afghan-Pakistani frontier region. Opium contributed to the Taliban's rapid rise to power out of the chaos and violent predation of the early 1990s. In its campaign to pacify the country and impose an extreme interpretation of Islam, the Taliban initially sought to ban opium cultivation on religious grounds. But faced with intense popular resistance rooted in the livelihood the poppy provided to so many, the group reversed course and came to not only tolerate but promote the opium economy. It banned the consumption of opiates, as well as alcohol and other drugs, but allowed the production and trading of opium.[170] This generated not only revenue for the Taliban cause but, perhaps most importantly, much-needed popular support, given how important the opium economy was to local sustenance.

Before capturing Kabul, the Taliban systematically conquered key opium-growing areas, including Qandahar and Helmand in the south in 1994 (the source of 56 percent of the country's opium), Herat in 1995, and Jalalabad and the eastern opium-growing region in 1996 (the source of 39 percent of the country's opium).[171] Opium funded the Taliban cause largely through taxes on growers and traffickers. The Taliban's primary rival, the Northern Alliance, was also involved in the opium trade (as well as other illicit trades, especially the smuggling of gemstones) but was disadvantaged by the fact that areas under its control represented only a small percentage of the country's overall cultivation.[172]

Once in power, the Taliban regime not only continued to allow the cultivation of opium poppy—and continued to systematically tax it (collecting a 10 percent tax from farmers at the point of production and a 20 percent tax on truckloads of opium at the point of export)[173]—but provided some semblance of stability for the illicit trade to greatly expand. While failing to provide some of the basic services of a full-fledged state, the Taliban was able to impose its authority over most of the country's roads, urban centers, airports, and customs posts, and this modicum of security and stability benefited cross-border traders, including opium exporters.[174] By the end of the decade, Afghanistan had become the source of three-fourths of the world's supply of opium, with areas under Taliban control in the south and east producing virtually all of the country's poppy crop.[175]

Such flagrant support for the booming opium trade contributed to the Taliban's growing international pariah status and reputation as a "narco-state." And opium in turn helped to sustain a defiant Taliban in the face of growing international isolation. Few countries recognized it as Afghanistan's legitimate government. But it was the Taliban's hospitality toward terrorists, not drug traffickers, that would ultimately bring it down—and it was opium that would help build it back up.

The United States invaded Afghanistan in October 2001 in retaliation for the September 11 terrorist attacks. The target was not only those responsible for bringing down the Twin Towers—Osama bin Laden and Al Qaeda—but their hosts and protectors, the Taliban regime. While the United States dropped bombs from the air, it paid a coalition of local warlords to lead the ground attack. This coalition, funded by the CIA, included both a group of Pashtun warlords near the Pakistani border and the Northern Alliance, a Tajik army with experience fighting the Soviets in the 1980s and the Taliban during the next decade. Both controlled opium-smuggling routes in their respective territories.[176] In other words, following the old Cold War pattern, the United States was once again more than willing to work with drug traffickers when it served larger strategic goals.

The Taliban quickly collapsed and scattered into the countryside, while bin Laden disappeared into the jagged Tora Bora Mountains. Although the Taliban had actually implemented a sweeping opium ban during its final year in power—apparently to try to win international recognition and respect, but also perhaps to drive up drug prices and benefit from stockpiled heroin—opium production made a dramatic comeback in the aftermath of the invasion, making up an estimated 62 percent of Afghanistan's gross domestic product in 2003.

By the end of 2004, it was not only the drug trade but also the Taliban that was resurgent, and the two would become increasingly intertwined. US officials initially paid little attention to the revival of the drug trade in Afghanistan but eventually came to push for an aggressive eradication campaign in the countryside. But by this time, opium cultivation was as entrenched in the rural economy as ever, and suppression efforts had the perverse and unintended consequence of driving the disgruntled local population right into the hands of the Taliban. Thus, the inescapable conundrum facing the United States and its allies was not only that opium was funding the guerrillas, but also that going after opium was creating new guerrilla recruits. By 2007, opium production had reached record levels, with the United Nations estimating that Afghanistan was the source of 93 percent of the world's illicit heroin supply. The UN also noted that the Taliban insurgents had "started to extract from the drug economy resources for arms, logistics, and militia pay."[177] In 2008 alone, "taxes" on the opium trade reportedly generated $425 million for the Taliban.

To make matters worse, the United States also found itself backing an extraordinarily corrupt government in Kabul, one that also had deep

Figure 4.6 A US Army colonel walks through an opium poppy field in Helmand Province in southern Afghanistan, April 2006 (John Moore/Getty Images).

ties to drug trafficking. As had been the case during the Cold War, a pragmatic calculus meant Washington was willing to overlook such ties and perhaps even take advantage of them. For instance, Ahmed Wali Karzai, the brother of the new Afghan president, was widely suspected of ties to the heroin trade before he was assassinated, but he was also allegedly on the CIA payroll.[178] The United States also turned a blind eye to the appointment of Asadullah Khalid as the Afghani director of the National Directorate of Security. Khalid was a former governor of Kandahar and was widely accused of "abuses of power," including murder, torture, and drug trafficking. The United States and its allies did not act on these allegations because, as Vanda Felbab-Brown puts it, "whatever his accountability deficiencies, Khalid had a proven record of being tough on the Taliban."[179]

At the same time, the United States faced blowback from its earlier backing of drug-dealing allies. This was embarrassingly evident in the case of the Haqqani network in Afghanistan and Pakistan, whose criminal activities included drug smuggling. This network had enjoyed covert CIA support while fighting Soviet forces in the 1980s, but in 2011 it was responsible for orchestrating a bold daylong attack on the American embassy in Kabul and was described as the most dangerous security threat to US forces in Afghanistan. As one press report put it, in the 1980s the network had been supplied with US missiles; now it was the target of CIA missiles. Texas representative Charlie Wilson, whose support for the mujahideen was the subject of the Hollywood film *Charlie Wilson's War*, had even described the elder Haqqani leader, Jalaluddin Haqqani, as "goodness personified."[180]

Fifteen years after the US invasion of Afghanistan—with Washington having spent more than $1 trillion and counting on military operations—the war had no end in sight. The Taliban's control over the drug trade continued to grow, expanding to cover much of Helmand Province, the heart of poppy cultivation in southern Afghanistan. But even in those Helmand districts where the government remained in charge, opium not only grew openly near military and police stations but was taxed by the local authorities. Despite the United States spending billions of dollars on antidrug efforts and billions more to curb corruption, local government officials had become so complicit in the drug trade that they were now apparently competing with the Taliban to profit from it. While the central government in Kabul repeatedly declared its commitment to fighting drugs and corruption, the reality on the ground in Helmand, as reported in the *New York Times*, was "a local narco-state administered directly by government authorities."[181]

Even though most of the drug profits may have stayed in the hands of local officials, payoffs reached up to the regional and national levels. Those complicit included key regional security and law enforcement commanders with ties to US military and intelligence officials. "Over the years, I have seen the central government, the local government and the foreigners all talk very seriously about poppy," observed Hakim Angar, a former head of police in Helmand Province. "In practice, they do nothing, and behind the scenes, the government makes secret deals to enrich themselves."[182]

AS WE'VE SEEN, THE centuries-old relationship between opium and war has been first and foremost about generating revenue, whether to fund imperial expansion, prop up warlord ambitions, or pay for insurgency and counterinsurgency campaigns. The shifting legal status of the drug, including its worldwide criminalization in the twentieth century, brought with it a more covert role as a funder of war. Consequently, the business of war and the business of crime became much more intertwined. The drug has also been consumed by combatants at various times and places, though beyond serving as a crucial pain medication, leaders have usually not promoted it as a facilitator of military performance.

We therefore now turn to a drug that is equally potent but has had an opposite history: more than any other mind-altering substance, amphetamines have been pushed first and foremost as battlefield performance enhancers rather than revenue makers. So while the relationship between opium and war has mostly been a story about war *through* drugs and war *for* drugs, the story of amphetamines and war is almost entirely a story of war *while on* drugs. As a fully synthetic drug, it is no coincidence that the industrial production and mass distribution of amphetamines occurred at the height of the industrialization of warfare in the twentieth century.

# 5

## Speed Warfare

IN *THE ART OF WAR*, Sun Tzu wrote that speed is "the essence of war." While he of course did not have amphetamines in mind, he would no doubt have been impressed by their powerful war-facilitating psychoactive effects. Amphetamines—often called "pep pills," "go pills," "uppers," or "speed"—are a group of synthetic drugs that stimulate the central nervous system, reducing fatigue and appetite and increasing wakefulness and a sense of well-being. Methamphetamine is a particularly potent and addictive form of the drug, best known today as "crystal meth." All amphetamines are now banned or tightly regulated. The quintessential drug of the modern industrial age, amphetamines arrived relatively late in the history of mind-altering substances—commercialized just in time for mass consumption during World War II by the leading industrial powers. Few drugs have received a bigger stimulus from war. As Lester Grinspoon and Peter Hedblom wrote in their classic 1975 study *The Speed Culture*, "World War II probably gave the greatest impetus to date to legal medically authorized as well as illicit black market abuse of these pills on a worldwide scale."[1] The story of this particular drugs–war relationship is therefore mostly about the proliferation of synthetic stimulant use during World War II and its speed-fueled aftermath.

*Killer High*, Peter Andreas. Oxford University Press (2020). © Peter Andreas.
DOI: 10.1093/actrade/9780190463014.001.0001

While produced entirely in the laboratory, amphetamines owe their existence to the search for an artificial substitute for the *ma huang* plant, better known in the West as ephedra. This relatively scarce desert shrub had been used as an herbal remedy for more than 5,000 years in China, where it was often ingested to treat common ailments such as coughs and colds and to promote concentration and alertness, including by night guards patrolling the Great Wall of China. In 1887, Japanese chemist Nagayoshi Nagai successfully extracted the plant's active ingredient, ephedrine, which closely resembled adrenaline, and in 1919, another Japanese scientist, A. Ogata, developed a synthetic substitute for ephedrine. But it was not until amphetamine was synthesized in 1927 at a University of California at Los Angeles laboratory by the young British chemist Gordon Alles that a formula became available for commercial medical use. Alles sold this formula to the Philadelphia pharmaceutical company Smith, Kline & French, which brought it to the market in 1932 as the Benzedrine inhaler (an over-the-counter product to treat asthma and congestion) before introducing it in tablet form a few years later. "Bennies" were widely promoted as a wonder drug for all sorts of ailments, from depression to obesity, with little apparent concern or awareness of their addictive potential and the risk of longer-term physical and psychological damage. And with the outbreak of another world war, it did not take long for such large-scale pill pushing to also reach the battlefield.[2]

### The Nazi Need for Speed

Nazi ideology was fundamentalist in its antidrug stance. Social use of drugs was considered both a sign of personal weakness and a symbol of the country's moral decay in the wake of a traumatic and humiliating defeat in World War I. Widespread drug use in Weimar Germany was viewed as decadent, hedonistic, and shameful, a habit that threatened to poison the Aryan "master race." Addicts not only were stigmatized and marginalized but could face severe punishment, including forced sterilization and being sent off to concentration camps. In Nazi propaganda, Jews were portrayed as drug abusers and pushers and therefore as a threat to the purity of the nation.[3]

But methamphetamine was the privileged exception. While other drugs were banned or discouraged, methamphetamine was touted as a miracle product when it appeared on the market in the late 1930s. Indeed, the little pill was the perfect Nazi drug: "Germany, awake!" the Nazis had commanded.[4] Energizing and confidence boosting, methamphetamine played into the Third Reich's obsession with physical and mental superiority. In sharp contrast to drugs such as heroin or alcohol, methamphetamines were not about escapist pleasure. Rather, they were taken for hyper-alertness and vigilance. Aryans, who were the embodiment of human perfection in Nazi ideology, could now even aspire to be superhuman—and such superhumans could be turned into super-soldiers. "We don't need weak people," Hitler declared, "we want only the strong!"[5] Weak people took drugs such as opium to escape; strong people took methamphetamine to feel even stronger.

The German chemist Friedrich Hauschild had been aware of the American amphetamine Benzedrine ever since the drug had been used as a doping product in the Olympic Games in Berlin in 1936.[6] The following year, he managed to synthesize methamphetamine, a close cousin of amphetamine, while working for Temmler-Werke, a Berlin-based pharmaceutical company. Temmler-Werke began selling methamphetamine under the brand name Pervitin in the winter of 1937. Partly thanks to the company's aggressive advertising campaign, Pervitin became well known within a few months. The tablets were wildly popular and could be purchased without a prescription in pharmacies.[7] One could even buy boxed chocolates spiked with methamphetamine. But the drug's most important use was yet to come.

Dr. Otto F. Ranke, director of the Research Institute of Defense Physiology (a section of the Military Medical Academy), had high hopes that Pervitin would prove advantageous on the battlefield. His goal was to defeat the enemy with chemically enhanced soldiers—soldiers who could give Germany a military edge by fighting harder and longer than their opponents. After testing the drug on a group of medical officers, Ranke believed that Pervitin would be "an excellent substance for rousing a weary squad. . . . We may grasp what far-reaching military significance it would have if we managed to remove natural tiredness using medical methods." He concluded that it was "a militarily valuable substance."[8] It also helped that methamphetamine pills

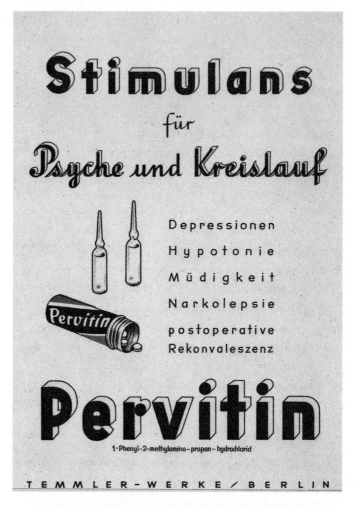

Figure 5.1 A German advertisement for Pervitin, which stimulates the psyche and circulation and has an undefined impact on depression, hypotonia, fatigue, narcolepsy, and post-operative depression (Landesarchiv Berlin).

were relatively cheap to produce, and base chemicals were readily available. Manufacturing the drug did not require imported raw materials and instead relied entirely on the country's pharmaceutical industry. Coffee, the main alternative stimulant used to fight sleep and fatigue, was far more expensive and would become scarce as a result of wartime import disruptions. As a coffee substitute, methamphetamine could be added to coffee-like drinks.[9]

Ranke himself was a daily user, as detailed in his wartime medical diary and letters. He wrote glowingly about the drug to a colleague: "It distinctly revives concentration and leads to a feeling of relief with regard to approaching difficult tasks. It is not just a stimulant, but clearly also a mood-enhancer. Even at high doses lasting damage is not apparent. . . . With Pervitin you can go on working for thirty-six to fifty hours without feeling any noticeable fatigue."[10] This allowed Ranke to work days at a time with no sleep. And his correspondence indicated that a growing number of officers were doing the same thing—popping pills to manage the demands of their jobs.[11]

Wehrmacht medical officers administered Pervitin to soldiers of the Third Tank Division during the occupation of Czechoslovakia in 1938.[12] But the invasion of Poland in September 1939 served as the first real military test of the drug in the field. Germany overran its eastern neighbor by October, with 100,000 Polish soldiers killed in the attack. Thousands of Polish civilians would also lose their lives by the end of the year.[13] The invasion introduced a new form of industrialized warfare, *Blitzkrieg*.[14] This "lightning war" emphasized speed and surprise, catching the enemy off guard by the unprecedented quickness of the mechanized attack and advance. It relied on German engineering in the form of Panzer divisions and Stuka dive bombers, as well as on German chemistry in the form of Pervitin. The weak link in the Blitzkrieg strategy was the soldiers, who were humans rather than machines and as such suffered from fatigue. They required regular rest and sleep, which, of course, slowed down the military advance. That is where Pervitin came in—part of the speed of the Blitzkrieg literally came from speed. As medical historian Peter Steinkamp puts it, "*Blitzkrieg* was guided by methamphetamine. If not to say that *Blitzkrieg* was founded on methamphetamine."[15]

As part of the invasion plan, the distribution of methamphetamine pills was not systematic but instead was left up to individual commanders, medical officers, and soldiers.[16] During the course of the invasion, reports of drug usage on the battlefield trickled in. According to the medical report of the 8th Panzer Division: "Own experience very favourable. . . . Effect on depressed mood excellent."[17] The 3rd Panzer Division reported: "Often there is euphoria, an increase in attention span, clear intensification of performance, work is achieved without difficulty, a pronounced alertness effect and a feeling of fresh-ness. Worked through the day, lifting of depression, returned to normal mood."[18]

The tank units seemed to especially benefit from the meth boost: "Everyone fresh and cheerful, excellent discipline. Slight eu-phoria and increased thirst for action. Mental encouragement, very stimulated. No accidents. Long-lasting effect. After taking four tablets, double vision and seeing colors." Moreover, "the feeling of hunger subsides. One particularly beneficial aspect is the appearance of a vig-orous urge to work. The effect is so clear that it cannot be based on imagination."[19] A medical officer from the IX Army Corps excitedly reported that "I'm convinced that in big pushes, where the last drop has to be squeezed from the team, a unit supplied with Pervitin is superior. This doctor has therefore made sure that there is a supply of Pervitin in the Unit Medical Equipment."[20] Another report read: "An increase in performance is quite evident among tank drivers and gun operators in the long-lasting battles from 1 to 4 September 1939 and the recon-naissance division, which has used this substance with great success on tough long journeys at night, as well as to maintain and heighten attentiveness on scouting patrol operations."[21] It then added: "We should particularly stress the excellent effect on the working capacity and mood among severely taxed officers at divisional headquarters, all of whom acknowledged the subjective and objective increase in perfor-mance with Pervitin."[22]

One senior military doctor from the 30th Infantry Division in Poland also recounted the effect of the drug on motorcyclists. Because of their importance as couriers and scouts in rough terrain and over long journeys, motorcyclists "in particular were burdened with enormous strain. The pills were distributed without com-ment. Owing to their remarkable effect, the troops came to know very soon what their purpose was."[23] Others reported that the ab-sence of Pervitin was a liability: one medic wrote that "among the drivers many accidents, mostly attributable to excessive fatigue, could have been avoided if an analeptic such as Pervitin had been administered."[24]

Medical officers were given general guidelines and warnings about Pervitin: "To apply them at random could endanger the health of the troops, if the time of rest is not used to sleep. The physician must be aware at all times that the whip of stimulants is allowed in exceptional cases only, when human damage is to be expected if this medication is not applied, and that it must remain restricted to people who are really in need of it."[25]

In his letters home from training and later from occupied Poland, one soldier regularly commented on the wonders of Pervitin. A letter dated November 9, 1939, read: "My duty is very strict, and you must understand when I write only every two or four days. Today I am mainly writing for *Pervitin*!" He followed up this correspondence with another letter a few months later, in which he asked, "Perhaps you could provide me with some *Pervitin* for my supply?"[26] His letters suggest a high dependence on the drug without awareness of any risks. "If next week goes as quickly as last, I'll be glad. Send me more Pervitin if you can; I use it on my many watches."[27] The soldier was Heinrich Böll, the 1972 Nobel Laureate in literature.

In late 1939 and early 1940, Leo Conti, the "Reich Health Führer," and others sounded the alarm bells about the risks of Pervitin, resulting in the drug being made available by prescription only.[28] But these warnings largely fell on deaf ears, and the new regulations were widely ignored. Use of the drug continued to grow. To Conti's dismay, the prescription requirement was never applied to the military, since his office was a civilian agency. "The Wehrmacht cannot renounce a temporary increase in performance or a defeat of fatigue, even through the use of medication," the Army Medical Inspector bluntly replied to Conti's appeal.[29]

Conti's effort to limit access to the drug was poorly timed, coinciding as it did with German military planning for the most critical stage of the Blitzkrieg. Military medical officers ordered that methamphetamine production be ramped up for the next phase of the war. At the Temmler-Werke factory, production revved into overdrive, pressing as many as 833,000 tablets per day.[30] Between April and July of 1940, German servicemen received more than 35 million methamphetamine tablets.[31] Restarting the Blitzkrieg meant having plenty of pills ready. The drug was even dispensed to pilots and tank crews in the form of chocolate bars known as *Fliegerschokolade* (flyer's chocolate) and *Panzerschokolade* (tanker's chocolate).[32] Ranke

Figure 5.2 Heinrich Böll was an enthusiastic user of Pervitin (Heinrich Böll Fotoarchiv).

observed that "a very large proportion of officers carries Pervitin on their person." Indeed, he expressed concern that the proliferation of the drug had gotten out of hand: "The question is not whether Pervitin should be introduced or not, but how to get its use back under control. Pervitin is being exploited on a mass scale, without medical checks."[33]

On April 13, 1940, the Army Medical Inspector sent the army's commander-in-chief, Field Marshal von Brauchitsch, a document labeled "The Pervitin question. Decree concerning careful, but necessary use in a special situation."[34] Ranke was tasked with writing a Wehrmacht instruction sheet for Pervitin, and he also ordered Temmler-Werke to ramp up its production of the drug. A "stimulant decree" written by Ranke and signed by von Brauchitsch was distributed to corps doctors and medical officers. It read:

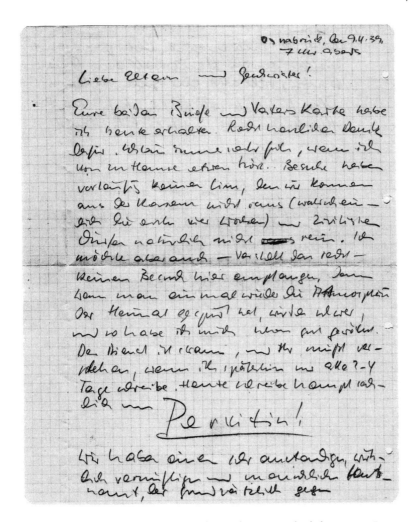

Figure 5.3 One of Heinrich Böll's many letters home in which he praises Pervitin. "Dear parents and grandparents . . . today I am writing mostly about Pervitin!" (Heinrich Böll Fotoarchiv).

The experience of the Polish campaign has shown that in certain situations military success was crucially influenced by overcoming fatigue in a troop on which strong demands had been made. The overcoming of sleep can in certain situations be more important than concern for any related harm, if military success is endangered by sleep. The stimulants are available for the interruption of sleep. Pervitin has been methodically included in medical equipment.[35]

The recommended dosage was a daytime tablet, plus two tablets at night. If the circumstances demanded it, an additional tablet or two could be taken after three or four hours.[36] "With correct dosage the feeling of self-confidence is clearly heightened, the fear of taking on even difficult work is reduced," the decree noted. "As a result inhibitions are removed, without the decrease in the sensory function associated with alcohol."[37]

Armies had long consumed various psychoactive substances, but this was the first large-scale use of a synthetic performance-enhancing drug. Historian Shelby Stanton comments: "They dispensed it to the line troops. Ninety percent of their army had to march on foot, day and night. It was more important for them to keep punching during the Blitzkrieg than to get a good night's sleep. The whole damn army was hopped up. It was one of the secrets of the Blitzkrieg."[38]

The Blitzkrieg depended on speed, relentlessly pushing ahead with tank troops, day and night. In April 1940, it quickly led to the fall of Denmark and Norway. The next month, the troops moved on to Holland, Belgium, and finally France. German tanks covered 240 miles of challenging terrain, including the Ardennes Forest, in eleven days, bypassing the entrenched British and French forces who had mistakenly assumed the Ardennes was impassable.[39] Paratroopers sometimes landed ahead of the advance, causing chaos behind enemy lines; the British press described these soldiers as "heavily drugged, fearless, and berserk."[40]

General Heinz Guderian, an expert in tank warfare and leader of the invasion, gave the order to speed ahead to the French border: "I demand that you go sleepless for at least three nights if that should be necessary."[41] The surprise attack was designed to catch the French off guard in the north of the country so that the Germans could cross into French territory before the army could redeploy the troops it had concentrated along the Maginot Line to the south or in Belgium (where the German attack had mistakenly been expected to come from).

General Graf von Kielmansegg had ordered 20,000 pills for the 1st Panzer Division, who swallowed them on the night of May 10. No one slept that night as the Germans began their invasion.[42] It took three days to reach the French border, with many soldiers not sleeping during the entire campaign.[43] When they crossed into France, French reinforcements had yet to arrive, and their defenses were overwhelmed by the German attack. Guderian was astonished: "I had ordered you not to sleep for forty-eight hours. You kept going for seventeen days."[44] Hitler was even more surprised, and indeed did not believe it when first informed that his troops were already in France. The reply to his general was: "Your message is a mistake."[45]

"I was dumbfounded," Churchill wrote in his memoirs, recalling the astonishing speed of the German forces and the collapse of the French defenses. "I had never expected to have to face . . . the overrunning of the whole of the communications and countryside by an irresistible incursion of armoured vehicles. . . . I admit this was one of the greatest surprises I have had in my life."[46] The speed of the attack was jaw-dropping. High on Pervitin, German tank and artillery drivers covered ground night and day, almost without stopping. Foreign commanders and civilians alike were caught entirely off guard.[47]

Ranke, who rode with General Guderian and his tanks for more than 500 kilometers in three days, kept a detailed military diary, which included passages revealing the importance of Pervitin. A medical officer of the Panzer troops reported to Ranke that units were taking two to five Pervitin tablets per driver each day. Ranke also noted that it was mostly the "General Staff officers . . . who knew and valued Pervitin and asked me for it."[48] The Waffen-SS, the elite corps of the Nazi Party, was also taking large doses of the drug: "Set off 10 o'clock via the reconnaissance route of the 10th Panzer Division. Took pictures of the SS, very disciplined in spite of long journey. Dropped off 2000 Pervitin there with troop doctor."[49]

Some users reported negative side effects of the drug. During the French invasion, these included a lieutenant colonel with the Panzer Ersatz Division I, who experienced heart pains after taking Pervitin four times daily for as many weeks; the commander of the Twelfth Tank Division, who was rushed to a military hospital due to the heart attack he suffered an hour after taking one pill; and several officers who suffered heart attacks while off duty after taking Pervitin.[50]

German airmen also turned to Pervitin during their nighttime bombing raids over Britain. As Britain downed more and more German planes, bombing missions during the day were deemed too dangerous.[51] Pervitin tablets, which the airmen nicknamed "pilot salt," "stuka pills," and "Göring pills," came in handy for long night flights.[52] One bomber pilot explained:

> The launch was very often late, ten o'clock, eleven o'clock, and then you were over London or some other English city at about one or two in the morning, and of course then you're tired. So you took one or two Pervitin tablets, and then you were all right again. . . . I had a lot of night operations, you know. And, of course, the commander always has to have his wits about him. So I took Pervitin as a precautionary measure. Imagine the commander being tired in battle! Uh, yes, please, that's not going to work. . . . One wouldn't abstain from Pervitin because of a little health scare. Who cares when you're doomed to come down at any moment anyway![53]

Another German pilot reported flying high on meth over the Mediterranean: "In my knee pocket there is a hand-length strip of linen covered with cellophane, with five or six milk-white tablets stuck to it, the size of a chocolate bar. The label reads: 'Pervitin.' Tablets against fatigue. I open the bag and tear first two, then three of these tablets from the pad, take the breathing mask off my face for a moment and start chewing the tablets. They taste repellently bitter and floury, and I've got nothing to wash them down with." Then the drug starts to take effect. "The engine is running cleanly and calmly. I'm wide awake, my heartbeat thunders in my ears. Why is the sky suddenly so bright, my eyes hurt in the harsh light. I can hardly bear the brilliance; if I shield my eyes with my free hand it's better. Now the engine is humming evenly and without vibration—far away, very far away. It's almost like silence up here. Everything becomes immaterial and abstract. Remote, as if I were flying above my plane."[54] Eventually he lands:

> I kept my course precisely, in spite of my euphoric indifference and my seemingly weightless state. Upon landing, I find the place in a state of complete stasis. Nothing moves, there's no one to be seen, rubble of the hangars forlornly looms . . . between the bomb craters. As I roll on to the squadron's stand my right tyre bursts. I've probably driven over a bomb splinter. Later I meet Dr Sperrling and ask him in passing what kind of "crap" this Pervitin really is, and whether it

mightn't be better to warn pilots in advance? When he learns that I've taken three tablets, he nearly faints, and forbids me to touch a plane, even from outside, for the rest of the day.[55]

Military physicians also kept themselves going on Pervitin.[56] On a visit to France in July 1940, Ranke collected reports on the personal experiences of twenty medical officers. More than two-thirds of them had used Pervitin. Of those, over half had consumed it with alcohol in an effort to drink even more, stay up later at a party, or remedy a hangover. These same physicians were responsible for dispensing the drug to the troops.[57]

At the same time, Conti continued to express concern about overusing Pervitin, stating in a 1940 speech to the National Socialist Medical Association, "Giving it to a top pilot who must fly for another two hours while fighting fatigue is probably right. It may not, however, be used for every case of tiredness where fatigue can in reality only be compensated by sleep. As physicians this ought to be clear to us immediately."[58] Though his warnings were largely ignored by the military, Conti nevertheless persisted, turning to a scientist friend to author an article critical of Pervitin. Titled "The Pervitin Problem," the article was published the following year and caught the attention of scientists and doctors alike.[59]

Amid growing worries about the addictive potential and negative side effects of overusing the drug, the German military began to cut back on allocations of methamphetamine by the end of 1940. Consumption declined sharply in 1941 and 1942, when the medical establishment formally acknowledged that amphetamines were addictive.[60] The German Health Ministry included Pervitin under the Opium Law in June 1941, making illicit consumption of the drug punishable by law. The following year, the military issued new guidelines to medical officers noting the danger of addiction, though the recommended dosage remained the same.[61]

Nevertheless, the drug continued to be dispensed on both the western and eastern fronts. Temmler-Werke, the maker of the drug, remained as profitable as ever, despite rising awareness of its side effects.[62] Indeed, Wehrmacht medical services sent 10 million methamphetamine tablets to the eastern front in the first half of 1942 alone.[63] Gerd Schmückle of the 7th Panzer Division recounted his experience with Pervitin while fighting in Ukraine in November 1943 as follows: "I could not sleep. During the attack I had taken too much Pervitin. We had all been dependent on it for a long time. Everyone swallowed the stuff, more frequently and in greater doses. The pills seemed to remove the sense of agitation. I slid into a world of bright indifference. Danger lost its edge. One's own power seemed to increase. After the battle one hovered in a strange state of intoxication in which a deep need for sleep fought with a clear alertness."[64]

The Wehrmacht high command and the Reich Ministry for Arms and Ammunition concluded shortly before the invasion of Russia that Pervitin was "decisive for the outcome of the war."[65] Immediate military necessity pushed aside all health concerns. Battling the Red Army and surviving the extreme conditions of the winter of 1941–1942 was of more immediate consequence than the longer-term health ramifications of chemical assistance. As a result, the production of Pervitin continued, and the tablets were shipped to the Russian front.[66]

The pills also came in handy as the war turned against Germany. When Panzer Captain Hans von Luck was transferred from Russia to the 3rd Reconnaissance Battalion of the Afrika Korps in January 1942, he told his comrade: "We'll drive without stopping until we're out of Russia. We'll relieve each other every 100 kilometers, swallow Pervitin and stop only for fuel."[67]

That same month, a group of 500 German soldiers were given Pervitin as they attempted to retreat from the Soviet Army encircling them in the northern sector of the eastern front. The escape was successful, as reported by the medical officer:

Many comrades showed signs of total exhaustion: staggering, a complete loss of interest and willpower, pain and cramps in the leg muscles, the calves and groin especially, palpitation, pain in the chest, and nausea. Around midnight (6 hours after the retreat had started) some of the troops repeatedly tried to lie down in the snow, their willpower could not be aroused despite vehement encouragement. These men were given 2 pills of Pervitin each. After half an hour the first men confirmed their improved state of health. They were marching properly again, stayed in line, were more confident and took notice of their surroundings. The pain in the muscles was borne more easily. Some proved to be in a slightly euphoric mood.[68]

As the end of the war neared, an increasingly desperate Germany looked for a pharmacological miracle. In March 1944, Vice-Admiral Hellmuth Heye met with pharmacists, chemists, and army commanders to come up with a new wonder drug.[69] Pharmacologist Gerhard Orzechowski was tasked with creating a pill to increase fighting endurance and boost self-esteem. D-IX was the result, a combination of five milligrams of cocaine, three milligrams of Pervitin, and five milligrams of a morphine-based pain reliever (a combination known today as a speedball).[70] The Allies invaded Germany before the drug could go into mass production. Orzechowski was nevertheless able to test the stimulant at the Sachsenhausen concentration camp, where prisoners were given D-IX and ordered to march continuously with forty-four-pound backpacks.[71]

Meanwhile, as the war ground on, Hitler himself became a junkie dictator. Publicly, the Führer chastised those who could not abstain from drugs: "The higher a man rises the more he has to be able to abstain. . . . If a street-sweeper is unwilling to sacrifice his tobacco or his beer, then I think, 'Very well, my good man, that's precisely why you're a street-sweeper and not one of the ruling personalities of the State!'"[72] Yet the head of state was an addict. While he avoided tobacco, alcohol, and caffeine, he was routinely injected with various painkillers and hormones, as well as mood- and mind-altering substances. Hitler's personal physician, Dr. Theodor Morell, who kept a detailed diary of his experience, gave the leader regular injections of a mixture of cocaine, amphetamines, synthetic morphine, glucose, testosterone, and corticosteroids, among other substances.[73] Hitler was reportedly given eighty-two different drugs during his years in power.[74]

## Pill-Popping Allies

The Germans were not the only ones doping up their soldiers. Allied forces, first the British and then the Americans, also became enthusiastic pill poppers, and their use of amphetamines increased even as the Germans were tapering off their dependence in response to health concerns.[75]

The British armed forces distributed 72 million standard-dose amphetamine tablets during the war.[76] Some sources suggest that the Royal Air Force first turned to the drug after a downed German pilot was found to have methamphetamine tablets on him during a bombing raid on Britain in June 1940.[77] Physiologist Henry Dale identified the tablets as methamphetamine and suggested further studies.[78] Word spread that the German war effort was chemically assisted. A September 13, 1940, Italian press report claimed that the Germans were using a "courage pill" as a secret weapon to keep their troops going, and the British Broadcasting Company followed up with a story about German pilots chemically enhanced by Pervitin.[79]

The British had their own strategic reasons for using stimulants: protecting the Atlantic sea convoys bringing supplies from the United States involved flying long-range planes for long hours, day and night, and anything that helped keep pilots awake and alert was welcomed. Some pilots had already been taking Benzedrine amphetamine tablets, nicknamed "co-pilots," on their own before the Royal Air Force began to distribute them. The recommended dose was two five-milligram Benzedrine tablets per long-range air patrol flight.[80] This dosage instruction was based on a report from R. H. Winfield, a Royal Air Force medical officer, who had tested the in-flight effects of the drug while accompanying crews on more than a dozen missions.[81]

The Royal Air Force had even more reason to promote amphetamine use once its pilots began high-altitude nighttime bombing raids over Germany. As these became more routine, Winfield was again tasked with testing the drug, flying along on twenty bombing missions between August 1941 and July 1942 to observe its effects. Winfield reported that pilots on Benzedrine were often more alert and less risk-averse— precisely what the Royal Air Force was hoping to find. Crucially, the drug also helped pilots stay awake on the long late-night return flight home. The drug, Winfield concluded, helped airmen achieve "peak efficiency." He advised that amphetamine pills be routinely distributed to all aircrews, and this recommendation was adopted as official policy in 1942.[82]

The British army also embraced the pills. As reflected in a paper by Brigadier Q.V.B. Wallace, the deputy director of medical services for the 10th Armoured Corps:

> "Pep" tablets, i.e. Benzedrine tablets, were used for the first time in the Middle East on a large scale. 20,000 tablets were issued to the ADMS [assistant director of medical services] of each division . . . who was responsible for their distribution and safe custody. The initial dose was 1.5 tablets two hours before the maximum benefit was required, followed six hours later by another tablet, with a further and final tablet for another six hours, if required. . . . I consider that "Pep" tablets may be very useful in certain cases, particularly where long-continued work is required over extended periods, i.e., staff officers, signallers, lorry drivers, transport workers, etc. The tablets must only be used when an extreme state of tiredness has been reached. The tablets have practically no ill-effects, and an ordinary night's sleep restores the individual to his original working capacity.[83]

General Bernard Montgomery, who assumed command of the 8th Army in North Africa in August 1942, promoted regular use of Benzedrine among his troops as a way to chemically enhance their will and capacity to go on the offensive against Erwin Rommel's Afrika Korps, the German expeditionary force on the continent. Preparations for his October 23, 1942, attack included the distribution of 100,000 Benzedrine pills. The Battle of El Alamein, the first significant British victory of the war, and one that marked a decisive shift in the military fate of North Africa, was clearly drug-assisted, even if the importance of the drug in determining its outcome is far less clear.[84]

The Americans were as eager as the British to exploit the performance-enhancing potential of amphetamines in wartime. Their usage started with the air force, which ordered large supplies of Benzedrine from Smith, Kline & French in late 1942. The Air Surgeons Office considered Benzedrine the most effective drug "for temporarily postponing sleep when desire for sleep endangers the security of the mission."[85] Benzedrine pills were included in the emergency kits of American bombers by 1943.[86] A March 25, 1945, *New York Times* article titled "With a B-29 over Japan—a Pilot's Story" revealed how the use of "bennies" had become routine for long-range bomber flights, during which the navigator "just rubs his tired eyes, takes some more Benzedrine and goes to work again."[87]

The army followed suit, adding amphetamine tablets to soldiers' medical kits in 1943, as did the navy. The naval base in San Diego even housed amphetamine factories to supply troops deployed to the South Pacific. Benzedrine tablets were included in their field kits.[88] At the bloody Battle of Tarawa, fought on a Japanese-held atoll in the Pacific between November 20 and 23, 1943, American troops reportedly took large doses of amphetamine.[89]

The total amount of Benzedrine consumed by the US military during World War II is unknown. What we do know is that the military bought $877,000 in Benzadrine Sulfate tablets from Smith, Kline & French during the war.[90] As Rasmussen points out, this was enough pills to put almost all 12 million US servicemembers operating abroad in contact with the drug.[91] The British also supplied US servicemen with almost 80 million additional Benzedrine tablets and pills.[92] One study at an American military hospital at the conclusion of the war indicated that a quarter of the patients abused amphetamines, and that almost all of them had been regular users of the drug while deployed.[93]

Smith, Kline & French not only ramped up production to keep up with the wartime demand but ran commercials praising Benzedrine's contribution to the war effort. One advertisement depicted a group of deployed American GIs with the line, "For Men in Combat When the Going Gets Tough." Another advertisement proudly announced, "Benzedrine inhaler is now an official item of issue in the Army Air Forces." Physicians in the armed forces were targeted with advertisements offering free Benzedrine inhalers for "personal use."[94]

## Kamikaze's Flying High and Japan's First Drug Epidemic

The Japanese imperial government also sought to give its fighting capacity a pharmacological edge, contracting out methamphetamine production to domestic pharmaceutical companies for use during the war.[95] The tablets, under the trade name Philopon (also known as Hiropin), were distributed to pilots for long flights and to soldiers for combat.[96] In addition, the government gave munitions workers and those laboring in other factories methamphetamine tablets to increase their productivity.[97] The Japanese called the war stimulants *senryoku zokyo zai*, or "drug to inspire the fighting spirits."[98] Workers in the defense industry and other war-related fields were compelled to take drugs to help boost their output.[99] Strong prewar inhibitions against drug use were pushed aside. The introduction of what is now the illegal drug of choice in Japan therefore began with state-promoted use during World War II.

It is not difficult to understand the appeal of methamphetamines in wartime Japan. Total war required total mobilization, from factory to battlefield.[100] Pilots, soldiers, naval crews, and laborers were all routinely pushed beyond their natural limits to stay awake longer and work harder. As one group of scholars notes, in Japan, "taking stimulants to enhance performance was a mark of patriotism."[101] Kamikaze pilots in particular took large doses of methamphetamine via injection before their suicide missions.[102] They were also given pep pills stamped with the crest of the emperor. These consisted of methamphetamine mixed with green tea powder and were called *Totsugeki-Jo* or *Tokkou-Jo*, known otherwise as "storming tablets."[103] Most kamikaze pilots were young men, often in their late teens. Before they received their injection of Philopon, the pilots undertook a warrior ceremony in which they were presented with sake, wreaths of flowers, and decorated headbands.[104]

Although soldiers on all sides in World War II returned home with an amphetamine habit,[105] the problem was most severe in Japan, which experienced the first drug epidemic in the history of the country.[106] Many soldiers and factory workers who had become hooked on the drug during the war continued to consume it into the postwar years. Users could get their hands on amphetamines because the Imperial Army's postwar surplus had been dumped into the domestic market.[107] At the time of its surrender in 1945, Japan had massive stockpiles of Hiropin in warehouses, military hospitals, supply depots, and caves scattered throughout the islands.[108] Some of the supply was sent to public dispensaries for distribution as medicine, but the rest was diverted to the black market rather than destroyed.[109] The country's Yakuza crime syndicate took over much of the distribution, and the drug trade would eventually become its most important source of revenue.[110]

Any tablets not diverted to illicit markets remained in the hands of pharmaceutical companies. The drug companies mounted advertising campaigns to encourage consumers to purchase the over-the-counter medicine.[111] Sold under the name "wake-a-mine," the product was pitched as offering "enhanced vitality."[112] According to one journalist, these companies also sold "hundreds of thousands of pounds" of "military-made liquid meth" left over from the war to the public, with no prescription required to purchase the drug. With an estimated 5 percent of Japanese between the ages of eighteen and twenty-five taking the drug, many became intravenous addicts.[113]

The presence of US military bases on the islands contributed to the epidemic. The national newspaper *Asahi Shinbun* wrote that US servicemen were responsible for spreading amphetamine usage from large cities to small towns. Indeed, the country's Narcotics Section arrested 623 American soldiers for drug trafficking in 1953. However, most drug scandals involving US soldiers garnered little coverage by the major papers out of "deference" to "American-Japanese friendship."[114]

By 1954, there were 550,000 illicit amphetamine users in Japan.[115] This epidemic led to strict state regulation of the drug.[116] The 1951 Stimulant Control Law banned methamphetamine possession, and penalties for the offense were increased in 1954.[117] In 1951 some 17,500 people were arrested for amphetamine abuse, and by 1954 the number had spiked to 55,600.[118] During the early 1950s, arrests in Japan for stimulant offenses made up more than 90 percent of total drug arrests.[119] In a 1954 Ministry of Welfare anonymous survey, 7.5 percent of respondents reported having sampled Hiropon.[120] Meanwhile, *Asahi Shinbun* published an estimate that 1.5 million Japanese used methamphetamine in 1954.[121] The high rates of amphetamine use in Japan began to subside by the late 1950s and early 1960s as economic growth began to create jobs.[122] Nevertheless, it is striking that methamphetamine would remain the most popular illicit drug in Japan for decades to come.[123]

Germany, meanwhile, did not experience the same postwar surge in stimulant use found in Japan, in part because the occupation dismantled domestic production. The area where Temmler-Werke had produced Pervitin came under Soviet occupation, and the factory was expropriated. At the same time, American pharmaceutical companies bought up the firm's production facilities in the western zones, and it would take years for Temmler-Werke to restart production in its new Marburg location. Moreover, Germany had already imposed tighter controls on Pervitin during the war, making it less accessible even before the war came to an end.[124]

## Superpower on Speed

In contrast to the tapering off of use in postwar Germany, amphetamine consumption in the United States took off. Pharmacologist Leslie Iversen writes that "the non-medical use of amphetamines spread rapidly in the 20 years after the Second World War. This was partly due to the attitude of the medical community to these drugs, which continued to view them as safe and effective medicines, and partly due to the widespread exposure of US military personnel to D-amphetamine during the war."[125] By the late 1950s, pharmaceutical companies in the United States were legally manufacturing 3.5 billion tablets annually— equivalent to twenty doses of five to fifteen milligrams for every American.[126]

Of all major powers in the decades after World War II, the United States stood out for its continued heavy use of speed in the military. Indeed, although amphetamines had been widely available to US servicemembers during World War II, they became standard issue during the Korean War (1950–1953).[127] Smith, Kline & French was more than happy to be the supplier of choice once again, although this time it was supplying the military with dextroamphetamine (sold under the brand name Dexedrine), which was almost twice as potent on a milligram basis as the Benzedrine used during World War II. The manufacturer insisted that the drug had no negative side effects and was nonaddictive.[128]

In addition to coming home hooked on speed, some servicemen returning from the Korean War also introduced to the United States new methods of ingesting the drug. Dr. Roger C. Smith, who ran the Amphetamine Research Project at the Haight-Ashbury Free Clinic, notes that the first reported case of Americans engaging in intravenous methamphetamine abuse involved servicemen based in Korea and Japan in the early 1950s. It is perhaps no coincidence that East Asia was at that time "awash in supplies of liquid meth left over from World War II."[129]

Moreover, returning soldiers may have been some of the first to build meth labs in the United States. Following numerous arrests in 1962 of California doctors who were illegally prescribing injectable methamphetamine to patients, and pharmaceutical companies' voluntary withdrawal of the drug from stores, those looking for a profit or a fix came up with a solution. Several Korean War veterans reportedly got together in the San Francisco Bay Area to build the first meth labs to take advantage of the scarcity of the drug after the recall of Methderine and Desoxyn.[130]

High levels of amphetamine use among the US armed forces persisted into the Vietnam War. Although the recommended dose was twenty milligrams of Dexedrine for forty-eight hours of combat-readiness, the reality was that the drug was handed out, as one soldier put it, "like candies," with little attention to dosage or frequency of use.[131] Elton Manzione, a member of a long-range reconnaissance platoon, acknowledged: "We had the best amphetamines available and they were supplied by the U.S. government." A navy commando noted, "When I was a SEAL team member in Vietnam, the drugs were routinely consumed. They gave you a sense of bravado as well as keeping you awake. Every sight and sound was heightened. You were wired into it all and at times you felt really invulnerable."[132]

The US military supplied its troops with more than 225 million doses of Dexedrine (and the French-manufactured Obestol) during the war.[133] Soldiers could also buy amphetamines over the counter in many cities and towns in Vietnam.[134] Grinspoon and Hedblom argue that all the attention given to illicit drug consumption by soldiers during the Vietnam War glossed over the more severe problem of amphetamine addiction.[135]

A key source of information on amphetamine use in Vietnam was the 1971 *Inquiry into Alleged Drug Abuse in the Armed Services*, a report of the House of Representatives Committee on Armed Services. The report noted that due to increased safety concerns, amphetamines had been removed from survival kits by 1971, and prescriptions of these drugs had sharply declined: in 1966 the US Navy issued the equivalent of 33 million ten-milligram capsules of amphetamine, but by 1970 this number had dropped to 7 million capsules.[136] Though these numbers demonstrated reductions in usage over time, they also revealed the high rates of amphetamine use in the US military during the Vietnam War.

According to another report published in 1971, *The Fourth Report by the Select Committee on Crime*, "Over the past 4 years, the Navy seems to have required more stimulants than any other branch of the services. Their annual, active duty, pill-per-person requirement averaged 21.1 during the years 1966–69. The Air Force has flown almost as high by requiring 17.5 ten milligram doses per person in those years. The Army comes in last, averaging 13.8 doses per person per year."[137] Grinspoon and Hedblom point out that these figures suggest that from 1966 to 1969, members of the US Army alone took more amphetamines than all British or American armed forces in the Second World War.[138] They note that even as the military launched a campaign against heroin, it continued to overlook amphetamine use, and indeed routinely supplied the drug to the troops in Southeast Asia as late as 1973.[139]

In the following years, even as amphetamines came to be tightly controlled at home, the US Air Force kept dispensing them to pilots.[140] Dexedrine was given to the crews of F-111 aircraft for their thirteen-hour-long missions to Libya during Operation El Dorado Canyon in mid-April 1986. The drug was again given out in late December 1989 during Operation Just Cause in Panama, and during the 1990–1991 Gulf War, almost two-thirds of fighter jet pilots in Operation Desert Shield and more than half in Operation Desert Storm took amphetamines.[141] Operations Desert Shield and Storm saw the deployment of aircraft from the continental United States to the Arabian Peninsula, a trip that required a fifteen-hour flight across five to seven time zones.[142] One pilot admitted, "Without go pills I would have fallen asleep maybe 10 to 15 times."[143]

In 1991 Air Force Chief of Staff General Merrill McPeak temporarily banned amphetamines, saying the pills were no longer needed with the ending of combat operations in Iraq. But in 1996 Air Force Chief of Staff John Jumper quietly reversed the ban.[144] At the turn of the century, supplying amphetamines to US aircrews remained standard practice, though the air force had its crews sign a consent form emphasizing that taking the pills was voluntary. The form appeared to both leave the decision of whether to take Dexedrine up to the pilot and compel the pilot to take the medication with him on the flight.[145]

A study of dextroamphetamine use during B-2 combat missions in Operation Iraqi Freedom revealed high rates of amphetamine use among pilots. The pilots flew B-2 bombers from either Whiteman Air Force Base in Montana or a forward deployed location to targets in Iraq. Pilots on the shorter missions used dextroamphetamine on 97 percent of their sorties, while those on the longer missions used the drug in 57 percent of sorties.[146] The puzzling difference between these two rates was partly explained by the fact that napping was more often possible on longer flights, reducing pilots' need for the drug.

Moreover, the US military's spending on stimulant medications, such as the amphetamine drugs Ritalin and Adderall, reportedly reached $39 million in 2010 alone, up from $7.5 million in 2001—a jump of more than 500 percent. Medical officers were writing 32,000 prescriptions for Ritalin and Adderall for active-duty servicemembers every year, up from only 3,000 five years earlier. It remains unclear whether these prescriptions were to counter attention-deficit/hyperactivity disorder (ADHD) or fatigue, but, as psychiatrist Richard A. Friedman notes, "short of an unlikely epidemic of that disorder among our soldiers, the military almost certainly uses the stimulants to help fatigued and sleep-deprived troops stay alert and awake."[147]

Meanwhile, US Air Force researchers continued to insist that pilot use of amphetamines enhanced their fighting capacity while decreasing accidents. Dr. John A. Caldwell, writing in *Air & Space Power Journal*, defended amphetamine use by arguing that for pilots in the War on Terror, "around-the-clock operations, rapid time-zone transitions, and uncomfortable sleep environments are common on the battle-field; unfortunately, these conditions prevent personnel from obtaining the eight solid hours of sleep required for optimum day-to-day functioning."[148]

### *Breaking Bad* in the Middle East

The use of amphetamines on the battlefield, a practice once largely monopolized by states, also increasingly extended to irregular combatants, ranging from Syrian rebels and Islamic State (IS) recruits to suicide bombers and child soldiers. Illicit supplies of Captagon became particularly popular battlefield stimulants, described as the "drug of choice" for fighters in the Syrian civil war.[149] Captagon is the trade name for fenetylline, an amphetamine-type stimulant developed in Germany in the 1960s to treat ADHD and other disorders but banned in most countries in the 1980s. The pills became a favorite party drug in Saudi Arabia, Kuwait, and the United Arab Emirates.[150] Although stamped "Captagon," most seized pills in the Middle East contained amphetamines that were easier and less expensive to produce than fenetylline. Costing only a few cents to make in Lebanon and Syria, each tiny counterfeit Captagon pill sold for as much as $20.[151] Syria's niche in Captagon manufacturing predated the outbreak of the war, perhaps due to the country's sizeable pharmaceutical industry with the requisite expertise and availability of precursor chemicals and pill-pressing machinery.[152]

Combatants could simultaneously energize and fund themselves with the drug. According to Reuters, "Reports of seizures and interviews with people connected to the trade suggest it generates hundreds of millions of dollars in annual revenues in Syria, potentially providing funding for weapons, while the drug itself helps combatants dig in for long,

Figure 5.4 Syrian police show seized Captagon pills in Damascus, January 2016 (Louai Beshara/AFP/Getty Images).

grueling battles."[153] Syrian state media frequently reported seizures of Captagon from captured fighters, with one officer commenting that interrogation techniques were changed to account for the effects of Captagon on prisoners: "We would beat them, and they wouldn't feel the pain. Many of them would laugh while we were dealing them heavy blows. . . We would leave the prisoners for about 48 hours without questioning them while the effects of Captagon wore off, and then the interrogation would become easier."[154]

A psychiatrist at a clinic that treated Captagon users in the government stronghold of Latakia noted that soldiers on both sides were likely users of the drug, "especially when they are assigned night duty or other long missions."[155] One former Syrian fighter described his amphetamine experience as follows: "So the brigade leader came and told us, 'this pill gives you energy, try it,'" he said. "So we took it the first time. We felt physically fit. And if there were 10 people in front of you, you could catch them and kill them. You're awake all the time. You don't have any problems, you don't even think about sleeping, you don't think to leave the checkpoint. It gives you great courage and power. If the leader told you to go break into a military barracks, I will break in with a brave heart and without feeling of fear at all—you're not even tired."[156]

The Islamic State was also allegedly distributing Captagon— nicknamed "the jihadists' drug"—and other stimulants to militants to boost their courage, motivation, and endurance, foster feelings of invincibility among fighters, and facilitate indoctrination.[157] Testimonials from Islamic State defectors pointed to the battlefield use of a Captagon-like drug:

> When we were fighting against nizam in Ras al-Ayn, there were loud sounds of explosions all around me and I was very scared. There was this guy from IS, he looked at me and realized that I was scared. Asked if I was afraid, I said, "Yes I am really scared." He gave me a tablet. It was very bitter and brown in color. I swallowed it. In thirty minutes, I became a different man—as if I am a hero. . . . It gave me so much power. I felt as if I am indestructible and unbeatable. I went back home on the fourth day without sleeping—after having taken this tablet. . . . Many of the IS members use this drug.[158]

Amphetamines have been the ultimate military performance-enhancing drug ever since they energized the battlefields of World War II. That war was not only the most destructive in human history but also the most pharmacologically enhanced. It was literally sped up by speed, with tens of millions of pills doled out to combatants to keep them fighting more and sleeping less. Despite their shift from being widely accessible to being strictly controlled in later decades, the pills have become the drug of choice for many combatants in the most war-ravaged region of the world and continue to be prescribed by the world's leading military power.

As we will see in the next chapter, it is thus striking that this same pill-popping military power went to war against another potent stimulant—cocaine. While the main war role of amphetamines was to stimulate soldiers, the main war role of cocaine was to stimulate the transformation of soldiers into antidrug warriors. In short, amphetamines turned soldiers into super-soldiers, but cocaine turned soldiering into policing. Our story therefore shifts from war *while on* drugs to the war *against* drugs.

# 6

## Cocaine Wars

NO DRUG HAS BEEN a target of war more than cocaine—and this striking distinction is therefore the main focus of this chapter. This also necessitates a focus on the United States and the Western Hemisphere, since Washington became the most enthusiastic promoter of a militarized regionwide campaign against cocaine in the last decades of the twentieth century. The US-led "war on drugs" went from metaphor to reality through cocaine-suppression efforts at home, at the border, and abroad. It was the cocaine boom that provided the rationale for officially classifying drugs as a threat to US national security for the first time in 1986 and for launching a war on cocaine that increasingly adopted the language and tactics of a real war. The obsession with cocaine drove the militarization of policing and the domestication of soldiering, blurring the lines between war fighting and crime fighting across the hemisphere. By the early 1990s, the drug war had come to replace the Cold War as the defining feature of US military relations with its southern neighbors, especially the cocaine-saturated Andean region. But before turning to this recent history, we need to briefly delve into the more distant past to see how we arrived at the point at which fighting a white powdery substance turned into a military crusade.

*Killer High*, Peter Andreas. Oxford University Press (2020). © Peter Andreas.
DOI: 10.1093/actrade/9780190463014.001.0001

## From Green Leaf to White Powder

The coca leaf—which in addition to many vitamins, proteins, and minerals contains small amounts of its principle psychoactive alkaloid, cocaine—was an integral part of Andean life long before the Spanish conquest of the Incas in 1532. Coca chewing dates back to at least 3000 BC, and the plant was one of the first to be domesticated in the Americas.[1] By the time the conquistadores arrived, the dried leaf of the coca shrub was considered sacred, enabling those who chewed it to overcome fatigue and heat exhaustion and ward off thirst and hunger. Users included Inca soldiers, who by chewing the leaf could travel farther and fight harder on fewer rations.[2] Coca also facilitated the Incas' pacification and co-optation of conquered tribal leaders, who were given bales of coca leaves once they pledged their loyalty to the Inca Empire.[3] Conquered communities also paid tribute to the Incas with gold, silver, and coca.[4]

The Spanish at first sought to ban coca but quickly reversed course, turning the leaf into a mass-consumption crop for the first time once they realized they could use it to motivate poorly fed native laborers in the fields and mines to work longer and harder. These benefits also had clear battlefield applications. Reports circulated that the Peruvian army was able to endure extreme cold and other hardships thanks to coca.[5] In the siege of La Paz in 1771, the besieged desperately turned to coca to survive, as retold by Golden Mortimer in his classic *History of Coca: The "Divine Plant" of the Incas*: "The inhabitants, after a blockade of several months, during a severe winter, ran short of provisions and were compelled to depend wholly on coca, of which happily there was a stock in the city. This apparently scanty sustenance was sufficient to banish hunger and to support fatigue, while enabling the soldiers to bear the intense cold."[6] General Miller, a British soldier embedded with the Peruvian army during Peru's War of Independence in the 1820s, similarly observed the positive impact that coca chewing had on the troops: "Their everyday pedestrian feats are truly astonishing. . . . A battalion, eight hundred strong, has been known to march thirteen or fourteen leagues in one day, without leaving more than ten or a dozen stragglers on the road."[7]

But the rest of the world was slow to embrace coca. Widely consumed in Peru and Bolivia as a benign workaday stimulant, the leaf did not catch on globally the way other psychoactive plants, such as tobacco, tea, and coffee, did. Part of the reason was that the leaves lost their potency during long-distance transport, and production remained confined to South America until the late nineteenth century. The typical method of ingestion may have also been off-putting, inhibiting colonists from taking to chewing coca the way they had to puffing tobacco—with the spread of the latter also undoubtedly aided by the fact that, unlike coca, tobacco was highly addictive.

Cocaine was first isolated from the coca plant in 1860 by Albert Niemann using Peruvian leaves from a carefully shipped thirty-pound package.[8] The German pharmaceutical company Merck began production of the drug in small batches in 1862, promoting it as "a stimulant which is peculiarly adapted to elevate the working ability of the body, without any dangerous effect."[9] Two decades later, the Bavarian army physician Theodore Aschenbrandt experimented with giving soldiers cocaine dissolved in water, and reported the drug's "eminent usefulness."[10] Those who took notice included medical student Sigmund Freud, who wrote to his fiancée that "a German has tested this stuff on soldiers and has reported that it has really rendered them strong and capable of endurance."[11] Freud purchased a gram of cocaine from Merck and in July 1884 published his famous essay *Über Coca*, which enthusiastically promoted the medical use of cocaine. He noted that small doses of the drug had done wonders for his own depression, with the effects described as "exhilaration and lasting euphoria."[12]

## World Wars and the Rise and Fall of Legal Cocaine

By the end of the nineteenth century, cocaine was widely embraced, a popular ingredient in patent medicines, drinks such as Coca-Cola, and other concoctions. The explosive growth in cocaine production made the drug far more accessible and affordable—prices fell sharply, from $280 per ounce in 1885 to approximately $3 in 1914—enabling a global epidemic that lasted until the mid-1920s.[13] Faster and more reliable transportation ensured that foreign markets could be supplied with the drug, with the crude alkaloid extracted in Peru for more efficient shipment to Europe. Before abruptly turning against the drug after 1910, the United States was the world's leading cocaine market, with most of the supply refined domestically from imported leaves (which, unlike crude cocaine, faced no import tariff).

Coca plant seedlings had also been brought to Java from Peru, and by the first years of the twentieth century the Dutch colony was producing a variety of coca rich in cocaine.[14] This propelled the rise of Nederlandsch Cocainefabrieck, an Amsterdam pharmaceutical company founded in 1900. During World War I, this firm took advantage of Holland's neutral status and proximity to the frontlines to sell cocaine to all sides.[15]

World War I was the first and only major armed conflict in which cocaine was widely consumed by combatants. Cocaine's short-lived historical moment on the battlefield was made possible by readily available legal supplies of the drug. Cocaine joined morphine as a popular pain medication but was also distributed to enhance combat performance. The drug was administered to the Australian Anzacs at the Battle of Gallipoli, and the British army handed out the first cocaine-based tablet on the market, manufactured by the London pharmaceutical company Burroughs Wellcome & Company under the trade name "Tabloid" or "Forced March." Tabloid was promoted with the promise that it "allays hunger and prolongs the power of endurance."[16]

At the same time, growing wartime public fear in Britain about the spread of recreational cocaine use, especially among soldiers, set off a moral panic that helped set the stage for more comprehensive drug bans after the war. London was the epicenter of the panic, where hundreds of thousands of troops were either on leave or passing through on their way to or from the Western Front. The media added fuel to the public hysteria over the availability of nonmedical cocaine, with the *Times* denouncing the drug as a threat even "more deadly than bullets." In early 1916 a number of prominent London stores, including Harrods and Savory & Moore, were fined for selling cocaine to soldiers. A few months earlier, Savory & Moore had advertised a mail-order medical kit that included cocaine and heroin. Harrods had promoted small packages of cocaine and morphine as "A Useful Present for Friends at the Front." The *Times*, which had earlier run ads for cocaine products, now denounced the drug as a threat to military effectiveness, with one of its journalists writing that cocaine provided a "terrible tempta- tion" to the soldier, offering short-term relief but ultimately rendering him "worthless as a soldier and a man." The *Daily Chronicle* added to the public outcry by reporting that cocaine could potentially turn soldiers mad.[17]

London prostitutes, popularly known as "cocaine girls" or "dope girls," were blamed as illicit distributors of the drug to vulnerable soldiers. Politicians, military leaders, and the media all pointed an ac- cusatory finger at Germany, blaming this pioneer in the development and production of cocaine for supplying the drug to military personnel as a secret weapon of war to weaken their will and capacity to fight. On May 11, 1916, the Army Council responded to mounting public pressure by prohibiting the unauthorized provision of cocaine, as well as a number of other drugs, to military personnel, with a penalty of six months in jail for violators. Additional cocaine-focused restrictions were imposed through Defence of the Realm Regulation 40B, issued on July 28, 1916.[18]

These wartime controls laid the groundwork for the postwar British ban that followed, the Dangerous Drugs Act of 1920, which applied to both military personnel and civilians.[19] Thus, the origin of British antidrug laws can be traced to the country's wartime drug experience, spurred by the public panic over cocaine.[20] These new restrictions brought Britain more in line with the type of drug controls strongly advocated by the United States.

Germany's defeat in the war brought with it a rollback of the country's pharmaceutical industry's once-dominant influence over the cocaine industry in Europe. As a result, Germany was now less equipped to push back against the mounting US-led international drive toward tighter controls. Germany also began to turn against the drug as a consequence of its own immediate postwar domestic abuse problem, which included a spike in cocaine-related hospital emer- gency room visits.[21] Adding to the momentum toward restriction was the Dutch government's decision to fully comply with the regulations of the 1925 International Convention Relating to Dangerous Drugs, signed in Geneva, which prompted a downsizing and diversification of Dutch cocaine producers.[22]

Meanwhile, Japan had become the main cocaine producer and distributor in East Asia, having cultivated coca and processed crude cocaine in substantial quantities on colonial Formosa (Taiwan) since the early 1920s. Japanese-owned companies also ran plantations in Java. Even as Japanese leaders paid lip service to the cocaine manufacturing restrictions outlined in successive Geneva conventions of the League of Nations, the country's pharmaceutical companies turned into the region's biggest cocaine supplier, through both licit and illicit channels.[23]

World War II and its aftermath killed off legal cocaine. The US military occupation wiped out the Japanese cocaine industry that had grown up in the 1920s and 1930s, and the United States also uprooted the last remnants of coca production in Java, which Japan had invaded during the war.[24] More generally, postwar US hegemony also meant the hegemony of the US antidrug agenda, including the global criminalization of cocaine. The United States had for decades been an antidrug crusader, but only with the postwar transformation of the geopolitical context did it finally have an opening to fully promote prohibition on a global scale. This included exerting its influence via the newly formed United Nations Commission on Narcotics Drugs (which in 1961 produced the UN Single Convention on Narcotic Drugs).

The hostility of US drug warriors toward cocaine had even blocked wartime exploration of potential new military uses of coca. For instance, shortly before Pearl Harbor, the US Army reached out to the Bureau of Narcotics about research on the possible benefits of coca chewing or coca tea, but the proposal was rejected.[25] And during the war, US drug tsar Harry Anslinger banned research on the physiology of coca and cocaine as a possible performance enhancer for high-altitude naval jet pilots.[26]

After the war, coca cultivation fully retreated to its Andean origins and its indigenous consumer base. Cocaine would only reemerge in later years as an illicit drug handled by criminal organizations rather than pharmaceutical companies. Having been heavily dependent on Germany and Japan as customers before war broke out and then having been entirely cut off from these Axis consumers during the war, Peru's already struggling crude-cocaine manufacturers were now put out of business. The US anticocaine agenda became Peru's agenda as the country moved swiftly, even if reluctantly, to criminalize the drug in the late 1940s. "At war's end," writes drug historian Paul Gootenberg, "legal cocaine came to its last crossroad, as Peru faced the United States alone on the global stage. Former German, Dutch, and Japanese cocaine networks now lay physically demolished by warfare or under U.S. occupation."[27]

### The Cold War Birth and Boom of Illicit Cocaine

But even as the legal cocaine industry became a casualty of war, an illegal cocaine industry slowly came to life in its Cold War aftermath. What began as a trickle of Andean cocaine measured in ounces and pounds in the late 1940s and early 1950s would turn into tens and then hundreds of kilos in the 1960s and a tidal wave of multiton shipments in the 1970s and beyond. The initial pioneers of illicit cocaine involved a loose network of Peruvians, Mexicans, Chileans, Argentines, and Cubans.[28]

Cuba served as the nascent hub of illicit cocaine culture and trafficking in the 1950s. Havana was one of the world's first "postwar global sin capitals," as Gootenberg describes it. "Havana's notorious gambling and pleasure clubs, and its freewheeling prostitution industry, became the era's pioneer test market of cocaine. The spreading modern taste for cocaine, including that of curious American tourists, was a Cuban invention."[29]

The 1959 Cuban Revolution profoundly disrupted and reconfigured the still-infant illicit cocaine trade. Havana's drug dealers fled as part of the diaspora of Cuban nationals, becoming the core players in the postrevolution pan-American cocaine business.[30] A November 1961 Federal Bureau of Narcotics memo on the cocaine trade noted that "in most of our cases, where we are able to trace the cocaine back to the source of supply in South America, there is usually a Cuban involved somewhere along the line. . . . It appears that Cubans are taking over as middlemen . . . smuggling cocaine into this country." Cubans were reportedly "the only people able to bring cocaine into this country in any quantity or regularity."[31]

Anslinger nevertheless attempted to publicly place the blame on Castro's Cuba, charging that Havana was "full of cocaine coming up from Bolivia."[32] He accused Cuba of not only profiting from cocaine but using it to drug dissidents.[33] Castro replied to Anslinger's insistence that Cuba deport its "hoodlums" by publicly proclaiming, "We are not only disposed to deport the gangsters but to shoot them. Send us that list and they will see. . . . Evidently the Commissioner has not heard that there has been a Revolution here."[34]

The reality was that Cuba's gangsters had already deported themselves, with a large contingent of them settling in Miami. Indeed, between 1959 and 1966, almost all of the Cubans busted in Florida for drug trafficking (mostly involving cocaine) had entered the state after Castro took power. Similarly, in New York during this same period, most of those convicted for cocaine trafficking were Cuban.[35] Far from colluding with Castro, these Cuban exiles were passionately anticommunist. Many were recruited and trained by the CIA for the Bay of Pigs operation but returned to Miami after its failure.

Meanwhile, cocaine use in America began to rise in the late 1960s and early 1970s, partly as the result of stricter federal controls over other stimulants such as amphetamines.[36] In 1979 the National Institute on Drug Abuse estimated that cocaine use in the United States had nearly tripled in two years.[37] By 1980, there were twice as many cocaine dealers as heroin dealers in New York City.[38] Initially, many cocaine users were middle class and affluent—powder cocaine was a relatively expensive "status drug"—although large numbers of lower-income drug users were inhaling it when they could afford it.[39]

Cocaine was considered by users, and even by many medical authorities, to be nonaddictive, because habitual users did not experience the physiological symptoms of heroin withdrawal.[40] As Time reported in July 1981, "Superficially, coke is a supremely beguiling and relatively risk-free drug—at least so its devotees innocently claim. A snort in each nostril and you're up and away for 30 minutes or so. Alert, witty and with it. No hangover. No physical addiction. No lung cancer. No holes in the arms or burned-out cells in the brain. Instead, drive, sparkle, energy."[41] The magazine's cover illustration—a martini glass filled with cocaine—captured its new status as America's most fashionable drug. Similarly, the Time story also captured the upbeat attitude toward the drug: "Whatever the price, by whatever name, cocaine is becoming the all-American drug. No longer is it a sinful secret of the moneyed elite, nor merely an elusive glitter of decadence in raffish society circles, as it seemed in decades past." It continued: "Today, in part precisely because it is such an emblem of wealth and status, coke is the drug of choice of perhaps millions of solid, conventional and often upwardly mobile citizens."[42]

Colombian smuggling entrepreneurs were perfectly positioned to feed America's growing appetite for cocaine, muscling their way into the increasingly profitable trade by ruthlessly pushing the Cubans out. Colombia first entered the cocaine business in the early 1970s, building on earlier illicit trades in marijuana and tax-evading contraband goods (especially cigarettes and whiskey). Medellin, the country's most industrialized and export-oriented city, soon became the most impor- tant center for the cocaine industry. This had an enormous economic ripple effect throughout the Andean region, fueling a coca cultivation boom in remote areas of neighboring Peru and Bolivia. Hundreds of thousands of Andean peasant farmers turned to growing the raw mate- rial that was then processed into Colombian cocaine for the US market. Coca was soon the region's most important export crop.[43]

Medellin's cocaine entrepreneurs, specializing in refining and whole- sale trafficking, led the way in turning cocaine into a mass-production industry capable of handling multiton shipments to the United States by the late 1970s. Medellin traffickers were also advantaged by the fact that many Colombians from the same region had migrated to the East Coast of the United States in the late 1960s and early 1970s—providing a ready-made distribution network.[44] Soon Medellin's old elites found themselves pushed aside by brash new narco-elites such as Pablo Escobar. Escobar, who began his criminal career stealing gravestones and cars, became the most recognizable face of the Colombian co- caine trade, even making the *Forbes* list of the top billionaires in the world. Escobar's fame, fortune, and bravado in directly challenging the Colombian government—including assassinating the country's justice minister in April 1984 and declaring war on the state—made him the world's best-known outlaw.[45]

One of Escobar's business partners, Carlos Lehder Rivas, is credited with pioneering the transportation of cocaine through the Caribbean to the United States by small aircraft. At the height of his trafficking career in the late 1970s and early 1980s, Lehder took over Norman's Cay, a tiny island in the Bahamas, and turned it into his own private airstrip. Government authorities in Nassau were suspected of taking hefty bribes to look the other way, tolerating Lehder's transport business until US pressure and media coverage finally prompted them to shut it down.

With the snowstorm of Colombian cocaine also came the myth that the whole business was tightly organized by a few hierarchical trafficking "cartels." The cartel myth was created and perpetuated by politicians, journalists, and law enforcement agents looking for a simple and easily identifiable target.[46] Over time, use of the term "cartel" became so common that it was permanently incorporated into the drug war vocabulary. But the reality was considerably more complex. By definition a cartel exerts sufficient control over a market to set prices. But the cocaine trade was in fact hypercompetitive—indeed, ruthlessly so, as evident by the violent competition for turf and market share. Cocaine prices plummeted and purity levels increased during the course of the decade, suggesting overproduction and a saturated market. For instance, a kilo of cocaine in Miami was worth between $47,000 and $60,000 in 1982, but by late 1987 its price had plummeted to between $9,000 and $14,000.[47] Overall, wholesale cocaine prices in the United States dropped by 75 percent between 1980 and 1988. Moreover, as law enforcement went after the most visible and well-known trafficking organizations, the cocaine business became even more fragmented and dispersed, based more on loose, flattened networks than centralized and hierarchical organizations.

As the main gateway to the US drug market in the late 1970s and early 1980s, South Florida became ground zero for both drug profits and drug violence, with competition between Colombians and Cubans over cocaine distribution turning the Miami area into the murder capital of the country. It is no surprise, then, that South Florida also became the main target of President Ronald Reagan's drug interdiction campaign. The South Florida Task Force, organized under the direction of Vice President George H. W. Bush, was launched with much fanfare in January 1982 to block air and sea drug-smuggling routes in the Southeast. Federal funding for interdiction doubled between 1982 and 1987, mostly concentrated in South Florida and the Caribbean.

Traffickers adjusted. As air interdiction improved, traffickers shifted away from direct flights into Florida and returned to sea routes, ferrying in cocaine loads by speedboat from mother ships waiting offshore. As sea interdiction then improved, traffickers turned to using airdrops rather than mother ships—with speedboat crews picking up floating cocaine packages and ferrying them back to shore. Over time, traffickers shifted not only their methods but also their routes, turning westward to move more of their drug shipments through Central America and Mexico.

America's rapidly growing cocaine habit provided a ready-made target for the Reagan-era conservative backlash. President Reagan's drug policy agenda was shaped by a large and vocal national constituency that had grown impatient with the permissive attitudes toward drug use and other counterculture activities of the previous decade. At the center of his domestic policy agenda was a set of social policies, articulated most powerfully by the so-called Moral Majority, that embodied a defense of traditional family values, conservative Christian morality, and patriotism.

President Reagan launched his drug war by using his executive power to revise executive-branch regulations, organizations, and lines of authority. By the end of his first year in office, Reagan had issued an executive order drafting the entire federal intelligence apparatus into the war on drugs and ordering its officials to provide guidance to civilian drug enforcement agencies. The president also opened the door for the first time to military involvement in the war against drugs by securing an amendment to the Posse Comitatus Act, which had outlawed military involvement in civilian law enforcement for more than a century. The Reagan administration successfully argued that the navy should be allowed to join civilian agencies, such as the Coast Guard, in interdicting smuggling vessels at sea, and that all branches of the military should be empowered to assist the US Customs Service, the Coast Guard, and the Drug Enforcement Administration (DEA) with training, equipment, and information.

In June 1982 Reagan put the federal bureaucracy on notice that the drug war was now a priority mission. The heads of eighteen federal agencies, the vice president, several military leaders, and the commissioner of the Internal Revenue Service were ordered to the White House for a special address, during which Reagan announced: "We're taking down the surrender flag that has flown over so many drug efforts. We're running up the battle flag. We can fight the drug problem, and we can win."[48] In his 1983 State of the Union address, Reagan confirmed, "The administration hereby declares an all-out war on big-time organized crime and the drug racketeers who are poisoning our young people."[49] The media helped fuel the president's effort, providing extensive coverage that built up the drug threat beginning in 1982. The administration intended to use "a scorched-earth policy" in drug enforcement, according to former associate attorney general Stephen S. Trott. It would not only send traffickers to jail but also lay claim under the new forfeiture laws to "everything they own—their land, their cars, their boats, everything."[50]

The introduction of a new cocaine derivative—"crack," the "poor man's coke"—added fuel to the drug war fire. Smokable cocaine had been around since the late 1970s as cocaine "free base," but not until the mid-1980s was it packaged and mass-marketed as crack, with a relatively affordable price that made it popular in poor urban neighborhoods. There was an important racial and class dimension to the public reaction to crack: as dealing and use of the drug became more visible in urban black and Latino neighborhoods, the crack trade and its related violence came to be powerfully tied to negative images of poor minority Americans.[51]

The national panic over the spread of crack cocaine made the drug war an even more potent issue in electoral politics. "My generation will remember how Americans swung into action when we were attacked in World War Two," President Reagan proclaimed as the November 1986 midterm elections approached. "Now we're in another war for our freedom."[52] He signed a national security decision directive classifying drugs as a national security threat. *Congressional Quarterly* commented: "In the closing weeks of the congressional election season, taking the pledge becomes a familiar feature of campaign life. Thirty years ago, candidates pledged to battle domestic communism. . . . In 1986, the pledge issue is drugs. Republicans and Democrats all across the country are trying to outdo each other in their support for efforts to crush the trade in illegal drugs."[53] Speaking of Senate efforts to increase the military role in the drug war in 1988, Arizona senator John McCain said, "This is such an emotional issue— I mean, we're at war here—that voting no would be too difficult to explain."[54]

One consequence of this escalating drug war was to propel the adoption of military technologies, training, funding, and methods by domestic law enforcement.[55] SWAT (Special Weapons and Tactics) teams dated back to the 1965 Watts riots, when the Los Angeles Police Department formed the first SWAT team, applying Vietnam counterinsurgency tactics to policing. But the cocaine-focused drug war fueled their rapid expansion elsewhere in later decades. The militarized nature of these units came from the training of their members directly with military personnel, hiring military personnel, and using military weaponry.[56] In the 1980s, about 3,000 SWAT teams were deployed nationwide, but this number had mushroomed to 30,000 by 1995. Journalist Radley Balko argues that this sharp increase can "almost exclusively" be attributed to the drug war.[57] As he puts it, "When you're carrying a hammer, everything looks like a nail. . . . Soon, just about every decent-sized city police department was armed with a hammer. And the drug war would ensure there were always plenty of nails for pounding."[58]

Beyond the proliferation of SWAT teams, the flow of military expertise and technology to domestic law enforcement agencies incentivized the latter to prioritize drug crimes. The 1988 Byrne Grant Program provided funding to local law enforcement agencies that were directly tied to antidrug activities. The Justice and Defense Departments also committed to a formal equipment- and technology-sharing agreement (the Joint Technology Program) that funneled military defense resources to local law enforcement and incentivized local agencies to hire military veterans.[59]

Meanwhile, as America's war against cocaine was ramping up, cocaine was quietly helping to fund a very different sort of war in Central America: the campaign by US-backed Contra rebels against Nicaragua's revolutionary Sandinista government. This episode had eerie echoes of the drug-financed anticommunist insurgents in Southeast Asia and Afghanistan. A three-year congressional investigation, headed by Massachusetts senator John Kerry, revealed that some of the same CIA-contracted air transport companies covertly hired to fly supplies to the Contras were also involved in transporting cocaine. For instance, the Honduran airline SETCO, created by cocaine trafficker Juan Ramon Matta Ballesteros, had been contracted to supply the Contras.[60] While the exact nature and extent of CIA knowledge and involvement in this trafficking is murky and steeped in controversy, the Kerry committee presented clear evidence that individual Contras, Contra supporters, and Contra suppliers had exploited their political protections as a convenient cover for cocaine-trafficking operations. This was at the same time that President Reagan was praising the Contras as the "moral equivalent of the Founding Fathers."[61]

It appears that the government routinely turned a blind eye to such activities, and that some individuals or branches actually suggested that money from cocaine be used to fund the Contras. As the Kerry report put it, "The logic of having drug money pay for the pressing needs of the Contras appealed to a number of people who became involved in the covert war. Indeed, senior U.S. policy makers were not immune to the idea that drug money was a perfect solution to the Contras funding problems." The report concluded that "it is clear that individuals who provided support for the Contras were involved in drug trafficking, the supply network of the Contras was used by drug trafficking organizations, and elements of the Contras themselves knowingly received financial and material assistance from drug traffickers. In each case, one or another agency of the U.S. government had information regarding the involvement either while it was occurring, or immediately thereafter."[62]

The Reagan White House attempted to undermine Kerry's investigation from the start, using methods ranging from discrediting witness testimony to stonewalling the committee when it requested evidence. The committee's probe was most embarrassing to Vice President George H. W. Bush, who was serving as the administration's point person for cocaine interdiction efforts.[63] The White House also apparently engaged in a behind-the-scenes effort to discourage and discredit media coverage of the Contra-cocaine connection, and when the Kerry report was released, it was largely ignored by the mainstream press.[64]

## Militarized Escalation

The cocaine-driven war against drugs was ramped up even further by Reagan's successor, George H. W. Bush, who drafted the military to take on a more frontline antidrug role. Holding up a bag of crack cocaine as a political prop, the president began his first prime-time address to the nation: "This is the first time since taking the oath of office that I felt an issue was so important, so threatening, that it warranted talking directly with you, the American people." He quickly declared a national consensus—"All of us agree that the gravest domestic threat facing our nation today is drugs"—and then called for a $1.5 billion increase in domestic law enforcement spending in the drug war and $3.5 billion for interdiction and foreign supply reduction.[65] A *Washington Post*/ABC News poll taken after Bush's speech indicated that 62 percent of those polled were willing to give up "a few of the freedoms we have in this country" to fight the war on drugs. Eighty-two percent said they were willing to permit the military to join the war on drugs.[66]

To a degree unmatched by previous presidents, Bush used his power as commander-in-chief to draft the US military into the drug war, elevating what had been a sporadic and relatively minor role in assisting civilian enforcement into a major national security mission for the armed forces. In the fall of 1989, Secretary of Defense Dick Cheney declared that fighting drugs was a high-priority mission of the Department of Defense. The fiscal 1989 National Defense Authorization Act charged

Figure 6.1  US President George H. W. Bush displays a bag of crack cocaine during his first televised address to the nation, September 5, 1989 (Bettman/Getty Images).

the Defense Department with three new responsibilities. It was to serve as the lead agency for detecting drug traffic into the country; integrate all command, control, and communications related to drug interdiction into an effective network; and approve and fund state governors' plans for using the National Guard in interdiction and enforcement. Funding for the military's drug enforcement activities jumped from $357 million in 1989 to more than $1 billion in 1992.[67]

The Pentagon became noticeably more enthusiastic about taking on drug war duties as the Cold War came to an end. A former Reagan official in the Pentagon commented that "getting help from the military on drugs used to be like pulling teeth. Now everybody's looking around to say, 'Hey, how can we justify these forces.' And the answer they're coming up with is drugs."[68] One two-star general observed in an interview: "With peace breaking out all over it might give us something to do."[69] The Pentagon inspector general found that a large number of officers considered drug control "an opportunity to subsidize some non-counternarcotics efforts struggling for funding approval."[70] In 1990, for example, "the Air Force wanted $242 million to start the central sector of the $2.3 billion Over-the-Horizon Backscatter radar network. Once a means of detecting nuclear cruise missiles fired from Soviet submarines in the Gulf of Mexico, Backscatter was now being sold as a way to spot drug couriers winging their way up from South America."[71] Some skeptics within the Pentagon viewed the military as too blunt an instrument for antidrug police work, but the shift in the political winds continued to push it in that direction.

The recycling of Cold War technologies for drug war missions provided a new growth area for defense contractors struggling to adapt to the changed security environment. In July 1990, government and corporate representatives gathered at what was called a "forecast" conference (formally known as Drug Summit I, sponsored by the Program Group of Washington, DC) to discuss the technological needs of the country's expanding antidrug campaign. More than 300 weapons makers, including representatives from the Pentagon's top twenty contractors, attended the $950 per person, three-day event. Many officials from federal weapons research labs, such as Los Alamos National Laboratory, the birthplace of the atomic bomb, also attended.[72] In the promotional mailing to advertise the event to industry leaders, the conference organizers highlighted four points:

(1) The war facing America right now, in our cities, streets and homes is the Drug War (*Federal Computer Week* calls it "the only war in town"), and funding for this war is going up.

(2) The technologies and ideas required to win this war are resident in your companies.

(3) The objective of this conference is to introduce you to the many different players of the Drug War, and their requirements, programs, and priorities. And to allow you to introduce yourself and your group's capabilities to them.

(4) The result: Give the Drug Warriors the Technological Edge of the Cold Warriors. And win the Drug War.[73]

Reflecting the mood of the time, Senator Joseph Biden argued in 1990 that "many of the most promising technologies [for drug control] have already been developed by the Defense Department over the last 10 years for military purposes," and he urged that these technologies be adapted and made available for drug enforcement. As part of this shift, Airborne Warning and Control System surveillance planes soon began to monitor international drug flights; the North American Aerospace Defense Command, which had been built to track incoming Soviet bombers and missiles, refocused some of its energies to track cocaine smugglers; X-ray technology designed to detect Soviet missile warheads in trucks was adapted for use by US Customs to find smuggled drugs in cargo trucks; researchers at Los Alamos National Laboratory started developing sophisticated new technologies for drug control; and the Pentagon's Defense Advanced Research Projects Agency (DARPA) began using its research on antisubmarine warfare to develop listening devices to detect drug smugglers. DARPA turned to its attention to modifying miniature receivers and transmitters developed for the military into tracking, eavesdropping, and recording instruments for antidrug operations.[74]

The intelligence community was also drafted to take on a more frontline role in the drug war. In 1989, the CIA created the Counter-Narcotics Center, and in 1990 it announced that "narcotics is a new priority."[75] Some observers no doubt found this rather ironic, given that the agency had since its creation shown a chronic willingness to subvert the fight against drugs in the name of fighting communists. The CIA's expanded involvement in antidrug activities in the region included providing analysis, training, and equipment for surveillance and intelligence gathering, and developing undercover sources. The full extent of the CIA role was obscured by secrecy and a classified budget.[76]

The drug war came to define Washington's post–Cold War military relations with its southern neighbors, especially the Andean cocaine-producing region, which surpassed Central America as the primary recipient of US military aid in the hemisphere. Reflecting the new priorities, the US Southern Command in Panama was transformed into a de facto forward base for cocaine interdiction. Its commander, General Maxwell Thurman, frankly observed that the drug war was "the only war we've got."[77] In 1989 the US military was authorized to arrest drug traffickers and fugitives on foreign territory without the approval of the host country.[78]

Drug control even provided part of the official rationale for Operation Just Cause—the late December 1989 military invasion of Panama and the indictment of Panamanian general Manuel Noriega on cocaine-trafficking charges. While US intelligence reports connecting Noriega to drug trafficking went back as far as the early 1970s, Washington tolerated and overlooked his shady dealings until he was no longer politically useful and had become too much of a liability and embarrassment.[79] Earlier in the decade, Noriega had been on the CIA payroll, collaborating with US efforts to undermine the Sandinista government in Nicaragua and stem communist influence in the region. Indeed, the CIA had cultivated Noriega as a source early in his military career during the late 1960s.[80] But the Panamanian leader proved to be as eager to cozy up to Medellin traffickers as he was to Washington officials. As Secretary of State George Shultz described him, "You can't buy him; you can only rent him."[81]

It took several weeks for the US military to hunt down and nab the deposed dictator, who finally surrendered on January 3, 1990, after taking refuge in the Vatican embassy in Panama City. Noriega was flown to Miami to stand trial; he received a forty-year jail sentence for drug trafficking, racketeering, and money laundering. Operation Just

Cause was heralded by the Bush administration as a major victory in the war on drugs, despite evidence that trafficking through Panama soon returned to pre-invasion levels.[82]

Meanwhile, the security situation in Colombia continued to deteriorate. After Pablo Escobar orchestrated the assassination of presidential candidate Luis Carlos Galan in August 1989, President Virgilio Barco responded by intensifying his crackdown on the drug trade, a campaign that included deploying the military in urban antidrug operations for the first time.[83] This in turn prompted Escobar to escalate his war against the state, which took the lives of hundreds of police officers, dozens of journalists and judges, and two other presidential candidates. More than 200 bombs were exploded in Bogota alone, while Medellin gained the reputation as the most violent city in the world. Adding to the violence was the fact that Escobar was not only at war with the authorities but also simultaneously engaged in an all-out war with his trafficking rivals from the city of Cali.

The government's war with Escobar culminated in a massive manhunt in 1992–1993, in which the CIA played a hands-on support role.[84] Journalist Mark Bowden, detailing the hunt for Escobar, recounts that "there were so many American spy planes over the city [Medellin], at one point 17 at once, that the Air Force had to assign an AWAC, an airborne command and control center, to keep track of them."[85]

Washington's drug warriors became increasingly alarmed by Colombia's escalating drug violence, with Charles Rangel, chairman of the House Select Committee on Narcotics Abuse and Control, even promoting a scary new version of the Vietnam-era domino theory: "If Colombia falls [to the cocaine cartels], the other, smaller, less stable nations in the region would become targets. It is conceivable that we would one day find ourselves an island of democracy in a sea of narcopolitical rule, a prospect as bad as being surrounded by communist regimes."[86]

The premise and methods guiding the US cocaine-suppression strategy were hardly new. "Going to the source" of the foreign supply had for years been viewed by Washington drug warriors as an effective means of curbing demand at home. What was new in the post–Cold War era was the unprecedented level of funding and the dramatically expanded antidrug role of US and Latin American military forces.

Through a newly announced Andean Initiative, the United States in 1991 increased its spending for international supply reduction efforts by 65 percent. The new initiative for the first time integrated Andean military forces directly into antidrug operations while simultaneously increasing the involvement of the US Department of Defense. Through diplomatic pressure, aid, and training, Washington pushed Andean militaries to take on domestic drug enforcement tasks that US military personnel were banned from doing at home, including searches and seizures, arrests and interrogations, surveillance operations, and forcing down suspicious aircraft.[87]

Military documents reveal that the Pentagon viewed the drug war as a new form of armed conflict, adapting well-worn counterinsurgency strategy and tactics from earlier conflicts in Vietnam and Central America. Drawing from military manuals and presidential national security directives, the Center for Low Intensity Conflict defined the counterdrug mission as a low-intensity conflict mission, and military officials confirmed that their antidrug training activities in the Andes closely resembled earlier anti-insurgency training in Central America. Colonel Robert Jacobelly, the head of special forces trainers in Central and South America, acknowledged that training for counterdrug operations was "basically the same" as training for counterinsurgency.[88] Some of the same military advisors who had been involved in Central American operations in the 1980s, including those who had covertly supported the Contra resupply effort, were now redeployed as part of the new antidrug campaign.[89]

Conveniently glossed over in the US Andean strategy was a pattern of complicity between elements of the region's militaries and cocaine traffickers. International human rights organizations documented the collaborative relationship between members of the Colombian security forces, for example, and cocaine-financed right-wing paramilitary groups responsible for the majority of the political killings that had occurred in Colombia.[90] Bank records located after the December 1989 capture and killing of Colombian trafficker Jose Gonzalo Rodriguez Gacha revealed that he had provided multimillion-dollar payoffs to entire brigades of the Colombian army.[91]

In Bolivia, meanwhile, the military had a notorious history of coups, corruption, and direct involvement in cocaine trafficking. It is little wonder, then, that the US strategy of drafting the military to fight cocaine was almost universally opposed by Bolivians. As one development worker from Cochabamba noted ironically, "To bring in the army [for drug control] would be the best way to promote drug trafficking in Bolivia."[92] Citizens still had fresh memories of the 1980 "cocaine coup," in which high-level military officers led by General Luis Garcia Meza had taken power with the support of drug traffickers. Even after being deposed, Garcia reportedly continued to move about freely in Bolivia and received his military pension, and many leaders from his regime remained in positions of power, including the minister of defense, Rear Admiral Alberto Saenz Klinsky.

After initially resisting such involvement and even publicly announcing that there was no need to draw the military into drug control efforts, Bolivian president Jaime Paz Zamora signed a military assistance agreement during a visit to Washington in May 1990. In April 1991 dozens of US special forces trainers arrived in Bolivia. An estimated 1,000 Bolivian troops participated in the first ten-week training session. Zamora tried to avoid domestic protest against the military assistance agreement by keeping it secret. However, details of the plan were leaked to the press, and well-organized federations of peasant coca growers staged protests denouncing it. Zamora promised that military units would not enter coca-growing areas and that they would target only drug traffickers, not coca farmers.

Competing priorities posed a further complication to military cooperation in the drug war in Colombia and Peru. The unambiguous objective of both militaries was to continue protracted campaigns against their countries' respective leftist insurgencies. In fact, Colombian military officials told US congressional staff in April 1990 that virtually all of that year's US antinarcotics military assistance would be used in a major counterinsurgency campaign in an area with no known drug-trafficking presence.[93]

Similarly, the Peruvian military's singular focus was its campaign against the Maoist Shining Path guerrillas. This insurgency had begun in the highlands of the Ayacucho region in 1980 but had spread rapidly throughout the country, coming to control large swathes of territory and engaging in increasingly bold attacks against the government. The guerrillas had gained a base of peasant support in the Upper Huallaga

Valley, the largest coca-producing zone in the world, by protecting peasant coca growers against government antidrug operations and demanding higher coca prices from Colombian traffickers on behalf of small producers. The escalation of drug control efforts in the valley brought a corresponding increase in peasant support for the insurgency. The military's counternarcotics strategy was therefore to drive a wedge between the peasants and the guerrillas by allowing the peasants to grow coca unimpeded. "There are 150,000 *campesinos cocaleros* [peasant coca growers] in the zone," stated General Alberto Arciniega, who served as regional commander in the valley until January 1989. "Each of them is a potential subversive [insurgent]. Eradicate his field and the next day he'll be one."[94] Arciniega further observed, "Most of my troops come from this area. . . . In effect, the police were wiping out the livelihood of their families, while I was asking them to fight Shining Path, which was sworn to protect the growers. Shining Path looked like heroes."[95] Peruvian defense minister General Jorge Torres bluntly summed up the situation in March 1991: "If we attack drug trafficking, we will convert the local population into our enemy."[96]

Peruvian military personnel at times actively obstructed US antidrug operations. For example, in two separate missions in March 1990, US-piloted helicopters carrying Peruvian antidrug police were fired upon by army soldiers. Pervasive drug-related corruption—including the use of military-controlled airfields by drug traffickers—further undermined the military's will to support the drug war. Nevertheless, US strategists continued to insist that this same military was the key to antidrug success in the Upper Huallaga Valley. To make matters worse, it would later be revealed that Peru's top intelligence official at the time, Vladimiro Montesinos, was simultaneously taking money from the CIA to combat drugs (through the antidrug unit he created and ran within the National Intelligence Service) and from drug traffickers to protect their shipments from the Huallaga region and elsewhere.[97]

President Bill Clinton's administration toned down the Reagan–Bush drug war rhetoric but did little to actually change drug laws or redirect federal drug control agencies. The drug war machinery created and built up by his predecessors continued to grind on. Overall, Clinton's cocaine-focused drug war looked little different than it had during the Bush era. Clinton even appointed as the new drug tsar the former head of the US Southern Command, General Barry McCaffrey, who brought dozens of military personnel with him to staff his office. Washington's relations with much of Latin America continued to be driven by drugs, primarily cocaine, with virtually all US military and police aid to the region provided under the rubric of drug control.

The growing overlap of US military, intelligence, and law enforcement forces and resources in the escalating cocaine-suppression effort was strikingly illustrated by the ambitious efforts in the 1990s to intercept drug-smuggling aircraft in Andean airspace. The CIA, DEA, FBI, Coast Guard, and Department of Defense–related institutions, such as the Joint Interagency Task Force–South, the Defense Intelligence Agency, the Office of Naval Intelligence, the National Mapping and Imagery Agency, and the National Security Agency, all joined in on this effort. Military personnel from the Andean countries were brought onto US drug surveillance aircraft, and local militaries were tasked with the job of shooting down drug planes.[98]

Ironically, Colombia's largest insurgent group, the Revolutionary Armed Forces of Colombia (FARC), was an unintended beneficiary of the US-sponsored antidrug offensive in the 1990s. The campaign to eradicate coca fields, which included aerial fumigation of coca crops, increasingly pushed peasant coca cultivation into remote FARC-held areas and made coca farmers more reliant on (and sympathetic toward) the guerrillas. At the same time, the US-backed dismantling of the Medellin and Cali trafficking organizations played into the FARC's hands by increasing its leverage over the cocaine industry. Together, these twin developments created greater opportunities for the FARC to tax the cocaine business to fund its war against the Colombian state. It is striking that in the early 1990s, only about 20 percent of Andean coca was cultivated in Colombia, but by the end of the decade this figure had increased to almost 75 percent—most of it in southern FARC strongholds. The FARC experienced tremendous expansion during the 1990s—its forces more than doubled in the second half of the decade—and its greater ability to generate revenue from the cocaine industry was a crucial part of that success. Whereas in the 1980s the insurgency had generated most of its funding through kidnapping and extortion, in the 1990s it derived an ever-increasing proportion of its revenue from the cocaine industry.[99]

Figure 6.2 Colombian soldiers examine a cocaine laboratory in El Aguila, a district of Putumayo, Colombia, October 2000. The lab belonged to the FARC rebel group and produced 300 pounds of cocaine base per week (Carlos Villalon/Newsmakers/Getty Images).

Although the FARC long predated Colombia's involvement in the cocaine trade, cocaine was now helping the insurgency to not only survive but thrive, making possible a significant upgrade of its military capabilities and control of larger swaths of territory. Officials increasingly labeled the FARC a "narco-guerrilla" group, helping to justify the merging of counternarcotics and counterinsurgency operations and setting the stage for an even greater influx of US military assistance at the turn of the century. Branding the FARC as "narco-guerrillas" was politically convenient, and the organization was certainly profiting from cocaine. But the label was also an oversimplification. Unlike criminal organizations, which used cocaine to enrich individual members, the FARC used cocaine to fund a political agenda. Far from being in a strategic alliance, cocaine traffickers and the FARC were often in intense conflict, so much so that traffickers formed their own paramilitaries (the largest of which was the United Self-Defense Forces of Colombia, or AUC) to wage war on the insurgents. The AUC commanded tens of thousands of heavily armed fighters, many of them former members of the military.

While engaging in mass atrocities, these drug-financed paramilitary groups were often aided and abetted by Colombia's security forces because they shared an anti-FARC agenda.[100] With their human rights record increasingly being scrutinized, the Colombian military could essentially outsource the dirtiest parts of its counterinsurgency campaign to the paramilitaries. According to Americas Watch, these paramilitary groups were so "fully integrated into the army's battle strategy, coordinated with its soldiers in the field, and linked to government units via intelligence, supplies, radios, weapons, cash, and common purpose that they effectively constitute[d] a sixth division of the army."[101]

Washington mostly looked the other way as it poured ever-increasing antidrug resources into the country, turning Colombia into the world's third-largest recipient of US military and police assistance by the end of the century.[102] By this time, around 200 US military advisors and 100 DEA and intelligence agents were reportedly operating in Colombia.[103] Total antidrug funding reached more than $1 billion in 2000 as part of "Plan Colombia." The antidrug package, the administration promised, would not "cross the line" between counternarcotics and counterinsurgency.[104] "As a matter of Administration policy, the United States will not support Colombian counterinsurgency efforts," General McCaffrey pledged in November 2000.[105] Whereas most US antidrug assistance until the late 1990s had gone to the police, now it mostly shifted to the Colombian military, providing new aircraft and equipment for the air force, expanding support for the navy's riverine operations, and channeling helicopters and funding to the army's new mobile counterdrug battalion in guerrilla-controlled southern coca-growing areas.[106] Intelligence from the US real-time satellite surveillance system was provided to the Colombians, and human intelligence on the ground was also gathered by elite spy units made up of a combination of US and Colombian personnel.[107]

Private military contractors from companies such as Military Professional Resources Incorporated, DynCorp, and Matcom also poured into Colombia, serving in roles ranging from spray plane pilots to radar site operators to intelligence analysts.[108] Former US ambassador to Colombia Myles Frechette explained the rationale behind this privatization: "Congress and the American people don't want any servicemen killed overseas. So it makes sense that if contractors want to risk their lives, they get the job."[109] Others challenged the trend. "Are we outsourcing in order to avoid public scrutiny, controversy, and embarrassment?" asked Representative Jan Schakowsky (D-IL) in 2001. "Is it to hide body bags from the media and thus shield them from public opinion?"[110] Heated political debate arose when a Peruvian military plane shot down a civilian airplane carrying an American missionary family. The Peruvian air force had been supported by intelligence provided by a CIA-contracted US company, Aviation Development Corporation. One veteran of antidrug efforts in the Andes complained that "there wasn't one person aboard that [CIA-commissioned] plane sworn to uphold the Constitution of the United States. They were all . . . businessmen!"[111]

## Mexico and the Border War

Washington's escalating drug war in the 1980s had focused mostly on the flow of Andean cocaine through the Caribbean to South Florida. The Maginot Line–style interdiction strategy that was adopted in South Florida did not significantly deter cocaine imports, but it did influence the location, methods, and organization of the traffic. Its most important impact was to push much of the flow to the US Southwest, making Colombian traffickers increasingly reliant upon their Mexican counterparts. In other words, the US drug war offensive had unintentionally empowered Mexican traffickers. The end result was a redistribution of wealth and influence within the cocaine trade—with the world's most powerful traffickers now next door across the border.[112]

Testifying at a Foreign Affairs Committee task force hearing in October 1987, Assistant DEA Administrator David Westrate noted that the enforcement crackdown in the Southeast had redirected more cocaine shipments through Mexico: "Now that's got a serious downside, other than it opens a major theater for us to address, which is the southwest border. . . . It also has produced a strong linkage between the Colombian major drug organizations and Mexican drug organizations—a connection we did not have before. And I think that clearly is something that's going to cause us fits in the next couple of years."[113]

Apparently, the main lesson learned from the experience in the Southeast was the need to replicate the strategy in the Southwest. Coast Guard Admiral Paul Yost testified: "The more money that you spend on it, the more success you are going to have in the interdiction area. . . . We did that in the Caribbean for the last two years, and I'm sure that what we're about to do on the southwest border will also be extremely successful. It is also going to be extremely expensive, and the success expense ratio is going to be a very direct one."[114]

But measuring such success was politically tricky. At a 1987 Senate hearing held in Nogales, Arizona, Senator Pete Domenici (R-NM) summarized the situation as follows: "Now, I understand that we're shooting at floating targets. I mean, you do well in the Southeast and they [traffickers] move to the Southwest. We'll load up the Southwest and what happens next? Nonetheless, we have to continue the war on drugs. And for us to sustain the resources, you have to have a few field victories of significant size that are measurable."[115] The reply by Customs Commissioner William Von Raab was predictable: "The seizures, which are your typical measure of success, are impressive." Pleased to hear that some progress was being made in controlling the border, none of the committee members questioned what these measures of success actually measured.[116] At the same hearing, Von Raab acknowledged that there was "good news and bad news" regarding increased drug seizures: "The good news is that we are catching more drugs because we are getting better at doing our jobs. We have more resources. The bad news is that we are catching more because more is coming across."[117]

The heightened role of cocaine in Mexican drug smuggling dramatically elevated the financial stakes of the trade. As long as the heroin and marijuana that traditionally dominated the business of drug smuggling across the southwestern border were produced within Mexico, Mexican drug smuggling remained primarily a local and regional business. The percentage of cocaine entering the United States through Mexico had been negligible in the early 1980s. But according to the State Department, by 1989 nearly a third of cocaine exports were being rerouted through Mexican territory, and that number increased to more than half by 1992 and in later years was as high as 75 to 80 percent.[118]

The militarized US interdiction offensive in the 1980s had disrupted not only the traditional routes for cocaine smuggling through the Caribbean and South Florida but also the favored method of such smuggling: light aircraft. The extension of the US radar net from the Southeast to the Southwest forced much of the trade out of the air. The United States had built what one senior customs official described as a "Maginot line of radar" across the border, which had the effect of drastically curtailing air smuggling.[119] Washington drug warriors boasted that the sharp drop demonstrated the effectiveness of interdiction. But the actual effect was to redirect rather than reduce the drug flow. With much of the traffic pushed out of the air, road transportation networks through Mexico to the US market became a much more integral part of the cocaine trade. And the Mexican organizations that controlled cocaine smuggling along these routes were more than willing to sell their services—offloading, storing, and smuggling—to Colombia's cocaine exporters.

When Carlos Salinas assumed the Mexican presidency in December 1988, he faced the daunting twin tasks of coping with a more powerful and internationally connected Mexican drug-smuggling business (thanks largely to the "success" of US interdiction in the Caribbean and South Florida) and meeting rising US political expectations that Mexico demonstrate much greater commitment to battling that trade. Salinas therefore launched an aggressive campaign to revitalize the Mexican antidrug program, declaring that drug trafficking was the number-one security threat facing the nation. He reorganized and greatly expanded the country's drug control apparatus, an accomplishment that was particularly impressive given that it occurred during a time of deep cuts in overall government spending. The resources devoted to drug control by the Mexican attorney general's office tripled from the late 1980s to the early 1990s. Drug control came to dominate the Mexican criminal justice system. Salinas also extended the antidrug role of the military, with about one-third of its budget devoted to the effort by the end of the 1980s. As in the United States, militarization fit well with the new emphasis on defining drugs as a national security threat.

As the Salinas government beefed up its efforts on the Mexican side of the border, US drug control strategists built up interdiction efforts on their side. The enforcement-induced shift in drug smuggling from the Southeast to the Southwest provided the main rationale for this push. As the Bush administration reported in 1991, "The success of interdiction in the southeastern United States and the Caribbean islands and Sea has caused drug smugglers to shift their focus towards Mexico as a primary transfer point into the United States." As a result, "resources have been enhanced along the Southwest Border." Concretely, that meant that the United States added 175 new Customs Service inspectors, 200 more Border Patrol agents, 23 more canine drug detection teams, and increased funds for "capital assets such as fencing, ground sensors, traffic checkpoints, aerostats, and other equipment to detect smugglers."[120]

The border also became more militarized. As part of the Pentagon's expanded interdiction role, Joint Task Force Six was established in the fall of 1989, based at Fort Bliss, Texas. The task force involved units of some seventy infantrymen armed with M-16 rifles who were divided into camouflaged four-man teams to cover designated thirty-mile segments of the border. In fiscal year 1990, the task force conducted twenty operations in support of border drug interdiction. By fiscal year 1992 the number of missions had increased to 408.[121] Teams of National Guardsmen were also drafted into antidrug work, deployed to remote border posts to monitor smuggling in rural areas and to ports of entry for cargo inspection. What began as a test program became a permanent presence. While prohibited from making arrests, military personnel were involved in a growing range of support activities, including reconnaissance and intelligence analysis, the construction and maintenance of roads and fences, weapons and communications training, and the operation of surveillance equipment. The army even used its tunnel detection skills developed along the Korean border to detect drug-smuggling tunnels under the US-Mexico border.[122]

Meanwhile, Mexican smugglers were renegotiating the terms of their partnership with Colombia's cocaine exporters. In the early years of this business alliance, the Mexicans were simply paid in cash for moving Colombian cocaine across the southwestern border, receiving $1,000 to $2,000 for every kilogram transported. But as the relationship matured and the Colombians faced growing government pressure at home and abroad, the leverage of the Mexican smugglers grew. As a result, they increasingly demanded payment in the form of product—40 to 50 percent of each cocaine shipment, which in turn expanded their own distribution networks, especially in the western parts of the United States. This increased the Mexican share of cocaine profits by five to ten times, dramatically changing the financial stakes of drug smuggling across the border.[123]

Mexico's growing stake in the cocaine trade produced more sophisticated and organized smuggling organizations in the border's main transportation hubs, the most prominent of which were the Gulf, Tijuana, and Juarez drug-trafficking groups. The Mexican government calculated that the gross revenue of Mexican drug-smuggling organizations reached $30 billion in 1994, while US officials estimated the profits at $10 billion—putting it ahead of Mexico's leading legal export, oil.[124]

As more cocaine flooded into Mexico on its way to the noses of US consumers and Mexican police forces became even more submerged in drug-related corruption, the government increasingly turned to the military to stem the tide. The antidrug role of the Mexican military, though dating back to the 1970s and enhanced during the Salinas years, expanded much further under President Ernesto Zedillo. By early 1998, military personnel occupied top law enforcement posts in two-thirds of Mexico's states.[125] For example, more than 100 military personnel were brought into the Federal Attorney General's Office in the border state of Chihuahua. In some states, such as Nuevo Leon, Federal Judicial Police forces were entirely replaced by soldiers.[126] Overall, by 1998 some 40 percent of the 180,000-member army was reportedly focused on drug control.[127] At the end of the decade, the Mexican secretaries of defense and the navy acknowledged that drug control had become the primary mission of their services.[128]

This new reliance on the military reaffirmed the Mexican government's definition of drug trafficking as "the most serious danger to national security."[129] In order to give the military new law enforcement powers, the Mexican government modified the nation's constitution and criminal codes. Generals were put in charge of the Federal Judicial Police, the National Institute to Combat Drugs, and the Center for the Planning of Drug Control. An active-duty officer also headed the uniformed branch of the Mexican federal customs service. Moreover, the military increasingly ran the Center for National Security and Investigation, the federal intelligence agency.

The militarization of drug control in Mexico also meant a greater militarization of US-Mexico relations and new cross-border military ties. Interaction between US and Mexican armed forces, which had been extremely limited in the past, became more intimate through the United States' provision of military assistance and training for antidrug programs. In addition, the CIA provided instruction, resources, and operational support for a Mexican army intelligence unit, the Center for Anti-Narcotics Investigations. These developments were particularly remarkable given that until the 1980s, Mexican military manuals had depicted the United States as Mexico's enemy. As part of this closer US-Mexico military antidrug relationship, Mexico's army received a large shipment of US helicopters, and thousands of Mexican army special forces airmobile groups were trained at Fort Bragg, North Carolina.[130] US military training then shifted to the Mexican navy's amphibious special forces groups.[131]

Yet the government's decision to send in the Mexican military in response to corruption within the police also brought with it greater risk of corruption within the military. Indeed, in early 1997 the head of the federal antidrug agency, General Jesus Gutierrez Rebollo, was arrested on charges of working for the Juarez trafficking organization. The agency, which had been patterned after the DEA when it first opened in 1993, was quickly dismantled. Just a few weeks before the scandal, the White House drug policy director, Barry McCaffrey, had described the general as "an honest man who is a no-nonsense field commander of the Mexican army who's now been sent to bring to the police force the same kind of aggressiveness and reputation he had in uniform."[132] Indeed, no other army commander had displayed more antidrug initiative. The problem was that he had a highly selective focus that largely left the Juarez traffickers untouched while aggressively targeting other trafficking groups. This scandal, although an unusually high-profile one, was not an isolated incident. The next month, General Alfredo Navarro Lara was arrested for offering $1 million a month to the top federal justice official in Baja California on behalf of the Tijuana drug-trafficking organization.[133] A 1997 White House report indicated that thirty-four senior Mexican military officers had been targeted for disciplinary action as a result of drug-related corruption.[134]

The Mexican government's response to such corruption, however, was to reinforce the militarization trend. This approach was partly oriented toward impressing and appeasing the United States. Such signaling came at politically opportune moments. Early in the morning of March 1, 1996—the deadline for the Clinton administration's decision on whether or not to certify Mexico as fully complying with US antidrug objectives—Mexican troops were deployed in a highly visible sweep of Tijuana neighborhoods in search of the Arellano Felix brothers, leaders of the "Tijuana drug cartel." By the end of the day, Mexico had received the certification blessing from Washington, and the troops returned to the barracks. The next year the ante was upped: one week before the US certification deadline, Mexico replaced the entire federal police force in the border state of Baja with military personnel.

Meanwhile, smugglers were increasingly hiding their cocaine shipments within the rising tide of commercial trucks, railcars, and passenger vehicles crossing the border. The boom in cross-border traffic encouraged by the North American Free Trade Agreement had the side effect of creating a much more challenging job for those border agents charged with the task of weeding out illegitimate flows from legitimate ones—a challenge that in turn provided the rationale for a further infusion of enforcement resources at official ports of entry. As the 1999 *National Drug Control Strategy Report* explained, "Rapidly growing commerce between the United States and Mexico will complicate our efforts to keep drugs out of cross-border traffic. Since the southwest border is presently the most porous of the nation's borders, it is there that we must mount a determined coordinated effort to stop the flow of drugs."[135]

The sheer volume of border crossings provided an ideal environment for drug smuggling. By 1997, over 200,000 vehicles were coming into the United States from Mexico every day. That year, US border officials searched more than a million commercial trucks and railway cars crossing from Mexico and found cocaine in only six.[136] The enforcement challenge, in other words, was the equivalent of finding a needle in a haystack—except the haystack kept getting bigger and the needle was actively trying to avoid detection. Trade between the United States and Mexico tripled between 1993 and 2000, most of which was transported via commercial cargo conveyances across the border. Such conveyances, of course, could carry illegal goods as easily as legal goods. One truck that was stopped near San Diego was smuggling eight tons of cocaine stuffed into cans of jalapeño peppers. US officials believed that the shipment belonged to the owner of one of Mexico's largest shipping companies.[137]

For political reasons, customs officials continued to proclaim that efforts to keep drugs out would not be sacrificed in order to keep legitimate trade moving, but commercial realities dictated that the border remain highly porous. The more intensive and intrusive the inspection process, the longer the wait at the border. As one Customs Service official warned, "If we examined every truck for narcotics arriving into the United States along the Southwest border . . . Customs would back up the truck traffic bumper-to-bumper into Mexico City in just two weeks—15.8 days. In 15.8 days, there would be 95,608 trucks backed up into Mexico. That's 1,177 miles of trucks, end to end."[138] By the end of the decade, 90 million cars and 4 million trucks and railcars were entering the United States from Mexico every year.

To keep generating drug seizures without stopping the rising flow of commercial traffic, US border control strategists increasingly turned to state-of-the-art technologies, many of which had initially been developed for the military. Giant backscatter X-ray machines large enough to drive a truck through were installed at more and more ports of entry along the border. In 1995 the Border Research Technology Center was opened in San Diego with the purpose of adapting various gadgets and gizmos previously restricted to military use to border control tasks. As McCaffrey put it, "Technology can help us stop drugs while facilitating legal commerce."[139]

And this military-aided search for a high-tech fix for the border was just getting started. In the next decade, major military contractors, including Boeing, Lockheed Martin, Raytheon, and Northrop Grumman, would be recruited to play a larger role in securing the border by, as one press report noted, "using some of the same high-priced, high-tech tools these companies have already put to work in Iraq and Afghanistan."[140] Reflecting the growing faith in high-tech solutions, the US Border Patrol began to use unmanned aerial vehicles, becoming the first civilian law enforcement agency in the world to do so. In September 2005 border officials in Arizona unveiled a new unmanned aerial surveillance system based on the satellite-controlled Predator-B drone used for military operations in the Middle East and elsewhere. By the end of the decade the Department of Homeland Security, which already operated hundreds of manned aircraft—the largest nonmilitary force in the world—also had its own small fleet of Predator drones along the border.

### Merging the War on Drugs with the War on Terror

In the aftermath of the September 11 terrorist attacks, US drug warriors who traditionally had had little or nothing to do with counterterrorism scrambled to adjust and redefine their mission in the suddenly transformed security environment. The DEA, for instance, quickly jumped on the counterterrorism bandwagon rather than be left behind. DEA officials pushed to integrate the war on drugs with the War on Terror through a renewed focus on "narcoterrorism," drawing greater attention to alleged links between drug trafficking and terrorist activities.[141] In late 2001, President George W. Bush remarked, "It's so important for Americans to know that the traffic in drugs finances the work of terror. If you quit drugs, you join the fight against terror."[142] The White House's Office of National Drug Control Policy (dubbed the "drug tsar's office") followed up this declaration with a television advertising campaign in early 2002 that depicted drug users as sponsors of terrorists. Terminology from the counterterrorism campaign became incorporated into the antidrug campaign: in 2003, Southern Command General James Hill repeatedly referred to drugs as a "weapon of mass destruction."[143]

The repackaging of the war on drugs as part of the war on terrorism was particularly critical in maintaining political support for growing levels of US security assistance to Colombia, where the line between fighting drugs and fighting guerrillas was becoming progressively blurred. "There's no difficulty in identifying [Osama bin Laden] as a terrorist, and getting everybody to rally against him," commented Secretary of State Colin Powell in October 2001. "Now, there are other organizations that probably meet a similar standard. The FARC in Colombia comes to mind, the Real IRA comes to mind . . . both of which are on our terrorist list down at the State Department."[144] A few months later, CIA director George Tenet noted that "the terrorist threat also goes beyond Islamic extremists and the Muslim world. The Revolutionary Armed Forces of Colombia poses a serious threat to U.S. interests in Latin America because it associates us with the government it is fighting against."[145]

In the 1990s, US officials had been careful to emphasize that Washington was supporting Colombia's antidrug campaign rather than its antiguerrilla campaign—with the Cold War over, the public was no longer so enthused about fighting communists. But the new emphasis on narcoterrorism made it less necessary for officials to publicly distance themselves from counterinsurgency. The term "narcoterrorism" was coined long before September 11 (dating back at least to the 1980s) but gained much wider currency and acceptance in the wake of the attacks. Labeling members of the FARC "narcoterrorists" became standard practice in Washington. As part of an increase in international antiterrorism funding in March 2002, Congress authorized support for the Colombian military in a "unified campaign" to combat both drugs and insurgents, making it possible for the United States to fund a variety of non-drug-related military and law enforcement operations in Colombia. In late 2002, the Bush administration also overturned an earlier executive order of the Clinton administration blocking the sharing of non-drug-related intelligence with Colombian security forces.[146] Any pretense of a distinction between fighting cocaine trafficking and fighting communist insurgents was now entirely gone.

The integration of the antidrug and antiterrorism missions had broader regional implications. As one observer commented, "For many in Washington, the war on drugs and the war on terror are virtually indistinguishable in Latin America."[147] US officials began to frame counterterrorism and counternarcotics efforts as part of a much larger security goal of imposing control over lawless zones. At a meeting with the region's defense ministers in November 2002, US Secretary of Defense Donald Rumsfeld told his counterparts, "In this hemisphere, narco-terrorists, hostage takers and arms smugglers operate in ungoverned areas, using them as bases from which to destabilize democratic governments."[148] By this logic, frontier zones that had long been viewed as hubs of drug trafficking and other criminal activities, such as the Darien Gap between Panama and Colombia, were now security priorities. Administration officials urged the regions' militaries to embrace a greater policing role to control these "ungoverned spaces."

In March 2003, General James Hill described the shift in perceived security threats as follows:

> Today, the threat to the countries of the region is not the military force of the adjacent neighbor or some invading foreign power. Today's foe is the terrorist, the narco-trafficker, the document forger, the international crime boss, and the money launderer. This threat is a weed that is planted, grown and nurtured in the fertile ground of ungoverned spaces such as coastlines, rivers and unpopulated border areas. This threat is watered and fertilized with money from drugs, illegal arms sales, and human trafficking. This threat respects neither geographical nor moral boundaries.[149]

As the United States began to retreat from its wars in Iraq and Afghanistan, some of the personnel, knowledge, tactics, and technologies used in those theaters were transferred to the drug war effort in the Americas. Forward operating bases "patterned on the forward bases in Iraq and Afghanistan" were created in Honduras to fight cocaine transshipment there, and military personnel returning from the Middle East took up new drug war positions in Central America. Several hundred US servicemembers were deployed to Honduras alone. A *New York Times* story described this shift: "The United States military has brought lessons from the past decade of conflict to the drug war . . . and showcases the nation's new way of war: small footprint missions with limited numbers of troops, partnerships with foreign military and police forces that take the lead in security operations, and narrowly defined goals, whether aimed at insurgents, terrorists or criminal groups that threaten American interests."[150] Yet this new development also echoed past experience: recall that as the coca and cocaine eradication efforts in the Andean region escalated in the late 1980s and 1990s, US military strategists applied old Cold War counterinsurgency methods and tools to the new counterdrug mission.

## Skyrocketing Violence

Meanwhile, it turned out that Mexico's drug war was just warming up. Escalating turf battles between increasingly well-armed traffickers placed growing pressure on the government to respond. President Vicente Fox initially resisted the temptation to further militarize the drug war. Indeed, he proposed sending the army back to the barracks, but in the face of pressure from Washington, particularly US drug tsar Barry McCaffrey, he changed his mind.[151] Clashes between traffickers for control of the border city of Nuevo Laredo in the fall of 2004 became particularly violent, made possible by a cocaine-funded buildup of firepower since the 1990s. In response, Fox launched Operation Mexico Seguro in June 2005, deploying some 700 soldiers and cops to Nuevo Laredo and then extending the operation elsewhere.[152] This strategy provided a hint of what was to come.

With much fanfare, Mexico's next president, Felipe Calderon, declared an all-out war on the country's leading drug traffickers when he took office in December 2006. "We will give no truce or quarter to the enemies of Mexico," Calderon instructed the troops at a military base in early 2007.[153] Some of the initial military successes were impressive. For instance, marines searching a container boat traveling from Colombia were responsible for the largest cocaine bust the world had ever seen, seizing more than 23.5 metric tons of the drug. But while Calderon's military-led antidrug offensive weakened the Tijuana, Juarez, and Gulf trafficking organizations—which since the 1990s had become much more powerful thanks to their expanded role in shipping and distributing cocaine across the border—these "successes" created opportunities for rival traffickers. The ensuing disorganization, disruption, and competitive scramble to control turf, routes, and market share fueled an unprecedented wave of drug violence in Mexico.[154]

Applauding Calderon's drug war offensive, Washington pledged $400 million in antidrug military and police assistance for Mexico in 2008 and took on an increasingly active role behind the scenes in Mexico. This included setting up a "fusion intelligence center" at a northern Mexican military base that was modeled on similar counterinsurgency centers in Iraq and Afghanistan; providing military and police training for thousands of Mexican agents; and deploying CIA operatives and military contractors to Mexico to gather intelligence, assist in wiretaps and interrogations, and help plan raids and other operations. The use of private US military contractors made it possible to get around Mexican laws prohibiting foreign military personnel from carrying out operations on Mexican territory. In early 2011 the Pentagon also began to deploy high-altitude Global Hawk drones deep into Mexican territory on drug surveillance missions.[155] More than ever before, US officials viewed the situation in Mexico as a security threat, with Secretary of State Hillary Clinton even going so far as to describe it as an insurgency.

Yet much to Mexico's frustration, Washington made only token efforts to curb the clandestine export of US firearms that was arming Mexican drug gangs.[156] Despite Mexico's protests, there was little domestic political pressure within the United States—and plenty of political obstacles—to more intensively police and restrict the bulk sale of weapons ranging from handguns to AK-47s by thousands of loosely regulated gun dealers in Texas and elsewhere near the border. In late 2011, J. Dewey Webb, the special agent responsible for curbing gun smuggling in Texas for the Bureau of Alcohol, Tobacco and Firearms, noted that "the United States is the easiest and cheapest place for drug traffickers to get their firearms."[157] Despite the proximity of the drug violence in Mexico and public anxiety about spillover, the southbound flow of arms generated far less attention and concern than the northbound flow of drugs.[158]

Washington provided sophisticated surveillance technology and expertise to help Calderon target and remove a growing number of high-profile traffickers. But as had been the case in the elimination of high-level Colombian traffickers in the 1990s, this decapitation strategy did not translate into a reduction in drug trafficking. Rather than reducing the drug flow, the crackdown did more to intensify brutal competition within and between a growing number of rival smuggling organizations and created a much more fluid and volatile—and therefore much more violent—market environment. While five criminal organizations dominated the trafficking of drugs into the United States in 2007, in 2012 there were nine, mostly spinoffs and remnants of the old organizations. And these new organizations were even more willing and able to use violence to protect and promote their business than their predecessors had been.

The most trigger-happy of the new groups, Los Zetas, was founded by former members of an elite US-trained Mexican antidrug military unit.[159] Los Zetas started out as enforcers for the Gulf trafficking organization but then broke away to form their own organization. Their emergence represented a turning point in the Mexican drug wars, in terms of not only military discipline, sophistication, and capacity but also willingness to routinely use extreme brutality. In Darwinian style, other trafficking organizations adapted and adopted similar methods or risked elimination.[160] Many of the new recruits were from the military. Los Zetas brazenly hung banners on bridges urging those with military backgrounds to join their organization. "The Zetas operations group wants you, soldiers and ex-soldiers," read one such banner. "We offer you a good salary, food, and attention for your family. Don't suffer hunger and abuse anymore."[161] Recruitment efforts extended into Guatemala to former members of the Kaibil counterinsurgency commandos, who had been responsible for some of the bloodiest government massacres during the country's brutal civil war. By 2010, Los Zetas reportedly had a fighting force of more than 10,000 soldiers.[162]

Each year, the drug killings in Mexico continued to mount. In 2012, drug-related deaths reached nearly 50,000 since Calderon had launched his drug war offensive at the end of 2006.[163] Brushing aside critics and insisting the violence was a sign of progress in the drug war, Calderon kept sending in more troops—at one point deploying as many as 96,000 army soldiers and 16,000 marines across a dozen states.[164] This only fueled the flames: death rates were significantly higher in states targeted by military campaigns than in nontargeted states.[165] Human rights abuses by the military also skyrocketed, provoking a growing public outcry. And the crackdown did not necessarily mean less corruption—in 2012, half a dozen senior military officers, including two generals, were charged with aiding drug trafficking.[166]

Meanwhile, rising fear of "spillover" violence from Mexico generated calls to further militarize the US side of the line. Alarm about spillover, Adam Isaacson notes, "has crept into official rhetoric, especially at the state and opposition-politics level, as a chief argument for further increasing US investment in border security, including greater

Figure 6.3 Mexican marines escort five alleged members of the Zetas drug-trafficking group past hand grenades, firearms, cocaine, and military uniforms seized during their arrest, June 2011 (Yuri Cortez/AFP/Getty Images).

use of military capabilities at the border."[167] A September 2011 Texas Department of Agriculture report authored by two retired generals declared that "conditions within these border communities along both sides of the Texas-Mexico border are tantamount to living in a war zone in which civil authorities, law enforcement agencies as well as citizens are under attack around the clock."[168] What was most remarkable, however, was how little spillover there actually was. Indeed, urban areas on the US side of the border had among the lowest crime rates in the country. In 2010, Juarez was one of the most violent cities in the world, while its counterpart just across the border, El Paso, was one of the safest in the United States.

When Enrique Peña Nieto assumed the Mexican presidency in 2012, there was widespread speculation that he might end or at least deescalate his predecessor's all-out drug war and turn his attention to other priorities. Indeed, one trafficking group, the Knights Templar, welcomed the new president with *narcomantas* ("narco-banners") that read: "If you honor your promise [to alter the course of the drug war], we will lay down our arms . . . otherwise we will continue to defend our territory."[169]

Figure 6.4 Military police stand guard at the scene of a murder in Juarez, Mexico, March 2010. Then-president Felipe Calderon sent 7,000 military troops to the border city to curtail drug violence (Spencer Platt/Getty Images).

But instead of retreating, Peña Nieto doubled down, deploying soldiers to even more states than his predecessor until eventually the military was patrolling the streets in a majority of Mexican states. Within a few years, drug violence had again skyrocketed, matching the peak levels of violence from 2010 to 2012. To make matters worse, as Vanda Felbab-Brown notes, the brutality not only continued to rage on in hotspots such as Guerrero, Michoacan, and Tamaulipas but returned to places such as Tijuana and Juarez where the violence had momentarily declined, and even extended into areas previously untouched by drug violence. She suggests that part of the new surge of violence was due to the infighting within the Sinaloa drug-trafficking organization after the 2016 recapture of its leader, Joaquin "El Chapo" Guzman, as well as to the encroachment of other trafficking organizations on Sinaloa territory along the northern border.[170]

Thus, while getting rid of El Chapo was certainly good public relations for the Mexican government and was cheered on by Washington, it unleashed still more bloody battles over turf and leadership. This was entirely predictable. After all, El Chapo himself had successfully

Figure 6.5 The world's most wanted drug trafficker, Joaquin "El Chapo" Guzman, is escorted in handcuffs by the Mexican marines, February 22, 2014, in Mexico City (STR/LatinContent/Getty Images).

risen to the top partly by ruthlessly taking advantage of the market opportunities created when his Colombian and Mexican business rivals were weakened or taken out by government crackdowns. The war on drugs helped give rise to El Chapo, and the war on drugs took him down because he had become too much of an embarrassment.[171] In the wake of his downfall, even more brutal and skilled criminal entrepreneurs, both within and outside of the Sinaloa organization, began muscling their way in to fill the power vacuum. The drug trade consequently became even more chaotic, fragmented, and difficult to contain. Levels of violence reached record levels in 2017 and again in 2018. With the mounting death toll and militarization of their society, more and more Mexicans suffered from drug war fatigue. Yet there was no end in sight. After years of making war on drugs, peace seemed as distant as ever.

Meanwhile, the militarized drug war continued to rage on elsewhere in the region. In Colombia, the demobilization of the FARC insurgency in 2016 was expected to be a blow to the cocaine industry. Yet production and trafficking actually went up in the wake of demobilization. Coca cultivation in the country reportedly reached record levels in 2017. Just as the FARC had been an unintended beneficiary of the dismantling of the Medellín and Cali trafficking organizations and the coca-suppression efforts in neighboring Peru and Bolivia in the 1990s, other players were now stepping in to take advantage of the vacuum created by the exit of the FARC. But perhaps most importantly, many former FARC rebels, facing bleak employment prospects, were turning to more full-time work in the criminal underworld, where their particular skills were still in demand.[172] For example, one crime group involved in cocaine trafficking near the Colombia-Ecuador border on the Pacific Coast, known as the United Guerrillas of the Pacific, was founded by defectors from the 2016 peace accord between the government and the FARC.[173] This development should not be surprising. After all, something similar had happened after the earlier disbanding of the country's major paramilitary groups, which subsequently splintered into criminal bands tied to the cocaine trade. So while the war against the cocaine-funded FARC insurgency was finally over, the war against cocaine continued on.

Farther south, the drug war in Brazil became progressively more militarized, with Rio de Janeiro as ground zero. With the influx of cocaine in the mid-1980s, Rio had transformed from mostly a stopover point for shipping cocaine to West Africa and Western Europe into a destination market for cocaine—with Brazil eventually becoming the world's second-largest consumer of the drug after the United States. In early 2018 Brazilian president Michel Termer placed the army in charge of Rio's police forces. He declared that only the military could carry out the "hard and firm responses" needed to defeat drug gangs and end their violent rivalries.[174] After years of heavy-handed police efforts to contain violent clashes between gangs competing for control of the retail drug trade, some 30,000 military troops were deployed to Rio's sprawling *favelas*, where almost a fifth of the city's residents lived. Previous military deployments—more than two dozen of which had occurred since 2001, including several in 2014 and 2016 during the Olympics and the World Cup—had had little lasting impact on the drug business, and there was little to indicate that this latest intervention would turn out differently.[175] The most immediate impact was a surge in violence: between March and September 2018, more than 900 people were killed by the police and the army in the state of Rio de Janeiro—a 45 percent jump from the same period the year before. And this may have only been the beginning. Jair Bolsonaro, a retired military officer elected in October 2018 as Brazil's new president, rose in popularity by promising to kill criminals. As Bolsonaro put it on the campaign trail, a "good criminal is a dead criminal."[176]

Such militarized crackdowns, popular among Brazil's middle and upper-middle classes, can be described as essentially a containment strategy, with the gangs squeezed and confined in particular spaces but still largely in charge. The main losers of this strategy, as Reginaldo Lima, who had worked as a mediator between rival gangs, noted, were the *favela* residents, who "now have to live in a permanent face-off with drug traffickers on the one side and military men on the other side, and risk being caught in crossfire."[177] Despite the deployment of troops into the *favelas* and the government's all-out declaration of war, there were no signs that the gangs and the drug trade that provides their biggest source of revenue were about to go out of business anytime soon.

Figure 6.6 Children walk near soldiers at the Complexo do Alemao favela, Rio de Janeiro, August 2018 (Carl de Souza/AFP/Getty Images).

IN THE FIRST DECADES of the twenty-first century, Latin America had become the murder capital of the world, with more than 2 million violent deaths since the year 2000—a number far exceeding the approximately 900,000 killed in the wars in Syria, Iraq, and Afghanistan combined. With only 8 percent of the world's population, approximately one-third of all murders were taking place there. Most strikingly, the world's top ten most violent cities were all in Latin America.[178] What was the cause of such startling numbers? Drugs and the drug war were only part of the answer, but especially in countries like Mexico, Colombia, and Brazil—three of the most violent places in the hemisphere—they were a crucial part of the answer. And no drug was more important in this regard than cocaine. As we've seen, from Rio to the Rio Grande, cocaine was both the leading funder of heavily armed traffickers and the leading target of ever-more militarized government suppression campaigns.

The type of organized violence involved in the cocaine wars is not conventionally classified as war, yet the extraordinary lethality involved in efforts to either profit from or suppress cocaine may signal a need to reconsider what qualifies as war. With soldiers turned into cops and criminals as heavily armed as soldiers, the distinction between military conflict and criminal conflict has become increasingly fuzzy.[179] But was this an endless war? And what of the fate of the drugs–war relationship more generally? In the concluding pages that follow, our centuries-long story ends with some speculative thoughts on what past and present trajectories may mean for the future.

# Conclusion: The Drugged Battlefields of the Twenty-First Century

BRINGING IN HISTORY TO understand the relationship between drugs and warfare is essential for a number of reasons: because it is so conspicuously absent from contemporary debates about the drugs–conflict nexus, because it corrects for the common tendency to view recent developments as entirely new and unprecedented, and because it helps us make sense of why we are where we are and even where we might be headed. In the early twenty-first century, the drugs–war relationship remains alive and well, with the six psychoactive substances highlighted in the previous chapters—alcohol, tobacco, caffeine, opium, amphetamines, and cocaine—still the leading "war drugs." This brief conclusion to our long story sums up how these drugs compare across the various dimensions of the drugs–war relationship and looks at what recent developments and trends may mean for the future.

Each of the drugs examined in this book has had a distinct and ever-evolving relationship to war. Alcohol has been the all-purpose drug with the greatest longevity: arriving with the introduction of grain agriculture, it dates back not only to ancient warfare but also to the origins of civilization itself. Drinking on the job has always been risky when it comes to war, but doing so has become less tolerable as war tasks in modern militaries have become more complex and involve the operation of increasingly sophisticated and expensive machinery. And as

*Killer High*, Peter Andreas. Oxford University Press (2020). © Peter Andreas.
DOI: 10.1093/actrade/9780190463014.001.0001

the tax base of states has shifted and diversified, alcohol is no longer the essential funder of war that it was in earlier centuries. Tobacco became globalized and popularized through warfare, with soldiers hooked on smoking and governments hooked on taxing it. Today, the leaf kills far more people than war itself, but unlike alcohol, tobacco is not considered an impediment to battlefield performance. Caffeine—mostly in the form of coffee and tea but also in carbonated sodas such as Coca-Cola and in an assortment of energy drinks—is long past its heyday as a stimulant for imperial expansion, but it continues to be the most widely used drug in the world, both on and off the battlefield. Opium, once the source of imperial war between Britain and China, remains as closely connected to war as ever, but the main beneficiaries are now armed nonstate actors such as Afghan insurgents and warlords. Beginning with World War II, the story of amphetamines has been almost entirely one of state-sponsored combatant drug use and its postwar aftermath, though nonstate combatants, including rebel fighters in Syria, have also turned to amphetamine-type stimulants in recent years. And finally, while cocaine has had various connections to war for more than a century, it stands out in recent decades as the top target of a highly militarized war against drugs.

These various war roles and their changes over time, as detailed in the previous chapters, are summed up in Table 7.1. Here we can briefly revisit the dimensions of the drugs–war relationship introduced at the beginning of the book. War *while on* drugs (drug use by combatants and civilians in wartime) has mostly involved alcohol, tobacco, caffeine, opium, and amphetamines.. Alcohol, tobacco, opium, and cocaine have played an especially prominent role in war *through* drugs (the use of drugs to finance war or to weaken the enemy). Opium and cocaine lead the way in war *for* drugs (war to secure drug markets) and war *against* drugs (the use of military means to suppress drugs or to attack or discredit enemies in the name of drug suppression). Notice that all six drugs score high in importance on at least two dimensions of the drugs–war relationship, and all score high in importance as drugs *after* war (drugs that are profoundly shaped by the aftermath of armed conflict). Although not part of the book, cannabis is included in the table for comparison. Despite this drug's widespread use and various links to war, what is most striking is that cannabis does not score high in

TABLE 7.1 Dimensions of the drugs–war relationship and its variation in importance across drugs

| | Alcohol | Tobacco | Caffeine | Opium | Amphetamines | Cocaine | Cannabis |
|---|---|---|---|---|---|---|---|
| **War *while on* drugs** | High | High | High | Moderate/High | High | Low/Moderate | Moderate |
| **War *through* drugs** | High | High | Moderate | High | Low | High | Moderate |
| **War *for* drugs** | Low | Low | Moderate | High | Low | High | Low |
| **War *against* drugs** | Low/Moderate | Low | Low | High | Low | High | Moderate |
| **Drugs *after* war** | High | High | High | High | High | High | Low |

importance on any single dimension. It would certainly have been next on the list of top war drugs, but is comparatively less consequential.

## Drugs and War as State-Making

One notable characteristic that these six drugs have in common is that they have all been instruments of state-making. Of course, guerrillas, traffickers, and other armed nonstate actors have also exploited drugs, often in ways that violently confront the state. In the contemporary era, this has prompted growing alarm about so-called narco-terrorists and narco-insurgents. But looking back not just years and decades but centuries, on balance it is clear that states have been the biggest beneficiaries of the drugs–war relationship. The term "narco-state" is typically used today to describe places such as Afghanistan that are deeply enmeshed in the illicit drug trade. Yet viewed from a longer historical perspective, all the major powers can actually be labeled "narco-states" in the sense that they have, at various times, in various ways, and to varying degrees, relied on drugs and drug revenue to carry out their state-making and war-making objectives. In some of the most prominent cases, this has even included empire building, as illustrated by imperial Russia's addiction to vodka revenue and imperial Britain's dominance of the tea and opium trades and heavy reliance on alcohol taxes.

As we've seen, these state-building projects did not always work out as planned and sometimes even backfired—the tsar used vodka money to build up the largest army in Europe, but his soldiers were often too drunk to fight. The subsequent vodka prohibition deprived the state of desperately needed funds to fight World War I, and that disaster in turn helped lay the groundwork for the Russian Revolution. Similarly, King Louis XVI imposed heavy tobacco and alcohol taxes on the French to help pay for his ever-more expensive military rivalry with Britain, but an intense public backlash contributed to the outbreak of the French Revolution and his beheading.

Even the contemporary war against drugs can in some ways be viewed as a state-making venture. After all, government leaders have often justified their antidrug campaigns as an effort to protect citizens, pacify violent nonstate challengers, secure borders, and impose law and order—quintessential state-making practices.[1] And even as the war against drugs has repeatedly failed, sometimes spectacularly so, the escalating war-making involved in it has greatly enlarged and empowered the security apparatus of the state. Policing, a core state function, has greatly expanded through the war against drugs, and in some places this has even involved turning soldiers into cops. One consequence has been to fundamentally challenge the traditional distinction between war fighting and crime fighting.[2]

And we should not forget that the war against drugs has involved substantial revenue extraction—another core state-making activity—through expansive asset forfeiture laws that have made policing highly profitable.[3] Since the mid-1980s, governments throughout the world have adopted legislation permitting the seizure and forfeiture of drug-trafficking assets, with the United States leading the way.[4] And there has been massive even if unrecorded informal revenue extraction in the form of bribes and payoffs, which can be thought of as a de facto tax on the drug trade.[5]

Writing about the rise of the modern state in Europe, historian and social scientist Charles Tilly argues that war-making and state-making went hand in hand. As he puts it, "States made war and war made states."[6] The enormous bureaucratic infrastructure and coercive power of the state was built up over time through the process of preparing for and engaging in warfare. Extending this dynamic to a very different context today, one could perhaps also say that "states make drug war and drug war makes states."[7] Benjamin Lessing, looking at militarized antidrug crackdowns in Latin America, rightly points out that this interactive dynamic necessarily prompts questions about what type of state is being built. As he warns, "One danger is that drug wars may lead to an over-strengthening of certain state actors, creating entrenched stakeholders with excessive authority and discretion, who are resistant to necessary adjustments of policy once drug violence has abated."[8] He also reminds us that a key and often-overlooked part of Tilly's argument is that the state, operating as a protection racket, can create the very security threat it then provides protection against. Although not what Tilly had in mind, this argument can be extended to the drug war: the state act of criminalizing drugs creates the threat—by sharply inflating drug profits and driving the business underground into the hands of heavily armed criminals—and this in turn provides the rationale for the state to respond with an increasingly militarized drug war. And since the eliminated traffickers and seized drugs that states use to measure their "success" are easily replaced and politicians and bureaucrats have powerful incentives to persist and escalate rather than reevaluate, the drug war grinds on.[9]

## The Future of Fighting Drugs

This leads us to wonder, then, where this is all headed. Drug war battles are won, but the war doesn't end. And the war has a perversely self-perpetuating dynamic: battlefield victories unintentionally create the conditions for more war—shutting down old routes and eliminating traffickers simply leads to the emergence of new routes and more traffickers. Moreover, the ensuing turf battles can further fuel the violence that sending in the military was supposed to quell. We've seen variations of this dynamic again and again. And if the past is any guide to the future, we can expect it to continue.[10]

In Mexico, where drug violence has taken an especially heavy toll and where the drug war has become the most militarized, one possible development that would certainly bring some relief to the country is a greater geographic dispersion of the drug trade, such as a move back to the Caribbean trafficking routes that were once the main gateway for US-bound Colombian cocaine. After all, it is largely intensified competition between Mexican traffickers to control drug shipments across the border—amid militarized government crackdowns—that has fueled such extraordinarily high levels of drug violence in the country.

There are already signs of a partial return of drug trafficking through the Caribbean, and this shift may increasingly take place via the use of GPS-guided submersible and semisubmersible vessels. This is an alarming trend from a US national security perspective, since such delivery mechanisms can transport more than drugs, but it is actually a positive development from the perspective of reducing drug violence and other collateral damage along trafficking routes. After all, the more removed the illegal drug trade is from legal commerce, population centers, and regular transportation channels, the better. For example, Guatemala and Honduras have been battered by their use as transshipment points for the flood of US-bound cocaine. It would be a change for the better if the trade were pushed more out to sea and even under the sea. If the use of submersibles and semisubmersibles really takes off, it may provide a rationale for the government to adapt and deploy the US Navy's latest submarine detection technologies for counterdrug purposes. To date, these submersibles have typically required a small crew, but one can easily imagine the development of unmanned remotely controlled vehicles.

This remote control scenario applies not only to sea transport but also to air transport. For instance, the proliferation of drones will certainly continue in the coming years, and drones have the potential to not only provide surveillance and targeted strikes but also carry high-value illicit cargoes such as drugs. There have already been scattered reports of traffickers turning to drones to ship their drugs, and as drones become capable of hauling heavier loads, this smuggling method may become more popular.[11] At the same time, governments have also started to incorporate drones into their antidrug arsenals. The US Department of Homeland Security already operates along the southern border a small fleet of satellite-controlled Predator-B drones that were originally used for military operations in the Middle East and elsewhere. The US Coast Guard has similarly begun to use ScanEagle—a ten-foot-long drone similar to one first used by the US military in Iraq—to detect drug-smuggling craft on the high seas. Farther south, Colombia has announced plans to deploy low-flying drones to undertake the aerial spraying of coca crops in the country's remote coca-growing regions.[12]

Meanwhile, the spread of new synthetics, potentially including synthetic cocaine, promises to undermine the traditional dominance of drugs derived from plants, with far-reaching repercussions for the international drug trade and the war against drugs. The advantages of synthetics, which are often manufactured in mobile clandestine laboratories, include their compactness and the minimal labor and territory required for their production. According to the latest UN estimates, production of the top three plant-based drugs—cannabis, heroin, and cocaine—are at all-time highs.[13] Nevertheless, it is safe to predict that the current trend toward the development and increased availability of a wide range of new synthetic substances will continue to accelerate, and that these will increasingly compete with and serve as substitutes for plant-based drugs that require vast tracts of land and are much more labor-intensive to produce.

This shift is already evident in the proliferation of prescription pills and synthetic opioids that have fueled the opioid crisis in the United States—with a record 72,000 drug overdose deaths in 2017—a crisis that now has the potential of going global.[14] Many US heroin users only turned to the drug after first becoming hooked on opioid prescription painkillers. The war against drugs, however, is a highly selective war, one that avoids any serious targeting of the pharmaceutical companies that have so aggressively pushed their addictive products.

Developments in drug production and consumption in China may prove particularly consequential in the years ahead. Ironically, while China lost two wars to Western opium pushers in the mid-nineteenth century, today it is becoming an increasingly important illicit exporter of synthetic drugs such as fentanyl (which distributors often mix with heroin) to Western countries. The main difference today is that China is not militarily forcing its way into foreign drug markets, and none of its producers come close to rivaling the British East India Company, which in its heyday enjoyed a virtual monopoly on illicit Indian opium imports into China.

China is also reemerging as a consumer market for illicit drugs, mirroring its development as a modern consumer society more generally. In a sense, then, China may be returning to its late-nineteenth-century status as both a top global drug producer and a top drug consumer. With an increasing drug problem, including a growing appetite for amphetamines, China is one of the world's most enthusiastic advocates of the war against drugs. However, there is little evidence to date that draconian Chinese drug laws and their enforcement, including public executions in some cases, will replicate the suppression results of Mao's sweeping postrevolution antidrug campaign.[15]

Of course, the old mantra of drug policy reformers remains as true as ever: trying to curb supply with increasingly militarized methods will ultimately do little without also curbing consumer demand, which has received considerably less policy attention. In this regard, it should be noted that even as new drugs, drug markets, drug routes, and drug transportation and production methods can be expected to proliferate, scientists are reportedly working on an "addiction vaccine."[16] And even if this proves illusory, scientists will likely continue to unlock the mysteries of addiction in ways that could greatly improve treatment and reduce the demand for drugs, both legal and illegal.

Drug war exhaustion has generated growing calls for peace, especially in Latin America. Until now, however, real movement in this direction has primarily involved cannabis, a soft drug that has a weaker connection to organized violence than its hard-drug counterparts. As the world's most drug war–ravaged country, Mexico presents a particularly critical test case. While on the campaign trail, Mexican president Andrés Manuel López Obrador boldly declared that he would deescalate the drug war. One of his campaign slogans was "abrazos, no balazos"— hugs, not gunfire—but once in office it was clear that there would be plenty of balazos.[17] He announced plans to create a specialized national guard force—to grow to 150,000-strong over three years—composed of members of the military and police under a single command. With much of the leadership coming from the ranks of the military, this move seemed to reflect more continuity rather than a radical break from the militarized approach of his immediate predecessors.[18] As one critic described it, "Mexico's law enforcement may get a different name and wear a different uniform under a new plan, but the essence, tactics, and command structure will continue to follow a military logic, in line with the prevailing security paradigm that has generated poor results."[19] The Mexican military itself may also be an obstacle to changing course, as its political influence and budgets have swelled thanks to the antidrug offensive. Indeed, as plans to create the national guard moved forward in early 2019, the army claimed that its latest buildup of military equipment was necessary to support the new force.[20]

For Mexico to demilitarize and push for an end to the drug war would also invite the wrath of Washington, further straining an already troubled bilateral relationship. Publicly making peace with the criminal organizations that feed America's seemingly insatiable appetite for illicit drugs is politically taboo and would invite even more intense Mexico bashing north of the border and generate even more calls to fortify it. An unlikely but alarming scenario could even involve US military intervention across the border. And this in turn would spark an intense anti-American backlash in Mexico. In *The Next War*, published more than two decades ago, former secretary of defense Caspar Weinberger describes five key potential future war scenarios for which US national security strategists should be ready. In the scenario closest to home, 60,000 American troops are deployed to the southwest border after a radical nationalist leader takes power in Mexico with the backing of drug traffickers and the resulting chaos turns the northward flow of people and drugs into a flood.[21] In retaliation, Washington launches a full-scale military invasion. While the likelihood of such an extreme scenario appears remote, US-Mexico relations may very well be headed in a more turbulent direction.

But what if the drug war were to somehow come to an end? Would the violence also end? Some see the declaration of peace as a sort of magic bullet, especially if it involves drug legalization. Legalization would strip the massive global illicit trade of its prohibition-inflated profits that fuel violence and fund terrorists and insurgents. Traffickers would likely diversify and turn to other illicit businesses—as mobsters did in the United States after the prohibition on alcohol was lifted—but their most important revenue stream would dry up. Similarly, in Afghanistan, other sources of insurgent and warlord financing would persist, but opium would no longer be the cornerstone of the illicit war economy.

The appeal of such an idea is understandable. Yet we should be careful not to oversell its potential pacifying effects. One drug war critic recently claimed that in gang-plagued San Salvador, described as the murder capital of the world, "the circumstances of these killings are disturbingly familiar. More often than not, illegal drugs are involved." He went on to say, "Ultimately, the only way to reliably reduce homicide in El Salvador—or anywhere in Latin America—is to end the war on drugs."[22] Such sweeping claims gloss over a much messier and more varied regional reality. Not all gang-related violence is drug-related, since the business of gangs extends well beyond drugs. This is especially true in El Salvador, where extortion is a more important gang revenue generator than drugs. While El Salvador is on the US-bound route for Colombian cocaine, much of the supply actually moves north off the coast rather than by land, where the violence is concentrated.[23]

Moreover, nearby Nicaragua and Costa Rica, countries that are also in close proximity to the cocaine transshipment corridor, have so far had comparatively low levels of drug violence. Meanwhile, an imploding

Venezuela has been rocked by extraordinarily high levels of violence, yet most of it has not been drug-related. At the same time, Bolivia and Peru are deeply enmeshed in the cocaine industry, yet drug violence in these two countries has remained strikingly low. Furthermore, with the decline of Colombia's FARC and Peru's Shining Path, the threat of drug-funded insurgencies has diminished in the region, despite a thriving drug trade.

Prohibition clearly matters in drug violence: business disputes are more likely to be resolved through violence or threats of violence if there are no legal protections—in other words, traffickers resort to killing rather than suing each other. Still, other forms of informal and largely nonviolent dispute resolution mechanisms have long existed. After all, most traffickers in most parts of the world are more sneaky than violent. This tendency holds true for their relations with the authorities: declaring an all-out war on the state, as Pablo Escobar did in Colombia, is the exception rather than the rule. Most of the time, traffickers want to evade and buy off the state rather than bully it.[24]

Drug prohibition and high volumes of drug trafficking, it should be remembered, long predated the recent surges in drug violence. Mexico, for example, had for decades been a favorite entry point into the US market for illegal drugs, including cocaine since the late 1980s, yet violence did not truly skyrocket until the government launched an all-out militarized offensive at the end of 2006. This suggests that it is not only prohibition and drug flows per se that shape violence, but the specific manner in which drug laws are enforced (or not enforced). And this raises the tricky issue of finding ways to make peace short of legalization—which at the moment remains a political nonstarter, at least for major illicit drugs beyond cannabis. Prohibition is necessary for the drug war, but the drug war is not necessary for prohibition. For instance, rather than continuing with its militarized antidrug crackdown, the Mexican government could do much more to prioritize curbing violence over curbing drugs. A greater shift toward more intensively targeting only the most violent trafficking organizations could create incentives for other traffickers to pull back their private armies. Those able to conduct their business with the least violence would be the least targeted. This strategy could reduce the killings—and help demilitarize Mexican society—even if it would not necessarily reduce the flow of drugs. Washington would not be pleased, but Mexico would be more peaceful.[25]

Implementing and sustaining such a shift would be logistically and politically challenging, to say the least.[26] Accommodation need not simply mean corruption, as has been the case in Mexico in the past.[27] Nevertheless, it would inevitably invite domestic and international accusations of corruption and complicity if the government were perceived as favoring one trafficking group over another and giving out free passes for good behavior. Unfortunately, these are the sort of political conundrums that tend to lead to policy persistence and escalation rather than a fundamental change in course. The morally charged politics of the drug war all too often crowds out more pragmatic approaches.[28]

### The Future of Fighting High

While modern militaries have been deployed to fight drugs on more and more fronts, they have also been fighting high on more and more drugs. Regardless of the battlefield applications of the robotics revolution, soldiers are still the primary participants in warfare, and boots are likely to be on the ground for years to come. Many of those responsible for the work of war will continue to seek drug assistance, whether prescribed or self-prescribed. While fighting high is an old story, more drugs are now available to more soldiers than ever before, and the state continues to be a primary pusher. Consider the sheer number of drug options made available to US troops. As one journalist has described it:

> Walk into any of the larger-battalion-aide stations in Iraq or Afghanistan today, and you'll find Prozac, Paxil, and Zoloft to fight depression, as well as Wellbutrin, Celexa, and Effexor. You'll see Valium to relax muscles (but also for sleep and combat stress) as well as Klonopin, Ativan, Restoril, and Xanax. There's Adderall and Ritalin for ADD and Haldol and Risperdal to treat psychosis; there's Seroquel, at subtherapeutic doses, for sleep, along with Ambien and Lunesta. Sleep, of course, is a huge issue in any war. But in this one, there are enough Red Bulls and Rip Its in the chow halls to light up the city of Kabul, and soldiers often line their pockets with them

before missions, creating a cycle where they use caffeine to power up and sleep meds to power down.[29]

Even more meds are then prescribed to help soldiers cope with the physical and mental scars they bring back from the battlefield. Those hooked on the pills include thousands of American soldiers returning home from Afghanistan and Iraq. "The troops, if they got hurt they'd just shove you a bag of pills," noted one soldier who had been deployed to Iraq. "You never got a bottle and knew what was in it; you always got a baggie."[30] Many of these drugs include opioids such as Percocet, hydrocodone, and oxycodone. The prescription rate for those in the military has been three times higher than the national average. In 2014, the Department of Veterans Affairs was prescribing opioids to some 650,000 veterans. Rates of opioid abuse among this group were greater than in the civilian population, and increased sharply during the wars in Iraq and Afghanistan. "We have a very large number of people coming home," noted Dr. Gavin West, head of the Opioid Safety Initiative at the Department of Veterans Affairs, which was created in 2013 in response to skyrocketing drug dependence among veterans. "We have people coming back that maybe in the past would not have survived these injuries, that have really significant pain syndromes from their injuries sustained on the battlefield."[31] To make matters worse, in the absence of adequate treatment, cutting back on opioid prescriptions has pushed many veterans to simply turn to the black market to self-medicate, either obtaining prescription pills illegally or switching to illicit opiates such as heroin.[32]

Meanwhile, despite its controversial use and strict controls, amphetamines have continued to have advocates within the military. Here again the United States has led the way. As two US Air Force researchers explain, "Technology has placed even higher demands on aircrews, so Go Pills likely will continue to be used to counter high levels of operational fatigue in the future."[33] Two commanders in the Medical Corps of the US Navy similarly write in their review of the military use of amphetamines: "As the nature of warfare changes, particularly as the US military moves towards nocturnal warfare and long duration missions, there will be continued pressure to use performance maintenance drugs in many settings." They go on to note:

Because of the wide-spread use of night-vision devices in all branches of US forces, the US military has a great advantage over many potential adversaries in undertaking night operations. However, by definition, night operations run against normal circadian rhythms. As such, forces might show diminished vigilance during those hours of the day when they will probably be called on to go into battle. Because of their effects on performance maintenance, amphetamines could be useful tactical adjuncts for such operations.[34]

Beyond amphetamine-type stimulants, the development of entirely new drugs aimed at soldiers' cognitive and performance enhancement is also sure to occur in the future. Indeed, the creation of a drugged-up super-soldier has long been a favorite fantasy. We've seen countless Hollywood versions, such as Jason Bourne in *The Bourne Legacy*. Comic books are also full of soldiers enhanced by drugs, with Captain America—injected with "Super Soldier Serum"—perhaps the most famous example. Villains, too, are often portrayed as drug-enhanced: the Green Goblin in the *Spider-Man* series gained strength, heightened reflexes, intelligence, and healing abilities by injecting himself with the Oz Compound—originally invented, thanks to a US government contract, to build up soldiers.

Outside of movies and comics, military researchers will no doubt continue investing in the development of drug-assisted soldiers and have been especially enthused about antifatigue drugs. Indeed, the MITRE Corporation (contracted by the Office of Defense Research and Engineering at the Pentagon), in a long-term threat assessment for the US military, reports: "The most immediate human performance factor in military effectiveness is degradation of performance under stressful conditions, particularly sleep deprivation. If an opposing force had a significant sleep advantage, this would pose a serious threat."[35] MITRE recommends that the Pentagon "monitor enemy activities in sleep research, and maintain close understanding of open source sleep research." Drawing on several military sleep studies, these researchers issue a warning: "Suppose a human could be engineered who slept for the same amount of time as a giraffe (1.9 hours per night). This would lead to an approximately *twofold* decrease in the casualty rate. An adversary would need an approximately 40 percent increase in the troop level to compensate for this advantage."[36] A report by the US Air Force Research Laboratory puts it more bluntly: "Forcing our enemies to perform continuously without the benefit of sufficient daily sleep is a very effective weapon." Such a strategy, however, requires us to "manage fatigue among ourselves."[37]

No wonder, then, that military researchers in a number of countries have been experimenting with ways to fight off sleep, with much of the interest in recent years focused on modafinil, a drug that is considered less addictive and has fewer negative side effects than amphetamines. To study modafinil, the US military has turned to its Air Force Research Laboratory, Army Aeromedical Research Laboratory, Army Medical Research and Materiel Command, Walter Reed Army Institute of Research, and Special Operations Command Biomedical Initiative Steering Committee. Military researchers in other countries have been equally excited about the drug, including at China's Second Military Medical University, Taiwan's National Defense Medical Center, South Korea's Air Force Academy, the Netherlands' Ministry of Defense, and India's Institute of Aerospace Medicine and Defence Institute of Physiology and Allied Sciences. The United States, Britain, and France have already been dispensing modafinil tablets to military personnel in the field for more than a decade.[38]

The drive to give troops a chemical edge is also sure to continue as the increasing complexity of combat and advances in technology have, in the words of MITRE Corporation researchers, "created a greater need to make rapid tactical decisions at lower command levels, and ha[ve] thereby spread the responsibility for making leadership decisions to more personnel."[39] They further report:

> New types of neuropharmaceuticals are being developed that more directly target synaptic firing, and thus impact brain plasticity far more effectively than existing drugs (e.g., modafinil, donepezil). When approved for use, these new drugs will certainly have extensive off-label use for improvement of memory and cognitive performance. . . . Depending on the ultimate performance of these drugs, adversaries might use them in training programs or field operations.[40]

At the same time, we can expect rebels, terrorists, and other non-state combatants to continue to turn to psychoactive substances for the same reasons that their state counterparts do—with the main difference being that they lack legal access to the ever-growing range of pharmacological options available to modern militaries. It is not hard to imagine, for example, why those on a suicide mission might be given a drug to calm their nerves, as kamikaze pilots were in an earlier era. Cocaine and other drugs were reportedly used by Islamist militants during the twelve coordinated bombings and shooting sprees they carried out over the course of four days in Mumbai in 2008. One official commented, "This explains why they managed to battle the commandos for over 50 hours with no food or sleep."[41] Reports also indicate that the Islamic State and Boko Haram routinely drugged their child soldiers before sending them off on suicide attacks.[42] The same was apparently the case with some teenage suicide bombers in Pakistan.[43]

Yet we should avoid jumping to conclusions about drugged-up terrorists. For some fighters, extremist ideology itself is apparently enough of a stimulant that no chemical assistance is needed. "Under the influence" can mean more than the influence of psychoactive substances. In 2015, a Belgian terror cell linked to the Islamic State carried out a series of coordinated attacks in Paris and surrounding areas, including suicide bombings and mass shootings. Witnesses described the terrorists as acting like crazed zombies, and several media accounts immediately jumped to the conclusion that they had been high on drugs such as Captagon. But the forensic reports later found no evidence of drugs. "It's true, it was reassuring to think they had taken drugs, that they weren't fully conscious of the massacre they were committing," noted Jean-Pol Tassin, an addiction specialist at the National Institute for Health and Medical Research, who initially promoted the notion that the killers had been drugged. "No doubt that's why one subscribes so rapidly to such theories."[44]

Moreover, some fundamentalist fighters can also be antidrug fundamentalists: Jabhat al-Nusra, an Al Qaeda–affiliated organization combating Assad in Syria, destroyed Captagon factories near the Lebanese border, citing its members' strict interpretation of Islamic law. And the most drug-free fighting force in the world may have been the foot soldiers of the Mexican drug-trafficking organization La Familia

Michoacana: "Its Bible-pounding leaders recruit young people from rehabilitation centers, insist that they throw off their dependence on alcohol, drugs, and other addictive substances, and, once clean, apply to join their organization. The novitiates must submit themselves to 2 months of brainwashing that includes scripture readings, exposure to motivational speakers, and long periods of silence and meditation."[45]

ONE FINAL NOTE: ALTHOUGH IT is well beyond our focus here, it should be recognized that war itself can be thought of as a drug—one that will likely endure even as the popularity of other drugs comes and goes. Soldiers can get "high on war," as many a helmet in Vietnam proclaimed. Combat produces an adrenaline rush, which is what amphetamines do, except that with amphetamines the rush is longer and the crash harder. If frequent and prolonged, combat can also "fry" soldiers' brains, in the sense of causing lasting and pathological neuronal changes—another thing drugs do. Many writers and artists have seized on the war-as-baddest-drug-of-all theme—think of Michael Herr's *Dispatches* or Kathryn Bigelow's *The Hurt Locker*.[46] In his book *War Is a Force That Gives Us Meaning*, former *New York Times* war correspondent Chris Hedges writes that "the rush of battle is a potent and often lethal addiction, for war is a drug, one I ingested for many years."[47] Countless war memoirs similarly describe war as a form of addiction, so much so that its absence can provoke intense withdrawal symptoms for combatants returning home. And many of them then turn to other drugs—both prescribed and self-prescribed, licit and illicit—to help them cope and recover.

In the end, war will likely be the hardest of all habits to kick. Despite a long-term historical trend toward fewer and less lethal wars, a world without war unfortunately seems about as realistic as a drug-free world. The one thing that we can therefore predict with some confidence is that drugs and war will continue their deadly embrace, making and remaking each other in the years and decades ahead.

# NOTES

<hr />

## Introduction

1. Although the interactive dynamic is rather different, this has echoes of Charles Tilly's notion that "states make war and war makes states." See Charles Tilly, *Coercion, Capital, and European States: AD 990–1992* (Oxford: Blackwell, 1992).
2. See, for instance, Paul Rexton Kan, *Drugs and Contemporary Warfare* (Dulles, VA: Potomac Books, 2009); Paul Rexton Kan, *Drugs and International Security* (Lanham, MD: Rowman & Littlefield, 2016).
3. Two recent exceptions, which focus mostly on drug use, are Lukasz Kamienski, *Shooting Up: A Short History of Drugs and War* (New York: Oxford University Press, 2016); and Dessa Bergen-Cico, *War and Drugs: The Role of Military Conflict in the Development of Substance Abuse* (Boulder, CO: Paradigm Publishers, 2012).
4. Much of the most relevant literature is cited throughout this book.
5. David T. Courtwright, *Forces of Habit: Drugs and the Making of the Modern World* (Cambridge, MA: Harvard University Press, 2001), 2.
6. Courtwright, *Forces of Habit*, 140.
7. Quoted in Courtwright, *Forces of Habit*, 141.
8. Quoted in Richard Kluger, *Ashes to Ashes: America's Hundred-Year Cigarette War, the Public Health, and the Unabashed Triumph of Philip Morris* (New York: Vintage, 1997), 63.
9. Quoted in Iain Gately, *Tobacco: A Cultural History of How an Exotic Plant Seduced Civilization* (New York: Grove Press, 2001), 181.
10. Margaret Levi, *Of Rule and Revenue* (Berkeley: University of California Press, 1989), 96.

11. War, involving the strategic use of organized violence, has varied enormously in form, intensity, and frequency across time and place. For a useful discussion of the definition of war, see Lawrence Freedman, "Defining War," in Julian Lindley-French and Yves Boyer, eds., *The Oxford Handbook of War* (New York: Oxford University Press, 2012).

12. Quoted in Frances Stead Sellers and Michael Scherer, "Oliver North, Incoming NRA Chief, Blames School Shootings on 'Culture of Violence,'" *Boston Globe*, May 20, 2018.

## Chapter 1

1. John Mueller, *The Remnants of War* (Ithaca, NY: Cornell University Press, 2004), 89–94, 97–99.

2. "Drunken militia bands" in Rwanda, writes journalist Philip Gourevitch, "were bused from massacre to massacre"; reporter Ed Vulliamy similarly describes boozy Serb fighters in Bosnia as having "inflammable breath." Quoted in Mueller, *Remnants of War*, 91, 99.

3. Bruce Bower, "Ancient Site Taps into Soldiers' Brew," *Science News*, December 10, 1994, 390.

4. Robert J. Braidwood, Jonathan D. Sauer, Hans Helbaek, Paul C. Mangelsdorf, Hugh C. Culter, Carleton S. Coon, Ralph Lenton, Julian Steward, and Leo A. Oppenheim, "Symposium: Did Man Once Live by Beer Alone?" *American Anthropologist* 55, no. 4 (1953): 515–526; Greg Wadley and Brian Hayden, "Pharmacological Influences on the Neolithic Transition," *Journal of Ethnobiology* 35, no. 3 (2015): 566–584.

5. Gavin D. Smith, *Beer: A Global History* (London: Reaktion Books, 2014), 7–11.

6. Tom Standage, *A History of the World in 6 Glasses* (New York:, 2005), 36–37.

7. Iain Gately, *Drink: A Cultural History of Alcohol* (New York: Gotham Books, 2009), 12.

8. Angelos Chaniotis, "Greeks Under Siege: Challenges, Experiences, and Emotions," in *The Oxford Handbook of Warfare in the Classical World*, ed. Brian Campbell and Lawrence A. Trittle (Oxford: Oxford University Press, 2013), 448.

9. Quoted in Robin Lane Fox, *Alexander the Great* (New York: Dial Press, 1974), 262.

10. Rod Phillips, *Alcohol: A History* (Chapel Hill: University of North Carolina Press, 2014), 36.

11. Gately, *Drink*, 36.

12. Standage, *History of the World*, 70.

13. Paul Lukacs, *Inventing Wine: A New History of One of the World's Most Ancient Pleasures* (New York: W. W. Norton, 2013), 18–19.

14. David Arscott, *Wine: A Very Peculiar History* (Brighton, UK: Book House, 2016), 15.

15. Arscott, *Wine*, 19.

16. Quoted in Gately, *Drink*, 38.
17. Gately, *Drink*, 37.
18. Gately, *Drink*, 38.
19. Gately, *Drink*, 52.
20. Arscott, *Wine*, 18.
21. Gately, *Drink*, 62.
22. Smith, *Beer*, 13.
23. Gately, *Drink*, 63.
24. Phillips, *Alcohol*, 78.
25. This paragraph is drawn from Phillips, *Alcohol*, 78.
26. Phillips, *Alcohol*, 101.
27. Phillips, *Alcohol*, 110.
28. Rudi Matthee, "Exotic Substances: The Introduction and Global Spread of Tobacco, Coffee, Cocoa, Tea, and Distilled Liquor, Sixteenth to Eighteenth Centuries," in *Drugs and Narcotics in History*, ed. Roy Porter and Mikulas Teich (Cambridge: Cambridge University Press, 1997), 44.
29. Gately, *Drink*, 95.
30. Lukacs, *Inventing Wine*, 86. Madeira wine had better immediate success— it was fortified by adding a distilled spirit made from cane sugar, making it more hardy and stable for travel. It was also certainly convenient that it was produced on a well-situated Portuguese island in the middle of transatlantic trade routes. It soon turned into a favorite upper-class drink. Lukacs, *Inventing Wine*, 119.
31. Standage, *History of the World*, 129.
32. Quoted in Standage, *History of the World*, 108.
33. Quoted in Gately, *Drink*, 144.
34. Ian Williams, *Rum: A Social and Sociable History* (New York: Nation Books, 2006), 229.
35. Quoted in Wayne Curtis, *And a Bottle of Rum: A History of the New World in Ten Cocktails* (New York: Three Rivers Press, 2006), 51. Note that Curtis questions whether temperance advocates may have made these up.
36. Curtis, *And a Bottle of Rum*, 51.
37. Quoted in Gately, *Drink*, 145.
38. Curtis, *And a Bottle of Rum*, 54.
39. James Pack, *Nelson's Blood: The Story of Naval Rum* (Annapolis, MD: Naval Institute Press, 1982).
40. Kerstin Ehmer and Beate Hindermann, *The School of Sophisticated Drinking: An Intoxicating History of Seven Spirits* (Vancouver: Greystone Books, 2015), 93.
41. Standage, *History of the World*, 109.
42. Standage, *History of the World*, 109–110.
43. Ralph L. Ketcham, ed., *The Political Thought of Benjamin Franklin* (Indianapolis, IN: Bobbs-Merrill, 2003 [1965]), 262. Italics in original.

44. John Adams to William Tudor, August 11, 1818, in Charles Francis Adams, ed., *The Works of John Adams, Second President of the United States: With a Life of the Author, Notes and Illustrations, by His Grandson Charles Francis Adams*, (Boston: Little, Brown, 1856), 10:345.

45. For more details, see Peter Andreas, *Smuggler Nation: How Illicit Trade Made America* (New York: Oxford University Press, 2013), 39–41.

46. Susan Cheever, *Drinking in America: Our Secret History* (New York: Twelve, 2015), 33.

47. Cheever, *Drinking in America*, 32; Eric Burns, *The Spirits of America: A Social History of Alcohol* (Philadelphia: Temple University Press, 2004), 7; Gately, *Drink*, 196.

48. Curtis, *And a Bottle of Rum*, 109.

49. Gately, *Drink*, 191.

50. Quoted in Gately, *Drink*, 195.

51. Williams, *Rum,* 170.

52. Curtis, *And a Bottle of Rum*, 110.

53. Quoted in Standage, *History of the World*, 120–121.

54. Quoted in Gately, *Drink*, 195.

55. David T. Courtwright, *Forces of Habit: Drugs and the Making of the Modern World* (Cambridge, MA: Harvard University Press, 2001), 140.

56. Gately, *Drink*, 196.

57. Cheever, *Drinking in America,* 66.

58. Quoted in Gately, *Drink*, 196.

59. Quoted in Williams, *Rum,* 175.

60. Richard Foss, *Rum: A Global History* (London: Reaktion Books, 2012), 54.

61. Gately, *Drink*, 196.

62. Williams, *Rum*, 228.

63. Curtis, *And a Bottle of Rum*, 111.

64. Quoted in Phillips, *Alcohol*, 167.

65. Courtwright, *Forces of Habit*, 141.

66. Sita Ram, quoted in Foss, *Rum*, 80.

67. Williams, *Rum,* 227. Also see John Keegan, *The Face of Battle* (New York: Viking Press, 1976), 181–182.

68. Lukasz Kamienski, *Shooting Up: A Short History of Drugs and War* (New York: Oxford University Press, 2016), 9.

69. Foss, *Rum*, 67–72.

70. Mark A. Vargas, "The Progressive Agent of Mischief: The Whiskey Ration and Temperance in the United States Army," *Historian* 67, no. 2 (2005): 204.

71. Charles Augustus Murray, *Travels in North America Including a Summer Residence with the Pawnee Tribe of Indians, in the Remote Prairies of the Missouri, and a Visit to Cuba and the Azore Islands* (London: Richard Bentley, 2 vols., 1854), 2:115.

72. Vargas, "Progressive Agent of Mischief," 202.

73. Cited in Vargas, "Progressive Agent of Mischief," 205–206.

74. Vargas, "Progressive Agent of Mischief," 216.

75. Quoted in Gately, *Drink*, 217–218.

76. Standage, *History of the World*, 122.

77. John Dos Passos, *The Ground We Stand On: The History of a Political Creed* (New Brunswick, NJ: Transaction, 2010), 464.

78. Cheever, *Drinking in America*, 68.

79. Quoted in Gately, *Drink*, 222.

80. Standage, *History of the World*, 126.

81. Peter C. Mancall, *Deadly Medicine: Indians and Alcohol in Early America* (Ithaca, NY: Cornell University Press, 1995), 68.

82. See John W. Frank, Roland S. Moore, and Genevieve M. Ames, "Public Health Then and Now: Historical and Cultural Roots of Drinking Problems Among American Indians," *American Journal of Public Health* 90, no. 3 (March 2000): 346. For a more general discussion, see National Institute on Alcohol Abuse and Alcoholism, *Alcohol Use Among American Indians and Alaska Natives: Research Monograph 37* (Washington, DC: US Department of Health and Human Services, 2002).

83. Quoted in Williams, *Rum*, 110.

84. Quoted in Williams, *Rum*, 110.

85. Williams, *Rum*, 111.

86. Williams, *Rum*, 99.

87. Quoted in Curtis, *And a Bottle of Rum*, 76.

88. Larzer Ziff, ed., *The Portable Benjamin Franklin* (New York: Penguin, 2005), 117.

89. Quoted in Williams, *Rum*, 101–102.

90. William E. Unrau, *White Man's Wicked Water: The Alcohol Trade and Prohibition in Indian Country, 1802–1892* (Lawrence: University Press of Kansas, 1996), x.

91. US Congress, *American State Papers: Indian Affairs*, vol. 4, pt. 2: *1832* (Whitefish, MT: Kessinger, 2005), 65.

92. Quoted in Unrau, *White Man's Wicked Water*, 24.

93. Quoted in Unrau, *White Man's Wicked Water*, 26.

94. Quoted in Gately, *Drink*, 312.

95. Cheever, *Drinking in America*, 111.

96. Quoted in Cheever, *Drinking in America*, 111.

97. Cheever, *Drinking in America*, 111.

98. Quoted in Gately, *Drink*, 313.

99. Cheever, *Drinking in America*, 114.

100. Quoted in Cheever, *Drinking in America*, 110.

101. Ryan M. Kennedy, " 'Drunk and Disorderly': The Origins and Consequences of Alcoholism at Fort Hays," *Kansas History: A Journal of the Central Plains* 36 (Summer 2013): 92.

102. Quoted in Kennedy, "Drunk and Disorderly," 94.

103. Kennedy, "Drunk and Disorderly," 101.

104. W. J. Rorabaugh, *Prohibition: A Concise History* (New York: Oxford University Press, 2018), 47.

105. W. Elliot Brownlee, *Funding the Modern American State, 1941–1995: The Rise and Fall of the Era of Easy Finance* (Washington, DC: Woodrow Wilson Center Press, 2002), 48.

106. John V. C. Nye, "Political Economy of Anglo-French Trade, 1689–1899: Agricultural Trade Policies, Alcohol Taxes, and War," American Association of Wine Economists Working Paper No. 38 (2009), 1–2.

107. Nye, "Political Economy of Anglo-French Trade," 2.

108. Mark Lawrence Schrad, "The First Social Policy: Alcohol Control and Modernity in Policy Studies," *Journal of Policy History* 19, no. 4 (2004): 440.

109. Kevin R. Kosar, *Whiskey: A Global History* (London: Reaktion Books, 2010), 46–47.

110. Kosar, *Whiskey*, 69.

111. Christopher Storrs, "Introduction: The Fiscal Military State in the 'Long' Eighteenth Century," in *The Fiscal-Military State in Eighteenth-Century Europe: Essays in Honor of P.G.M. Dickson*, ed. Christopher Storrs (Farnham: Ashgate, 2009), 4.

112. Patrick Karl O'Brien, "The Triumph and Denouement of the British Fiscal State: Taxation for the Wars Against Revolutionary and Napoleonic France, 1793–1815," in *The Fiscal-Military State in Eighteenth-Century Europe*, ed. Christopher Storrs (Farnham: Ashgate, 2009), 169, 200.

113. John V. C. Nye, *War, Wine, and Taxes: The Political Economy of Anglo-French Trade, 1689–1900* (Princeton, NJ: Princeton University Press, 2007), 73.

114. Nye, *War, Wine, and Taxes*, 71.

115. Nye, *War, Wine, and Taxes*, xiv.

116. Curtis, *And a Bottle of Rum*, 85.

117. Nye, *War, Wine, and Taxes*, 42.

118. On the birth of the London beer industry, see especially Peter Mathias, *The Brewing Industry in England, 1700–1830* (Cambridge: Cambridge University Press, 1959).

119. Brian Harrison, *Drink and the Victorians: The Temperance Question in England 1815–1872* (Edinburgh: Edinburgh University Press, 1997), 333.

120. Harrison, *Drink and the Victorians,* 61.

121. Harrison, *Drink and the Victorians,* 333.

122. Patricia Herlihy, *Alcoholic Empire: Vodka and Politics in Late Imperial Russia* (New York: Oxford University Press, 2002).

123. Patricia Herlihy, *Vodka: A Global History* (London: Reaktion Books, 2012), 46.

124. Mark Lawrence Schrad, *Vodka Politics: Alcohol, Autocracy, and the Secret History of the Russian State* (Oxford: Oxford University Press, 2014), 10–11.

125. Schrad, *Vodka Politics*, 113.
126. Herlihy, *Alcoholic Empire*, 57.
127. Herlihy, *Alcoholic Empire*, 56.
128. Quoted in Herlihy, *Alcoholic Empire*, 55.
129. Schrad, *Vodka Politics*, 152.
130. Quoted in Schrad, *Vodka Politics*, 153.
131. Quoted in Don Kladstrup and Petie Kladstrup, *Champagne: How the World's Most Glamorous Wine Triumphed over War and Hard Times* (New York: Harper Perennial, 2006), 66.
132. Kladstrup and Kladstrup, *Champagne*, 66.
133. Kladstrup and Kladstrup, *Champagne*, 67.
134. Napoleon was not a big drinker, but he was a big fan of champagne, declaring: "In victory you deserve it, in defeat you need it" (quoted in Kladstrup and Kladstrup, *Champagne*, 65). His secretary noted that "a single glass of champagne was enough to restore his strength and produce cheerfulness of spirit" (quoted in Kladstrup and Kladstrup, *Champagne*, 65).
135. Quoted in Kladstrup and Kladstrup, *Champagne*, 68.
136. Schrad, *Vodka Politics*, 149.
137. Quoted in George E. Snow, "Alcoholism in the Russian Military: The Public Sphere and the Temperance Discourse, 1883–1917" in *Jahrbücher für Geschichte Osteuropas* 65 (1997): 420–421.
138. Schrad, *Vodka Politics*, 156.
139. Quoted in Herlihy, *Alcoholic Empire*, 53. Herlihy notes that receipts after 1904 for vodka almost doubled, producing a net increase of 500 million rubles.
140. Quoted in Herlihy, *Alcoholic Empire*, 54.
141. Schrad, *Vodka Politics*, 161.
142. Herlihy, *Alcoholic Empire*, 54.
143. Quoted in Schrad, *Vodka Politics*, 161.
144. Schrad, *Vodka Politics*, 167.
145. Quoted in Herlihy, *Alcoholic Empire*, 52.
146. Quoted in Schrad, *Vodka Politics*, 162.
147. Quoted in Kamienski, *Shooting Up*, 13.
148. Quoted in Schrad, *Vodka Politics*, 167.
149. Quoted in Kamienski, *Shooting Up*, 13.
150. Quoted in Herlihy, *Alcoholic Empire*, 52.
151. Quoted in Herlihy, *Alcoholic Empire*, 52.
152. Schrad, *Vodka Politics*, 176–177.
153. Quoted in Schrad, *Vodka Politics*, 178.
154. Quoted in Schrad, *Vodka Politics*, 196.
155. Schrad, *Vodka Politics*, 190.
156. Herlihy, *Alcoholic Empire*, 64–65.
157. Quoted in Herlihy, *Alcoholic Empire*, 67.
158. This paragraph is drawn from Herlihy, *Alcoholic Empire*, 67.

159. Herlihy, *Alcoholic Empire*, 67. See also David Christian, "Prohibition in Russia, 1914–1425," *Australian Slavonic and East European Studies* 9, no. 2 (1995): 101.
160. Schrad, *Vodka Politics*, 191.
161. Schrad, *Vodka Politics*, 191.
162. Quoted in Schrad, *Vodka Politics*, 192.
163. Schrad, *Vodka Politics*, 181.
164. Schrad, *Vodka Politics*, 194–195.
165. Quoted in Schrad, *Vodka Politics*, 200.
166. Quoted in Schrad, *Vodka Politics*, 200.
167. Quoted in Schrad, *Vodka Politics*, 202.
168. Reprinted in John Reed, *Ten Days that Shook the World* (New York: Random House, 1935), 309.
169. Quoted in Schrad, *Vodka Politics*, 198.
170. Quoted in Boris M. Segal, *The Drunken Society: Alcohol Abuse and Alcoholism in the Soviet Union: A Comparative Study* (New York: Hippocrene Books, 1990), 25.
171. Quoted in Schrad, *Vodka Politics*, 204.
172. Herlihy, *Vodka*, 59.
173. Quoted in Schrad, *Vodka Politics*, 220.
174. Schrad, *Vodka Politics*, 233.
175. Quoted in Phillips, *Alcohol*, 241.
176. Gately, *Drink*, 364.
177. Gately, *Drink*, 365.
178. Phillips, *Alcohol*, 242.
179. Kamienski, *Shooting Up*, 18.
180. Quoted in Kamienski, *Shooting Up*, 18.
181. Kamienski, *Shooting Up*, 18.
182. Quoted in Kamienski, *Shooting Up*, 19.
183. Quoted in Kamienski, *Shooting Up*, 19.
184. Quoted in Kamienski, *Shooting Up*, 19.
185. Phillips, *Alcohol*, 245.
186. Gately, *Drink*, 366.
187. Phillips, *Alcohol*, 254.
188. Philipp Blom, *Fracture: Life and Culture in the West, 1918–1938* (New York: Basic Books, 2015), 61.
189. Quoted in Burns, *Spirits of America*, 164, 166–167.
190. Gately, *Drink*, 370.
191. Quoted in Gately, *Drink*, 371.
192. Mark Lawrence Schrad, "The First Social Policy: Alcohol Control and Modernity in Policy Studies," *Journal of Policy History* 19, no. 4 (2007): 434, 440; James F. Mosher and Dan E. Beauchamp, "Justifying Alcohol Taxes to Public Officials," *Journal of Public Health Policy* 4, no. 4 (1983): 423–424.
193. Burns, *Spirits of America*, 164–165.

194. Quoted in Phillips, *Alcohol*, 250.
195. Lukacs, *Inventing Wine*, 193.
196. Quoted in Kladstrup and Kladstrup, *Champagne*, 187.
197. Quoted in Kladstrup and Kladstrup, *Champagne*, 188.
198. Quoted in Kladstrup and Kladstrup, *Champagne*, 6.
199. Kladstrup and Kladstrup, *Champagne*, 187.
200. Quoted in Kladstrup and Kladstrup, *Champagne*, 188.
201. Kladstrup and Kladstrup, *Champagne*, 209–210.
202. This paragraph is drawn from Kladstrup and Kladstrup, *Champagne*, 210–211.
203. Quoted in Kladstrup and Kladstrup, *Champagne*, 211–212.
204. Quoted in Gately, *Drink*, 387.
205. Quoted in Kamienski, *Shooting Up*, 21.
206. Quoted in Don Kladstrup and Petie Kladstrup, *Wine and War: The French, the Nazis, and the Battle for France's Greatest Treasure* (New York: Broadway Books, 2002), 41.
207. F. A. McKenzie, *Pussyfoot Johnson: Crusader, Reformer, a Man Among Men* (London: Hodder & Stoughton, 1920), 146. I thank Mark Schrad for this reference.
208. Kamienski, *Shooting Up*, 21.
209. Quoted in Gately, *Drink*, 403.
210. Quoted in Kamienski, *Shooting Up*, 22.
211. Pack, *Nelson's Blood*, 94–95.
212. Pack, *Nelson's Blood*, 94–95.
213. This paragraph is drawn from Lisa Jacobson, "Beer Goes to War: The Politics of Beer Promotion and Production in the Second World War," *Food, Culture, and Society* 12, no. 3 (2009): 275–312.
214. Quoted in Gately, *Drink*, 406.
215. Gately, *Drink*, 406.
216. Quoted in Pete Brown, *Man Walks into a Pub: A Sociable History of Beer* (London: Pan Books, 2010), 207.
217. Brown, *Man Walks into a Pub*, 204.
218. Gately, *Drink*, 407.
219. Quoted in Brown, *Man Walks into a Pub*, 216.
220. Gately, *Drink*, 407.
221. Gately, *Drink*, 401–402.
222. Quoted in Phillips, *Alcohol*, 297.
223. Quoted in Kamienski, *Shooting Up*, 22.
224. Quoted in Kamienski, *Shooting Up*, 22.
225. James Walter, *Becoming Evil: How Ordinary People Commit Genocide and Mass Killing* (New York: Oxford University Press, 2007), 245.
226. Phillips, *Alcohol*, 297.
227. Edward B. Westermann, "Stone-Cold Killers or Drunk with Murder?: Alcohol and Atrocity During the Holocaust," *Holocaust and Genocide Studies* 30, no. 1 (2016): 1–19.

228. Quoted in Edward B. Westermann, "Drunk on Genocide: How the Nazis Celebrated Murdering Jews," *Aeon*, February 16, 2018.
229. Quoted in Westermann, "Stone-Cold Killers," 9.
230. Quoted in Gately, *Drink*, 405.
231. Quoted in Gately, *Drink*, 404–405.
232. Gately, *Drink*, 405.
233. Kladstrup and Kladstrup, *Champagne*, 245–246.
234. Gately, *Drink*, 404; Kladstrup and Kladstrup, *Champagne*, 247–248.
235. Quoted in Kladstrup and Kladstrup, *Wine and War*, 94.
236. Quoted in Kladstrup and Kladstrup, *Champagne*, 247.
237. Gately, *Drink*, 404.
238. Kladstrup and Kladstrup, *Champagne*, 250.
239. Kladstrup and Kladstrup, *Wine and War*, 104.
240. Gately, *Drink*, 409.
241. Quoted in Kamienski, *Shooting Up*, 23.
242. Quoted in Gately, *Drink*, 410.
243. Gately, *Drink*, 410.
244. Quoted in Gately, *Drink*, 411.
245. Quoted in Kamienski, *Shooting Up*, 24.
246. Chris Foran, "Our Back Pages: When Schlitz, Blatz Bought Korean War Soldiers a Brew—1.2 Million of Them," *Milwaukee Journal Sentinel*, February 14, 2017.
247. Gately, *Drink*, 437.
248. Quoted in Kamienski, *Shooting Up*, 25.
249. Quoted in Kamienski, *Shooting Up*, 25.
250. Quoted in Kamienski, *Shooting Up*, 25.
251. Quoted in Kamienski, *Shooting Up*, 26.
252. Edgar Jones and Nicola T. Fear, "Alcohol Use and Misuse Within the Military: A Review," *International Review of Psychiatry* 23 (April 2011): 169.
253. Mark McDonald, "Keeping Alcohol out of War Zones," *New York Times*, March 19, 2012.
254. Paul Von Zielbauer, "In Iraq, American Military Finds It Has an Alcohol Problem," *New York Times*, March 12, 2007.
255. Kamienski, *Shooting Up*, 27.
256. Cheever, *Drinking in America*, 123.
257. Cheever, *Drinking in America*, 123–124.
258. Quoted in Kamienski, *Shooting Up*, 27.
259. Quoted in Schrad, *Vodka Politics*, 151.
260. Quoted in Kamienski, *Shooting Up*, 223.
261. Herlihy, *Vodka*, 27.
262. Quoted in Kamienski, *Shooting Up*, 26.
263. Kamienski, *Shooting Up*, 26.
264. Kamienski, *Shooting Up*, 27.
265. Quoted in Kamienski, *Shooting Up*, 27.

266. Quoted in Schrad, *Vodka Politics*, 304.
267. Quoted in Jason Lyall, "Does Indiscriminate Violence Incite Insurgent Attacks?: Evidence from Chechnya," *Journal of Conflict Resolution* 53, no. 3 (2009): 345.
268. Quoted in Lyall, "Does Indiscriminate Violence Incite Insurgent Attacks?," 345.
269. Lyall, "Does Indiscriminate Violence Incite Insurgent Attacks?," 345.
270. Schrad, *Vodka Politics*, 303.
271. High levels of alcoholism and alcohol-related deaths extended well beyond the Russian military. Stan Fedun, "How Alcohol Conquered Russia," *Atlantic*, September 25, 2013.

## Chapter 2
1. Quoted in Cassandra Tate, *Cigarette Wars: The Triumph of "The Little White Slaver"* (New York: Oxford University Press, 1999), 67.
2. Tate, *Cigarette Wars*, 68.
3. Sander L. Gilman and Zhou Xun, "Introduction," in *Smoke: A Global History of Smoking*, ed. Sander L. Gilman and Zhou Xun (London: Reaktion Books, 2004), 9; Iain Gately, *Tobacco: A Cultural History of How an Exotic Plant Seduced Civilization* (New York: Grove Press, 2001), 3.
4. Gately, *Tobacco*, 5; Frances Robicsek, "Ritual Smoking in Central America," in *Smoke: A Global History of Smoking*, ed. Sander L. Gilman and Zhou Xun (London: Reaktion Books, 2004), 32; Marcy Norton, *Sacred Gifts, Profane Pleasures: A History of Tobacco and Chocolate in the Atlantic World* (Ithaca, NY: Cornell University Press, 2008), 22.
5. Gately, *Tobacco*, 5.
6. Richard Kluger, *Ashes to Ashes: America's Hundred-Year Cigarette War, the Public Health, and the Unabashed Triumph of Philip Morris* (New York: Vintage Books, 1996), 8–9; Gately, *Tobacco*, 13.
7. Gately, *Tobacco*, 18.
8. Gately, *Tobacco*, 23–24.
9. W. D. Wills and H. O. Wills, "Smoking Through the Ages," in *A History of Tobacco Around the World: A Collection of Historical Articles on the Origins, Industry, and Uses of Tobacco* (UK: Read Books, 2011), 20; N. A. Hunt, "Tobacco Manual," in *A History of Tobacco Around the World*, 336–337; Gately, *Tobacco*, 21–36; Burns, *Smoke of the Gods*, 14–21.
10. Gately, *Tobacco*, 35–36.
11. Norton, *Sacred Gifts, Profane Pleasures*, 203.
12. Gately, *Tobacco*, 80.
13. Wills and Wills, "Smoking Through the Ages," 21.
14. Eric Burns, *The Smoke of the Gods: A Social History of Tobacco* (Philadelphia: Temple University Press, 2007), 25, 28.
15. Burns, *Smoke of the Gods*, 54.

16. Field Museum of Natural History, Department of Anthropology, "The Introduction of Tobacco into Europe," in *A History of Tobacco Around the World* , 88.

17. Gately, *Tobacco,* 81.

18. Gately, *Tobacco*, 86.

19. Gately, *Tobacco*, 57.

20. Rudi Mathee, "Exotic Substances: The Introduction and Global Spread of Tobacco, Coffee, Cocoa, Tea, and Distilled Liquor, Sixteenth to Eighteenth Centuries," in *Drugs and Narcotics in History*, ed. Roy Porter and Mikulas Teach (Cambridge: Cambridge University Press, 1997), 26.

21. Carol Benedict, *Golden-Silk Smoke: A History of Tobacco in China, 1550–2010* (Berkeley: University of California Press, 2011), 61.

22. Timothy Brook, "Smoking in Imperial China," in *Smoke: A Global History of Smoking*, ed. Sander L. Gilman and Zhou Xun (London: Reaktion Books, 2004), 84–85.

23. Brook, "Smoking in Imperial China," 86.

24. Gately, *Tobacco*, 87.

25. Quoted in Burns, *Smoke of the Gods*, 33. Also see Carol Benedict, "Between State Power and Popular Desire: Tobacco in Pre-Conquest Manchuria, 1600–1644," *Late Imperial China* 32, no. 1 (2011): 13–48.

26. Rudi Matthee, "Tobacco in Iran," in *Smoke: A Global History of Smoking*, ed. Sander L. Gilman and Zhou Xun (London: Reaktion Books, 2004), 58–60.

27. Kātib Chelebi [Hajji Kalfa], *The Balance of Truth*, trans. G. L. Lewis (London: George Allen and Unwin, 1957 [1656]), 52.

28. Kluger, *Ashes to Ashes*, 11.

29. Burns, *Smoke of the Gods*, 93.

30. Burns, *Smoke of the Gods*, 72–73.

31. Susan Wagner, *Cigarette Country: Tobacco in American History and Politics* (New York: Praeger, 1971), 24–25.

32. Allan M. Brandt, *The Cigarette Century: The Rise, Fall, and Deadly Persistence of the Product that Defined America* (New York: Basic Books, 2007), 23.

33. Kluger, *Ashes to Ashes*, 12.

34. Quoted in Burns, *Smoke of the Gods*, 70.

35. Burns, *Smoke of the Gods*, 70.

36. Gately, *Tobacco*, 140.

37. Gately, *Tobacco*, 142.

38. Burns, *Smoke of the Gods*, 73, 95; Gately, *Tobacco*, 142; Wagner, *Cigarette Country*, 24–25.

39. Quoted in Burns, *Smoke of the Gods*, 94.

40. Burns, *Smoke of the Gods*, 93–95.

41. Gately, *Tobacco*, 142.

42. Burns, *Smoke of the Gods*, 95; Wagner, *Cigarette Country*, 24–25.

43. Burns, *Smoke of the Gods*, 105.
44. Thomas J. Sargent and François R. Velde, "Macroeconomic Features of the French Revolution," *Journal of Political Economy* 103, no. 3 (1995): 477.
45. Quoted in Michael Kwass, *Contraband: Louis Mandrin and the Making of a Global Underground* (Cambridge, MA: Harvard University Press, 2014), 44–45.
46. Kwass, *Contraband*, 321; Gately, *Tobacco*, 143.
47. Kwass, *Contraband*, 52–53.
48. Kwass, *Contraband*, 46, 48, 324. Also see Suzanne Desan, "Internalizing the French Revolution," *French Politics, Culture, and Society* 29, no. 2 (2011): 137–160.
49. Kwass, *Contraband*, 328–329.
50. Kwass, *Contraband*, 333–334.
51. Noelle Plack, "Liberty, Equality and Taxation: Wine in the French Revolution," *Social History of Alcohol and Drugs* 26, no. 1 (2012): 5.
52. Kwass, *Contraband*, 346.
53. Gately, *Tobacco*, 143.
54. Gately, *Tobacco*, 144.
55. Kluger, *Ashes to Ashes*, 13; Gately, *Tobacco*, 143.
56. Gately, *Tobacco*, 143.
57. Gately, *Tobacco*, 144.
58. Field Museum of Natural History, "Introduction of Tobacco into Europe," 76–77.
59. Gately, *Tobacco*, 146–147.
60. Field Museum of Natural History, "Introduction of Tobacco into Europe," 76–77; Gately, *Tobacco*, 150–152.
61. Gately, *Tobacco*, 155–156.
62. Gately, *Tobacco*, 157–158.
63. Gately, *Tobacco*, 160, 181–182.
64. Gately, *Tobacco*, 182.
65. Gately, *Tobacco*, 183.
66. Wills and Wills, "Smoking Through the Ages," 26; Wagner, *Cigarette Country*, 33; Kluger, *Ashes to Ashes*, 12–13; Tate, *Cigarette Wars*, 12, 68; Burns, *Smoke of the Gods*, 130.
67. Kluger, *Ashes to Ashes*, 13.
68. Tate, *Cigarette Wars*, 68.
69. Wagner, *Cigarette Country*, 33.
70. Kluger, *Ashes to Ashes*, 13.
71. Wagner, *Cigarette Country*, 33; Kluger, *Ashes to Ashes*, 14–16; Brandt, *Cigarette Century*, 25; Barbara Hahn, *Making Tobacco Bright: Creating an American Commodity, 1617–1937* (Baltimore: Johns Hopkins University Press, 2011), 2.
72. Wagner, *Cigarette Country*, 28, 37, 47; Burns, *Smoke of the Gods*, 126–127; Kluger, *Ashes to Ashes*, 22.

73. Frank L. Olmstead, "The Tobacco Tax," *Quarterly Journal of Economics* 5, no. 2 (1891): 193–194; Davis Rich Dewey, *Financial History of the United States* (New York: Longmans, Green & Co., 1918), 300–301.

74. Olmstead, "Tobacco Tax," 195–196.

75. Jan-Willem Gerritsen, *The Control of Fuddle and Flash: A Sociological History of the Regulation of Alcohol and Opiates* (Leiden: Brill, 2000), 107.

76. Burns, *Smoke of the Gods*, 125.

77. Burns, *Smoke of the Gods*, 125.

78. Burns, *Smoke of the Gods*, 125.

79. Tate, *Cigarette Wars*, 68.

80. Burns, *Smoke of the Gods*, 131.

81. Burns, *Smoke of the Gods*, 132–133; Wills and Wills, "Smoking Through the Ages," 26–27; Norton, *Sacred Gifts, Profane Pleasures*, 264.

82. Quoted in Brandt, *Cigarette Century*, 46.

83. Tate, *Cigarette Wars*, 20.

84. Tate, *Cigarette Wars*, 20.

85. Gately, *Tobacco*, 216.

86. Tate, *Cigarette Wars*, 65–66; Brandt, *Cigarette Century*, 45–50; Lee J. Alston, Tomas Nonnenmacher, and Ruth Dupre, "Social Reformers and Regulation: The Prohibition of Cigarettes in the United States and Canada," *Explorations in Economic History* 39, no. 4 (2002): 432–433.

87. Patrizia Russo, Giulio Alzetta, Candida Nastrucci, and Clara Szalai, "Tobacco Habit: Historical, Cultural, Neurobiological, and Genetic Features of People's Relationship with an Addictive Drug," *Perspectives in Biology and Medicine* 54, no. 4 (2011): 557–577; Tate, *Cigarette Wars*, 66.

88. Burns, *Smoke of the Gods*, 157; Tate, *Cigarette Wars*, 91; Gately, *Tobacco*, 233–234.

89. Tate, *Cigarette Wars*, 71–72.

90. Quoted in Burns, *Smoke of the Gods*, 157; Tate, *Cigarette Wars*, 71.

91. See Tate, *Cigarette Wars*, 70–71 for a discussion of both pro- and anticigarette doctors' arguments.

92. Quoted in Burns, *Smoke of the Gods*, 157.

93. Tate, *Cigarette Wars*, 88.

94. Tate, *Cigarette Wars*, 68.

95. Quoted in Tate, *Cigarette Wars*, 69.

96. Tate, *Cigarette Wars*, 90–91.

97. Quoted in Tate, *Cigarette Wars*, 91.

98. Tate, *Cigarette Wars*, 66.

99. Tate, *Cigarette Wars*, 75.

100. This paragraph is drawn from Tate, *Cigarette Wars*, 66, 75. See also Russo et al., "Tobacco Habit," 563.

101. This paragraph is drawn from Tate, *Cigarette Wars*, 66, 73–74.

102. See Elizabeth A. Smith and Ruth E. Malone, "Everywhere the Soldier Will Be: Wartime Tobacco Promotion in the U.S. Military," *American Journal of Public Health* 99, no. 9 (1999): 1595.

103. Tate, *Cigarette Wars*, 75–76, 91.

104. Tate, *Cigarette Wars*, 76; see also Alston, Dupre, and Nonnenmacher, "Social Reformers and Regulation," 433.

105. Alston, Dupre, and Nonnenmacher, "Social Reformers and Regulation," 432; Tate, *Cigarette Wars*, 7, 66, 76–83, 103; Gately, *Tobacco*, 231; Brandt, *Cigarette Century*, 51–52; Burns, *Smoke of the Gods*, 158–159.

106. Quoted in Tate, *Cigarette Wars*, 89–90.

107. Tate, *Cigarette Wars*, 82.

108. Kluger, *Ashes to Ashes*, 63; Tate, *Cigarette Wars*, 7, 66, 76–77, 79; Brandt, *Cigarette Century*, 51–52; Burns, *Smoke of the Gods*, 158.

109. Quoted in Tate, *Cigarette Wars*, 78, 89.

110. Quoted in Burns, *Smoke of the Gods*, 158.

111. Quoted in Brandt, *Cigarette Century*, 51.

112. Quoted in Matthew Hilton, "Smoking and Sociability," in *Smoke: A Global History of Smoking*, ed. Sander L. Gilman and Zhou Xun (London: Reaktion Books, 2004), 198.

113. Kluger, *Ashes to Ashes*, 65–66; Tate, *Cigarette Wars*, 107.

114. Wagner, *Cigarette Country*, 50–51; Kluger, *Ashes to Ashes*, 58.

115. Tate, *Cigarette Wars*, 85–86.

116. Tate, *Cigarette Wars*, 86–87; Gately, *Tobacco*, 235; Brandt, *Cigarette Century*, 53–54.

117. Quoted in Russo et al., "Tobacco Habit," 563.

118. Tate, *Cigarette Wars*, 85.

119. Kluger, *Ashes to Ashes*, 63–64.

120. Burns, *Smoke of the Gods*, 164.

121. Tate, *Cigarette Wars*, 66, 80, 92; Burns, *Smoke of the Gods*, 160, 163.

122. Gately, *Tobacco*, 231–232; Burns, *Smoke of the Gods*, 159.

123. Quoted in Burns, *Smoke of the Gods*, 161.

124. Richard Doll, "Uncovering the Effects of Smoking," *Statistical Methods in Medical Research* 7, no. 2 (1998): 88.

125. Gately, *Tobacco*, 237.

126. Hilton, "Smoking and Sociability," 131–132.

127. Gately, *Tobacco*, 238.

128. Wagner, *Cigarette Country*, 74; Kluger, *Ashes to Ashes*, 112–113; Gately, *Tobacco*, 255–257; Burns, *Smoke of the Gods*, 197–198; Russo et al., "Tobacco Habit," 563–564.

129. Quoted in Gately, *Tobacco*, 254.

130. See Robert N. Proctor, *The Nazi War on Cancer* (Princeton, NJ: Princeton University Press, 2000).

131. Quoted in Tracy Brown Hamilton, "The Nazis' Forgotten Anti-Smoking Campaign," *Atlantic*, July 9, 2014.

132. Henner Hess, "The Other Prohibition: The Cigarette Crisis in Post-War Germany," *Crime, Law, and Social Change* 25 (1996): 44.
133. This paragraph is drawn from Gately, *Tobacco*, 254–257.
134. Hess, "Other Prohibition," 46.
135. Quoted in Hess, "Other Prohibition," 46.
136. Gately, *Tobacco*, 258, 261.
137. Kluger, *Ashes to Ashes*, 112.
138. Quoted in Kluger, *Ashes to Ashes*, 113.
139. Gately, *Tobacco*, 257, 265.
140. Russo et al., "Tobacco Habit," 563–564.
141. Gately, *Tobacco*, 256.
142. Burns, *Smoke of the Gods*, 210–211.
143. Gately, *Tobacco*, 257–258.
144. Gately, *Tobacco*, 255.
145. Quoted in Gately, *Tobacco*, 255–256.
146. Wagner, *Cigarette Country*, 74–75.
147. Gately, *Tobacco*, 257.
148. Burns, *Smoke of the Gods*, 199.
149. Kluger, *Ashes to Ashes*, 117; Gately, *Tobacco*, 263–264.
150. Gately, *Tobacco*, 261–262.
151. R. A. Bradford, "The Economic Organization of a P.O.W. Camp," *Economica* 12, no. 48 (1945): 194.
152. Quoted in Burns, *Smoke of the Gods*, 202.
153. Wagner, *Cigarette Country*, 74–75; see also Brandt, *Cigarette Century*, 100; Burns, *Smoke of the Gods*, 204–205.
154. Hess, "Other Prohibition," 51–52.
155. Hess, "Other Prohibition," 52, 59.
156. Burns, *Smoke of the Gods*, 204–205.
157. Burns, *Smoke of the Gods*, 206.
158. Kluger, *Ashes to Ashes*, 113.
159. Kluger, *Ashes to Ashes*, 113–114, 336.
160. Kluger, *Ashes to Ashes*, 113.
161. Kluger, *Ashes to Ashes*, 150–151; Brandt, *Cigarette Century*, 244–245.
162. Quoted in Gilman and Xun, "Smoking and Sociability," 198.
163. Quoted in Gately, *Tobacco*, 308.
164. Gately, *Tobacco*, 309.
165. Gately, *Tobacco*, 302.
166. Gately, *Tobacco*, 303.
167. Smith and Malone, "Everywhere the Soldier Will Be," 1598.
168. This paragraph is drawn from Peter Andreas, *Blue Helmets and Black Markets: The Business of Survival in the Siege of Sarajevo* (Ithaca, NY: Cornell University Press, 2008), 84.
169. This paragraph is drawn from Andreas, *Blue Helmets and Black Markets*, 85.

170. This paragraph is drawn from Andreas, *Blue Helmets and Black Markets*, 84–85.
171. Quoted in Michael Mechanic, "Is the World's Most Powerful Military Defenseless Against Big Tobacco?," *Mother Jones*, May 22, 2014.
172. Andrew Tobin, "Israel Army Has a Smoking Problem, New Study Finds," *Jewish Telegraphic Agency*, January 23, 2017.
173. Robert Beckusen, "Russia Fears Its Troops Will Riot If Cigarette Rations End," *Wired*, March 5, 2013.
174. Rukmini Callimachi, "After ISIS, Smoking Openly to Feel Free," *New York Times*, April 22, 2017; Nabih Bulos, "Islamic State: Smoking Will Kill You, One Way or Another," *Los Angeles Times*, February 12, 2015.

## Chapter 3

1. Bennett Alan Weinberg and Bonnie K. Bealer, *The World of Caffeine: The Science and Culture of the World's Most Popular Drug* (New York: Routledge, 2001), xiv.
2. Weinberg and Bealer, *World of Caffeine*, xiii.
3. Alan Macfarlane and Iris Macfarlane, *Green Gold: The Empire of Tea* (London: Ebury Press, 2003), 259–260.
4. Macfarlane and Macfarlane, *Green Gold*, 32.
5. Victor H. Mair and Erling Hoh, *The True History of Tea* (London: Thames & Hudson, 2009), 55.
6. Mair and Hoh, *True History of Tea*, 70–72, 77.
7. Quoted in Mair and Hoh, *True History of Tea*, 72.
8. Quoted in Mair and Hoh, *True History of Tea*, 74.
9. Beatrice Hohenegger, *Liquid Jade: The Story of Tea from East to West* (New York: St. Martin's Press, 2006), 28.
10. Mair and Hoh, *True History of Tea*, 74–75.
11. Mair and Hoh, *True History of Tea*, 77.
12. Mair and Hoh, *True History of Tea*, 78.
13. Mair and Hoh, *True History of Tea*, 80–81, summarizing a Ming government memorandum of 1505.
14. For more on Sanetomo, see Weinberg and Bealer, *World of Caffeine*, 134.
15. For more on tea utensils, see Mair and Hoh, *True History of Tea*, 95, 98.
16. Hohenegger, *Liquid Jade*, 42.
17. Laura C. Martin, *Tea: The Drink that Changed the World* (Rutland, VT: Tuttle Publishing), 68–69.
18. Quoted in Martin, *Tea*, 69.
19. Weinberg and Bealer, *World of Caffeine*, 136.
20. Weinberg and Bealer, *World of Caffeine*, 135–136.
21. Weinberg and Bealer, *World of Caffeine*, 5.
22. Quoted in Weinberg and Bealer, *World of Caffeine*, 4–5.
23. Mark Pendergrast, *Uncommon Grounds: The History of Coffee and How It Transformed Our World* (New York: Basic Books, 2010), 7.

24. Weinberg and Bealer, *World of Caffeine*, 13.
25. Anthony Wild, *Coffee: A Dark History* (New York: W. W. Norton, 2004), 55; Pendergrast, *Uncommon Grounds*, 6.
26. Weinberg and Bealer, *World of Caffeine*, 15.
27. This account is drawn from Pendergrast, *Uncommon Grounds*, 9–10.
28. Several authors question the authenticity of this well-known account of the heroics of Kolschitzky in saving Europe. In particular, see Wild, *Coffee*, 62.
29. William H. Ukers, *All about Coffee* (New York: Tea and Coffee Trade Journal Company, 1922), 50.
30. Quoted in Weinberg and Bealer, *World of Caffeine*, 86.
31. Weinberg and Bealer, *World of Caffeine*, 86–87.
32. Quoted in Tom Standage, *A History of the World in 6 Glasses* (New York: Walker Publishing, 2005), 144–145.
33. Standage, *History of the World*, 145.
34. Quoted in Standage, *History of the World*, 169–170.
35. Standage, *History of the World*, 170.
36. Quoted in Pendergrast, *Uncommon Grounds*, 14.
37. Ukers, *All about Coffee*, 111; Suzanne Von Drachenfels, *The Art of the Table: A Complete Guide to Table Setting, Table Manners, and Tableware* (New York: Simon & Schuster, 2000), 487.
38. Quoted in Mair and Hoh, *True History of Tea*, 7.
39. Quoted in Benjamin L. Carp, *Defiance of the Patriots: The Boston Tea Party and the Making of America* (New Haven, CT: Yale University Press, 2010), 72.
40. Carp, *Defiance of the Patriots*, 77.
41. Niall Ferguson, *Empire: The Rise and Demise of the British World Order and the Lessons for Global Power* (New York: Basic Books, 2004), 72.
42. Benjamin Woods Labaree, *The Boston Tea Party* (New York: Oxford University Press, 1964), 164, 253; Pendergrast, *Uncommon Grounds*, 15.
43. Quoted in Pendergrast, *Uncommon Grounds*, 15.
44. Quoted in John Griffiths, *Tea: A History of the Drink that Changed the World* (London: Carlton Publishing Group, 2011), 93.
45. Pendergrast, *Uncommon Grounds*, 15.
46. Pendergrast, *Uncommon Grounds*, 15.
47. Pendergrast, *Uncommon Grounds*, 21.
48. Ukers, *All About Coffee*, 468.
49. Ellis, Coulton, and Mauger note that "it has been calculated that revenue from the tea excise met nearly two-thirds of the annual cost of the civil establishment in Britain in the 1830s, including the Crown." Markman Ellis, Richard Coulton, and Matthew Mauger, *Empire of Tea: The Asian Leaf that Conquered the World* (London: Reaktion Books, 2015), 219.
50. Jane Pettigrew and Bruce Richardson, *A Social History of Tea: Tea's Influence on Commerce, Culture & Community* (Danville, KY: Benjamin

Press, 2014), 17; Roy Moxham, *Tea: Addiction, Exploitation, and Empire* (London: Constable & Robinson, 2004), 87–88.

51. Standage, *History of the World*, 195; William H. Ukers, *All About Tea* (New York: Tea and Coffee Trade Journal Company, 1935), 75; Mair and Hoh, *True History of Tea*, 183.

52. Mair and Hoh, *True History of Tea*, 183.

53. Mair and Hoh, *True History of Tea*, 183–184.

54. Ellis, Coulton, and Mauger, *Empire of Tea*, 214–215.

55. Quoted in Ellis, Coulton, and Mauger, *Empire of Tea*, 216.

56. Quoted in Ellis, Coulton, and Mauger, *Empire of Tea*, 216.

57. Quoted in Mair and Hoh, *True History of Tea*, 193–194.

58. Quoted in Mair and Hoh, *True History of Tea*, 194.

59. Mair and Hoh, *True History of Tea*, 195; Griffiths, *Tea*, 100.

60. Mair and Hoh, *True History of Tea*, 195–196.

61. Griffiths, *Tea*, 104.

62. As Griffiths notes, the British were not the only ones who developed an opium-for-tea trade, nor were they the only nation eager to find an alternative to Chinese tea. On a smaller scale, the Dutch replicated the British strategy, exchanging illicit opium for tea and ultimately growing their own tea in the Dutch East Indies. Having smuggled tea seeds out of China between 1827 and 1833, the Dutch soon set up successful tea plantations in Java and Sumatra. And indeed, the tea export business in these lands flourished until the Japanese invasion in early 1942 brought it to a sudden halt. Griffiths, *Tea*, 106–108.

63. Moxham, *Tea*, 93–94, 98; Mair and Hoh, *True History of Tea*, 211.

64. Erika Rappaport, *A Thirst for Empire: How Tea Shaped the Modern World* (Princeton, NJ: Princeton University Press, 2017), 8, 92.

65. This point is forcefully made in Macfarlane and Macfarlane, *Green Gold*, 180–181.

66. Griffiths, *Tea*, 113–114; Macfarlane and Macfarlane, *Green Gold*, 119.

67. Moxham, *Tea*, 104–105.

68. Macfarlane and Macfarlane, *Green Gold*, 185–186.

69. Stewart Lee Allen, *The Devil's Cup: A History of the World According to Coffee* (New York: Ballantine Books, 1999), 210.

70. Pendergrast, *Uncommon Grounds*, 46.

71. Quoted in Pendergrast, *Uncommon Grounds*, 46–47.

72. William Force Scott, *The Story of a Cavalry Regiment: The Career of the Fourth Iowa Veteran Volunteers, from Kansas to Georgia, 1861–1865* (New York: G. P. Putnam's Sons, 1893), 379–382.

73. Jon Grinspan, "How Coffee Fueled the Civil War," *New York Times*, July 9, 2014.

74. Quoted in Grinspan, "How Coffee Fueled the Civil War."

75. Quoted in Grinspan, "How Coffee Fueled the Civil War."

76. Quoted in Grinspan, "How Coffee Fueled the Civil War."

77. "If War Is Hell, Then Coffee Has Offered U.S. Soldiers Some Salvation," *National Public Radio*, July 25, 2016.

78. Grinspan, "How Coffee Fueled the Civil War."

79. Quoted in Kim A. O'Connell, "Soldiers Loved a Refreshing Cup of Coffee," *Civil War Times Magazine*, August 2016.

80. Quoted in Grinspan, "How Coffee Fueled the Civil War."

81. Scott, *Story of a Cavalry Regiment*, 380.

82. Quoted in Grinspan, "How Coffee Fueled the Civil War."

83. Franz A. Koehler, *Coffee for the Armed Forces: Military Development and Conversion to Industry Supply* (Washington, DC: Historical Branch, Office of the Quartermaster General, 1958), 1, 11.

84. As Pendergrast points out, "Until the conflict, the ports of Hamburg and Le Havre, and to a lesser degree Antwerp and Amsterdam, had commanded over half of the world's coffee. Because German coffee growers and exporters dominated much of Latin America, German importers traditionally had received the prime growths. Europeans also were willing to pay more for good coffee, leaving Americans with lower grades." Pendergrast, *Uncommon Grounds*, 133.

85. Pendergrast, *Uncommon Grounds*, 135.

86. Pendergrast, *Uncommon Grounds*, 135.

87. Pendergrast, *Uncommon Grounds*, 136.

88. Quoted in Pendergrast, *Uncommon Grounds*, 136.

89. Pendergrast, *Uncommon Grounds*, 136.

90. Ukers, *All About Coffee*, 539.

91. E. F. Holbrook, "Coffee for Our Soldiers Abroad and at Home," *Simmon's Spice Mill: Devoted to the Interests of the Coffee, Tea and Spice Trades* 42, pt. 2 (1919): 1182.

92. Koehler, *Coffee for the Armed Forces*, 16.

93. Quoted in Pendergrast, *Uncommon Grounds*, 137.

94. Pendergrast, *Uncommon Grounds*, 137.

95. Pendergrast, *Uncommon Grounds*, 137–138.

96. Pendergrast, *Uncommon Grounds*, 138.

97. Quoted in Pendergrast, *Uncommon Grounds*, 138.

98. Holbrook, "Coffee for Our Soldiers," 1183.

99. See *Simmon's Spice Mill: Devoted to the Interests of the Coffee, Tea and Spice Trades* 42, no. 2 (1919): 837.

100. Quoted in Pendergrast, *Uncommon Grounds*, 144.

101. Pendergrast, *Uncommon Grounds*, 203.

102. The author adds in a footnote that there are two other theories regarding the origins of the term "cuppa Joe": that it "derived from a combination of Java and Mocha, or that it was named after Josephus Daniels, who served as secretary of the U.S. Navy from 1913 to 1921 and who banned wine at the officers' mess, so that coffee became the strongest available drink." Pendergrast, *Uncommon Grounds*, 205.

103. Koehler, *Coffee for the Armed Forces*, 53

104. Pendergrast, *Uncommon Grounds*, 204.

105. Pendergrast, *Uncommon Grounds*, 205.

106. Wild, *Coffee*, 200.

107. Quoted in Pendergrast, *Uncommon Grounds*, 208.

108. Pendergrast, *Uncommon Grounds*, 211, 220.

109. Pendergrast, *Uncommon Grounds*, 211.

110. Koehler, *Coffee for the Armed Forces*, 39–40.

111. Pendergrast, *Uncommon Grounds*, 205.

112. Pendergrast, *Uncommon Grounds*, 195.

113. Pendergrast, *Uncommon Grounds*, 205.

114. Pettigrew and Richardson, *Social History of Tea*, 171.

115. Rappaport, *Thirst for Empire*, 305.

116. Quoted in Rappaport, *Thirst for Empire*, 316.

117. Griffiths, *Tea*, 364.

118. Griffiths, *Tea*, 366.

119. Griffiths, *Tea*, 372.

120. Griffiths, *Tea*, 365.

121. Griffiths, *Tea*, 367.

122. Griffiths, *Tea*, 365.

123. Quoted in Ellis, Coultron, and Mauger, *Empire of Tea*, 259.

124. Ellis, Coultron, and Mauger, *Empire of Tea*, 259.

125. Griffiths, *Tea*, 368.

126. Quoted in Rappaport, *Thirst for Empire*, 326.

127. Griffiths, *Tea*, 370.

128. Ellis, Coultron, and Mauger, *Empire of Tea*, 260–261.

129. Griffiths, *Tea*, 371.

130. Griffiths, *Tea*, 367.

131. Rappaport, *Thirst for Empire*, 323.

132. Quoted in Pendergrast, *Uncommon Grounds*, 220.

133. Pendergrast, *Uncommon Grounds*, 220.

134. Allen, *Devil's Cup*, 212.

135. Wild, *Coffee*, 200–201.

136. Wild, *Coffee*, 201.

137. Mark Pendergrast, *For God, Country, and Coca-Cola: The Definitive History of the Great American Soft Drink and the Company That Makes It* (New York: Basic Books, 2013), 184.

138. Quoted in Pendergrast, *For God, Country, and Coca-Cola*, 28, 56.

139. Quoted in Pendergrast, *For God, Country, and Coca-Cola*, 28.

140. Pendergrast, *For God, Country, and Coca-Cola*, 22, 53–54, 115, 148.

141. Quoted in Standage, *History of the World*, 251; quoted in Pendergrast, *For God, Country, and Coca-Cola*, 184.

142. Quoted in Standage, *History of the World*, 252; quoted in Pendergrast, *For God, Country, and Coca-Cola*, 185.

143. Pendergrast, *For God, Country, and Coca-Cola*, 186.
144. Pendergrast, *For God, Country, and Coca-Cola*, 193.
145. Pendergrast, *For God, Country, and Coca-Cola*, 186–187.
146. Pendergrast, *For God, Country, and Coca-Cola*, 187.
147. Pendergrast, *For God, Country, and Coca-Cola*, 187.
148. Standage, *History of the World*, 253.
149. Quoted in Standage, *History of the World*, 253.
150. Quoted in Standage, *History of the World*, 254; quoted in Pendergrast, *For God, Country, and Coca-Cola*, 188.
151. Quoted in Bartow J. Elmore, *Citizen Coke: The Making of Coca-Cola Capitalism* (New York: Norton, 2015), 159.
152. Standage, *History of the World*, 255.
153. Quoted in Pendergrast, *For God, Country, and Coca-Cola*, 189.
154. Quoted in Standage, *History of the World*, 255; quoted in Pendergrast, *For God, Country, and Coca-Cola*, 191.
155. Quoted in Standage, *History of the World*, 255.
156. Pendergrast, *For God, Country, and Coca-Cola*, 192–193.
157. Elmore, *Citizen Coke*, 107.
158. Standage, *History of the World*, 255.
159. Quoted in Standage, *History of the World*, 255.
160. Standage, *History of the World*, 256.
161. Standage, *History of the World*, 257–258.
162. Standage, *History of the World*, 260.
163. Jeffery M. Paige, *Coffee and Power: Revolution and the Rise of Democracy in Central America* (Cambridge, MA: Harvard University Press, 1997), 3. Paige shows how patterns of landownership and class relations between the coffee elite and the peasantry shaped revolutions and subsequent regime types in Nicaragua, Costa Rica, and El Salvador.
164. Robert G. Williams, *States and Social Evolution: Coffee and the Rise of National Governments in Central America* (Chapel Hill: University of North Carolina Press, 1994), 2, 4–5.
165. Williams, *States and Social Evolution*, 4–5, discussing Barrington Moore Jr., *Social Origins of Dictatorship and Democracy: Lord and Peasant in the Making of the Modern World* (Boston: Beacon Press, 1966).
166. Paige, *Coffee and Power*, 87.
167. Pendergrast, *Uncommon Grounds*, 31.
168. Pendergrast, *Uncommon Grounds*, 170.
169. Pendergrast, *Uncommon Grounds*, 228–229.
170. Quoted in Pendergrast, *Uncommon Grounds*, 229.
171. Quoted in Pendergrast, *Uncommon Grounds*, 229.
172. Piero Gleijeses, *Hope Shattered: The Guatemalan Revolution and the United States, 1944–1954* (Princeton, NJ: Princeton University Press, 1991), 155–156; Pendergrast, *Uncommon Grounds*, 230–231.
173. Pendergrast, *Uncommon Grounds*, 231.

174. Pendergrast, *Uncommon Grounds*, 37.
175. Pendergrast, *Uncommon Grounds*, 168–169. Also see Liisa North, *Bitter Grounds: Roots of Revolt in El Salvador* (Westport, CT: Lawrence-Hill, 1985), 38–39.
176. Quoted in Pendergrast, *Uncommon Grounds*, 169.
177. Paige, *Coffee and Power*, 4.
178. Pendergrast, *Uncommon Grounds*, 317.
179. Elisabeth Jean Wood, *Insurgent Collective Action and Civil War in El Salvador* (New York: Cambridge University Press, 2003), 73, 148–149.
180. Pendergrast, *Uncommon Grounds*, 321.
181. Pendergrast, *Uncommon Grounds*, 322.
182. Pendergrast, *Uncommon Grounds*, 321.
183. Pendergrast, *Uncommon Grounds*, 322.
184. Wild, *Coffee*, 239.
185. Pendergrast, *Uncommon Grounds*, 37–38.
186. Pendergrast, *Uncommon Grounds*, 170.
187. Pendergrast, *Uncommon Grounds*, 299; Alan Riding, "Nicaragua Gets Loan to Meet Interest Debt," *New York Times*, December 14, 1982.
188. Zachary Sklar, "Bringing the War Home in Nicaragua," *Nation*, February 9, 1985.
189. Stephen Kinzer, "Nicaragua's Bitter Harvest: War in Coffee Fields," *New York Times*, December 23, 1983.
190. Quoted in Stephen Kinzer, "Nicaraguan Rebels Step Up Raids in Coffee Areas as Harvest Nears," *New York Times*, November 23, 1984.
191. Quoted in Pendergrast, *Uncommon Grounds*, 319.
192. See Murray Carpenter, *Caffeinated: How Our Daily Habit Helps, Hurts, and Hooks Us* (New York: Hudson Street Press, 2014), 147–160.
193. Tom McLellan, Lyndon A. Riviere, Kelly W. Williams, Dennis McGurk, and Harris R. Lieberman, "Caffeine and Energy Drink Use by Combat Arms Soldiers in Afghanistan as a Countermeasure for Sleep Loss and High Operational Demands," *Nutritional Neuroscience*, March 2018.
194. Tim Hsia, "The Performance-Enhanced Military," *New York Times*, May 7, 2010.

## Chapter 4

1. The name "heroin," the trademark for which was registered by Friedrich Bayer & Co., derived from the German *heroisch*, which meant "heroic."
2. Martin Booth, *Opium: A History* (New York: St. Martin's Press, 1996), 18–20.
3. Booth, *Opium*, 22–23.
4. Alfred McCoy, "Heroin as a Global Commodity: A History of Southeast Asia's Opium Trade," in *War on Drugs: Studies in the Failure of U.S. Narcotics Policy*, ed. Alfred W. McCoy and Alan A. Block (Boulder, CO: Westview Press, 1992), 240.

5. Quoted in Booth, *Opium*, 25.
6. Francois Bernier, *Bernier's Travels in the Mogul Empire* (Washington, DC: Ross & Perry, 2001), 39–40.
7. David T. Courtwright, *Forces of Habit: Drugs and the Making of the Modern World* (Cambridge, MA: Harvard University Press, 2001), 140.
8. Booth, *Opium*, 109–110.
9. Booth, *Opium*, 120–121.
10. Lukasz Kamienski, *Shooting Up: A Short History of Drugs and War* (New York: Oxford University Press, 2016), 60.
11. William O. Walker III, *Opium and Foreign Policy: The Anglo-American Search for Order in Asia, 1912–1954* (Chapel Hill, NC: University of North Carolina Press, 1991), 5.
12. Quoted in Kamienski, *Shooting Up*, 61.
13. Yongming Zhou, *Anti-Drug Crusades in Twentieth-Century China: Nationalism, History, and State Building* (Lanham, MD: Rowman & Littlefield, 1999), 15; Kathryn Meyer and Terry Parssinen, *Webs of Smoke: Smugglers, Warlords, Spies, and the History of the International Drug Trade* (Lanham, MD: Rowman & Littlefield, 1998), 9.
14. Yangwen goes so far as to argue that "opium had demilitarized the fighting machine" by undermining troop morale; Zheng Yangwen, *The Social Life of Opium in China* (Cambridge: Cambridge University Press, 2005), 91–92.
15. Booth, *Opium*, 139.
16. Booth, *Opium*, 141.
17. Quoted in Booth, *Opium*, 145.
18. Zhou reports that "opium revenues were used to pay for capital defense expenses; for the Beijing police; for new navy gunboats; for making machinery, guns, cartridges, and percussion caps; for soldier's wages and sundries; and to pay off foreign loans for new arms." But they also contributed to surging production and use. Zhou, *Anti-Drug Crusades*, 19–20.
19. Alfred McCoy, *The Politics of Heroin: CIA Complicity in the Global Drug Trade*, 2nd ed. (Chicago: Lawrence Hill Books, 2003), 80.
20. McCoy, *Politics of Heroin*, 88.
21. Edward R. Slack, *Opium, State, and Society: China's Narco-Economy and the Guomindang, 1924–1937* (Honolulu: University of Hawai'i Press, 2001), 6.
22. Quoted in Eric Jay Dolin, *When America First Met China: An Exotic History of Tea, Drugs, and Money in the Age of Sail* (New York: Liveright, 2012), 215.
23. Quoted in Dolin, *When America First Met China*, 254.
24. Dolin, *When America First Met China*, 288–289. Dolin also notes that US involvement in the opium business went into sharp decline and came to an end by 1880, largely because of heightened competition from foreign traders with lower operating costs.

25. See especially David T. Courtwright, "Opium Addiction as a Consequence of the Civil War," *Civil War History* 24, no. 2 (1978): 101–111; and David T. Courtwright, *Dark Paradise: A History of Opiate Addiction in America* (Cambridge, MA: Harvard University Press, 1982), 54–55.

26. See especially Frank Dikotter, Lars Laamann, and Zhou Xun, *Narcotic Culture: A History of Drugs in China* (Chicago: University of Chicago Press, 2004), ch. 6.

27. Booth, *Opium*, 180; Thomas Dormandy, *Opium: Reality's Dark Dream* (New Haven, CT: Yale University Press, 2012), 201.

28. United Nations Office on Drugs and Crime, "The Shanghai Opium Commission," January 1, 1959, https://www.unodc.org/unodc/en/data-and-analysis/bulletin/bulletin_1959-01-01_1_page006.html.

29. William B. McAllister, *Drug Diplomacy in the Twentieth Century: An International History* (New York: Routledge, 2000), 28–29. For a more detailed account of the global turn against opium, see Steffen Rimner, *Opium's Long Shadow: From Asian Revolt to Global Drug Control* (Cambridge, MA: Harvard University Press, 2018).

30. Booth, *Opium*, 159.

31. Kathryn Meyer, "From British India to the Taliban: Lessons from the History of the Heroin Market," in *One Hundred Years of Heroin*, ed. David F. Musto (Westport, CT: Auburn House, 2002), 205.

32. McAllister, *Drug Diplomacy*, 25; Slack, *Opium, State, and Society*, 6.

33. Slack, *Opium, State, and Society*, 65.

34. Alan Baumler, *The Chinese and Opium under the Republic* (Albany: State University of New York Press, 2007), 90.

35. For example, according to Bianco, "the control over Shanghai traffic in both national and Indian opium (the latter providing enough revenues to finance three army divisions) was the most important factor triggering the 1924 war between Jiangsu and Zhejiang. Guangxi's location made it a favorite exit route for Yunnan and Guizhou opium, especially since Sichuan's victory had closed the northern route through Sichuan. It was partly in order to open the Guangxi route for Yunnanese opium that Yunnan warlord Tan Jiyao attacked the New Guangxi clique late in 1924." Lucien Bianco, "The Responses of Opium Growers to Eradication Campaigns and the Poppy Tax, 1907–1949," in *Opium Regimes: China, Britain, and Japan, 1839–1952*, ed. Timothy Brook and Tadashi Wakabayashi (Berkeley: University of California Press, 2000), 293.

36. For example, "after the ousting of Tan Jiyao's troops, revenues from opium traffic became so important to the New Guangxi leaders that they worked to prevent the recurrence of hostilities with either of their opium-producing neighbors, Yunnan and Guizhou, both of which were also concerned about business." Bianco, "Responses of Opium Growers," 294.

37. Huang Shaoxiong, "Opium and Warlordism," in *Modern China and Opium: A Reader*, ed. Alan Baumler (Ann Arbor: University of Michigan Press, 2004), 110.
38. Baumler, *Chinese and Opium*, 91.
39. Baumler, *Chinese and Opium*, 90.
40. Quoted in Baumler, *Chinese and Opium*, 92.
41. For a detailed discussion, see Bianco, "Responses of Opium Growers."
42. Quoted in Yangwen, *Social Life of Opium*, 191–192.
43. Yangwen, *Social Life of Opium*, 191–192.
44. Booth, *Opium*, 159.
45. Quoted in Booth, *Opium*, 161.
46. Meyer, "From British East India to the Taliban," 209. For more details on the Green Gang, see Brian Martin, *The Shanghai Green Gang: Politics and Organized Crime, 1919–1937* (Berkeley: University of California Press, 1996).
47. Jonathan Marshall, "Opium and the Politics of Gangsterism in Nationalist China, 1927–1945," *Bulletin of Concerned Asian Scholars* 8, no. 3 (1976): 32.
48. Booth, *Opium*, 165.
49. Marshall, "Opium and the Politics of Gangsterism," 34.
50. Meyer, "From British India to the Taliban," 210.
51. Meyer, "From British India to the Taliban," 211.
52. Booth, *Opium*, 167.
53. Marshall, "Opium and the Politics of Gangsterism," 20.
54. Quoted in Marshall, "Opium and the Politics of Gangsterism," 20.
55. Marshall, "Opium and the Politics of Gangsterism," 37.
56. Dikotter, Laamann, and Xun, *Narcotic Culture*, 143–144.
57. Zhou, *Anti-Drug Crusades*, 172.
58. Meyer, "From British India to the Taliban," 217–218.
59. Baumler, *Chinese and Opium*, 217.
60. Marshall, "Opium and the Politics of Gangsterism," 41.
61. Kamienski, *Shooting Up*, 124–126.
62. Quoted in Kamienski, *Shooting Up*, 127.
63. Meyer, "From British India to the Taliban," 214.
64. Booth, *Opium*, 163.
65. Marshall, "Opium and the Politics of Gangsterism," 24. Also see McCoy, *Politics of Heroin*, 266–267.
66. Meyer, "From British India to the Taliban," 216.
67. Meyer, "From British India to the Taliban," 216.
68. McCoy, *Politics of Heroin*, 106.
69. Dikotter, Laamann, and Xun, *Narcotic Culture*, 150.
70. Quoted in Timothy Brook, "Opium and Collaboration in Central China, 1938–1940," in *Opium Regimes*, ed. Timothy Brook and Bob Tadashi Wakabayashi (Berkeley: University of California Press, 2000), 323.
71. As historian Timothy Brook writes, "It is not difficult to understand why the Japanese revived the opium trade in Shanghai: both the Japanese

army and the Reformed Government faced heavy financial burdens administering central China under wartime conditions." He goes on to note that while "it is impossible to deny that Japan was not only engaged in, but directed and sustained, a substantial opium traffic in China," there is no evidence "that there was a plot to narcotize the Chinese people, although many Japanese regarded the extent of addiction in China as grounds for treating Chinese with contempt." Timothy Brook, "Opium and Collaboration in Central China," in *Opium Regimes*, ed. Timothy Brook and Bob Tadashi Wakabayashi (Berkeley: University of California Press, 2000), 329, 339–340.

72. Quoted in Meyer, "From British India to the Taliban," 219.

73. Quoted in Walker, *Opium and Foreign Policy*, 167.

74. Kamienski, *Shooting Up*, 126.

75. Quoted in Kamienski, *Shooting Up*, 127.

76. Quoted in Motohiro Kabayashi, "An Opium Tug-of-War: Japan Versus the Wang Jingwei Regime," in *Opium Regimes*, ed. Timothy Brook and Bob Tadashi Wakabayashi (Berkeley: University of California Press, 2000), 351–352.

77. See, for example, Chen Yung-fa, "The Blooming Poppy under the Red Sun: The Yan'an Way and the Opium Trade," in *New Perspectives on the Chinese Communist Revolution*, ed. Tony Saich and Hans van de Ven (New York: M. E. Sharpe, 1995).

78. Baumler, *Chinese and Opium*, 92–93.

79. Walker, *Opium and Foreign Policy*, 151.

80. Yangwen, *Social Life of Opium*, 200.

81. Quoted in Yangwen, *Social Life of Opium*, 198.

82. For more details, see Rodney Campbell, *The Luciano Project: The Secret Wartime Collaboration of the Mafia and the U.S. Navy* (New York: McGraw Hill, 1977); Tim Newark, *Mafia Allies: The True Story of America's Secret Alliance with the Mob in World War II* (St. Paul, MN: Zenith, 2007), ch. 7.

83. James Cockayne, *Hidden Power: The Strategic Logic of Organized Crime* (New York: Oxford University Press, 2016), ch. 6; also see Campbell, *Luciano Project*; Newark, *Mafia Allies*.

84. Quoted in Tim Newark, *Lucky Luciano: The Real and the Fake Gangster* (New York: St. Martin's Press, 2010), 147.

85. Quoted in Cockayne, *Hidden Power*, 152.

86. Cockayne, *Hidden Power*, 152.

87. Quoted in Cockayne, *Hidden Power*, 157.

88. Cockayne, *Hidden Power*, 158.

89. Quoted in Newark, *Lucky Luciano*, 156.

90. Quoted in Jill Jonnes, *Hep-Cats, Narcs, and Pipe Dreams: A History of America's Romance with Illegal Drugs* (Baltimore: Johns Hopkins University Press, 1996), 146.

91. See US Department of the Army, *Urban Operations*, Field Manual No. 3-06 (Washington, DC: US Department of the Army, 2003), 16.

92. Cockayne, *Hidden Power*, 159–160.

93. Quoted in Cockayne, *Hidden Power*, 161.

94. Quoted in Cockayne, *Hidden Power*, 162.

95. Cockayne, *Hidden Power*, 162.

96. Newark, *Lucky Luciano*, 163.

97. Quoted in Newark, *Lucky Luciano*, 173.

98. Quoted in Jonnes, *Hep-Cats, Narcs, and Pipe Dreams*, 167.

99. Dormandy, *Opium*, 235–236.

100. Quoted in Jonnes, *Hep-Cats, Narcs, and Pipe Dreams*, 177.

101. Quoted in Newark, *Lucky Luciano*, 207.

102. David F. Musto, *The American Disease: Origins of Narcotic Control*, 3rd ed. (New York: Oxford University Press, 1999), 231.

103. Quoted in Yongming Zhou, "The Antidrug Crusade in the People's Republic, 1949–1952," in *Opium Regimes*, ed. Timothy Brook and Bob Tadashi Wakabayashi (Berkeley: University of California Press, 2000), 382.

104. McCoy, *Politics of Heroin*, 14.

105. Quoted in Zhou, *Anti-Drug Crusades*, 107.

106. Zhou, *Anti-Drug Crusades*, ch. 6.

107. Booth, *Opium*, 279.

108. McCoy, *Politics of Heroin*, 269.

109. McCoy, *Politics of Heroin*, 128.

110. Pierre-Arnaud Chouvy, *Opium: Uncovering the Politics of the Poppy* (Cambridge, MA: Harvard University Press, 2010), 15.

111. Richard M. Gibson with Wenhua Chen, *The Secret Army: Chiang Kai-Shek and the Drug Warlords of the Golden Triangle* (Singapore: J. Wiley & Sons Asia, 2011).

112. Quoted in McCoy, *Politics of Heroin*, 129.

113. Booth, *Opium*, 258–259.

114. Gibson with Chen, *Secret Army*.

115. McCoy, *Politics of Heroin*, 162.

116. McCoy, "Heroin as a Global Commodity," 258.

117. For more details, see McCoy, *Politics of Heroin*, 105.

118. Booth, *Opium*, 261.

119. Booth, *Opium*, 262.

120. McCoy, *Politics of Heroin*, 186, 191.

121. McCoy, *Politics of Heroin*, 113.

122. McCoy, *Politics of Heroin*, 112.

123. McCoy, *Politics of Heroin*, 114.

124. McCoy, *Politics of Heroin*, 115.

125. Booth, *Opium*, 265.

126. Booth, *Opium*, 267–268.

127. McCoy, *Politics of Heroin*, 291.

128. McCoy, *Politics of Heroin*, 130.

129. McCoy, *Politics of Heroin*.

130. Chouvy, *Opium*, xii.

131. Booth, *Opium*, 270–271.

132. Booth, *Opium*, 233; Dormandy, *Opium,* 239.

133. Booth, *Opium*, 271, 273.

134. Booth, *Opium*, 271.

135. Booth, *Opium*, 272.

136. Kamienski, *Shooting Up*, 195.

137. Quoted in Kamienski, *Shooting Up*, 212.

138. Quoted in Kamienski, *Shooting Up*, 211.

139. Quoted in Jeremy Kuzmarov, *The Myth of the Addicted Army: Vietnam and the Modern War on Drugs* (Amherst: University of Massachusetts Press, 2009), 2.

140. Quoted in Kamienski, *Shooting Up*, 209.

141. Quoted in Kuzmarov, *Myth of the Addicted Army*, 3.

142. Kamienski, *Shooting Up*, 210.

143. Quoted in Kuzmarov, *Myth of the Addicted Army*, 1.

144. Quoted in Kuzmarov, *Myth of the Addicted Army*, 9.

145. See Lee N. Robbins, Darlene H. Davis, and David N. Nurco, "How Permanent Was Vietnam Drug Addiction?," *American Journal of Public Health* 64, supp. (1974): 38–43; Lee N. Robbins, "Vietnam Veterans's Rapid Recovery from Heroin Addiction: A Fluke or Normal Expectation?," *Addiction* 88, no. 8 (1993): 1041–1054.

146. Kamienski, *Shooting Up*, 215

147. Booth, *Opium*, 274.

148. Booth, *Opium*, 275.

149. Quoted in Booth, *Opium*, 277.

150. Thomas Fuller, "Khun Sa, Golden Triangle Drug King, Dies at 73," *New York Times,* November 5, 2007.

151. McCoy, *Politics of Heroin*, 18.

152. Quoted in Elaine Sciolino with Stephen Engleberg, "Fighting Narcotics: U.S. Is Urged to Shift Tactics," *New York Times,* April 10, 1988.

153. Gretchen Peters, *Seeds of Terror: How Drugs, Thugs, and Crime Are Reshaping the Afghan War* (New York: Picador, 2010), 35.

154. Peters, *Seeds of Terror*, 37.

155. Vanda Felbab-Brown, "War and Drugs in Afghanistan," *World Politics Review*, October 25, 2011.

156. Vanda Felbab-Brown, *Shooting Up: Counterinsurgency and the War on Drugs* (Washington, DC: Brookings, 2010), 119.

157. McCoy, *Politics of Heroin*, 479.

158. McCoy, *Politics of Heroin*, 480.

159. Quoted in Peters, *Seeds of Terror*, 38.

160. Peters, *Seeds of Terror*, 40.

161. Letizia Paoli, Victoria Greenfield, and Peter Reuter, *The World Heroin Market: Can Supply Be Cut?* (New York: Oxford University Press, 2009), 123–124; McCoy, *Politics of Heroin*, 486.

162. Quoted in Peters, *Seeds of Terror*, 41.

163. McCoy, *Politics of Heroin*, 475, 480.

164. Quoted in Peters, *Seeds of Terror*, 45.

165. Quoted in Peters, *Seeds of Terror*, 45.

166. Quoted in McCoy, *Politics of Heroin*, 479.

167. Quoted in Peters, *Seeds of Terror*, 53.

168. Quoted in Peters, *Seeds of Terror*, 59.

169. McCoy, *Politics of Heroin*, 484.

170. Vanda Felbab-Brown, Harold Trinkunas, and Shadi Hamid, *Militants, Criminals, and Warlords: The Challenge of Local Governance in an Age of Disorder* (Washington, DC: Brookings, 2018), 36.

171. Barnett Rubin, *Afghanistan from the Cold War Through the War on Terror* (New York: Oxford University Press, 2013), 61–62.

172. Paoli, Greenfield, and Reuter, *World Heroin Market*, 125.

173. Peters, *Seeds of Terror*, 88.

174. Rubin, *Afghanistan from the Cold War*, 54; Michael Pugh and Neil Cooper, with Jonathan Goodhand, *War Economies in a Regional Context* (Boulder, CO: Lynne Rienner, 2004), 53; Aisha Ahmad, *Jihad & Co.: Black Markets and Islamist Power* (New York: Oxford University Press, 2017), ch. 4.

175. Rubin, *Afghanistan from the Cold War*, 52, 60.

176. Alfred McCoy, "How the Heroin Trade Explains the US-UK Failure in Afghanistan," *Guardian*, January 9, 2018.

177. Quoted in McCoy, "How the Heroin Trade Explains."

178. Dexter Filkins, Mark Mazzetti, and James Risen, "Brother of Afghan Leader Said to Be Paid by CIA," *New York Times*, October 27, 2009.

179. Vanda Felbab-Brown, *Aspiration and Ambivalence: Strategies and Realities of Counterinsurgency and State-Building in Afghanistan* (Washington, DC: Brookings, 2013), 116.

180. Mark Mazzeti, Scott Shane, and Alissa J. Rubin, "Brutal Haqqani Crime Clan Bedevils U.S. in Afghanistan," *New York Times*, September 24, 2011.

181. Azam Ahmed, "Tasked with Combating Opium, Afghan Officials Profit from It," *New York Times*, February 15, 2016.

182. Quoted in Ahmed, "Tasked with Combating Opium."

## Chapter 5

1. Lester Grinspoon and Peter Hedblom, *The Speed Culture: Amphetamine Use and Abuse in America* (Cambridge, MA: Harvard University Press, 1975), 18.

2. This paragraph is drawn from Frank Owen, *No Speed Limit: The Highs and Lows of Meth* (New York: St. Martin's Press, 2007), 79–83.

3. Norman Ohler, *Blitzed: Drugs in Nazi Germany* (London: Allan Lane, 2016), 20–21, 23.
4. Quoted in Ohler, *Blitzed*, 47.
5. Quoted in Lukasz Kamienski, *Shooting Up: A Short History of Drugs and War* (New York: Oxford University Press, 2016), 114.
6. Ohler notes that after World War II, Hauschild and his institute at the University of Leipzig were behind East Germany's sports doping program, and in 1957 he was honored with the National Prize. Ohler, *Blitzed*, 35.
7. Peter Steinkamp, "Pervitin (Metamphitamine) Tests, Use and Misuse in the German Wehrmacht," in *Man, Medicine, and the State: The Human Body as an Object of Government Sponsored Medical Research in the 20th Century*, ed. Wolfgang U. Eckart (Stuttgart, Germany: Franz Steiner Verlag, 2006), 61; Leslie Iversen, *Speed, Ecstasy, Ritalin: The Science of Amphetamines* (New York: Oxford University Press, 2006), 71–72; Owen, *No Speed Limit*, 84.
8. Quoted in Ohler, *Blitzed*, 57.
9. Ohler, *Blitzed*, 57, 73.
10. Quoted in Ohler, *Blitzed*, 71.
11. Ohler, *Blitzed*, 72.
12. Steinkamp, "Pervitin (Metamphetamine) Tests," 63.
13. Alan Taylor, "World War II: The Invasion of Poland and the Winter War," *Atlantic*, June 26, 2011.
14. Nicolas Rasmussen, *On Speed: The Many Lives of Amphetamine* (New York: New York University Press, 2008), 53.
15. Quoted in Ohler, *Blitzed*, 89.
16. Stephen Snelders and Toine Pieters, "Speed in the Third Reich: Metamphetamine (Pervitin) Use and a Drug History from Below," *Social History of Medicine* 24, no. 3 (2001): 689; Steinkamp, "Pervitin (Metamphetamine) Tests," 64.
17. Quoted in Ohler, *Blitzed*, 65.
18. Quoted in Ohler, *Blitzed*, 63.
19. Quoted in Ohler, *Blitzed*, 64.
20. Quoted in Ohler, *Blitzed*, 65.
21. Quoted in Ohler, *Blitzed*, 65.
22. Quoted in Ohler, *Blitzed*, 65–66.
23. Quoted in Steinkamp, "Pervitin (Metamphetamine) Tests," 64.
24. Quoted in Ohler, *Blitzed*, 66.
25. Quoted in Steinkamp, "Pervitin (Metamphetamine) Tests," 65–66.
26. Quoted in Steinkamp, "Pervitin (Metamphetamine) Tests," 61.
27. Quoted in Ohler, *Blitzed*, 49.
28. Steinkamp, "Pervitin (Metamphetamine) Tests," 64–65; Rasmussen, *On Speed*, 54–55; Snelders and Pieters, "Speed in the Third Reich," 692.
29. Quoted in Ohler, *Blitzed*, 74.
30. Ohler, *Blitzed*, 79.

31. Owen, *No Speed Limit,* 84; Steinkamp, "Pervitin (Metamphetamine) Tests," 65.
32. Kamienski, *Shooting Up,* 111; Mick Farren, *Speed-Speed-Speedfreak: A Fast History of Amphetamine* (Port Townsend, WA: Feral House, 2010), 24.
33. Quoted in Ohler, *Blitzed,* 70–71.
34. Quoted in Ohler, *Blitzed,* 77.
35. Quoted in Ohler, *Blitzed,* 78.
36. Ohler, *Blitzed,* 78.
37. Quoted in Ohler, *Blitzed,* 79.
38. Quoted in Kamienski, *Shooting Up,* 114.
39. Rasmussen, *On Speed,* 53.
40. Quoted in Rasmussen, *On Speed,* 53.
41. Quoted in Karl-Heinz Frieser, *The Blitzkrieg Legend: The 1940 Campaign in the West* (Annapolis, MD: Naval Institute Press, 2013), 118.
42. Frieser, *Blitzkrieg Legend,* 119.
43. Frieser, *Blitzkrieg Legend,* 112, 114, 118–119.
44. Quoted in Ohler, *Blitzed,* 103.
45. Quoted in Ohler, *Blitzed,* 106.
46. Winston S. Churchill, *The Second World War* (London: Bloomsbury Academic, 2013), 244.
47. Rasmussen, *On Speed,* 53–54; Kamienski, *Shooting Up,* 111.
48. Quoted in Ohler, *Blitzed,* 108.
49. Quoted in Ohler, *Blitzed,* 109.
50. Steinkamp, "Pervitin (Metamphetamine) Tests," 66; Kamienski, *Shooting Up,* 111; Ohler, *Blitzed,* 109.
51. Rasmussen, *On Speed,* 59.
52. Megan Garber, " 'Pilot Salt': The Third Reich Kept Its Soldiers Alert with Meth," *Atlantic,* May 31, 2013; Ohler, *Blitzed,* 115.
53. Quoted in Ohler, *Blitzed,* 114.
54. Quoted in Ohler, *Blitzed,* 115.
55. Quoted in Ohler, *Blitzed,* 116.
56. Snelders and Pieters, "Speed in the Third Reich," 691.
57. Steinkamp, "Pervitin (Metamphetamine) Tests," 66.
58. Quoted in Steinkamp, "Pervitin (Metamphetamine) Tests," 67.
59. Ohler, *Blitzed,* 123. For more on Conti's concerns about Pervitin and Speer's article, see also Steinkamp, "Pervitin (Metamphetamine) Tests," 67.
60. Rasmussen, *On Speed,* 55.
61. Steinkamp, "Pervitin (Metamphetamine) Tests," 68–69.
62. Steinkamp, "Pervitin (Metamphetamine) Tests," 65.
63. Kamienski, *Shooting Up,* 114.
64. Quoted in Kamienski, *Shooting Up,* 114.
65. Quoted in Ohler, *Blitzed,* 124.
66. Kamienski, *Shooting Up,* 114; Steinkamp, "Pervitin (Metamphetamine) Tests," 68.

67. Hans von Luck, *Panzer Commander: The Memoirs of Colonel Hans von Luck* (New York: Dell Publishing, 1989), 84.

68. Quoted in Steinkamp, "Pervitin (Metamphetamine) Tests," 69.

69. Kamienski, *Shooting Up*, 115.

70. Owen, *No Speed Limit*, 84; Farren, *Speed-Speed-Speedfreak*, 27.

71. Farren, *Speed-Speed-Speedfreak*, 27–28.

72. Quoted in Ohler, *Blitzed*, 262.

73. Farren, *Speed-Speed-Speedfreak*, 45–47.

74. Kamienski, *Shooting Up*, 107.

75. Rasmussen, *On Speed*, 55.

76. Grinspoon and Hedblom, *Speed Culture*, 18

77. Owen, *No Speed Limit*, 83; Farren, *Speed-Speed-Speedfreak*, 33; Kamienski, *Shooting Up*, 116.

78. Rasmussen, *On Speed*, 59.

79. Ohler, *Blitzed*, 121–122.

80. Kamienski, *Shooting Up*, 117; Rasmussen, *On Speed*, 61.

81. Kamienski, *Shooting Up*, 117; Rasmussen, *On Speed*, 61.

82. Kamienski, *Shooting Up*, 118.

83. Quoted in Kamienski, *Shooting Up*, 119.

84. Kamienski, *Shooting Up*, 119–120.

85. Quoted in Owen, *No Speed Limit*, 83.

86. Kamienski, *Shooting Up*, 123.

87. Quoted in Kamienski, *Shooting Up*, 124.

88. Owen, *No Speed Limit*, 83.

89. Kamienski, *Shooting Up*, 122.

90. Rasmussen, *On Speed*, 287n63.

91. Rasmussen, *On Speed*, 84.

92. Grinspoon and Hedblom, *Speed Culture*, 18.

93. Kamienski, *Shooting Up*, 121–122.

94. Quoted in Owen, *No Speed Limit*, 83.

95. Michael S. Vaughn, Frank F. Y. Huang, and Christine Rose Ramirez, "Drug Abuse and Anti-Drug Policy in Japan: Past History and Future Directions," *British Journal of Criminology* 35, no. 4 (1995): 498.

96. Miriam Kingsberg, *Moral Nation: Modern Japan and Narcotics in Global History* (Berkeley and Los Angeles: University of California Press, 2014), 182; Chauncey D. Leake, *The Amphetamines: Their Actions and Uses* (Springfield, IL: Charles C. Thomas, 1958), 112, 136.

97. Owen, *No Speed Limit*, 84.

98. Vaughn, Huang, and Ramirez, "Drug Abuse and Anti-Drug Policy," 497.

99. Kamienski, *Shooting Up*, 128.

100. Kamienski, *Shooting Up*, 128.

101. Vaughn, Huang, and Ramirez, "Drug Abuse and Anti-Drug Policy," 497.

102. Owen, *No Speed Limit*, 84; Farren, *Speed-Speed-Speedfreak*, 30.

103. Kamienski, *Shooting Up*, 129.

104. Farren, *Speed-Speed-Speedfreak*, 30–31.
105. Iversen, *Speed, Ecstasy, Ritalin*, 72.
106. David Sulzer, Mark S. Sonders, Nathan W. Poulsen, and Aurelio Galli, "Mechanisms of Neurotransmitter Release by Amphetamines: A Review," *Progress in Neurobiology* 75 (2005): 410; Kamienski, *Shooting Up*, 131.
107. Michael Flaum and Susan K. Schultz, "When Does Amphetamine-Induced Psychosis Become Schizophrenia?," *American Journal of Psychiatry* 1, no. 2 (1996): 209; Leake, *Amphetamines*, 113, 136.
108. Thomas Dormandy, *The Worst of Evils: The Fight Against Pain* (New Haven, CT: Yale University Press, 2006), 416; Kingsberg, *Moral Nation*, 182; Vaughn, Huang, and Ramirez, "Drug Abuse and Anti-Drug Policy," 498.
109. Kingsberg, *Moral Nation*, 182.
110. Kamienski, *Shooting Up*, 131.
111. Iversen, *Speed, Ecstasy, Ritalin*, 107.
112. Owen, *No Speed Limit*, 85.
113. Owen, *No Speed Limit*, 85.
114. Kingsberg, *Moral Nation*, 187.
115. Sulzer et al., "Mechanisms of Neurotransmitter Release," 410.
116. Flaum and Schultz, "When Does Amphetamine-Induced Psychosis Become Schizophrenia?," 209.
117. Kamienski, *Shooting Up*, 131–132.
118. Kamienski, *Shooting Up*, 131.
119. Vaughn, Huang, and Ramirez, "Drug Abuse and Anti-Drug Policy," 499.
120. Kingsberg, *Moral Nation*, 184.
121. Kingsberg, *Moral Nation*, 184.
122. Kingsberg, *Moral Nation*, 198.
123. Iversen, *Speed, Ecstasy, Ritalin*, 110.
124. H. Richard Friman, *Narcodiplomacy: Exporting the U.S. War on Drugs* (Ithaca, NY: Cornell University Press, 1996), 90; for an exception, see Snelders and Pieters, "Speed in the Third Reich," 696, who write that Pervitin "remained part of German drug consumption until the 1960s."
125. Iversen, *Speed, Ecstasy, Ritalin*, 91.
126. Grinspoon and Hedblom, *Speed Culture*, 20.
127. Iversen, *Speed, Ecstasy, Ritalin*, 72; Grinspoon and Hedblom, *Speed Culture*, 18.
128. Kamienski, *Shooting Up*, 145–146, 189.
129. Owen, *No Speed Limit*, 98–99.
130. Owen, *No Speed Limit*, 100.
131. Quoted in Kamienski, *Shooting Up*, 189.
132. Quoted in Kamienski, *Shooting Up*, 189.
133. Farren, *Speed-Speed-Speedfreak*, 39.
134. Grinspoon and Hedblom, *Speed Culture*, 19.
135. Grinspoon and Hedblom, *Speed Culture*, 19.

136. Committee on Armed Services, "Inquiry into Alleged Drug Abuse in the Armed Services in the 91st Congress, 2d Session," in *Report of a Special Subcommittee of the Committee on Armed Services House of Representatives* (Washington, DC: US Government Printing Office, 1971), 2191–2193, 2197, 2228.

137. Quoted in Grinspoon and Hedblom, *Speed Culture*, 19.

138. Grinspoon and Hedblom, *Speed Culture*, 19.

139. Grinspoon and Hedblom, *Speed Culture*, 19.

140. Joseph Albright, "Amphetamines for Fighter Pilots Banned," *Austin American-Statesman*, April 22, 1992; John A. Caldwell and Lex Brown, "Runnin' On Empty?," *Flying Safety* 59, no. 3 (2003): 4.

141. Kamienski, *Shooting Up*, 268–269.

142. David L. Emonson and Rodger D. Vanderbeek, "The Use of Amphetamines in U.S. Air Force Tactical Operations During Desert Shield and Storm," *Aviation Space and Environmental Medicine* 66, no. 3 (1995): 260.

143. Quoted in Kamienski, *Shooting Up*, 269.

144. Kamienski, *Shooting Up*, 269–270.

145. Iversen, *Speed, Ecstasy, Ritalin*, 73.

146. David Kenagy, Christopher Webber, Christopher Bird, and Joseph Fischer , "Dextroamphetamine Use During B-2 Combat Missions," *Aviation Space and Environmental Medicine* 75, no. 5 (2004): 381–382, 385.

147. Richard A. Friedman, "Why Are We Drugging Our Soldiers?," *New York Times*, April 22, 2012.

148. John A. Caldwell, "Go Pills in Combat: Prejudice, Propriety, and Practicality," *Air & Space Power Journal* 22, no. 3 (2018): 100.

149. Sulome Anderson, "These Are the People Making Captagon, the Drug ISIS Fighters Take to Feel 'Invincible,'" *New York Magazine*, December 9, 2015.

150. Aryn Baker, "Syria's Breaking Bad: Are Amphetamines Funding the War?," *Time*, October 28, 2013.

151. Global Initiative Against Transnational Organized Crime, *Captured by Captagon?: Lebanon's Evolving Illicit Drug Economy* (Geneva: Global Initiative Against Transnational Organized Crime, May 2017), vi; Global Initiative Against Transnational Organized Crime, *The Nexus of Conflict and Illicit Drug Trafficking: Syria and the Wider Region* (Geneva: Global Initiative Against Transnational Organized Crime, 2016).

152. Chavala Madlena and Radwan Mortada, "Syria's Speed Freaks, Jihad Junkies, and Captagon Cartels," *Foreign Policy*, November 19, 2015.

153. Stephen Kalin, "Insight: War Turns Syria into Major Amphetamines Producer, Consumer," *Reuters*, January 12, 2014.

154. Quoted in Kalin, "Insight."

155. Quoted in Kalin, "Insight."

156. Quoted in Peter Holley, "Captagon: The Tiny Amphetamine Pill Fueling the Syrian Civil War and Turning Fighters into Superhuman Soldiers," *Washington Post*, November 19, 2015; John Henley, "Captagon: The Amphetamine Fuelling Syria's Civil War," *Guardian*, January 13, 2014.
157. Mirren Gidda, "Drugs in War: What Is Captagon, the 'Jihad Pill' Used by Islamic State Militants?," *Newsweek*, May 12, 2017.
158. Quoted in Anne Speckhard and Ahmet S. Yayla, "Eyewitness Accounts from Recent Defectors from Islamic State: Why They Joined, What They Saw, Why They Quit," *Perspectives on Terrorism* 9, no. 6 (2015): 105–106.

## Chapter 6

1. David T. Courtwright, *Forces of Habit: Drugs and the Making of the Modern World* (Cambridge, MA: Harvard University Press, 2001), 46.
2. Dominic Streatfeild, *Cocaine: An Unauthorized Biography* (New York: Picador, 2001), 18.
3. W. Golden Mortimer, "The History of Coca," in *Drugs in the Western Hemisphere*, ed. William O. Walker III (Wilmington, DE: Scholarly Resources, 1996), 3.
4. William O. Walker III, *Drug Control in the Americas* (Albuquerque: University of New Mexico Press, 1989), 3.
5. Streatfeild, *Cocaine*, 63.
6. Mortimer, "History of Coca," 7.
7. Quoted in Streatfeild, *Cocaine*, 64.
8. Courtwright, *Forces of Habit*, 47.
9. Quoted in Lukasz Kamienski, *Shooting Up: A Short History of Drugs and War* (New York: Oxford University Press, 2016), 93.
10. Quoted in Kamienski, *Shooting Up,* 93.
11. Quoted in Kamienski, *Shooting Up,* 93.
12. Quoted in Edward Brecher and the Editors of Consumer Reports, *Licit and Illicit Drugs* (Boston: Little, Brown & Co., 1972), 273.
13. Courtwright, *Forces of Habit,* 50.
14. Courtwright, *Forces of Habit,* 50.
15. Kamienski, *Shooting Up,* 96.
16. Quoted in Kamienski, *Shooting Up,* 97.
17. This paragraph is drawn from Kamienski, *Shooting Up,* 99–101; and Marek Kohn, "Cocaine Girls: Sex, Drugs, and Modernity in London During and after the First World War," in *Cocaine: Global Histories*, ed. Paul Gootenberg (New York: Routledge, 1999).
18. Kohn, "Cocaine Girls," 118.
19. Kamienski, *Shooting Up,* 101–102.
20. See Kohn, "Cocaine Girls," 110–118.
21. H. Richard Friman, "Germany and the Transformations of Cocaine, 1860–1920," in *Cocaine: Global Histories*, ed. Paul Gootenberg (New York: Routledge, 1999), 99.

22. For more on the Dutch role in the cocaine trade, see Marcel de Kort, "Conflicting Interests in the Netherlands," in *Cocaine: Global Histories*, ed. Paul Gootenberg (New York: Routledge, 1999).

23. Steven B. Karch, "Japan and the Cocaine Industry in Southeast Asia, 1864–1944," in *Cocaine: Global Histories*, ed. Paul Gootenberg (New York: Routledge, 1999).

24. Paul Gootenberg, *Andean Cocaine: The Making of a Global Drug* (Chapel Hill: University of North Carolina Press, 2008), 140.

25. Mark Pendergrast, *For God, Country, and Coca Cola: The Definitive History of the Great American Soft Drink and the Company that Makes It*, rev. ed. (New York: Basic Books, 2013), 185.

26. Paul Gootenberg, "Reluctance or Resistance?: Constructing Cocaine (Prohibitions) in Peru, 1910–1950," in *Cocaine: Global Histories*, ed. Paul Gootenberg (New York: Routledge, 1999), 68.

27. Gootenberg, *Andean Cocaine*, 230.

28. Gootenberg, *Andean Cocaine*, 245.

29. Gootenberg, *Andean Cocaine*, 264.

30. Gootenberg, *Andean Cocaine*, 265–266.

31. Quoted in Gootenberg, *Andean Cocaine*, 267.

32. Gootenberg, *Andean Cocaine*, 267.

33. Gootenberg, *Andean Cocaine*, 268.

34. Quoted in Gootenberg, *Andean Cocaine*, 268.

35. Eduardo S. Rovner, *The Cuban Connection: Drug Trafficking, Smuggling, and Gambling in Cuba from the 1920s to the Revolution* (Chapel Hill: University of North Carolina Press, 2008), 149.

36. Brecher et al., *Licit and Illicit Drugs*, 302–305. Brecher and his co-editors write: "The decade [of the 1960s] began with almost all stimulants being supplied by reputable manufacturers; their low-cost amphetamines had almost driven cocaine off the market. The withdrawal of intravenous amphetamines from the legal market opened the door for the illicit speed labs. The Drug Abuse Control Amendments of 1965 curbed the direct diversion of legal amphetamines to the black market; this opened the door for the smuggling of exported amphetamines back into the United States. By 1969, law-enforcement efforts had raised black market amphetamine prices and curbed amphetamine supplies sufficiently to open the door for renewed cocaine smuggling."

37. According to the National Institute on Drug Abuse (NIDA), 4.4 million people had used cocaine within the past thirty days, at least 9.7 million had used it within the past year, and at least 15 million had used it at least once at some time in the past. These figures, which represent a 250 to 300 percent increase over the findings of the NIDA survey in 1977, were considered low by other official estimates. Steven Wisotsky, *Beyond the War on Drugs: Overcoming a Failed Policy* (Amherst, NY: Prometheus Books, 1990), 12–14.

38. Bruce D. Johnson and John Muffler, "Sociocultural Aspects of Drug Use and Abuse in the 1990s," in *Substance Abuse: A Comprehensive Text*, ed. Joyce Lowinson, Pedro Ruiz, and Robert Millman (Baltimore: Williams and Wilkins, 1992), 124.

39. Johnson and Muffler, "Sociocultural Aspects of Drug Use."

40. See Musto, *The American Disease: Origins of Narcotic Control* (New York: Oxford University Press, 1987), 274; and Wisotsky, *Beyond the War on Drugs*, 7.

41. Quoted in Ryan Grim, *This Is Your Country on Drugs: The Secret History of Getting High in America* (Hoboken, NJ: Wiley, 2009), 73–74.

42. Quoted in Grim, *This is Your Country*, 73.

43. On the history and development of the Andean cocaine industry, see especially Gootenberg, *Andean Cocaine*. On the 1980s cocaine boom and its implications for US policy, see Peter Andreas and Coletta Youngers, "U.S. Drug Policy and the Andean Cocaine Industry," *World Policy Journal* 6, no. 3 (1989): 529–562.

44. On the rise of Medellin as a cocaine export center, see Mary Roldan, "Colombia: Cocaine and the 'Miracle' of Modernity in Medellin," in *Cocaine: Global Histories*, ed. Paul Gootenberg (New York: Routledge, 1999), 166–167; and Angelica Duran Martinez, *The Politics of Drug Violence: Criminals, Cops, and Politicians in Colombia and Mexico* (New York: Oxford University Press, 2018), ch. 4.

45. The importance of the threat of extradition in fueling violence in this period is emphasized by Benjamin Lessing, *Making Peace in Drug Wars: Crackdowns and Cartels in Latin America* (Cambridge: Cambridge University Press, 2018), ch. 5.

46. On the mythical nature of Colombia's "drug cartels," see Michael Kenney, *From Pablo to Osama: Trafficking and Terrorist Networks, Government Bureaucracies, and Competitive Adaptation* (University Park: Pennsylvania State Press, 2008), 88–90.

47. Paul Eddy with Hugo Sabogal and Sarah Walden, *The Cocaine Wars* (New York: Norton, 1988), 98.

48. Quoted in Arnold S. Trebach, *Great Drug War* (New York: Macmillan, 1987), 152.

49. Quoted in "Major Crime Package Cleared by Congress," *Congressional Quarterly Almanac* 40 (1984): 213–224.

50. Quoted in Trebach, *Great Drug War*, 184.

51. See, for example, the discussion in Craig Reinarman and Harry Levine, "Crack in Context: Politics and Media in the Making of a Drug Scare," *Contemporary Drug Problems* 16, no. 4 (1989): 537–539, 555–559.

52. Quoted in Ioan Grillo, *El Narco: Inside Mexico's Criminal Insurgency* (New York: Bloomsbury Press, 2011), 68.

53. Quoted in "Four Key Issues Playing Role in Congressional Contests," *Congressional Quarterly*, October 18, 1986, 2599.

54. Quoted in Chris Adams, "Second Thoughts on the Military as Narcs," *Washington Post*, June 15, 1988.

55. See especially Peter B. Kraska, ed., *Militarizing the American Criminal Justice System: The Changing Roles of the Armed Forces and the Police* (Boston: Northeastern University Press, 2001). On the punitive trend more generally during this period, see Peter Andreas, "The Rise of the American Crimefare State," *World Policy Journal* 14, no. 3 (1997): 37–45.

56. Radley Balko, *Rise of the Warrior Cop: The Militarization of American Police Forces* (New York: Public Affairs, 2013), 53, 62–63.

57. Balko, *Rise of the Warrior Cop*, 207.

58. Balko, *Rise of the Warrior Cop*, 133.

59. Balko, *Rise of the Warrior Cop*, 192–195. This trend continued into the late 1990s with the creation of the 1033 program, which was carried out by yet another agency tasked with further facilitating the movement of military apparatus to local law enforcement agencies. See Balko, *Rise of the Warrior Cop*, 209.

60. Grillo, *El Narco*, 69–70.

61. Quoted in John M. Goshko, "U.S. War by Proxy at an End," *Washington Post*, February 27, 1990.

62. See Senate Committee on Foreign Relations, Subcommittee on Terrorism, Narcotics and International Operations, *Drugs, Law Enforcement and Foreign Policy* (Washington, DC: US Government Printing Office, 1989). Also see Peter Dale Scott and Jonathan Marshall, *Cocaine Politics: Drugs, Armies, and the CIA in Central America* (Berkeley: University of California Press, 1998); Robert Parry, *Lost History: Contras, Cocaine, the Press and Project Truth* (Arlington, VA: Media Consortium, 1999); Leslie Cockburn, *Out of Control: The Story of the Reagan Administration's Secret War in Nicaragua, the Illegal Arms Pipeline, and the Contra Drug Connection* (New York: Atlantic Monthly Press, 1987); and Alexander Cockburn and Jeffrey St. Clair, *Whiteout: The CIA, Drugs, and the Press* (New York: Verso, 1998).

63. Robert Parry, "How John Kerry Exposed the Contra-Cocaine Scandal," *Salon*, October 25, 2004.

64. Peter Kornbluh, "Crack, the Contras, and the CIA: The Storm over 'Dark Alliance,'" *Columbia Journalism Review* January/February (1997): 33–39.

65. "Text of Address by President Bush," *Washington Post*, September 6, 1989.

66. Poll cited in Tom Wicker, "The Wartime Spirit," *New York Times*, October 3, 1989.

67. White House, "National Drug Control Strategy: Budget Summary" (Washington, DC: White House, 1992), 23; Office of National Drug Control Policy, *National Drug Control Strategy Budget Summary* (Washington, DC: US Government Printing Office, 1994), 184–185.

68. Assistant Secretary of Defense Lawrence Korb, quoted in "Faced with Peace, Pentagon Wants to Enlist in Drug War," *State* (Columbia, SC), December 17, 1989.

69. Quoted in "Faced with Peace." Military officials have made similar arguments. For example, Lieutenant Charley L. Diaz explained: "DoD [Department of Defense] should consider expanding its funding justification to include increased federal funds for its 'new' drug detection and monitoring mission. . . . Shifting the emphasis of a portion of DoD's budget toward its new peace-time mission will help DoD retain certain resources and manpower while satisfying domestic pressure to increase the drug interdiction effort." Quoted in "DoD Plays in the Drug War," *Proceedings/Naval Review* 116, no. 5 (1990): 84, 86.

70. Quoted in David C. Morrison, "Police Action," *National Journal* 24, no. 5 (1992): 267–270.

71. Quoted in Morrison, "Police Action," 268.

72. Frank Greve, "Ailing Defense Contractors Urged to Arm the Drug War," *Miami Herald*, July 15, 1990.

73. Quoted in Peter Andreas and Richard Price, "From War-fighting to Crime-fighting: Transforming the American National Security State," *International Studies Review* 3, no. 3 (Autumn 2001): 40.

74. Eric Schmitt, "Colorado Bunker Built for Cold War Shifts Focus to Drug Battle," *New York Times*, July 18, 1993; William Matthews, "Toys Dusted Off for War on Drugs," *Federal Times*, April 16, 1990; "DOD Studies X-Ray Techniques for Examining Cargo Containers," *Drug Enforcement Report*, May 23, 1994; Frank Greve, "Ailing Defense Contractors."

75. Jeff Gerth, "CIA Shedding Its Reluctance to Aid in Fight Against Drugs," *New York Times*, March 25, 1990.

76. Adam Isaacson, "The U.S. Military in the War on Drugs," in *Drugs and Democracy in Latin America*, ed. Coletta Youngers and Eileen Rosen (Boulder, CO: Lynne Rienner, 2005), 42.

77. Quoted in Isaacson, "U.S. Military," 28.

78. Michael Isikoff and Patrick E. Tyler, "U.S. Military Given Foreign Arrest Powers," *Washington Post*, December 16, 1989.

79. Elaine Sciolino and Stephen Engelberg, "Fighting Narcotics: U.S. Is Urged to Shift Tactics," *New York Times*, April 10, 1988. More generally, see John Dinges, *Our Man in Panama* (New York: Random House, 1991).

80. Julie Marie Bunck and Michael Ross Fowler, *Bribes, Bullets, and Intimidation: Drug Trafficking and the Law in Central America* (State College: Pennsylvania State Press, 2012), 329–330.

81. Quoted in Bunck and Fowler, *Bribes, Bullets, and Intimidation*, 334.

82. Bunck and Fowler, *Bribes, Bullets, and Intimidation*, 346.

83. This was an important shift. In 1984, the military created a battalion in Medellin with a counterinsurgency mission but avoided becoming

involved in counternarcotics. As Colonel Augusto Bahamon, who set the battalion up, explained it, "Back then, the army was not interested in waging a war that they knew in advance they were going to lose with a high toll in lives and prestige, because the mission of the army differs from that of the police, and this was very clear to all our superiors." Quoted in Angelica Duran Martinez, *Politics of Drug Violence*, 122.

84. For a detailed account, see Mark Bowden, *Killing Pablo: The Hunt for the World's Greatest Outlaw* (New York: Penguin, 2002).

85. Quoted in Isaacson, "U.S. Military," 45.

86. Charles Rangel, "We Can Do Something for Colombia," *Washington Post*, August 24, 1989.

87. Isaacson, "U.S. Military," 23.

88. See Washington Office on Latin America, *Clear and Present Dangers: The U.S. Military and the War on Drugs in the Andes* (Washington, DC: WOLA, 1991), ch. 3. For a critique of early 1990s US antidrug efforts in the Andean region, see Peter Andreas, Eva Bertram, Morris Blachman, and Kenneth Sharpe, "Dead-End Drug Wars," *Foreign Policy*, Winter (1991–1992): 106–128.

89. See Frank Greve, "Contra Advisers in Peru," *Philadelphia Inquirer*, May 30, 1990.

90. See Americas Watch Report, *The Killings in Colombia* (New York: Americas Watch, 1989).

91. Andreas et al., "Dead-End Drug Wars," 118.

92. Quoted in Peter R. Andreas and Kenneth E. Sharpe, "Cocaine Politics in the Andes," *Current History*, February (1992): 76.

93. US House Committee on Government Operations, *Report on Operation Snowcap* (Washington, DC: US Government Printing Office, August 1990).

94. Quoted in Michael Massing, "In the Cocaine War . . . The Jungle Is Winning," *New York Times Magazine*, March 4, 1990, 90.

95. Quoted in John McClintock, "Poverty Complicates Cocaine War in Huallaga Valley," *Baltimore Sun*, October 24, 1989.

96. Quoted in Andreas and Sharpe, *Cocaine Politics in the Andes*, 78.

97. Marguerite Cawley, "Montecinos Is Gone, but Peru's Narco-Political Brokers Continue Tradition," *Insight Crime*, October 20, 2014.

98. Cornelius Friesendorf, *Pushing Drugs: The Displacement of the Cocaine and Heroin Industry as a Side Effect of U.S. Foreign Policy* (Ph.D. diss., University of Zurich, 2005), 106–108.

99. This paragraph is drawn from Mark Peceny and Michael Durnan, "The FARC's Best Friend: U.S. Antidrug Policies and the Deepening of Colombia's Civil War in the 1990s," *Latin American Politics and Society* 48, no. 2 (2006): 95–116.

100. Adam Isaacson, "Mission Creep: The U.S. Military's Counterdrug Role in the Americas," in *Drug Trafficking, Organized Crime, and Violence*

*in the Americas Today*, ed. Bruce M. Bagley and Jonathan D. Rosen (Gainesville: University Press of Florida, 2015), 92.

101. Quoted in Nicholas Barnes, "Criminal Politics: An Integrated Approach to the Study of Organized Crime, Politics, and Violence," *Perspectives on Politics* 15, no. 4 (2017): 977. The AUC would formally demobilize in 2006, but many AUC commanders either did not go through the demobilization ceremony or did so disingenuously and quickly regrouped into what came to be dubbed neo-paramilitaries, operating as criminal bands (*bandas criminales*) deeply enmeshed in the cocaine trade. Jeremy McDermott, "The 'Victory' of the Urabenos: The New Face of Colombian Organized Crime," *Insight Crime*, May 2014.

102. Winifred Tate, "Accounting for Absence: The Colombian Paramilitaries in U.S. Policy Debates," in *Sex, Drugs, and Body Counts: The Politics of Numbers in Global Crime and Conflict*, ed. Peter Andreas and Kelly M. Greenhill (Ithaca, NY: Cornell University Press, 2010).

103. Friesendorf, *Pushing Drugs*, 150.

104. Isaacson, "Mission Creep," 94.

105. Quoted in Isaacson, "U.S. Military," 47.

106. Isaacson, "U.S. Military," 46.

107. Jim Rochlin, "Plan Colombia and the Revolution in Military Affairs: The Demise of the FARC," *Review of International Studies* 37, no. 2 (2011): 728, 732.

108. Isaacson, "U.S. Military," 43; Rochlin, "Plan Colombia," 725–728.

109. Quoted in Friesendorf, *Pushing Drugs*, 150.

110. Quoted in Isaacson, "U.S. Military," 44.

111. Quoted in Friesendorf, *Pushing Drugs*, 121.

112. More generally, Gootenberg argues that the unintended cumulative impact of US drug enforcement over many decades was to push the cocaine trade ever closer to the United States. See Paul Gootenberg, "Cocaine's Long March North, 1900–2010," *Latin American Politics and Society* 54, no. 1 (2012): 159–180.

113. Quoted in John Moore, "No Quick Fix," *National Journal* 19 (November 1987): 2957.

114. Testimony of Admiral Paul Yost, US Coast Guard, before the House Select Committee on Narcotics Abuse and Control, *U.S. Narcotics Control Efforts in Mexico and on the Southwest Border*, 99th Cong., 2d sess., July 1986, 34.

115. See Senate Subcommittee, *Southwest Border Law Enforcement and Trade* (Washington, DC: US Government Printing Office, August 19, 1987), 25.

116. Senate Subcommittee, *Southwest Border Law Enforcement*, 25, 191, 200.

117. Senate Subcommittee, *Southwest Border Law Enforcement*, 191, 202.

118. State Department estimates cited in Peter H. Smith, "Semiorganized International Crime: Drug Trafficking in Mexico," in *Transnational Crime in the Americas*, ed. Tom Farer (New York: Routledge, 1999), 195.

119. Congressional Research Service, *Drug Interdiction: U.S. Programs, Policy, and Options for Congress* (Washington, DC: Senate Caucus on International Narcotics Control, September 1996).

120. Office of National Drug Control Policy, *National Drug Control Strategy* (Washington, DC: US Government Printing Office, February 1991), 102–103.

121. Oversight Hearing on Border Drug Interdiction, Senate Subcommittee on Treasury, Postal Service, and General Government, Committee on Appropriations, *Border Drug Interdiction*, 103d Cong., 1st sess., February 25, 1993, 133.

122. Dale E. Brown, "Drugs on the Border: The Role of the Military," *Parameters* 21 (1991): 56.

123. Tim Golden, "Mexico and Drugs: Was U.S. Napping?," *New York Times*, July 11, 1997.

124. General Accounting Office, *Drug Control: Counternarcotics Efforts in Mexico: Appendix II: Comments from the Drug Enforcement Administration* (Washington, DC: GAO, June 1996), 26.

125. "Time for Retreat?," *Economist*, March 8, 1997, 44–47.

126. Donald Schulz, *Between a Rock and a Hard Place: The United States, Mexico, and the Agony of National Security*, Strategic Studies Institute Special Report (Carlisle Barracks, PA: Strategic Studies Institute, US Army War College, June 1997), 4.

127. See George W. Grayson, "Civilians Order Army Out of the Barracks," *Hemisfile* 9, no. 5 (1998): 8.

128. Department of State, *International Narcotics Control Strategy Report* (Washington, DC: Department of State, March 1999).

129. *National Drug Control Program: 1995–2000* (Mexico City: Mexican Government, October 1995), 6.

130. Isaacson, "Mission Creep," 92.

131. Isaacson, "U.S. Military," 41.

132. Press conference with Barry McCaffrey, director of the Office of National Drug Control Policy, and Jorge Madrazo, Mexican attorney general, Washington DC, January 29, 1997.

133. Andrew Reding, "Facing Political Reality in Mexico," *Washington Quarterly* 20, no. 4 (1997): 103–117.

134. Cited in Peter Andreas, *Border Games: Policing the U.S.-Mexico Divide* (Ithaca, NY: Cornell University Press, 2009), 68.

135. Office of National Drug Control Policy, *National Drug Control Strategy Report* (Washington, DC: Government Printing Office, 1999), 69–70.

136. Christopher S. Wren, "U.S. Drug Chief Seeks Overhaul of Strategy to Stop Illegal Flow from Mexico," *New York Times*, September 20, 1998.

137. See Peter Andreas, "When Policies Collide: Market Reform, Market Prohibition, and the Narcotization of the Mexican Economy," in *The Illicit*

*Global Economy and State Power*, ed. H. Richard Friman and Peter Andreas (Lanham, MD: Rowman & Littlefield, 1999), 134.

138. Remarks of Harvey G. Pothier, deputy assistant commissioner of the Office of Air Interdiction, US Customs Service, in Congressional Research Service, *Drug Interdiction*, 22.

139. Testimony of Barry R. McCaffrey, House Subcommittee on Criminal Justice, Drug Policy, and Human Resources, Government Reform and Oversight Committee, 106th Cong., 1st sess., February 25, 1999.

140. Eric Lipton, "Bush Turns to Big Military Contractors for Border Control," *New York Times*, May 18, 2006.

141. Federal Documents Clearing House, FDCH Political Transcripts, "U.S. Senator Orrin Hatch (R-UT) Holds Hearing on International Drug Trafficking and Terrorism," May 20, 2003.

142. Quoted in Ginger Thomson, "Trafficking in Terror," *New Yorker*, December 14, 2015.

143. Quoted in Isaacson, "U.S. Military," 48.

144. Quoted in Isaacson, "U.S Military," 48.

145. Quoted in Isaacson, "U.S Military," 48.

146. Isaacson, "U.S. Military." Also see Washington Office on Latin America, *Blurring the Lines: Trends in U.S. Military Programs with Latin America* (Washington, DC: Washington Office on Latin America, 2004).

147. Isaacson, "U.S. Military," 50.

148. Quoted in Isaacson, "U.S. Military," 49.

149. Quoted in Washington Office on Latin America, *Blurring the Lines*.

150. Thom Shanker, "Lessons of Iraq Help U.S. Fight a Drug War in Honduras," *New York Times*, May 5, 2012.

151. Lessing, *Making Peace in Drug Wars*, 219; Grillo, *El Narco*, 92.

152. Lessing, *Making Peace in Drug Wars*, 220.

153. Quoted in Grillo, *El Narco*, 113.

154. For detailed and nuanced accounts, see Guillermo Trejo and Sandra Ley, "Why Did Drug Cartels Go to War in Mexico?: Subnational Party Alternation, the Breakdown of Criminal Protection, and the Onset of Large-Scale Violence," *Comparative Political Studies* 51, no. 7 (2018): 900–937; and Angélica Durán-Martínez, *The Politics of Drug Violence: Criminals, Cops and Politicians in Colombia and Mexico* (New York: Oxford University Press, 2018).

155. Ginger Thompson, "U.S. Widens Role in Battle Against Mexican Drug Cartels," *New York Times*, August 6, 2011.

156. Randal C. Archibold, "2-Nation Border Conference Discusses Gun Trafficking," *New York Times*, August 16, 2008.

157. Quoted in Chris McGreal, "How Mexico's Drug Cartels Profit from the Flow of Guns Across the Border," *Guardian*, December 8, 2011.

158. On the domestic obstacles to curbing gunrunning to Mexico, see especially James Verini, "Mexican Roulette," *Foreign Policy*, August 30, 2011.

159. For an overview, see June S. Beittel, *Mexico's Drug Trafficking Organizations: Source and Scope of the Rising Violence* (Washington, DC: Congressional Research Service, January 2011).

160. Jeremy McDermott, "Militarisation of the Drug War in Latin America: A Policy Cycle Set to Continue?," in *Militarised Responses to Transnational Organised Crime*, ed. Tuesday Reitano, Lucia Bird Ruiz-Benitez de Lugo, and Sasha Jepperson (London: Palgrave Macmillan, 2018), 265. Also see George Grayson, "Los Zetas: The Ruthless Army Spawned by a Mexican Drug Cartel," Foreign Policy Research Institute, May 2008.

161. Quoted in Grillo, *El Narco*, 104–105.

162. Grillo, *El Narco*, 105, 128.

163. The Justice in Mexico Project at the Trans-border Institute of the University of San Diego has carried out the most careful and detailed tracking of Mexican drug violence.

164. Ioan Grillo, *Gangster Warlords: Drug Dollars, Killing Fields, and the New Politics of Latin America* (New York: Bloomsbury Press, 2016), 269.

165. David Shirk and Joel Wallman, "Understanding Mexico's Drug Violence," *Journal of Conflict Resolution* 59, no. 8 (2015): 1363.

166. Lessing, *Making Peace in Drug Wars*, 237.

167. Adam Isaacson, "Northbound 'Threats' at the United States–Mexico Border: What Is Crossing Today, and Why?," in *American Crossings: Border Politics in the Western Hemisphere*, ed. Maiah Jaskoski, Arturo C. Sotomayor, and Harold A. Trinkunas (Baltimore: Johns Hopkins University Press, 2015), 139.

168. Quoted in Isaacson, "Northbound 'Threats,'" 139.

169. Quoted in Benjamin Lessing, "Logics of Violence in Criminal War," *Journal of Conflict Resolution* 59, no. 8 (2015): 1492.

170. Vanda Felbab-Brown, "Hooked: Mexico's Violence and U.S. Demand for Drugs," *Brookings Blog*, May 30, 2017.

171. Peter Andreas, "We Will Miss El Chapo: He Was Easy to Blame for Our Drug War Failures," *Guardian*, January 12, 2016.

172. James Bargent, "Reports Show Ex-FARC Criminal Cells Taking Shape Around Colombia," *Insight Crime*, August 1, 2017.

173. Mike LaSusa, "FARC Dissident Leader's Death Could Shake Up Colombia's Pacific Coast," *Insight Crime*, September 11, 2018.

174. Quoted in Nicholas Barnes and Stephanie Savell, "Life in a War Zone: Putting the Military in Control of Rio de Janeiro's Policing Threatens Brazilian Democracy," *U.S. News & World Report*, February 23, 2018.

175. Dom Phillips, "Brazil Military's Growing Role in Crime Crackdown Fuels Fears Among Poor," *Guardian,* February 27, 2018.

176. Ernesto Londono and Manuela Andreoni, "'We'll Dig Graves': Brazil's New Leaders Vow to Kill Criminals," *New York Times*, November 1, 2018.

177. Quoted in Andres Schipani, "Brazil Gets Tough in War on Crime in Rio's Slums," *Financial Times*, March 11, 2018.
178. David Luhnow, "Latin America Is the Murder Capital of the World," *Wall Street Journal*, September 20, 2018.
179. For a more general discussion, see especially Nicholas Barnes, "Criminal Politics: An Integrated Approach to the Study of Crime, Politics, and Violence," *Perspectives on Politics* 15, no. 4 (2017): 967–987; Benjamin Lessing, "The Logic of Violence in Criminal War," *Journal of Conflict Resolution* 59, no. 8 (2015): 1486–1516; and Vanda Felbab-Brown, "Crime-War Battlefields," *Survival* 55, no. 3 (2013): 147–166.

## Conclusion

1. This point is well made by Benjamin Lessing, *Making Peace in Drug Wars: Crackdowns and Cartels in Latin America* (Cambridge: Cambridge University Press, 2017), 278.
2. In the US case, see Peter Andreas and Richard Price, "From War-fighting to Crime-fighting: Transforming the American National Security State" *International Studies* Review, 3, no. 3 (Autumn 2001): 31–52.
3. See Lessing, *Making Peace in Drug Wars*, 282.
4. US federal revenue forfeitures totaled $96.7 billion in 1986 but by 2014 had skyrocketed to $4.5 billion. See Dick Carpenter, Lisa Knepper, Angela Erickson, and Jennifer McDonald, *Policing for Profit: The Abuse of Civil Asset Forfeiture*, 2nd ed. (Arlington, VA: Institute of Justice, November 2015), 5.
5. For an earlier discussion of drug corruption as a form of taxation in the case of Mexico, see Peter Andreas, "The Political Economy of Narco-Corruption in Mexico," *Current History* 97 (1998): 160–165.
6. Charles Tilly, "War Making and State Making as Organized Crime," in *Bringing the State Back In*, ed. Peter B. Evans, Dietrich Rueschemeyer, and Theda Skocpol (Cambridge: Cambridge University Press, 1985).
7. Partly inspired by Tilly, in an earlier work I argue more broadly that "the state makes smuggling and smuggling makes the state." See Peter Andreas, *Smuggler Nation: How Illicit Trade Made America* (New York: Oxford University Press, 2013).
8. Lessing, *Making Peace in Drug Wars*, 280–281.
9. For a more detailed analysis of the politics that sustains this dynamic, see Eva Bertram, Morris Blachman, Kenneth Sharpe, and Peter Andreas, *Drug War Politics: The Price of Denial* (Berkeley: University of California Press, 1996).
10. Cornelius Friesendorf, *U.S. Foreign Policy and the War on Drugs: Displacing the Cocaine and Heroin Industry* (London: Routledge, 2007).
11. Pauline Repard, "In New Tactic, Smugglers Use Drone to Fly Meth over Mexican Border into San Diego, Officials Say," *Los Angeles Times*, August

19, 2017; Gina Harkins, "Illicit Drone Flights Surge along U.S.-Mexico Border as Smugglers Hunt for Soft Spots," *Washington Post*, June 24, 2018; Christopher Woody, "Colombian Traffickers Have Added Drones to Their Smuggling Arsenal," *Business Insider*, November 18, 2016.

12. Jim Wyss, "Colombia's Latest Weapon in the War on Drugs?: Crop-Killing Drones," *Miami Herald*, June 27, 2018.

13. United Nations Office on Drugs and Crime, *World Drug Report 2018* (Vienna: United Nations Office on Drugs and Crime, 2018), 8.

14. Keith Humphreys, Jonathan P. Caulkins, and Vanda Felbab-Brown, "Opioids of the Masses," *Foreign Affairs*, May/June 2018.

15. Dan Levin, "Despite a Crackdown, Use of Illegal Drugs in China Continues Unabated," *New York Times*, January 24, 2015.

16. Keith Humphreys, "A Vaccine to Curb Addicts' Highs," *Wall Street Journal*, November 23, 2012.

17. David Agren, "Mexican President-Elect's New Plan to Fight Crime Looks Like the Old Plan," *Guardian*, November 21, 2018.

18. For a more detailed analysis, see Vanda Felbab-Brown, "AMLO's Security Policy: Creative Ideas, Tough Reality" (Washington, DC: Brookings Institution, March 2019).

19. Gustavo A. Flores Macias, "Mexico's New President Wants a New National Guard to Address Violent Crime. Will It Work?," *Washington Post*, December 19, 2018.

20. Patrick Corcoran, "Is Mexico's New National Guard Just Another Uniform?" *Insight Crime* March 20, 2019.

21. Caspar Weinberger, *The Next War* (Washington, DC: Regnery Publishing, 1998).

22. Robert Muggah, "It's Official: San Salvador Is the Murder Capital of the World," *Los Angeles Times*, March 2, 2016.

23. This paragraph is drawn from David Holiday, "Parsing the Evidence on 'Drug-Related' Violence in the Northern Triangle: Implications for Policy Implementation," presentation at the Annual Convention of the Latin American Studies Association, Barcelona, Spain, May 2018.

24. On the relationship between violence and illicit markets in general, see the special September 2009 issue of *Crime, Law & Social Change*, guest edited by Peter Andreas and Joel Wallman.

25. Something along these lines is suggested by Mark Kleiman, "Surgical Strikes in the Drug Wars," *Foreign Affairs*, September/October 2011.

26. For the most detailed discussion of this in the Latin American context, see Lessing, *Making Peace in Drug Wars*, especially part III. Lessing calls such accommodations "conditional repression."

27. See Andreas, "Political Economy of Narco-Corruption."

28. See Bertram et al., *Drug War Politics*.

29. Jennifer Senior, "The Prozac, Paxil, Zoloft, Wellbutrin, Celexa, Effexor, Valium, Klonopin, Ativan, Restoril, Xanax, Adderall, Ritalin, Haldol,

Risperdal, Seroquel, Ambien, Lunesta, Elavil, Trazodone War," *New York Magazine*, February 6, 2011.

30. Quoted in Quil Lawrence, "A Growing Number of Veterans Struggles to Quit Powerful Painkillers," *All Things Considered* (National Public Radio), July 10, 2014.

31. Quoted in Lawrence, "Growing Number of Veterans."

32. Valerie Bauerlein and Arian Campo-Flores, "The VA Hooked Veterans on Opioids, Then Failed Them Again," *Wall Street Journal*, December 29, 2016.

33. John A. Caldwell and Lex Brown, "Runnin' on Empty?: 'Go Pills,' Fatigue and Aviator Safety," *United States Air Force Flying Safety Magazine* 59, no. 3 (2003): 4–11.

34. Eric A. Bower and James Phelan, "Use of Amphetamines in the Military Environment," *Lancet*, December (2003): 18–19.

35. MITRE Corporation, *Human Performance*, JSR-07–625 (McLean, VA: MITRE Corporation, March 2008), https://fas.org/irp/agency/dod/jason/human.pdf.

36. MITRE Corporation, *Human Performance*.

37. Quoted in Will Saletan, "The War on Sleep," *Slate*, May 29, 2013.

38. Saletan, "War on Sleep."

39. MITRE Corporation, *Human Performance*.

40. MITRE Corporation, *Human Performance*.

41. Quoted in Damien McElroy, "Mumbai Attacks: Terrorists Took Cocaine to Stay Awake During Assault," *Telegraph*, December 2, 2008.

42. Ludovica Iaccino, "Why Tramadol Is the Suicide Bomber's Drug of Choice," *Newsweek*, December 13, 2017.

43. Iftikhar Firdous, "What Goes into the Making of a Suicide Bomber," *Express Tribune* (Pakistan), July 20, 2010.

44. Quoted in Mike Jay, "Don't Fight Sober," *London Review of Books*, January 5, 2017.

45. George W. Grayson, *La Familia Drug Cartel: Implications for U.S.-Mexican Security* (Carlisle, PA: Strategic Studies Institute, U.S. Army War College, 2010), vii.

46. I thank one of the external reviewers for this description of "war as drug." Also see Lukasz Kamienski, *Shooting Up: A Short History of Drugs and War* (New York: Oxford University Press, 2016), 304–309.

47. Chris Hedges, *War Is a Force that Gives Us Meaning* (New York: Public Affairs, 2002), 3.

# INDEX

For the benefit of digital users, indexed terms that span two pages (e.g., 52–53) may, on occasion, appear on only one of those pages.